BUSINESS JOURNALISM

COMMITTEE ON AMERICAN LEGISLATURES
American Political Science Association

BUSINESS JOURNALISM

SECOND REVISED EDITION

by Julien Elfenbein

With a preface to the Greenwood reprint by the author

GREENWOOD PRESS, PUBLISHERS
NEW YORK

First Greenwood Reprinting 1969

Library of Congress Catalogue Card Number 72-91759

SBN 8371-2433-6

PRINTED IN UNITED STATES OF AMERICA

To my colleagues
in the
FÉDÉRATION
INTERNATIONALE
DE LA
PRESSE PÉRIODIQUE

1. To collect a body of factual data upon which to base conclusions and recommendations for reorganization that will meet the needs of the states or will serve as a basis for adaptation for specific legislatures.
2. To encourage the study of the state legislative processes, particularly in college undergraduate and graduate courses of political science and law.
3. To stimulate the appropriation of more generous state funds for study of individual state legislatures by their own research agencies.
4. To enlist the aid of government officials, The Council of State Governments, and civic organizations in encouraging state legislative reform.
5. To encourage the establishment of a citizens' clearing house, aided by the mass media of communication to keep alive interest in state legislative reform as a continuing process.
6. To stimulate broader research in the legislative process with the assistance of foundation and government funds.

This report is, then, only a first step in achieving these objectives. The Committee hopes that all cooperating groups will study not only the informational data presented in this report but especially the recommendations at the close of the chapters.

The Committee wishes to thank the executive council, officers, and staff of the American Political Science Association for their sympathetic cooperation. The Committee deeply appreciates the assistance rendered by the staffs of the Bureau of Public Administration of Boston University, The Council of State Governments, the Legislative Reference Service of the Library of Congress, the state legislative libraries and councils, the National Municipal League, and the library of Brooklyn College.

Grateful acknowledgement is also due Winston W. Crouch of the University of California at Los Angeles, George B. Galloway of the Library of Congress, Edward H. Litchfield of Cornell University, Lloyd M. Short of the University of Minnesota, Harvey Walker of the Ohio State University, and Herbert L. Wiltsee of The Council of State Governments. The Committee records with sorrow the death of its esteemed member, Professor Joseph P. Chamberlain of Columbia University.

BELLE ZELLER

December, 1953

Contents

List of Tables and Figures

PRE-WORLD WAR II STEPS TOWARD LEGISLATIVE REORGANIZATION

Although a number of important steps have been taken in the twentieth century in the direction of improving state legislative organization and procedure, little or nothing was done before World War I. However, the legislative reference services, now existing in some form in nearly all states, did begin their significant services to the legislatures late in the nineteenth century; the New York State Library led the way in 1890 and was followed by the Massachusetts State Library in 1892. The idea was expanded and developed in Wisconsin beginning in 1901, under the leadership of Charles McCarthy, and the Wisconsin Legislative Reference Bureau celebrated its fiftieth anniversary in 1951. The original twofold purpose of supplying information to members and rendering assistance in the drafting of bills still holds in many jurisdictions, although the tendency in late years has been in the direction of separate agencies for reference and for bill-drafting work.

The split session, with which a number of states have experimented—in some cases by constitutional provision, in others by legislative practice—has been in use in California since 1911. It was subsequently adopted constitutionally, and later abandoned, in West Virginia and New Mexico. The split session was an effort to reduce confusion during the session and give members a better opportunity to study, and obtain constituents' reaction to, pending legislation. The same purpose can be achieved—and has been in some states—merely through agreement to adjourn until some specified date. Whichever the method used, however, careful students of the results indicate a good deal of doubt that the objectives have actually been attained.

Prominent among the developments of the post-World War I period was the first appearance in 1921 of the *Model State Constitution*, whose important recommendations relating to state legislatures are considered on page 10.

The early 1930's witnessed some further advances. The state legislative councils, now existing in more than two-thirds of the states, owe their origin to the precedent established in Kansas in 1933. The council plan achieves the objectives of closer coordination between the executive and legislative branches and provision of machinery for

Preface

The book jacket of the first edition of this now world-famous standard text and reference work described *Business Journalism* as "The Story of Know-How." The know-how in every field of human activity is first transmitted by the technical, professional and business press. All activity is encompassed in the world-word—Business.

In 1960, in the last revised edition of the book, the author updated and largely rewrote the text, adding new knowledge and including brief histories of the business press of fifteen leading countries as well as the United States.

This text is required reading in every journalism school in our country, in Canada, and abroad—even in such far-flung places as Tokyo University and the University of Helsinki.

The author, Professor Julien Elfenbein, introduced the course on Business Journalism at New York University and taught classes there for a quarter century. At the same time he acted as chief editor, successively, of eight leading national business magazines. He is the holder of seven national editorial achievement awards, and many honors from government, industry and his profession. He also served as director of technical publications in the School of Engineering and Science at N.Y.U.

Professor Elfenbein now acts as a communications consultant to corporations and government, and as an arbitrator of commercial disputes.

JULIEN ELFENBEIN
1969

Foreword to First Edition

By Stanley A. Knisely
EXECUTIVE VICE-PRESIDENT OF
THE ASSOCIATED BUSINESS PAPERS, INC.

Here, at last, is a work on business journalism that builds a monument worthy of its famous history and points a future in keeping with the magnitude and importance of so vital an influence in helping the world make an ever-better living.

No stodgy, orthodox, dry-as-dust textbook confined to a weary recital of mere mechanics or techniques—and doomed to gather dust, unopened, on musty library shelves.

How many business executives have ever leaned back in their swivel chairs for as much as a minute and asked themselves:

"Where would my business—my personal fortunes—be today had it not been for the business press?" and—

"What would happen to my business—my personal fortunes—if the business press closed its doors tonight and threw away the keys?"

Business historians may well attribute the phenomenal growth of industry and commerce in this country to the fact that we have had a business press of outstanding virility—at least one, and frequently two or more papers, devoted to each and every important phase of agriculture, mining, manufacture, transportation, and marketing. There are the professional business papers for the doctor, lawyer, and architect; merchandising papers for dealers and jobbers in every line; institutional papers in the hotel, school, hospital, and restaurant fields; specialized papers in the fields of sales, advertising, and marketing; and industrial papers covering every important branch of manufacturing activity.

True, the colonists found here unlimited wealth in natural resources, but other countries had similar wealth. Our pioneers found a vast, undeveloped area awaiting only the ingenuity and toil of man to transform it into gold; but the same is true of Russia, China, and other parts of the world. Our American Indians did not develop these resources. The American Indian slaved to lay up venison and maize for the winter while his squaw worked all summer to weave one blanket.

Why is it, then, that, starting only a few hundred years ago—after many nations of the world had been at it for centuries—we caught up with the leaders and passed them in so relatively short a time? Why is the United States the wealthiest nation? Why does it surpass all others in the fields of manufacture, transportation, and communications? In short, what has American business possessed that was not generally available to business throughout the world?

Broadly, we possessed these things: a sound democratic form of government, an economic system of competitive enterprise, and the largest, most active, unbiased independent and authoritative business press in the world. Many thousands of foreign businessmen and technicians subscribe regularly to American business papers. Japan, Germany, and Italy were heavy subscribers but were cut off following Pearl Harbor to prevent technical "knowhow" from reaching enemy hands. Japan's special envoy Saburo Kurusu tried vainly to subscribe for American aviation papers even after he was incarcerated in Greenbrier, West Va., in the early days of World War II.

In this country, hardly a machine or a material or a process but owes much of its rapid development and speedy acceptance to the fact that the business press picked it up out of its crib, nursed it along in its creeping stages, and spread the news of its birth and growth.

And today, what do we find? A new low-alloy high-tensile steel is developed by the metallurgists who are constantly studying their businesspapers; and before you can turn around, thousands of mechanical and design engineers, thousands of top business executives, and thousands upon thousands of other important key men in all lines of industry know all about it, how it is made, how you can form it into myriad shapes, and how it saves millions of dollars in the transportation industry alone.

So it is with every development—plastics, magnesium, electronics, a helicopter, a new hair-do. No matter what it is, or in what line of activity, the business executive, master mechanic, airplane designer, or buyer in a lingerie store in Los Angeles, Amarillo, Spokane, or Duluth, knows all about it—all the details, figuratively speaking, almost overnight. How?- Through the highly specialized business press, the information railway that transports know-how from where it is to where it is needed.

Does this mean anything to industry and trade?

Suppose the business press did close its doors tonight and throw away the keys. What other channel of public information and education now functioning could take over this highly technical service?

When we check them over—the colleges, newspapers, general magazines, radio, movies—we quickly discern their inability to man adequately the lines of business communication. What would result? The rate of progress in industry and trade would falter alarmingly. The standard of living would level off and start to decline. If we believe that true wealth in our nation depends upon ever-increasing production and ever-wider distribution at ever-lower costs and prices, we can readily understand what national retrogression would ensue if the business communication lines were cut.

Mr. Elfenbein's thesis that high-level employment will depend on more efficient distribution of the world's goods and services, under the guidance and inspiration of the specialized business press, is developed with an understanding that comes from eighteen years of practical experience as a working business journalist in the fields of distribution. He left the law school of the University of Texas twenty-seven years ago to join the U.S. Army Intelligence Service during World War I. In the quarter-century interregnum between wars he was newspaper reporter, commercial artist, advertising agency copywriter and account executive, trade association official, and businesspaper editor. When we entered World War II, Donald Nelson appointed him a member of the Business Paper Editors Advisory Council of the War Production Board. He is a former chairman of the New York Business Paper Editors. He is a member of the executive committee of the National Conference of Business Paper Editors and chairman of its postwar committee on distribution. He has lectured on business journalism at a number of universities and on business practice in many national forums.

Remember, the business press begins where the schools and col-

leges and textbooks leave off. The businesspaper is a new textbook, and a new, self-conducted examination every month. Who can say how much of our progress is due to a more universal burning of the midnight oil and the fact that the business press has helped mightily to provide us with the oil to burn and the information on how to burn it?

February 1, 1945

Preface to Second Revised Edition

More than a decade has passed since the first revised edition of *Business Journalism* was published. They have been eventful years for the world business press. In the United States the business press proved to be the nation's number one growth industry, making greater strides than any of the industries covered by the business press. Its growth was greater than the United States economy as a whole. The only other communications industry to approach it was television (Chapter V), and television has been slipping.

The author's colleagues in many other countries also report excellent progress in the same period for their own business press, particularly in the Federal Republic of Germany.

The specialized, professional, technical, scientific, industrial, or trade press, or business press, as it is variously called, has always commanded the respect of the business community. With the acceleration in technological development, however, businessmen and especially professionals everywhere have come to depend more heavily on the business press not only as a source of objective reporting, new knowledge, and technical know-how, but for interpretation, guidance, and leadership in a changing world that grows more complex every year.

In 1948, leading American businesspapers went back to school. The late J. K. Lasser, for many years consultant to businesspaper publishers, collaborated with the author in drawing up a sequence of workshop and orientation seminars. These seminars were sponsored by Northwestern University (Chicago campus) and New York University. Everyone from publishers to office boys had an opportunity to learn what made the businesspaper tick. The materials used in these courses fell into the author's lap to edit and organize, and four years later, in 1952, Harper & Brothers published a volume called

Businesspaper Publishing Practice. This second book, supplementing the first volume, *Business Journalism*, provided schools of journalism with what they had been asking for: an adequate body of knowledge on which to set up sequences for teaching business journalism to students who wished to make a career of it. The two books are also said to be useful to students in schools of business administration, advertising, marketing, and public relations and are used extensively by the working business press for on-the-job training.

Under the auspices of the publishers' and editors' associations, seminars and workshops continue in editorial, circulation, advertising, promotion, production, and administrative practice in New York City and Chicago.

During the past decade delegates of sixteen foreign countries, representing two hundred leading technical publications, attended three postwar congresses of the International Federation of the Periodical and Technical Press. The first, in 1950, was held in Paris, the Federation's headquarters. The second Congress met in Brussels in 1953, and the third in Copenhagen in 1956. United States, Canadian, and British businesspaper publishers, although not members of the Federation, have sent observers to each Congress. Magazine Publishers Association of New York, through the efforts of its treasurer, George Hecht, joined the International Federation of the Periodical & Technical Press in 1958, and will send an official delegation to the Berlin Congress in 1960. It is noteworthy that the first magazine publishers' association of an English-speaking nation to join is the largest in the United States, if not in the world, in point of number of titles, circulation, revenue, and capital investment represented by its membership.

It is hoped the Canadian and British businesspaper publishers will eventually sense the value of giving their support to this international group and send delegates to its congresses.

In 1958 there were forty-six colleges and universities with accredited schools of journalism, carrying some courses in magazine and business journalism. Not impressive when one knows there are two thousand colleges and universities in the United States. About 250 additional universities and colleges offer one or more courses in magazine journalism. Still not impressive. Apathy of the magazine press is partly responsible, due in some degree to the need of many businesspaper editors or consumer magazine editors for better educated people than come from some journalism schools.

The business press has begun to show some interest in journalism graduates as potential staff members. In November of 1952, John Philip Sousa III of *Time* magazine and the author, serving as a subcommittee, recommended to the other members of the Policy Committee of the Magazine Publishers Association a program of interneships for college journalism faculty members and students in accredited schools and in selected departments of journalism in smaller colleges. *Time, Life,* and *Look* magazines have had such programs on a limited scale. Journalism professors spend a month with these magazine staffs during the summer (all expenses paid), studying at firsthand the operation of a publishing house. They spend one week each in editorial, advertising, circulation, and promotion. *Red Book* and *The Saturday Evening Post* have taken student internes. The American Association of Industrial Editors (house magazines) have arranged interneships for journalism teachers with several of their member corporations for several summers.

Interneships of this nature have been used by the Council on Radio Journalism and the National Association of Radio and Television Broadcasters, The American Newspaper Publishers Association, and the Newspaper Advertising Executives Association for several years.

The interneship program was again proposed to MPA in May 1956 by Professor Floyd G. Arpan, Chairman of Magazine Sequences, Northwestern University, and by Professor Roland Wolseley, chairman of the Magazine Department, Syracuse University. In 1957, Robert Kenyon, President of MPA, established an interneship program.

Both the business press and the schools of journalism stand to profit from such a relationship with journalism teachers and graduates.

Journalism teaching in the United States is scarcely more than fifty or sixty years old, and that has been mainly newspaper journalism. Magazine journalism, and particularly business journalism, has been taught for less than two decades. Indeed, it was Dr. Frank Luther Mott's Pulitzer prize-winning four-volume *History of American Magazines,* first published in 1939, that stimulated leading American schools of journalism to set up courses in magazine journalism. We hope the business press and the consumer magazine press will see the wisdom of plowing back a percentage of their earnings into accredited schools of journalism as the newspaper and radio-television press have done. Sample copies of businesspapers are being supplied to some school of journalism libraries. A number of journalism schools have been admitted as "academic members" in the business press publishing associations, and several grants have been made to schools of journalism. These efforts must be intensified.

Many American editors and publishers have gone on business missions to other countries in recent years, either independently or under the sponsorship of the United States Department of Commerce. In addition, 32 traveling libraries of American businesspapers have been sent to 23 foreign countries by the Commerce department.

Since the launching of the first Sputnik, our country has shown a growing disposition to translate into English some of the many technical publications that come here from other countries, and thus benefit from other people's achievements and know-how.

Exchanges of businesspaper editors would prove as valuable to the cause of peace and understanding as the current exchange of college students.

Moreover, the United States Department of Commerce should include leading businesspaper editors on its teams of business leaders for foreign missions.

This edition sets up a universal nomenclature for both business and the journalism of business in an effort to improve communications between members of the world business press as well as the world business community.

We are happy to note that the United States digital code, Standard Industrial Classification, brought to the attention of the business press in our first edition (1945) was adopted by Business Publications Audit of Circulations, Inc., in 1958 and by *Industrial Marketing* for the *1959 Market Data and Directory* (July 25, 1958) and has been recommended by the Association of Industrial Advertisers' Media Practice Committee.

In this new edition we are able to bring together for the first time statistics of the world business press (Chapters I and VII). Unfortunately, the historically independent business press in certain European countries—East Germany, Czechoslovakia, Jugoslavia, Austria, Poland—is no longer independent. Businessmen in these iron-curtain countries avidly seek out and digest the contents of any independent businesspapers of free countries covering their fields they can obtain.

In this way they try to assess the veracity of the editorial content of their own government-controlled business press.

We have eliminated Book Two which appeared in earlier editions of this volume, because our follow-up volume, *Businesspaper Publishing Practice,* (1952) gives greater coverage-in-depth to the same subject: the functions of the various departments of a businesspaper publishing organization, particularly the editorial department. Detailed descriptions of eighteen executive positions are included in Chapter VII of this new edition.

These two volumes, the new edition of *Business Journalism* and *Businesspaper Publishing Practice,* are recommended for joint use by teachers and students of business journalism.

A third volume, in preparation, will furnish background for all students who plan careers in the fields of communications and communications engineering.

J. E.

Greenhaven, Rye, New York
September 1959

NORMAL LAWMAKING PROCEDURES

As the blueprint of the framework of government the constitution must provide for the organization and powers of the three branches of government—legislative, executive, and judicial. Although there is a separate article relating to each branch, the article relating to the legislature ordinarily contains but a small portion of the provisions affecting that body, restrictive provisions being scattered throughout the remainder of the document. Moreover, the detail in the rest of the document is frequently more important than the legislative article in determining the area within which the legislature may act.

These facts, so familiar to the student of constitutional law, are frequently not at all clear to the layman. The state legislature is a repository of the residual powers of the people. Unless restricted by provisions in the state constitution itself, it can do anything that has not been delegated to the national government or expressly or impliedly denied to the states by the federal Constitution. Grants of power to the federal government operate as restrictions upon the otherwise plenary powers of the state legislature, even though stated not in terms of limitation. In addition a doctrine of implied limitation applied by the courts in the interpretation of state constitutions removes from legislative judgment and decision many matters of governmental organization and powers that were fixed in the constitution in an earlier period in the history of the state and that now require constitutional amendment to effect needed changes.

The constitutional basis for the legislature, consequently, cannot be understood without careful examination of the provisions of all of the other articles of the constitution: the structure of the executive department and the judicial department; provisions as to local government, education, taxation, budget procedure, and other aspects of finance; and limitations in the bill of rights and specific prohibitions against the abuse of legislative power. The more detailed these articles, the more the legislature will be restricted in its ability to meet future problems in these fields.

In all constitutions or constitutional amendments adopted by 1850, and for more than fifty years thereafter, the emotional basis upon

Acknowledgments

THE author is deeply grateful for the cooperation he has received in bringing this work up to date.

The author owes a debt of gratitude for criticism and comment on the definition of business in Chapter I to the following: Lewis Mumford, Stuart Chase, Bernard Baruch, Edward Bernays, Lowell B. Mason, Dean Donald K. David, Justice Thurman Arnold, Henry A. Wallace, Robert A. Nathan, Professor Sumner H. Slichter, Paul Hoffman, Norman H. Strouse, Henry Ford II, T. V. Houser, Louis Engel, Dr. Robert G. James, W. Homer Turner, J. Ward Keener, C. R. Cox, and D. J. McCanney, and to the Editors of *Encyclopedia Britannica* for permission to reproduce this definition.

To Elmer J. Tangerman, editor of *Product Engineering*, for his comprehensive paper on small business and his report on Russia.

To Ralph Smith, former editorial director, and Henry G. Lord, honorary chairman of the finance committee, McGraw-Hill.

To Godfrey Lebhar (chain stores) and M. M. Zimmerman (supermarkets) for information about the fields they pioneered.

To Bernard Gallagher (salary survey).

To H. B. Bachrach, communication specialist, General Electric Company; chairman, International Council of Industrial Editors.

The author wishes to express his gratitude to these college teachers of magazine journalism, who offered valuable suggestions for changes in the new edition: Professor DeWitt C. Reddick, University of Texas; Professor Donald D. Burchard, Agricultural and Mechanical College of Texas; Professor Roland E. Wolseley, Syracuse University; Professor Louis Alexander, University of Houston; Professor Hillier Krieghbaum, New York University.

For statistical information on the world business press (Chapter VI) special thanks are due the following:

ACKNOWLEDGMENTS

Belgium: Robert Bodson of Brussels; Dr. Jan-Albert Goris, Belgian Information Service of New York; Lubertus Smilde, J. Walter Thompson Co., New York; J. Ricquier, Brussels, president of the Union of the Belgian Periodical Press; President, F.I.P.P.

France: Urbain J. Thuau, General Secretary and Founder, International Federation of the Periodical Press, Paris; M. T. Louveau, Director of Media, Elvinger Conseils en Vente et an Publicité, Paris.

Japan: Seiji Chihara, manager, Dentsu Advertising, Tokyo.

Great Britain: T. Ward Grice, Angmering-on-sea, Sussex; W. L. Hill and John Wheatley, London.

Netherlands: W. H. Van Baarle and G. M. Vander Mark, Netherlands Organization of Periodical Publishers, The Hague; Ph. J. Gomperts, executive secretary, Netherlands Chamber of Commerce in the United States, New York.

West Germany: Christoph Ledermann, German-American Chamber of Commerce, New York; Mengele & Dehmel, of Carl Gabler Werbegesellshaft, München; H. A. Kluthe *Frankfurte Illustrierte*, Frankfurt am Main; Arnold Miethe, Verbund Deutscher Zeitschriftenverlager.

Russia: V. Alkhimov, Commercial Counselor, Embassy of the Union of Soviet Socialist Republics, Washington, D. C.

Denmark: C. H. W. Hasselriis, director, Danish Information Office, New York.

Canada: Alan C. Ball, *Canadian Advertising,* Toronto; George Mansfield, Business Newspapers Association, Toronto.

Czechoslovakia: M. Valenta and Jerome Horoly, The Czechoslovak Foreign Institute in Exile, Chicago.

Norway: Jon Embretsen, manager, Norwegian Information Service, Embassy of Norway, New York.

Australia: Oswald Mingay, managing director, *Australian Advertising Rate & Data Service,* Sidney, Australia, and publisher of *Electrical Weekly* of Australia.

Sweden: A. Hörnquist, Tidningsstatistik Aktiebolag T. S., Solna (Swedish ABC) and publishers of the *Swedish Advertising Rate Book;* Gunnar Hambraeus, editor, *Teknisk Tidskrift,* and president, Swedish Association of The Periodical Press.

Switzerland: Vice Consul Rudolf M. Neeser, The Consulate General of Switzerland, N. Y.

Italy: David James, J. Walter Thompson Co., S.R.L., Milan, Italy;

ACKNOWLEDGMENTS

Ugo Morabito, Commercial Counsellor, Italian Embassy, Washington, D.C.

United States: Messrs. Walter E. Botthof and Laury Botthof, Dr. H. P. Alspaugh, Jay Dee Loomis of *Standard Rate & Data Service*, Evanston, Illinois; Angelo R. Venezian, vice president, McGraw-Hill Book Co., New York; William B. Lanier, McGraw-Hill Book Co.; the Editors of *Printers' Ink*; Irene Pearson, Associated Business Publications; Robert E. Harper, president, National Business Publications, Washington.

Grateful appreciation to Miss Marie Puglis, the author's assistant, for her invaluable help.

the fundamental constitutional basis of the legislature as originally intended in the earlier editions of the model constitution, but merely attempts to implement that provision so that it will operate, as it is failing rather completely to do in the modern period.

This question of reapportionment has been a stumbling block in various constitutional conventions in past years, but recommendations for more fundamental changes in the principle of representation are still largely in the academic stage, as they are not understood by the layman and are opposed by overrepresented districts that would undoubtedly lose representation on the basis of any change that might be made. Even where reapportionment takes place in accordance with the constitutional mandate, the existence of constitutional requirements with regard to minimum representation for counties may prevent representation of the people on a fair and equitable basis.

Effect of Restrictive Provisions

Most of the present state constitutions were framed in an era of fear and distrust of state legislatures, and past history provided much evidence for this distrust on a rational basis. The modern legislature, however, requires an entirely different psychological approach, aimed at freeing the legislature from the numerous limitations of most constitutions, indicated in Chapter 1, and permitting more discretion in the light of the very different history of most state legislatures in the last fifty years.

Considerable research is desirable to present concrete evidence of the effect of restrictions or to demonstrate that legislative power is not abused in states lacking such restrictions, in order to develop a general awareness of the reasons why the experts in this particular field do feel confident that a shift in the present constitutional basis would be wise and sound. Some monographs do exist, but the variations in the forty-eight state jurisdictions are so great that much more specific work needs to be done within each jurisdiction; also needed are complete cross references to other states for comparative purposes on the basis of somewhat similar studies. To the student it seems clear that the present constitutional restrictions have handicapped the

BUSINESS JOURNALISM

CHAPTER I

HOW WE DEFINE THE BUSINESS PRESS

1. Magnitude of the World Business Press

THE businesspaper is the most potent kind of *continuing education* in our adult world. No other medium, moreover, is as effective or economical for reaching and influencing the majority of prime decision-makers.

Every industrialized country has a business press of some sort. Our survey of the business press of 16 such countries, including the United States (see Table 1), shows that in 1957-58 there were published in these countries 14,507 different titles, with a combined readership estimated to be over 138 million.

In European countries many publishers are reticent about revealing their advertising revenue or circulation figures (for reasons best known to themselves).[1] In Japan, Italy, Russia, and Czechoslovakia we had to guess at the circulation.

We estimate that if the actual circulation figure of the entire world business press were available it would be in excess of 150 million.

Six countries, West Germany, Sweden, The Netherlands, England, Canada and the United States, furnish complete statistical information about their business press: number of titles published, total paid and free circulation, and annual advertising revenue in dollars.

Any accurate estimate of advertising revenue of the entire world business press is, therefore, impossible. In Table 1, however, you will see that the combined advertising revenue of these six countries alone is more than $916,000,000. It would be a fair guess to say that the world business community spends over a billion dollars a year to

[1] See Chap. IV, section 5.

TABLE 1. Statistics of World Business Press (1957-58)*

Country	Titles	Circulation	Advertising Revenue (*Dollars*)	House Organs
Australian	360	420,224	———	———
Belgian	335	2,614,918	———	———
British	2,280	25,000,000 A	108,600,000	305
Canadian	423	5,000,000 AC	27,845,625	———
Czechoslovakian	143	1,000,000 E	———	———
Danish	452	1,928,036	———	———
Dutch	576	3,250,000	16,000,000	———
French	317	3,092,543	———	———
West German	1,703	23,069,800 A	232,700,000	600
Italian	2,000	10,000,000 E	———	———
Japanese	939	5,000,000 E	———	———
Norwegian	125	650,000	———	———
Swedish	1500	6,500,000	7,150,000	———
Swiss	700	6,000,000 E	———	———
Soviet	561	5,000,000 E	———	———
United States	2,093	43,135,742 AC	524,700,000	8,000
	14,507	138,459,257	919,850,000 A	8,905 A

* See Chap. VII for later figures in some countries
E: Estimate
A: Accurate for those periodicals for which figures were furnished
AC: Accurate and complete

underwrite the world business press, with advertising and subscriptions, in order to get the rich know-how and know-what the business press digs up and processes.

The categories which each country designated with the information supplied to us are fairly standard, although not broken down into as many specialized fields as are used in United States and Canadian periodical directories. In some countries the classifications rarely go beyond these: trade, engineering, transportation, communication, education, agriculture, medical and industrial sciences, construction, religion, labor, jurisprudence. More than 160 distinct classifications are used to identify the United States business press.

In some countries businesspaper publishers practice the same kind of secrecy as the business firms they serve, instead of setting an example for the business community. Failure of these publishers to exchange information with each other on accounting for profit and loss and on other administrative practices, added to their reluctance to pool their statistics on number of readers served, purchasing power of the readership, and the income derived from advertising net billings, subscriptions, and miscellaneous services, is a two-edged sword: this isolationism cuts down their influence in the business community, especially with the advertising agency group. It cuts down their own growth as publishers. We can only advance if we exchange good and bad experiences with one another.[2] Business, like science, starves in an atmosphere of secrecy.

Detailed information on the business press of each country in the survey will be found in Chapter VII.

An estimated world readership for the business press of 150 million is about 6 per cent of the earth's population, estimated to be about two and a half billion people (1957). This small group make the policy and operating decisions which determine the present and future welfare of the remaining 94 per cent of the people on earth, a rather awesome fact. It serves to emphasize the heavy moral, social, and economic responsibility with which the publishers and editors of business periodicals are charged, since they are acknowledged to exert so strong an influence on the primary decision-makers of the world.

With so many decision-makers in every field of human activity continuously studying reports of other experiments and contributing the results of their own findings in the business press, the world's leadership is able to keep pace with its own specializations. The leaders are also able, by reading the business press, to get some feeling of coherence and orientation with the fast-moving outside world. Herein lies a hopeful sign for universal understanding and permanent peace through professional business journalism.

2. The Journalism of Business

Business journalism is the organized, systematic, and periodic extraction of news-information, know-how, and know-what from the most authentic sources, its transformation into intelligence, and its timely distribution to the prime decision-makers and the labor force in all fields of human activity by competent editors, reporters, technical contributors, and publishers.

Businesspaper is the generic term applied to independent technical periodicals published in either magazine or newspaper format and

[2] See J. K. Lasser, C.P.A., "Fundamentals in Businesspaper Accounting," *Businesspaper Publishing Practice* (New York, Harper & Brothers, 1952), pp. 26-53.

issued in regularly specified frequencies (at least four times a year) to serve special fields of private or public enterprise and not directed to the public at large.

These are minimal definitions. This entire chapter is the definition. Businesspapers have been and are variously identified by such prefixes as follows (for example, "Trade Journal," "Product Paper," etc.):

Trade-	Class-	Financial-
Industrial-	Professional-	Educational-
Merchandising-	Marketing-	Export-Import-
Scientific-	Agricultural-	Military-
Service-	Religious-	Naval-
Institutional-	Medical-	Specialized-
Managerial-	Legal-	Product-
Engineering-	Technical-	Commercial-

3. Nomenclature of Publishing

Dr. Frank Luther Mott, Pulitzer Prize Winner for his monumental four-volume *History of American Magazines,* distinguishes between the terms publication, periodical, magazine, review, journal, and paper, as follows:

Publication: any issue of the press bound or unbound.

Periodical: issued at intervals, more or less regular, of a variety of reading matter.

Magazine: a storehouse or collection (also once known as a "museum" and sometimes as a "repository" or "casket") bound and issued more or less regularly; today the most popular and meaningful general term.

Review: originally a periodical containing a number of long articles, mainly book reviews. Today, review of current thought.

Journal: originally meant daily (diurnal); now connotes a serious or technical periodical.

Paper: a publication without stapling, stitching, or cover. Newspapers are referred to as "papers" by the public, and a typed or printed speech read before a group or organization is called a "paper." Such "papers" are often reprinted in journals.[3]

Businesspaper is the term most frequently used by the independent business press of the United States and Canada, just as newspaper is the term most frequently used by the independent daily consumer press.

[3] Frank Luther Mott, A *History of American Magazines,* 4 vols. (Cambridge, Harvard University Press, 1939-1956), Vol. I, pp. 5-9.

Throughout this text it will be noted that businesspaper is spelled as one word, without hyphen, just as newspaper is universally spelled as one word.

Businesspapers are also distinguished in these eight ways:

1. *By commodity group:* producers' goods and services (sometimes called capital goods) and consumers' goods and services.

2. *By circulation:* character, quality, and type of reader, which will identify him with some kind of industry; but this bracket also is used to indicate whether the reader pays for the paper or gets it free, and what kind of audit determines those facts.

3. *By geography:* international, national, regional, sectional, or local.

4. *By format:* magazine size (large and standard), newspaper size (large and tabloid), pocket size.

5. *By frequency:* daily, weekly, biweekly, semimonthly, monthly, bimonthly, quarterly.

6. *By subject matter:* one businesspaper directory, *Standard Rate & Data Service,* has 160 classifications by subject matter, from Advertising, Air Conditioning, Amusements, and Architecture through the remainder of the alphabet to Water Supply, Welding, Wire Products, and Woodworking. This index is sometimes called "Market Classification."

7. *By title:* Every periodical directory has an alphabetical index by title, and the title of most businesspapers indicates the subject matter and/or "market" covered.

8. *Horizontal or vertical:* businesspapers that circulate across the broad width of an industry or cover a single function common to all industry are called horizontal; businesspapers which serve a single industry or field or special operation in depth are called vertical.

In the "Standard Industrial Classification" (S.I.C.) of economic activities of the United States, the Government has given "Industry Code Numbers" to the Printing, Publishing, and Allied Industries and these numbers are used uniformly by all Government agencies.[4]

These are the S.I.C. codes and titles used by the Government Census Bureau, for example:

Code	*Title*
2711	Newspapers
2721	Periodicals

[4] See Chapt. I, section 12, for more detail on "Standard Industrial Classification."

2731	Books, publishing and printing
2732	Book printing
2741	Miscellaneous publishing (Directories, racing forms, sheet music, almanacs, maps, etc.)

The Census Bureau treats the term newspaper (Industry 2711) "including those publications issued at regular frequencies which *contain news of interest to the general public.*" (ITALICS MINE.)

Publications are classified as periodicals (Industry 2721) rather than newspapers "if their news and editorial presentations *do not appear to be directed to the public at large.*" (ITALICS MINE.)

The Census Bureau says:

> Among the types of publications sometimes considered newspapers, but treated in the Census as periodicals, are the following: trade journals; house organs; local church or school papers and like publications with very limited or specialized news treatment. Generally, publications issued by non-profit organizations (educational, religious, charitable, labor, business, professional, etc.) are classified as periodicals.
>
> This Industry (2721) [the Census Bureau continues], comprises establishments primarily engaged in publishing periodicals, or in preparing, publishing and printing periodicals. These establishments carry on the various operations necessary for issuing periodicals but may or may not perform their own printing. Establishments not engaged in publishing periodicals, but which print or lithograph periodicals for publishers, are classified in Industry 2751, Commercial Printing, or 2761, Lithographing, depending on the primary printing process employed.[5]

The term publisher is used by the Census Bureau to designate "the person *or organization* by whom or in whose name newspapers, periodicals and other publications are listed.[6] (ITALICS MINE.)

A multiple publisher or group publisher is "one who publishes three or more different periodicals."[7]

4. Businesspaper Compared with Other Media

Consider these essential differences in comparing the independent businesspaper with other carriers of information.

[5] U.S. Bureau of the Census, *U.S. Census of Manufactures, 1954,* Industry Bulletin MC-27A, pp. 1, 2, Newspapers, Periodicals, Books and Miscellaneous Publishing (Washington, D. C., U.S. Government Printing Office), 20 cents.

[6] Ibid.

[7] *Industrial Marketing* (1959 Market Data and Directory Number), June 25, 1958.

The newspaper: spot news of interest to the general public, politics, crime, finance, social or "society" events and gossip, foreign correspondence, columnists on almost every subject, woman's page, sports, amusement, comics, crossword puzzles, menus, astrology, and cheesecake.

The general magazine: fiction and non-fiction for popular entertainment or information, amusement, or relaxation of the public at large, such as *The Saturday Evening Post.*

The specialized magazine for consumers: dealing with hobbies, sports, travel, adventure, etc., such as *Yachting, Popular Mechanics, Field & Stream, Holiday, Gourmet, Boy's Life,* and *Popular Science.*

The news weekly: digests of general news events, war, politics, crime, general economics with or without popular interpretations, such as *Time* or *Newsweek.*

The women's magazines: fiction, fashions, home economics, household and garden equipment, decoration, humor, theater, music, ballet, cinema, such as *Ladies' Home Journal* or *McCall's.*

Radio: soap opera and grand opera, disc jockeys, quiz programs, news, sports, weather, panels, interviews, announcements.

Television: old movies, live drama, grand and soap opera, quiz shows, animated cartoons, variety, ballet, sports, weather, news, education, interviews, panels.

Organization bulletins and publications: spokesman for special interest groups. These do not publish criticism of their sponsors but serve a useful purpose in distributing information.

Dictionaries, encyclopedias, thesauri: definitions and explanations.

Directories and data books: information tabulated for easy reference.

Catalog files: bound collections of catalogs by manufacturers and dealers.

House organs: internal (employee) and external (for stockholders and customers, suppliers, etc.) issued by private corporations and concerned with policies, products, and services.

Technical books, yearbooks, manuals: excellent reference source but some of its material is out of date by the time it leaves the bindery.

Equipment periodicals: brief reports of products, components, materials, such as *Product Design and Development.*

Publications of Governmental Agencies: often valuable, not always timely.

Businesspaper: avoids partisan politics, crime, social gossip, scandal, comics, fiction, sports; is the current textbook of adult education in business economics; publishes the know-how and know-what (technologies) for making a living—improving the job, solving problems, making decisions. Has an editorial page in every issue on which the editor is not afraid to be critical. Reports new processes, procedures, policies, new materials, new ideas. Primary objective is to advance the status of the field; secondary objective is to make new knowledge available. Businesspaper screens out inaccurate information; supplements incomplete data; reports on research and development; evaluates, analyzes, interprets; trains managers in the principles as well as the technics of management. Independent, it welcomes and publishes criticism of itself.

As one businesspaper editorial director said: "We forward men's life's work, out of which come the means to all other satisfactions in life . . . from indulging in marriage when you are young, to financing a hobby when you are old."[8]

5. The Readers Are the Prime Decision-Makers

Businesspapers are published for people on the managerial level who need *continuing* education and knowledge because they have to continuously make the prime decisions—not only for themselves but for the millions in every field of human activity in a rapidly changing world.

In the United States the destiny of 174 million people (1957) is in the hands of 38 million prime decision-makers (the readership of the United States business press in 1957).

In the entire world two and a half billion people depend on the decisions of 150 million decision-makers (the estimated readership of the world business press in 1957) who are the managers of all human enterprise.

The President of the United States asked, at a recent conference in New York:

> What is our economy anyway? Emphatically it is not the Federal Reserve System, or the Treasury, or the Congress, or the White House.
>
> This nation of 43,000,000 families, 174,000,000 people, is what we all think and what we do. This is our economy.

[8] Ralph Smith, editorial director of McGraw-Hill Book Co., at the Jesse Neal Editorial Awards Dinner, Washington, D. C., April, 1956.

Our economy is the result of millions of decisions we all make every day about producing, earning, serving, investing, spending. Both our individual prosperity, and our nation's prosperity, rest directly on the decisions all of us are making now.[9]

6. Know-How Is a Universal Continuum

Throughout this text the editorial content of the businesspaper is frequently referred to as know-how. On the jacket and in promotional mailing pieces for the first edition back in 1946 the publishers described this volume as "The Story of Know-How."

What exactly is meant by know-how?

An Oxonian (and a college president) in a booklet widely distributed nearly a decade ago made some disparaging remarks about the term know-how.

"As to our famous know-how," he wrote, "I think that word (which is pompous gobbledegook for 'skill') has already done our thinking enough harm. It always implies that scientific knowledge and industrial technique can be found only in America."[10]

There is some basis for this critic's opinion. A lot of people have grown up in the belief that Americans are responsible for all modern inventions and know everything better than people of any other nationality.

If many citizens have always regarded know-how as a strictly American brand name, it may be because they were taught in grade school and high school (even in some colleges) that Americans invented everything from steam boats, automobiles, telephones, and airplanes, to atomic bombs.

The author, sometime before the advent of Sputnik I, attended a press party given by an American distillery in the Hotel Waldorf-Astoria, New York, where the host staged a tableau to prove (quite seriously) that Americans had invented vodka.

The Russians, tongue-in-cheek, have in turn themselves laid claim to most modern inventions, perhaps to offset American propaganda of this type.

Know-how is a product of every country on earth. For much of our modern know-how all the world must thank the great mathematicians,

[9] Dwight D. Eisenhower, at the Economic Mobilization Conference, New York City, May 20, 1958.

[10] Stringfellow Barr, *Let's Join the Human Race* (Chicago, University of Chicago Press), 1950.

astronomers, and physicists of ancient Egypt, Assyria, Phoenicia, Greece, Babylon, Mesopotamia, Rome, and the land of the "inevitable priority," China.

"The great cultures of the East cannot be walled off by impassable seas and defects of understanding based on ignorance and unfamiliarity," says Dr. Robert Oppenheimer. "Neither our integrity as men of learning nor our humanity allows that."[11]

Which country's know-how gave us nuclear energy? Was it "American," meaning the United States? Was it England? Was it Sweden? If you check, you will find such names as O. R. Frisch and Niels Bohr (Denmark); Enrico Fermi (Italy); Isador Isaac Rabi (Austria); Lise Meitner, Fritz Strassman, Otto Hahn, Albert Einstein (Germany); Marie Curie, Frederic Joliot, L. Kowarski (France); Leo Szilard (Hungary); Arthur H. Compton, Ernest O. Lawrence, Harold C. Urey, J. Robert Oppenheimer, Linz W. Alvarez, Richard P. Feynman, James R. Coe, Jr,., H. T. Wensel (United States).

Look again at the names. What were the origins of these people? These are but a few of the scientists of many nationalities, races, religions, and creeds who "invented" the atom bomb. Englishmen really set the stage for it: Dr. J. J. Thomson discovered electrons in 1897. Dr. Ernest Rutherford gave us the theory of the atomic nucleus in 1913. Professor Chadwick of Cambridge discovered the neutron in 1932. In Germany, Dr. Max Planck announced the quantum theory in 1900.

Each scientist contributed the accumulated know-how of his country, his race, his environment, his experience and observation, his education, his inheritance. This know-how was based, in turn, on the accumulated know-how of astronomers, chemists, mathematicians, physicists and metaphysicists, anthropologists, neurologists, engineers, instrument makers, yes, even poets and philosophers, of centuries past. Every invention is an accretion of universal know-how.

The term know-how is standard universal usage to denote a special kind of intelligence, as distinguished from mere skill, no matter where in the world you find it.

Know-how is something more than skill. Skill is a word that means experience in execution or performance, like the skill of a mechanic or the skill of a surgeon. Know-how is *unending* knowledge gained—

[11] J. Robert Oppenheimer, *The Open Mind* (New York, Simon and Schuster, Inc., 1955), p. 144.

a *continuum.* Take two skilled mechanics, for example: they work in the same plant for ten years. The first remains a skilled mechanic. The second becomes superintendent of the plant and in time president of the company. The second mechanic acquired the know-how to rise above his skill. He was not content in his skill as a mechanic.

In time the first mechanic, in spite of his skill, was replaced by an electronic machine. He found himself out of work. The second mechanic, who became president, installed the machine.

A surgeon may have the skill to remove an appendix but not have the know-how to recognize and treat cancer. His diagnosis could be a death sentence for the patient.

Know-how involves wider comprehension: knowing something thoroughly, perceiving its relationship to other facts and ideas. You keep on learning more about it and around it (like the mechanic who became superintendent). You work out new combinations, you test out new theories, you observe, you distinguish, you relate. You read or hear or watch what others do. You reproduce their experiments, you learn, learn, learn, that's how you acquire know-how. It is a *continuing* context of knowledge.

What matters as much as the *know* is the *how* and the *what.* The *how* embraces the *when* and *where* and *what with* and *what for.* And the *why.*

"There is one quality more important than know-how," says Dr. Wiener, "and we cannot accuse the United States of any undue amount of it. This is 'know-what': by which we determine not only how to accomplish our purposes, *but what our purposes are to be.*"[12] (ITALICS MINE.)

MacIver lists four kinds of knowing:

1. *Knowing how to do.*
2. *Knowing what to do.*
3. *Knowing how to think.*
4. *Knowing what to think.*

Dr. MacIver says:

> The knowledge how to do is training in techniques. . . . as for knowing what to do . . . that depends on knowing what to think. You notice I

[12] Norbert Wiener, *The Human Use of Human Beings* (Boston, Houghton Mifflin Co., 1950), p. 210. Dr. Wiener is Professor of Mathematics at Massachusetts Institute of Technology. Also available, a revised paperbound edition, Doubleday & Co., N.Y. 1956.

speak of *knowing*, not remembering. Too much of our education is memorizing, drill on memory, so you remember and then forget—that's all it amounts to. And that goes for some so-called higher education, too.

We do not teach people to think . . . sometimes we teach them how to avoid thinking. To think is, first, to distinguish things, and then to relate them. That's how to find the truth of things—to distinguish, to relate, and, through relating, to see things together, and thus to comprehend, to appreciate them. We learn when we discover a meaning in its context, a sound in its harmony of sounds, a star in its constellation, an event in its setting, a human action in the complex of character, a human being in his group, a group in its community. Thus we reach out to our world, and, if we learn it right, we become one with it.

We need, I contend, much less of this memorizing business and much more of this essential training—to distinguish, to relate, to understand, to appreciate.[13]

7. The Definition of Definition

The most useless place to look for a satisfactory definition is a dictionary. A frustrating experience is to try to win an argument with a dictionary.

The meaning of a word is in *time*—the time in which it is used, as Mr. Justice Holmes observed:

"*A word is not a crystal, transparent and unchanged; it is the skin of a living thought and may vary greatly in color and content according to the circumstances and the time in which it is used.*"

To repeat, the real meaning of a word is in time—in "the instant."

José Ortega y Gasset wrote:

Nobody will make bold to maintain that the meaning of a word can be gathered from dictionaries. A dictionary furnishes, at best, a general scheme in which the manifold actual significations a word admits of may be inserted. But the real meaning of a word appears when the word is uttered and functions in the human activity called speech. Hence we must know who says it to whom, when and where. Which indicates that meaning, like all things human, depends on circumstance. . . .

What the word fails to say, circumstance mutely adds. Language is a text that calls for illustrations. The illustrations are furnished by the lived and living reality out of which a man speaks, a reality essentially unstable

[13] "What Should Be the Goals of Education?" an address over the National Broadcasting Company network, September 24, 1948, by Dr. R. M. MacIver, Lieber Professor of Political Philosophy and Sociology, Columbia University. See also *1948 Report of Conference on Science, Philosophy and Religion* (New York, Harper & Brothers, 1949).

and fleeting, emerging and vanishing never to return. The real meaning of a word is not in the dictionary; it is in the instant. . . .[14]

Korzybski stated:

If we enquire about the "meaning" of a word we find it depends upon the "meaning" of other words used in defining it and if we ask the meaning of the words used in the definition we eventually arrive at "the undefined terms" which, at a given period, can not be elucidated any further.[15]

Says Hayakawa:

Ultimately, no adequate definition of apple pie can be given in words—one has to examine and taste an actual apple pie.[16]

And Keyser:

If he contend, as sometimes he will contend, that he has defined all his terms and proved all his propositions, then either he is a performer of logical miracles or he is an ass; and, as you know, logical miracles are impossible.[17]

Finally, Dorothy Lee:

This thing which I hold in my hand as I write *is* not a pencil; I *call* it a *pencil*. And it remains the same whether I call it a *pencil, molyvi, bleistift,* or *siwiqoq*. These words are different sounding complexes applied to the same reality; but is the difference merely one of sound-complex? Do they refer to the same perceived reality? Pencil originally meant little tail; it delimited and named the reality according to form. *Molyvi* means lead and refers to the writing-element. *Bleistift* refers both to the form and the writing element. *Siwiqoq* means painting-stick and refers to observed function and form. Each culture has phrased the reality differently.[18]

But we also speak of a *pencil* of light, a styptic *pencil*, an eyebrow *pencil*, a *pencil* post bed.

The march of time and the march of language make obsolete the judgments of those who write dictionaries. The dictionary writer is

[14] José Ortega y Gasset, *Concord and Liberty*, (New York, W. W. Norton & Co., 1932).

[15] Alfred Korzybski, *Science and Sanity*, (2nd ed.; Lancaster, Pa., Science Press Printing Co., 1941), p. 21.

[16] S. I. Hayakawa, *Language in Thought and Action* (New York, Harcourt, Brace, & Co., 1949).

[17] Cassius J. Keyser, *Mathematical Philosophy*. Boston, E. P. Dutton, 1922.

[18] Dorothy Lee, "Psychosomatic Medicine," *ETC*, Quarterly of the International Society of General Semantics, Vol. VIII, No. One, Autumn 1950, p. 13.

just a mortal man and he relies on the works of well-know authors and writers for help in writing his definitions *at that moment.*

Always check the date of a dictionary or any other reference book, chart, map, or other reference. The first dictionary of English was written about 1440.[19]

8. Definition of the Businesspaper[20]

The businesspaper (*ca.* 1950-1959) is the continuous textbook of adult education for managers, both in its editorial and advertising columns. It is the up-to-the-minute, automatically self-correcting textbook in every technical and professional field. The good businesspaper does five specific things for decision-makers. It provides:

1. Practical economics for advancing the status of every industry and profession.

2. The know-how and know-what for stimulating and preserving fair competition, for increasing production, improving methods and technics, lowering costs, and elevating the working and living standards of employees.

3. The distribution technologies for delivering a higher standard of living to more family units and a consequent higher purchasing power for goods and services.

4. The training, discipline, and inspiration for human leadership.

5. The impartial, documented, pragmatic editorial criticism which is the prophylaxis of the private competitive free enterprise system.

9. Functions of the Businesspaper

The independently owned businesspaper is both a private profit enterprise and a quasi-public medium of communications. As a privately owned and operated business for profit it functions like most other private businesses. As a communications utility it is vested with a public interest and performs these basic functions:

1. *Adult education function:* providing the technical "know-how": information on management, maintenance, materials handling, methodology, marketing, and merchandising.

2. *News function:* gathering, processing, and disseminating busi-

[19] Geoffrey The Grammarian, *Promptorium Parvulorum sive Clericorum,* (Pynson, London, 1499).

[20] *Advertising Agency Magazine,* a businesspaper in the field of marketing and advertising, in April 1950, gave prominence to our definition of a businesspaper as it appeared in the first edition. Reading it, we can see no need to improve that definition in opening the first chapter of this new edition.

ness news-intelligence: news of products and services, materials and methods, research, equipment, and processes; news of people.

3. *Editorial function:* criticizing, interpreting, guiding, crusading, and pioneering to advance the status of the individual and the industry, trade, or profession of which he is a part. Interpreting the meaning of news events and forecasting trends.

4. *Forum function:* Town Hall-in-print. A meeting place in the editorial columns for discussion and criticism by the readers of all phases of business and professional enterprise, including criticism of the businesspaper itself.

5. *Advertising function:* selling and merchandising goods and services in print and enlarging the know-how of industry by means of paid advertising messages.

6. *Research function:* periodic engagement in and publication of market analyses, audience and readership surveys, research and product development studies, and studies of buying, selling, and operating procedure and performance.

7. *Public relations function:* giving information to its various "publics": advertisers and potential advertisers, readers, advertising agencies, news associations, wire services, other media, trade associations, institutions, research groups, government, labor, its own employees, stockholders, investors, and the ultimate consumer.

8. *Public utility function:* the responsibility to give the reader all sides of important questions; to keep the columns open as a forum for the readers; the responsibility to provide continuous service at fair rates in return for the *franchise from the public* which guarantees freedom to the press to print the truth without fear or prejudice or revelation of sources.

9. *Integrating function:* the performance of this function depends upon the *attitudes* of publishers as well as editors: an awareness of their social responsibilities, a sense of public trusteeship, a sense of identification with and appreciation of the *interdependence* of all human industry, of the relationship of the parts to the whole economic system, a devotion to what is known in law as the "public interest." To put the larger interest above any sectional, group or private interest is to perform the function of statesmanship, whether one is a journalist or any other kind of public servant.[21] The journalist is a public servant.

[21] See *Businesspaper Publishing Practice* for detailed explanation of these functions.

10. Qualifications of a Business Journalist

1. *Know how to think:* how to distinguish, to relate, to understand, appraise, appreciate, and discriminate between values; have the ability to judge what is first rate, to tell good from bad or mediocre; be able to reflect, to contemplate; apply an orderly process to creativity; possess a lively imagination.

2. *Know how to express oneself:* have the ability to write well, speak well, to make others understand your meanings; have some training in teaching and in the technics of journalism; have the ability to make decisions, to voice a considered opinion.[22]

3. *Know how to research:* how to apply specific, logical, scientific method to investigation; know how to listen, how to observe, know where to go for documentation, how to check and verify; know how to separate fact from fantasy, the real from the phony; be disciplined in general semantics; be able to distinguish between proper and "impropaganda."

4. *Know what to think:* have a clear picture of objectives, purposes, significance; have a synthesis of knowledge of the complex world we live in; have a sense of humor.

5. *Be professional in attitude:* be dedicated to journalism as a career, not as a stepping-stone to something else; have a respect for professional standards of practice, a sense of deep obligation to society, a feeling of great responsibility to the reader; have the courage to stand up for the truth; publish both sides of controversial issues.

11. Alphabets of Communication

An alphabet is any orderly or logical arrangement of signs or symbols.

Five elementary alphabets helped establish communication between men and made possible our societal organizations: One was the numbers alphabet (1, 2, 3, 4). A second was the letters alphabet (A, B, C). The third was the calendar (days, weeks, months, years). The fourth was space maps, and the fifth, the musical scale.

With the numbers men worked out systems of weights and meas-

[22] "Lucidity, simplicity, and euphony" are the three qualities recommended by Somerset Maugham, *The Summing Up* (New York, Doubleday & Co., 1938). A good handbook for any writer—fiction or non-fiction.

ures and mathematical formulae and made possible the business enterprise system.

With the letters men formed words, phrases, sentences, chapters, books, and libraries of ideas and information.

With the calendar time was organized.

With the maps men charted the lands and the seas, recorded the latitudes and longitudes, mapped out villages, towns, cities, counties, states, nations, continents, and a world state.

With the one dozen notes in the chromatic scale the creative musician has 1,302,061,344 possible combinations with which to produce melodic meaning, and in horizontal, vertical, and counterpoint the realm of music extends to 127,000 "googols."[23]

These elementary alphabets are no longer sufficient. As we progress they have to be supplemented by other alphabets such as the profile of technics: eotechnic, paleotechnic, neotechnic, biotechnic.[24]

Scientists, for example, have set up all kinds of alphabets: the sequence of stellar spectra, planets of the solar system, animal societies, classes of mammalia, the major phyla of animals and plants, a classification of material systems, a geological time-table, a periodic table of elements, the radiation sequence.[25]

The new alphabet of business (Table 2) and the classification of the business press along parallel lines (Chapter II) was originally set forth in the first edition of this book in 1945.

Dr. Frank Thayer, Professor of Journalism, University of Wisconsin, who wrote the chapter on business journalism for the *New Survey of Journalism,* had this to say of our alphabet of business and the journalism of business:

"Probably the most scientific classification of business papers is one that parallels the classification of industry. The basic divisions of this fourfold classification are extractive, transformative, contributive and distributive."[26]

[23] Leonard Bernstein, over the Columbia Broadcasting System, Feb. 22, 1959. In a note to the author, Music Director Bernstein of the New York Philharmonic, says: ". . . googol . . . was invented to express in shorthand any number consisting of a digit followed by 100 zeros—much the same way as astronomers use the word *light year* to avoid having to spend their valuable time mumbling endless numerical expressions."

[24] Lewis Mumford, *The Culture of The Cities* (New York, Harcourt Brace & Co., 1938), pp. 495-496.

[25] Harlow Shapley, *Of Stars and Men* (Boston, Beacon Press, 1958), p. 28.

[26] George Fox Mott, *et al.*, Eds., *New Survey of Journalism,* College Outline Series (4th ed., New York, Barnes & Noble, Inc., 1958), p. 318.

Upon the framework we have provided, anyone can coordinate his knowledge of business and business journalism, communicate more intelligently, and perhaps develop and spread other ideas.

TABLE 2. THE PROPER CLASSIFICATION OF BUSINESS

I. Extractive Industry

Agriculture (General, dairy, grain, livestock, and truck farms; horticulture; hunting; trapping)	Fisheries (Commercial fishing, fish farms and hatcheries, frog farms)	Forestry (Timber tracks, logging camps, nurseries)	Mines
			Wells
			Pits
			Banks
			Quarries

II. Transformative Industry

Apparel	Food	Machinery & tools	Photographic and optical goods
Cement	Furniture	Neutrons	Plastics
Chemicals	Gas	Non-ferrous metals	Primary Metals
Communication equipment	Heat, light, and power	Ordnance	Printing
Consumer goods	Inert gases	Packaging and Fixturing	Radium
Drugs	Isotopes	Paper	Stone, clay, glass
Electronic and electrical equipment	Instruments	Petroleum	Tobacco
	Leather		Transportation equipment
	Lumber		

III. Distributive Industry

Agents and brokers	Discount stores	Manufacturers representatives	Service and limited function wholesalers (including importers and exporters)
Assemblers of farm products	Drug & food chains	Miscellaneous independent retailers etc.	Stamp redemption centers
Buying syndicates	Farm cooperatives	Motor vehicle dealers	Super markets
Catalog houses	Farmers markets	Petroleum bulk tank stations	Transportation lines
Club and party plan operators	Facilitating market agencies	Pipelines	Variety chains
Communication lines	Filling stations	Premium operators	Vending machine operators
Company stores	Hardware-housewares stores	PX stores	Warehousing and storage
Consumer cooperatives	House-to-house installment	Restaurants	
Department store chains	Industrial stores		
	Mail order houses		

IV. Contributive Industry

Accounting
Advertising, merchandising
Agricultural Services
Amusement & recreation
Animal husbandry
Armed Services
Architecture & design
Art galleries
Artists
Ballet
Broadcasting
Construction
Direct mail
Display
Education
Engineering
Engravers
Entertainment
Federal Bureau of Investigation
Finance, insurance, & real estate
Fire prevention
Government
Hotel industry
Intelligence operatives
Journalism
Labor unions
Legal services
Librarians
Management
Marketing
Medical & health services
Museums
Music
Observatories
Organized charities
Personal services
Philosophers
Photographers
Playwrights
Poets
Police
Political organizations
Private investigators
Publicity
Public relations
Publishing
Religious organizations
Repair organizations
Scientists
Selling & promotion
Shippers
Technicians
Testing services
Trade & professional Associations
Water & sanitary services
Writers
Zoological gardens

SOURCE: Based, with certain modifications, on the *Standard Industrial Classification*, Executive Office of the President (3rd ed.; Washington, D.C., Bureau of the Budget, 1957).

12. The World Definition of Business

Business is all human life engaged in its own service of supply. Business refers to the activities the more than two and a half billion inhabitants of this planet are busy performing: exchanging labor, services, and goods by the use of money.

The marketplace is everywhere these exchanges are made. We are all traders. We trade what we have for something we want more, or cannot make ourselves.

In primitive times barter was the direct exchange of labor, commodities, or services for three basic human wants: food, shelter, clothing. Contemporary man wants more: health, security, freedom, communication, understanding, transportation, recreation, education, inspiration. Money is the medium by which we make our exchanges easier (But money is only a medium). The total volume of all these exchanges determines the degree of material well-being of organized society which in turn determines the opportunity for social, intellectual, and spiritual development of the individual.

The four basic ways that man makes his living are:

1. *Extractive:* man extracts raw materials from land, water and air, as, for instance, in mining, drilling, farming, fishing, forestry and chemistry. In scientific laboratories man extracts from the air such gases as oxygen, nitrogen, and argon and such rare gases, for instance, as helium, neon, xenon, freon, and krypton; from sea water man gets magnesium; from sand comes silicon. In the laboratories atoms and molecules are rearranged into new chemical patterns offered to industry in the form of metals, carbon products, gases, chemicals, and plastics.

2. *Transformative:* man in the capacity of processor, fabricator, formulator, etc., transforms raw materials into semi-finished and finished goods and services, as, for instance, when petroleum becomes gasoline or electric power; when ore becomes stainless steel or a radioisotope; when krypton becomes an atomic light bulb; when natural gas becomes textile fiber; when chemicals become plastics. Mills and factories, refineries and refractories, and industrial laboratories, are types of transformative industry.

3. *Distributive:* man, in the capacity of assembler, warehouseman, forwarder, distributor, wholesaler, jobber, importer, exporter, retailer or house-to-house salesman, disperses goods and services into markets over such transportation networks as railways, airways, waterways, highways, pipeways, wireways, and ideaways.

4. *Contributive:* workers of all nationalities collectively and cooperatively search for scientific knowledge which is then provided, in the form of improved skills, applied science, or know-how, to all human enterprise by men and women (in such technical and professional capacities as inventors, entrepreneurs, impressarios, authors, poets, musicians, mathematicians, engineers, scientists, educators, researchers, the clergy, designers and architects, entertainers, government and military officials, medical, legal, advertising, public relations, investment and insurance brokers and counsellors, accountants and bankers, administrators, overseers, supervisors, and other types of managers) who direct, coordinate, and service the whole business process.

Its network of intercommunication is the life blood of business. Scientific and technical writers and business journalists pool facts, ideas and know-how. They transmit this intelligence about men, materials, machines, methods, markets, media, money, and mores by means of (1) *ideaways*, such as businesspapers, newspapers, newsletters, house organs, magazines, records, tape, film, punched cards, books, monographs, brochures, pamphlets; (2) *instruments*, such as printing press, camera, telephone, telegraph, teletype, television, radio, radar, electronic, and other devices which project, magnify, measure, regulate, compute, record, track, guide, file, sort and process; store, recall, associate, sense, learn, beckon, observe, decide, act, and command. (3) *folkways*, such as congress, court, church, college, clinic, council, convention, conclave, conference.

Continuous cross-fertilization by the world's business press enables the managers of human enterprise to make policy and operating decisions to guide the rest of humanity in their decisions at the cash register, ballot box, vending machine, and instrument panel.

Objective of the whole business process is to bring together natural resources, labor, capital and management in a compatible pattern with science, invention, technology and scholarship so as to apply new knowledge for the fulfillment of man's needs and to guide man toward a common goal of making life longer, more secure, more pleasant and peaceful, more comprehensible.[27]

13. Proper Classification of Businesspapers

The definition of business lays the foundation for the proper classification of the technical press which serves all business.

Business, as we see, falls into four major divisions, in this logical and proper sequence:

1. Extractive industry;
2. Transformative industry;
3. Distributive industry;
4. Contributive industry.

Semantically, we arrange all businesspapers within the same four brackets:

1. Businesspapers serving the fields of extraction;
2. Businesspapers serving the fields of transformation;
3. Businesspapers serving the fields of distribution;
4. Businesspapers serving the fields of contribution.

[27] This definition of business was originally prepared by the author as an entry for the *Encyclopedia Britannica*, in 1947, at the request of its chief editor, Walter Yust, and was accepted the following year, although it has not appeared in print. It is published here for the first time, in revised form, with permission of the *Britannica*. The definition has been exposed to the critical appraisal of leaders in many professions and fields of business (see Acknowledgements) and is a composite of their helpful suggestions.

Semantics—the systematic study of meaning, of language and behavior—has these objectives: (1) To help the individual evaluate the world he lives in; (2) To improve communication between individuals and groups; (3) To cure abnormal mental and nervous conditions.

Uniform nomenclature is just as essential to the proper understanding of both business and business journalism as it is to the understanding of science.

For communication between A and B to be successful, both A and B must use symbols which have the *same meaning* to both A and B. In business journalism (as in science, which has been defined as the most exact kind of reporting) any experiment which A communicates to B must be so clear that B can repeat it and reach the same conclusion. The description of the experiment, therefore, may be said to be almost as important as the experiment itself.

Scientific communication is established between scientists by international systems of mathematical symbols, weights and measures, botanical and zoological terminology, and new alphabets, so that scientists anywhere in the world can reproduce each other's experiments and add to a common reservoir of knowledge or know-how; and thus, as Hayakawa puts it, "acquire collective control over their environment."[28]

Each of us, scientist or layman, must learn to use symbols which have the same meaning for those with whom we want or need to maintain communications.

14. Standard Industrial Classification

The classification of industry, in our definition of business, is based to some extent on the Standard Industrial Classification (S.I.C.) already referred to in Chapter I, sections 3 and 11. It is a digital coding system, sponsored by the Executive Office of the President of the United States and the Bureau of the Budget. It was prepared by The Technical Committee on Industrial Classification, Office of Statistical Standards, and is available in handbook form.[29]

The S.I.C. was first worked out in 1939, to eliminate inaccuracies,

[28] S. I. Hayakawa, *Language Meaning and Maturity* (New York, Harper & Brothers, 1954).

[29] *Standard Industrial Classification Manual* (1st ed., 1945, 2nd ed., 1949, 3rd ed., 1957; Washington 25, D. C., Supt. of Documents, U.S. Government Printing Office), $2.50.

confusion, and differences of opinion in the definition of terms by the various government bureaus and agencies to make it easier to collect, tabulate, present, and analyze data and promote uniformity and comparability. The S.I.C. manual (1957) is based *on the structure of the United States economy in 1957.*

As time and industry march on, this manual, too, will change. The S.I.C. code was brought to the attention of the United States business press in the first edition of this volume in 1945. Since then this code has been adopted by a circulation audit bureau and a business press directory and has been recommended by the Media Practices Committee of the Association of Industrial Advertisers.[30] It is, of course, used by all federal agencies of government.

The S.I.C. code brackets more than 1,500 different *types* of industry into *ten* major divisions which we reduce to *four* groups in our Classification of Business (see Table 2): Extraction (digitals 1 to 17); Transformation (digitals 19 to 39); Distribution (digitals 40 to 59); Contribution (digitals 60 to 94). We believe the use of these four major or basic divisions invoke the least complexity.

By placing all current technology in these four divisions and all technical know-how periodicals in the same four divisions we are able to clear our minds of harmful obstructions, and evaluate realistically the business world we live in. We are also able to communicate our ideas about business or businesspapers to others anywhere in the world and make comparisons without the mental confusion which has existed in the past. For example, in securing information on the Japanese business press, we learned that "technical" and "engineering" publications occupied two different brackets in Japanese thinking.

We would not want to leave the impression that these four divisions of human technology are rigid, fixed, unchangeable. Stuart Chase points out that "every great development in science involves a crisis in communications . . . Einstein used fresh mathematics to talk about relativity."[31]

Outer-space technology, as it adds to our know-how of communications between the earth and its satellites and between the earth and other planets will no doubt require new categories.

[30] Business Publications Audit of Circulations and *Industrial Marketing*'s Market Data Directory (July 1958) use the S.I.C. system.

[31] Stuart Chase, *Power of Words* (Harper & Brothers, New York), pp. 111-112.

The communications theory[32] as it borrows from the human nervous system to improve automation, may set up new categories.

The government may have foreseen such contingencies when it set up in the S.I.C. Manual, "Division J: Nonclassifiable Establishments."

15. All Businesspapers Are Technical

Having replaced such more or less synonymous and (semantically) confusing words as trade, industry, commerce, traffic, barter, exchange, and finance, with one master-word, business, let us now consider the familiar adjective, *technical.*

There is no such thing as a non-technical businesspaper or non-technical group of businesspapers, any more than there is a non-technical business activity. All businesspapers are technical publications because they are all concerned with the *technics* of our modern civilization. The Greek word is *technikos;* the Latin, *technicus.* From two Greek words, *techne* (art) and *logos* (discourse), come the term technology. The dictionaries define *technic* as a method or style of performance, *technics* as the branches of learning relating to the arts and sciences, and *technology* as "the terminology used in arts, profession, handcraft, business, science and the like."

Bergen and Cornelia Evans, in *The Dictionary of Contemporary Usage* (Random House, N. Y., 1957) prefer the spelling *technique* (French) and define it as "the description of method of performance." They describe technology as "the branch of knowledge that deals with the industrial arts; the sciences of the industrial arts."

Lewis Mumford digs deeper for a definition. He says: "Technics is a translation into appropriate, practical forms of the theoretic truths, implicit or formulated, anticipated or discovered, of science."

Mumford sees science and technology as "two independent yet related worlds: sometimes converging, sometimes drawing apart." He calls the machine "a counterfeit of nature, nature analyzed, regulated, narrowed, controlled by the mind of men." He describes as the ultimate goal "not nature's conquest but her resynthesis: dismembered by thought, nature was put together again in new combinations: material syntheses in chemistry, mechanical syntheses in engineering."[33]

[32] Norbert Wiener, *The Human Use of Human Beings* (New York, Doubleday, 1956).

[33] Lewis Mumford; *Technics and Civilization* (New York, Harcourt Brace & Co., 1938), p. 52.

Every sphere of human activity develops problems as well as knowledge: new knowledge out of problems. Problems out of new knowledge. The businesspaper, specializing in any particular field of technics, reports that field's problems and the technics for solving the problems, describes experiments, publishes formulae and solutions. The businesspaper will often report how more or less similar problems were approached and solved in other fields. This is the continuous cross-fertilization referred to in our definition of business. Such interpretive and analytical reporting enables the readers of businesspapers, who are the managers of all human enterprise, to become more responsible decision-makers at both policy and operating levels.

16. How Technical Periodicals Serve Small Business

The growth, and stamina and persistence of small business is one of the amazing phenomena of this world of giant corporations and syndicates.[34]

In the United States, for example, unincorporated business firms account for 85 per cent of all business firms. Since a large percentage of corporate firms are also businesses, the businessmen of this country are chiefly small businessmen (although many think big).

There are in the United States more than 4,300,000 business establishments (1957). More than 98 per cent of them have less than 50 employees. Of the total only 11 per cent are incorporated and only 8 per cent are in manufacturing.

When it comes to assets and income, the giant corporations, of course, stand out. But the big business corporation is often a small business in a small country that grew into a big business in a big country. That is the story of Du Pont, Great Atlantic and Pacific Tea Co., Westinghouse, General Motors, and General Electric. On the other hand, some small businesses such as General Dynamics and International Business Machines, grow big almost overnight.

The five hundred largest corporations in the United States employ almost 9 million people. Sixty million are employed by the remainder or are self-employed.

A century ago there were no big corporations. The need did not exist.

[34] *The Persistence of Small Business*, a study of unincorporated enterprise, prepared by Eugene C. McKean for W. E. Upjohn Institute for Community Research, Kalamazoo, Mich., March 1958.

Today the large private corporation is an integral part of the modern economic system of the free world. And it is vital to our national security system.

We do not measure military strength by manpower and weapons alone. The capabilities of large private corporations for research and development, for mass production, are the first measure of national security in a modern world. Most of the $8 billion spent for research in 1957 in the U. S. was spent by these large corporations.

The 9 million people who work for the corporate giants of the U. S. together with their families add up to 35 million people.

The large corporations which we see listed on the financial pages of *The Wall Street Journal* are owned collectively by the 10 million stockholders who have directly invested their savings in the stocks and bonds of these companies. (See Chapter III, section 8.)

Additional millions of people are indirect shareholders in these large corporations because their savings are in banks, building and loan associations, and insurance companies, which hold huge portfolios of stocks and bonds of private corporations.

Does this mean these millions of people control these private corporations? Only insofar as public opinion controls the fate of all institutions. The technical decisions, the operating and policy decisions, are made by management. The actual managers of a large corporation often own a very small percentage of the stock.

The 10 million or more majority stockholders simply supplied their surplus money (instead of spending it) to these corporations so the managers could buy modern tools—the complicated and expensive plants and machines modern industry uses in place of human power—to do the nation's work; to coordinate the work of many specialists and scientists in research and development; and to translate new know-how into a variety of useful labor-saving and time-saving products and services.

The primary service of the technical press, from the beginning, has been to the management of small companies. Larger corporations can and do provide themselves with special communications and research facilities.

The managers in the big corporations, nevertheless, are probably the most avid readers of the business press because their creative people depend on fast, objective information which is reported in the independent businesspaper. They also use the businesspaper as a vehicle for transmitting their information to small business, on whom they rely for their own survival.

Take a large automobile manufacturer, for example. It will depend on as many as 2,500 suppliers for the components for the end-product which is an automobile. There are 8,500 parts and hundreds of separate skills built into a finished automobile. The parts and the skills come from the forests of Canada or the northwest of the United States, from textile mills in the deep South or New England, from iron deposits in the Mesabi range, from rubber plantations in Java or synthetic plants in Delaware, from the plains of China, the sulphur mines of Texas, the chemical laboratories of New Jersey, and from electronic industries in Michigan and California.

All the big and little producers in turn use their particular technical press to convey messages to General Motors' purchasing agents, managers, supervisors, researchers, designers, decision-makers.

General Motors in turn uses hundreds of different business periodicals to convey its own message to hundreds of industries from which it buys components and materials and to which it sells cars, trucks, diesel locomotives, electro-motive freight locomotives, spark plugs, batteries, refrigerators, and other things. More than 45,000 firms are suppliers to the General Electric Company, and 17,000 firms participate in the company's military defense assignments.

Examples of usefulness of technical periodicals to small business could fill a volume. Elmer Tangerman, editor of *Product Engineering,* cited many examples at a recent President's Conference in Washington:

> Our experience has been that the most effective technical editorial content we can provide is that describing new ideas developed in big companies. Subscribers in big companies want it because it is faster, more objective, and more certain than their own house organs; those in small companies recognize it as information they couldn't afford to develop themselves unless they combined to do it.
>
> In addition to providing regular reports, the [business] magazine is a sort of screening device. While it presents all data of value to its particular reader group, it winnows out the trivial, explains the confusing, supplements the incomplete, questions or corrects the inaccurate, discards the old and outmoded. It is a combination of "bush telegraph," censor, and clearing house.
>
> That these services are appreciated is shown by studies which indicate that four out of five subscribers read every issue, and that by far the

greatest proportion pick up their copies to read a second and a third time. More than twice as many read an issue through as read consumer magazines through. They rate business magazines as three times as helpful to them as mail, trade shows, or sales literature of any sort, hence spend one to two hours reading each issue, and pass copies around for as long as a year. It is not a unique experience for coupons offering some particular booklet or piece of information to be returned as much as ten years after they were published.

One magazine, for example, *Electronics,* has undertaken extensive research for its industry. Members of that staff built the first remote TV tuner, transistor piano, and civilian radio in the megacycle range, reported results—and these have now become familiar commercial products. *American Fur Breeder* researched the genetics of fur-bearing animals, thus taught mink farmers how to direct their "sports" into mutation mink instead of discarding them. *Electrical World* and *American Machinist* both have provided statistical data for years that are the standard of their industries. *Engineering News-Record* reports new projects and gives costs and prices. Its editors also surveyed Spanish sites and conditions three months before the airbase treaty, so its readers could bid. *Engineering & Mining Journal* provides a metal-price and availability service so basic that public laws and taxes are based upon it. *Oil & Gas Journal* provides completion data on oil wells that are reprinted by the U.S. Bureau of Mines, and weekly world-wide crude-oil production figures that are standard. *Modern Packaging* literally built an industry itself. *Modern Plastics* showed the glass-fiber reinforced polyester-plastic industry how to convert its annual 4-million-pound military business into a 30-million-pound civilian one.[35]

Free interchange of technological know-how between large and small companies constantly surprises visitors to the United States from other countries, even the British. The carefully guarded secret is often an obstruction to the kind of progress in which everyone could profit. We repeat—*business, like science, starves in an atmosphere of secrecy.* This is particularly true of small business and explains why small business survives and thrives in the United States.

The businesspaper, in every industrialized country of the world, is the low-cost information carrier for small independent private enterprises. Some of these small businesses of today, largely on the

[35] Elmer Tangerman, "How Technical Magazines Help Small Business," a paper read before The President's Conference on Technical and Distribution Research, called by President Dwight Eisenhower in Washington, September 24, 1957.

know-how acquired from the editorial and advertising pages of businesspapers, will grow into tomorrow's giants. But whether they grow big or remain small, competitive private enterprise is able to survive and prosper in an atmosphere of mutual confidence and exchange of information. That is why small business is willing to assume risks.

In his paper, Mr. Tangerman cautioned businessmen:

No magazine seeks information for publication that is of interest and of value only to the source company. Editors are seeking information for readers, not just publicity releases, so they are likely to ask some fairly penetrating questions. If you are willing to share your know-how with your industry, the editors will be glad to help, and the resulting publicity will amaze you.

The transistor, a dozen drugs, a hundred chemicals, a thousand merchandising ideas—these have been reported with similar results. Most of them are not yet in books—for books take time to prepare. Only the business press can move fast enough to analyze, evaluate, interpret and report the pace of today's scientific, technological and merchandising development.

These are but random examples of such services as providing primary industry data, doing original research, and building industries done by the business press. George Westinghouse, reading of the use of air to dig the Mount Cenis tunnel, got his idea for the airbrake. Henry Ford, reading of the Kane-Pennington engine, adapted those ideas for his first automobile engine in November, 1897. There are dozens of modern inventors and developers who testify to similar ideas utilized—among them new blasting powders, drugs, mining methods, food technology, management methods, metalcutting processes, and a host of others. A recent spectacular example is the widespread use of the transistor—originally an idea of Bell Labs—and of ceramic cutting tools, with American development based on English and Russian applications.

Much to his own amazement, Dr. Hollis Godfrey, president of the Engineering-Economics Foundation, discovered 25 years ago that "the business press has led the production of wealth in America." Solid statistics proved this, and that wealth of a nation is the direct result of the growth of education. Members of a British Productivity Team, a few years ago, were also amazed at the free interchange of ideas and technical know-how in American business magazines. In England, such information is carefully guarded as a business secret, so progress is slower.

Beyond the published article or paper, the business magazine provides many other services. One of the more unique ones is to act as a vehicle of communication for all the other services available to small business. The magazine carries advertising that brings information, of course, but it also describes, lists—and in many cases offers to get for readers—booklets, books, charts and other useful data. It also provides a directory of representatives, consultants, associations and societies in its pages. In many cases, it has been instrumental in establishing associations and societies, and in carrying the news of smaller ones to their membership. One technical magazine, for example, was instrumental in the formation of both the American Society of Mechanical Engineers and the American Ordnance Association.

Magazines have also sponsored research, provided scholarships, and plumped for vital legislation, or regulation. *Power*, for example, carried on the fight for uniform boiler codes in all states for some 20 years, thus eventually succeeded in minimizing the once-common hazard of boiler explosions. *Electronics* similarly pointed out the dangers of a hazardous circuit so strongly that it has since been abandoned.[36]

[36] Ibid.

CHAPTER II

HOW INDUSTRY IS SERVED BY BUSINESSPAPERS

WE WERE concerned, in Chapter I, with the definition of the businesspaper and the definition of business. Both the business press and industry served by the business press fell into four major divisions:

1. Businesspapers serving extractive industries;
2. Businesspapers serving transformative industries;
3. Businesspapers serving distributive industries;
4. Businesspapers serving contributive industries.

We turn now to a closer examination of each of these four major divisions of business in order to understand the scope of the specialized businesspapers that serve within each division and to learn something of the background from which such businesspapers have emerged.

Let us remember: the term business is a generic word for a host of other words which, while they are used in an attempt to be more specific, only create more confusion in the minds of people who want to be specific. We refer to such words as industry, commerce, and trade, production and consumption, economics, or the economy, used without a referent.

Business is the master word, according to Professor Anshen of Harvard University:

Business is the way men make their living and because there are many men, with many talents, and skills, the ways of making a living can be counted by the thousands. They are bound up with every activity of life. The complex sum of these activities we call the business world . . . this multitude of activities, so interrelated and cross-bound that every human unit in our society is inescapably allied to other human units seems at first glance to be an impenetrable maze.[1]

The complex sum of all human activity is the business world. That includes the activity of the teacher, the preacher, the poet, the professional man of law, medicine, or science, and the professional soldier or actor. Everyone.

The business press is an information railway linking together these activities and those engaged in them.

Labor force: The total employment of a country is known as the labor force. Some people erroneously associate the word labor with manual effort, like that of the farmer, ditch digger, or coal miner, but government statisticians have defined the term "labor force" to embrace everyone working for a living.

In the United States the labor force increased from 54 millions of people in 1940 to 69 millions of people in 1957. The entire population of the United States stood at 170 million in 1957. In other words, in 1957, there were 101 million people who were not in the labor force: children, students, retired workers, housewives, the aged and disabled, people in institutions, and the temporarily unemployed.

The labor force is not evenly distributed among the four divisions—extractive, transformative, distributive and contributive. Much more than half the labor force used to be in extractive and transformative industries. Today the shift is to distributive and contributive industries. Incidentally, the United States labor force expands at the rate of more than a million workers a year.

Mechanization and automation are two factors which have influenced the shift in the labor force into the fields of distribution and contribution.

The *Standard Industrial Classification Manual* (see Chapter I, section 14) undertakes to define "industry" as "a group of establishments primarily engaged in the same or similar lines of economic activity." It defines an "establishment" as "an economic unit which produces goods or services."

Let us consider the four major divisions of business, as we have designated them, in more detail:

[1] Melvin Anshen, *An Introduction to Business* (New York, The Macmillan Co., 1942).

1. Extractive Industry

This group of industries as a whole is concerned with the drawing out, removal, digging up, growing, and *extracting* of raw material. The extraction usually requires one or more processes: manual, mechanical, or chemical. Other things may have to be added. Some things may have to be extracted or subtracted. In some cases the raw material is itself consumers' goods.

There are four major extractive industries: agriculture, forestry, fisheries, mining.

Agriculture: Farmers' net earnings in 1958 were expected to total 5 to 10 per cent better than their $11.5 billion income in 1957. In 1958 there were about 10,000 farm co-ops in the United States. They market an increasing amount of the country's food and fiber output and are expanding into the processing industries.[2]

Farmers and their families spend around forty billion dollars a year for farm equipment and consumer goods.[3]

Farm operating expenses in 1958 were 30 per cent higher than in 1948. There are an estimated 4,855,800 farms in the United States. Dairy products were $4.6 billion in 1957.

About 45,000 farmers produce horticultural specialty crops and nursery products and are responsible for the major portion of the nearly $60 million increase in farm value since 1949.

Forestry: Reforestation, conservation and research continue to be the major trends in this extractive industry. Present demand is 12 billion cubic feet a year. There are 489 million acres of potential woodland in the United States. Lumber output in 1957 totaled 33.4 billion board feet, lower than any year since 1949. Exports in 1957 were 812 million board feet.[4]

About 17,000 trained foresters are currently employed in the United States, of which 7,000 are in government employ.[5]

Fisheries: Total 1957 catch by United States fishermen was esti-

[2] *Industrial Marketing* (1959 Market Data and Directory Number) June 25, 1958, p. 518-539. See also, Agricultural Marketing Service, Bureau of the Census, U.S. Department of Agriculture.

[3] "How Farm Families Spend $40 Billion a Year—and How To Get Your Share of It," Agricultural Publishers Association, 333 N. Michigan Ave., Chicago, Ill.

[4] Sources: *Forest Products Journal; The Timberman; The Lumberman;* National Lumber Manufacturers Association; Forest Service, U.S. Department of Agriculture; American Forest Products Industries Association, Washington, D. C.

[5] *Industrial Marketing,* June 25, 1958, p. 540.

mated at 4.75 billion pounds, half a billion pounds under the 1956 catch. The value of the 1957 catch was $351 million. The capital valuation of the fishing industries is almost $11.2 billion.[6]

The capital investment in commercial fisheries is about $900 million; this includes freezing and processing, wholesale and retail fish houses and dealers, however.[7]

Mining: Over-all mineral output of the United States in 1957 reached $18.3 billion. Of this, metals was $2.08 billion and non-metallic minerals $16.2 billion. Non-metallic minerals include such fuels as petroleum, natural gas, natural gas liquids, asphalt and related bitumens, carbon dioxide, anthracite, bituminous and lignite coal, peat, and helium.[8]

The only structural metal extracted from sea water, magnesium, rose to 81,000 tons in 1957.

Uranium production reached an annual rate of nearly 10,000 tons of oxide in 1957, as compared with 6,000 tons in 1956. About 130,000 pounds of fissionable isotope of uranium (U-235) was made available for peaceful uses, bringing the 1956-1957 total to 220,000 pounds, valued at $1.7 billion.

Many important United States businesspapers serve the extractive industries. The farm journals are a very important group (see Chapter V, section 10). Here are titles of some of the businesspapers in this division, in addition to those already mentioned:
Canada Lumberman (Ontario); *American Forests* (Washington, D. C.); *Chain Saw Age* (Portland, Ore.); *National Fisherman* (Goffstown, N. H.): *American Nurseryman,* and *Pit & Quarry* (Chicago); *Coal Age* and *National Petroleum News* (New York); *Offshore Drilling* and *Oil* (New Orleans); *Oil & Gas Equipment* and *Oil & Gas Journal* (Tulsa); *Journal of Petroleum Technology* (Dallas); *Fur Trade Journal of Canada* (Toronto); *American Poultry Journal* (Chicago). After 84 years a horizontal periodical, *Poultry Journal,* split into three business periodicals in 1958: *The Egg Producer, The Broiler Producer, The Turkey Producer.* That is specialization.

2. Transformative Industry

This division includes those power utilities, plants, factories, foundries, mills, commercial laboratories and ordnance establishments,

[6] Sources: U.S. Fish and Wildlife Service; *Southern Fisherman.*

[7] *Industrial Marketing, loc. cit.,* p. 538.

[8] Source: *Industrial Marketing, loc. cit.,* p. 293; U:S. Bureau of Mines; *Engineering and Mining Journal.*

cyclotrons and reactors, engaged in the mechanical or chemical *transformation* of organic or inorganic substances into new products. These establishments, characteristically, use power-driven machines and materials-handling equipment. Establishments engaged in assembling component parts or manufactured products also are considered manufacturing if the new product is neither part of the structure nor other fixed improvement. The final product of a manufacturing establishment may be "finished," in the sense that it is ready for utilization or consumption, or "semi-finished," to become raw material for an establishment engaged in further manufacturing. For example, the product of a copper smelter is a raw material used in electrolytic refineries; refined copper is a raw material used by electrical equipment manufacturers to make, let us say, an electric toaster or an automatic blanket. Copper wire is also sold in hardware stores to the consumer.

Transformative Industry (S.I.C. Division D) includes groups 19 to 39, as follows: Ordnance; Food; Tobacco; Textiles; Apparel; Lumber and Wood Products; Furniture; Paper; Printing; Chemicals; Petroleum; Rubber; Leather; Stone, Clay and Glass; Primary Metal; Fabricated Metal; Machinery; Electrical Equipment; Transportation Equipment; Instruments, Photography, Optical Goods, Watches and Clocks; Miscellaneous (including nuclear components).

Some of the hundreds of titles of businesspapers serving in this division are *Ceramic Age; Gas Age; Iron Age; Rubber Age; Automotive Age; Aviation Age; Railway Age; Steel; Packer; Petroleum Refiner; Machinery* (for all metal-working plants); *Furniture Manufacturer; Paper Mill News; Food Processing; Chemical Processing; Canner & Freezer; Textile World; Electrical World; Drug & Cosmetic Industry; Electrified Industry; Nucleonics*; etc.

Some companies have vertical set-ups so that they function as extractors of raw materials, transformers of materials into finished and semi-finished goods, and distributors of goods. Example: The Aluminum Company of America owns ore deposits where bauxite is *extracted;* the bauxite ore goes to refineries where it is *transformed* into aluminum ingots bearing the stamp "Alcoa"; these ingots are further transformed into cooking utensils in their subsidiary, Aluminum Cooking Utensil Company, bearing the trademark "Wear-ever." The utensils and ingots are *distributed* to South America on the Alcoa Steamship Line. The talents of their research people, engineers, chemists, plant managers, sales managers, advertising and marketing experts, ship captains, pilots, and navigators *contribute* to the efficiency of the Alcoa operation.

3. Distributive Industry

The establishments in this division are concerned with the *distribution* and transport of goods and services from where they are to where they are needed or wanted. A businesspaper like *Railway Age* covers the activities of establishments manufacturing locomotives, freight cars, and Pullmans, as well as the activities of railroad companies engaged in the transport of people and goods.

All enterprises are included in this division which are engaged in passenger and freight transportation by railway, highway, waterway, or airway, or in furnishing services related to transportation; pipeline transportation; telephone and telegraph communication services; radio broadcasting and television; and the supplying of electricity, gas, steam, water, or sanitary services. Many establishments in this division are legally held to be "affected with a public interest" (quasi-public in character) and are regulated by public service commissions or other public authorities as to rates or prices charged, schedules, and services rendered.

Communication lines: The communication *lines* distribute the intelligence by which our modern complex business community is sustained, and include enterprises that furnish communication services, audibly or visually, by wire or wireless: cable, telephone, telegraph, radio broadcasting and television, radiotelephone, radio telegraph, radar; teletypewriter and ticker tape service; facsimile, telephoto, and phototransmission; automatic language translation; quotation services recording or reporting price and volume of transactions on security and commodity exchanges; news syndicates and press associations, publishing, printing, and allied industries. Some 40,000 firms are engaged in the graphic arts, turning out products every year valued at $10 billion, not counting the value of the advertising carried.

Many national business periodicals serve this bracket.

The printing industry, for example, has a number of businesspapers guiding it. *The American Pressman, The American Printer Lithographer, Book Production, Graphic Arts Monthly, Lithographers Journal, Offset Duplicator Review,* and *Printing Equipment Engineer* are some of them.

Radio and television industry have *Audio, Broadcasting-Telecasting, Hi-Fi Tape Recording, Radio-Electronics, Radio & Television News,* among others.

Telephony, Telephone Engineer and Management, Telegraph Delivery Spirit, and *Wire & Radio Communications* are some of the businesspapers concerned with the wire services overhead, underground, and undersea. Our nation is laced with a network of 65 million telephone sets, 260 million miles of wire, employs 750,000 people, and represents an $18 billion capital investment (1958).

Transportation lines: Businesspapers such as *Pipeline Engineer, Oil & Gas Journal, Pipeline Construction,* and *Pipeline Industry* serve the 400,000 mile system that distributes fuels to home and factory—an $8 billion industry (1958).

To provide the know-how for such carriers as ships, barges, canal boats, tug boats, railroads, trucks, buses, streetcars, and taxicabs there are a host of specialized periodicals: *Shipping Management, Shippers Guide, Marine Engineering, Motorship, Traffic World, Transport Topics, Distribution Age, Traffic Bulletin, Railway Age, Modern Materials Handling, Pacific Air & Truck Traffic, Railway Freight Traffic, Mass Transportation.*

Highways: More than 650,000 miles of highway and thruway give our nation new mobility for automobile and truck transport. An additional network of 41,000 miles will be added by 1965. About 79 million United States citizens drive cars (1958) and 2.7 million people are employed in their manufacture, design, distribution, and service. Some of the businesspapers in this field are *Automotive News, Automotive Chain Store, Automotive Retailer, Fleet Owner, Automotive Industries, Taxicab Industry, Automotive Service Digest, Gasoline Retailer.*

Aviation: Nearly 100,000 miles of Federal airways crisscross the United States, linking up 7,000 air fields and serving 53 commercial airlines operating 1,850 planes. In addition, private corporations and private individuals operate 60,000 aircraft. To this the military establishment adds 40,000 planes. CAA airport towers handle 1,700,000 takeoffs or landings a month. The Air Force at its own bases averages a million such operations a month (1958).[9]

To service the immense aviation market, estimated to be $11

[9] "Billion Dollar Modernization of U. S. Air Traffic Control," a research study by Goodbody & Co., N. Y., June 9, 1958.

billion dollars in 1958, here are the titles of some of the many excellent businesspapers providing specialized guidance and information: *Aviation Age, American Aviation, Air Cargo, Air Age, Aeronautical Purchasing, Aviation Week, Air Force, Aeronautical Engineering Review, Air Facts, Contact, Flying, Jet Propulsion.*

Electronic Engineering: Overcrowding of the airways—an acute problem—has opened new markets for radar, navigational devices, electronic data handling equipment, servo-mechanisms, anti-collision equipment, communication networks, and control products not yet conceived. Traffic problems on highways, seaways, and telephone lines increase the market potential.

First impetus to the commercial electronics industry was the perfection of wireless telegraphy by Marconi (1906), made possible by the transmission of voice sounds. The commercial radio industry went into action.

Next boost was radar, the instantaneous military tracking device used in World War II. This led to electronically controlled sight and sound and gave us the television industry.

The growth of electronic devices in industry and the guided missile systemology of the military establishment caused the electronic industry of the U. S. to soar from $2.5 billion dollars in annual sales to $13 billion in 1958.[10] It jumped from 49th place in 1939 to fifth place in 1958, topped only by chemicals, automotive, electricals, and steel.

Today the electronic industry ranges from radio, television, broadcasting systems, instrumentation, X-ray, radar, telephony, fire controls, circuitry, servo mechanisims, digital computers, fuel injectors, ultrasonic equipment, to all kinds of automation for factory, office, and home.

Fortune, a prominent horizontal businesspaper estimated that the electronic industry of the United States will be selling $16 billion of goods and services in 1960.[11]

One fifth of all the engineers in the United States are in electronics and the demand for talent and know-how is nothing less than frantic, as an examination of any Sunday want-ad supplement of *The New York Times* will reveal.[12]

[10] *Trend Analysis*, Francis I. Du Pont & Co., N.Y., January 14, 1958.
[11] "The Electronic Business" *Fortune*, April 1957, p. 137.
[12] See Chap. VIII, section 4.

Newer businesspapers created to serve this rapidly expanding field are *Automation, Control Engineering, Electronic Advertiser, Electronic Engineering, Electronic Equipment, Electronic Industries, Electronic News, Electronic Week, Electronics, Military Automation, Military Electronics, Electronic Technician* and *Circuit Digests, Machine Accounting and Data Processing, Management and Business Automation, Instrument Manufacturing, ISA Journal* (Instrument Society of America), *Electronic Design, Electronics and Communications.*

Electric Power: An industry which did not exist a hundred years ago has created three million jobs in the United States, one out of every twenty in the labor force. It now produces 600 billion kilowatt-hours a year (1958) and is spending $3 billion a year on new facilities. Prominent among the businesspapers serving this industry are the following: *Power Industry, Power Engineering, Power, Electric Light & Power, Electrical World, Electrical Equipment, Electrical Construction and Maintenance, Electrical Merchandising, Housewares Review, Electric Heat & Air Conditioning, Electrical Manufacturing.*

Nucleonics: In the expanding nuclear market which reached $3.5 billions a year in 1957, buyers and management personnel in atomic power, nuclear engineering, and applied radiation read and contribute to such businesspapers as *Nucleonics, Industrial Laboratories, Journal of Applied Physics, Science, Review of Scientific Instruments,* and numerous related periodicals concerned with nucleonic technologies.

Outerspace: By 1958, to serve and develop this new market (which is also called aerospace) a number of businesspapers had been organized such as *Missiles & Rockets, Aircraft & Missiles, Nucleonics, Astronautics* (American-Rocket Society), *Space Digest* (published by the Air Force Association as a 32-page insert within *Air Force,* "The Magazine of Aerospace Power").

Many older businesspapers revamped their editorial content to bring this market within their province and some changed their titles. *Aviation Age* is now *Space Aeronautics* (1958). *Aviation Engineering* is now *Aerospace Engineering,* and *Aviation Week* has added to its title "Space Technology."

Wholesale trade: As defined by the S.I.C. it includes all establishments or places of business engaged primarily in selling merchandise to retailers, to industrial or commercial users, or to other wholesalers, or acting as agents in buying merchandise for, or selling merchandise to, such persons or companies. The principal types of establishments included are service wholesalers (wholesale merchants, industrial distributors, voluntary-group wholesalers, and exporters and importers); limited-function wholesalers (cash and carry, drop shippers, wagon distributors, and retailer-cooperative warehouses); sales branches and sales offices (but not retail stores) maintained by manufacturing enterprises apart from their plants for the purpose of marketing their products; converters; auction companies; agents, merchandise or commodity brokers, and commission merchants; exporters and importers; petroleum bulk tank stations; assemblers, buyers, and cooperative marketing associations of farm products (grain elevators, packers, shippers); and chain store warehouses.

The chief functions of establishments included in wholesale trade are selling goods to trading establishments or to industrial users maintaining inventories of goods; extending credit; physically assembling, sorting, and grading goods in large lots; breaking bulk and redistributing in smaller lots; and bringing buyer and seller together. Other service activities include delivery, refrigeration, and various types of promotion, such as advertising, label designing, etc.

An establishment is classified in wholesale trade if its predominant activity is marketing merchandise to retailers, to industrial users, or to other wholesalers, whether or not it is engaged in auxiliary manufacturing or retailing.

The S.I.C. bulks together printing, publishing, and allied industries as a "manufacturing" group, failing to make a clear distinction between the functions of gatherers, conveyers, and purveyors of news information and editorial opinion, and those establishments which simply do commercial publishing and printing, typesetting, engraving, bookbinding, or perform other functions necessary in the process of completing communication from one point to another.

Recent addition to the ranks of the United States business press is *Industrial Supplier and Distributor News* (1959), published by Leonard Wasserbly, who acts as its editor. This businesspaper serves as a companion to *Industrial Maintenance and Plant Operation* (founded in 1940), another Wasserbly periodical. Mr. Wasserbly, only 38 in 1959, has talents in engineering and mathematics as well as experience in journalism. The latest U.S. Census showed there were

10,139 organizations distributing industrial materials, machinery, equipment and supplies, with annual sales over $5.5 billion.

A great many industries and trades are served by exclusively wholesale periodicals at both the capital goods and consumer goods levels. *Wholesale Drug Salesman* has a sworn paid circulation (1958) of more than 3,600 drug wholesalers, their executives and salesmen. *Wholesale Grocer News* has a sworn paid circulation (1958) of more than 6,500 grocery wholesale houses, their executives, department heads, and buyers.

Most businesspapers covering the activities of retail buyers in certain consumer goods categories also cover the activities of the "distributors," wholesalers, and jobbers in the same product categories, in spite of the many specialized wholesaling periodicals in the same fields. There are many reasons for this. For one thing, whole salers exert influence on both manufacturers and retailers. They exert an influence on the manufacturer's selection of media in which to place his trade and consumer advertising. They exert a heavy influence on all retail stores they serve. Businesspaper editors who were not thoroughly familiar with wholesale and jobbing practices would be ill-prepared to guide either manufacturers or retailers in their fields.

Export and import: There are many businesspapers specializing in the technics of exporting and importing goods and services. The overseas market for United States businesspapers is estimated at $15 billion (1958). It is expected that many new businesspapers will appear in this field and that the coverage of these markets will expand.

International editions: McGraw-Hill International Corporation, Gillette Publishing Company, Pan American Publishing Company, Simmons-Boardman Company, and many others publish international businesspapers for both hemispheres. Pan American publishes *America Clinica* (Western and European editions), *El Hospital, Textiles Americanos* and *Textiles Hispanoamericanos* (published in Spain). The *American Automobile* is the McGraw-Hill International magazine of the automotive industry, with an ABC circulation (1958) of over 15,000 copies a month. *Camenos y Construccion Pesada* is Gillette's highway industry and heavy construction businesspaper, printed in Spanish. *Efectos De Escritorio* is a Davidson directory in Spanish covering office equipment and suppliers. *Ingineria Inter-*

nacional Construccion is a McGraw-Hill businesspaper on engineering construction in Spanish with a companion publication, *Ingeneria Internacional Industrica.* Another McGraw-Hill international businesspaper is *Management Digest* (see complete listings in *Business Publication Rates and Data,* published monthly by Standard Rate & Data Service, Inc., Evanston, Ill.

Advertising Age published figures on the advertising of 100 leading United States corporations in 36 internationally circulated periodicals. The total expenditure of these companies in 1957 in the 36 top international periodicals was put at $8,481,371. Excluding *Readers' Digest, Newsweek, Time,* and *Life,* the remaining 32 were all business papers. The businesspaper list follows:

Agricultura de las Americas, American Automobile, El Automovil Americano, American Exporter, El Exportador Americano, Automotive World, Automotive World en Espanol, Caminos y Construction Pesada, El Embotellador, El Farmaceutico, Guia, Hablemos, Industria Avicola, Ingenieria Internacional, Construccion, Ingenieria International Industria, Management Digest, Mecanica Popular, Petroleo Interamericano, Pharmacy International (all foreign editions except Canadian), *Revista Area Latinoamericano, Revista Industrial, Servicios Publicos, Transporte Moderno, Visao, Vision, World's Business* and *World Construction.*[13]

Retail Trade: Out of some 4,300,000 separate business establishments of all kinds in the United States (1957), retail trade has the largest number with 2,500,000 establishments. Wholesale and retail trade together employ 18 per cent of the entire peacetime labor force of 69 million people (1957). Mostly small businesses (98 per cent), the independent retailers and wholesalers often refer to their businesspapers as their "bibles." They are guided by their businesspapers, not only in their buying and selling but also in the intricate matters of cost accounting, credit, financing, and even the smallest details of operating a business profitably.

Buying goods for resale to the consumer is a characteristic of retail trade establishments, but there are some exceptions cited by S.I.C. Farmers, for example, who sell their produce to the public at the farm, are not considered retailers by the S.I.C. On the other hand, retail lumber yards who do most of their business with contractors, and establishments selling machinery, feed, and fertilizer to farmers,

[13] *Advertising Age,* May 12, 1958.

are classified as retailers by the S.I.C. Establishments selling gasoline, typewriters, stationery, etc., to institutional or industrial users are not classified as retail trade.

Some processing may be done by retailers. Restaurants, for example, process food into meals. Delicatessens roast chickens. Feed stores grind feed and groceries grind coffee. Some fish stores even prepare chowder.

Retail trade is bracketed with wholesale trade as Division F in the S.I.C. manual, and is identified by eight major groups: Group 52—Building Materials, Hardware, and Farm Equipment; Group 53—Department Stores, Mail Order Houses, Limited Price Variety Stores, Merchandise Vending Machine Operators, Direct Selling Organizations, Miscellaneous General Merchandise Stores; Group 54—Grocery Stores, Meat and Fish Markets, Fruit and Vegetable Markets, Candy, Nut, Confectionery Stores, Dairy Product Stores, Retail Bakeries, Egg and Poultry Dealers; Group 55—Automotive Dealers and Gasoline Service Stations; Group 56—Apparel and Accessories Shops; Group 57—Home Furnishings Stores; Group 58—Eating and Drinking Places; Group 59—Miscellaneous, which includes drug, liquor, antique, camera, pipe and tobacco, jewelry, and garden supply stores.

The titles of some of the businesspapers serving the retail trade, for example, indicate the specialized service rendered small business: *Retail Bookseller, Retail Apparel Outlook, Poultry & Eggs Weekly, Home Furnishings Daily, Housewares Review, Retail Lumberman, Department Store Economist, American Druggist, Milk Dealer, Meat Dealer, Automotive Retailer, Beer Distributor, Retail Tobacconist, Toys & Novelties, Pet Shop Management, Sports Age,* etc.

When historians look back on the twentieth century it will not be the noise of wars or politics that gets the major attention but the quiet revolution in skills and mechanics for the mass distribution of goods and services.

"There are few in America today who realize that distribution is the largest single element in our economy," Harry W. Ketchum of the U.S. Department of Commerce told the largest retail association in our country at their convention in January 1958.[14]

[14] "The Importance of Distribution in Our Economy" by Harry W. Ketchum, Director, Office of Distribution, U.S. Department of Commerce, Washington, D.C., at the Distributive Education Session, 47th Annual Convention, National Retail Merchants Association, New York, January 8, 1958.

This holds true, Mr. Ketchum pointed out, whether you measure the distributive function by income, number of persons employed or engaged, or by the distribution component in retail prices, expressed in terms of either costs or values added.

One hundred years ago, 66 per cent of the work in the United States was performed by physical labor of men and animals. Today 99 per cent of the work is done by the energy of water and fuel. With 7 per cent of the world's land area and population, the United States produces and consumes more than 33 per cent of the world's total volume of goods and services and produces 50 per cent of the world's product and energy. U.S. Gross National Product (G.N.P.) was about $438 billion in 1958.

This was accomplished by the *contribution* of technical know-how applied to power plus machinery—but more importantly, it was achieved by the revolutionary changes in the distribution of goods and services.

Performing this important distributive function are 300,000 wholesalers, 2,500,000 retailers and service outlets, tens of thousands of agents and brokers, all employing vast storage facilities, assembly plants, warehouses, bulk terminals, tank stations, communication and transportation lines, advertising and marketing agencies, and banking and credit facilities. While this vast division is characterized as "distributive," the managers who guide its various operations with their talents and skills are themselves in a distinct division of their own.

It is the "contributive" division.

4. Contributive Industry

This industry involves such diverse functions as management, engineering, education, journalism, government, scientific research, the practice of medicine, etc.

In this division professional and semi-professional managers of all kinds *contribute* their talents, technics, and facilities to make the other three major divisions function smoothly and efficiently. (See Table 2, Proper Classification of Business). One important contribution made by business (including government) is scientific research. Eight billion dollars was invested in 1957 in this country for research.

The managers, as we have said, are the "reading public" of the businesspaper. They are known by many titles: operating executives, administration engineers, superintendents, supervisory technicians, personnel engineers, traffic managers, sales managers, merchandise managers, advertising managers. Some are theatrical producers, religious directors, police superintendents, funeral directors, admirals, college deans, major generals, major domos, chefs, and *Chefs de Cabinet.*

Editors are managers, usually assisted by managing editors. Lawyers, doctors, and accountants are managers. Chemists, bankers, and architects are managers. Labor union leaders are managers.

In government, the managers are chairmen or chiefs of bureaus and committees, commissioners, commissars, administrators, secretaries, cabinet officials, consuls, ambassadors. Presidents and vice-presidents are managers, whether in political government or in business government.

Whatever the title, the managers are decision-makers in some specialized phase of human activity in one of the three major divisions outlined. They all need and use some businesspaper devoted to their special activity.

For example: *Journal of Accountancy, Sanitary Maintenance, Legal Intelligencer, Savings Bank Journal, Journal of Dental Research, Journalism Quarterly, Architecture & Design, Mortuary Management, Show Business, American School & University, Editor & Publisher, Construction Methods, Church Management, Circulation Management, Sales Management, Consulting Engineer, Law & Order, National Sheriff, American City, Army-Navy-Air Force Journal, Marine Corps Gazette,* etc.

Standard Industrial Classification Manual already referred to (Chapter I, section 14) groups Finance, Insurance, and Real Estate in one division, called Division G (digitals 60 to 67). This includes banking, 60; credit agencies other than banks, 61; security and commodity brokers, dealers exchanges and services, 62; insurance carriers, 63; insurance agents, brokers, and services, 64; real estate, 65; combinations of real estate, insurance, loans and law offices, 66; holding and other investment companies, 67.

Division H of S.I.C. includes many contributive services: medical, legal, educational, and personal (repairs, hotels, etc.). Digitals 70 to 89 cover Division H.

Division I is government and Division J is "non-classifiable."

The business press itself may be described as a microcosm of business:

1. It *extracts* its information and ideas from many sources.

2. It *transforms* this information and knowledge into a magazine or newspaper.

3. It *distributes* the product (magazine or newspaper) to the managerial level in all four major divisions of business.

4. It *contributes* the talents and facilities of its editors and others within its organization and outside specialists to help the entire process.

CHAPTER III

MARKETPLACE—MAINSTREAM OF BUSINESS NEWS

1. Peddler to Vending Machine

"Trade is as universal as the human race, as ancient as the first barter when two men got what both wanted and each gained while neither lost."[1]

British artistocrats once looked down their noses at people "in trade." On the other hand, Napoleon (of peasant stock) spoke with contempt of England as "a nation of shopkeepers."

The truth is, without trade neither the British aristocracy nor Napoleon would have lasted as long as they did. Trade sustained them. Trade provides the sinews of war and of peace.

As we explained in the definition of business (Chapter I) we are all traders, exchanging some skill or talent or product or possession or know-how, for money or for something else of value we need or want or cannot produce ourselves.

All these exchanges of goods or services for money take place in some specific marketplace, and create business news.

There are commodity markets: grain, food, sugar, textiles, metals, rubber, hides, coal, oil, etc.

There are stock and bond markets, money markets, diamond markets, gold and silver and fish markets, black markets, secondhand book markets, antique markets, labor markets, and supermarkets.

Favorites of tourist and decorator are the antique markets: in London it is Petticoat Lane and the Thieves Market; in Paris, The Flea Market; in Madrid, El Rastro; in Rome, Via del Barbuino and

[1] *Mercantile Agency Annual* (R. G. Dun & Co., 1871).

Via Margutta; in New Orleans, the native quarter; in New York City, Second and Third Avenues and Upper Madison Avenue. In Amsterdam, the secondhand book market is rivaled only by the book stalls on the Left Bank in Paris.

Black markets exist where there is a public demand for some commodity that is temporarily scarce or illegal. Such markets have flourished in cigarettes, narcotics, penicillin, scrap iron, steel, French francs, gold.

Pushcart peddlers flourish today in the ghettos and slums of big cities just as they did centuries ago, and house-to-house selling is a billion-dollar business, to remind us how persistent some market traditions are, in spite of great changes in distribution.

Students of business journalism should glance backward sometimes and note the changing trends in distribution. The first merchants were the itinerant peddlers, hawkers, and chapmen, who brought the goods to the people. Besides the peddlers (or pedlars) of goods, others traveled the highways with services: tinkers, menders, and journeymen from the brotherhoods and guilds.

The peddler carried his merchandise in a pack (ped or pad) or sack over his shoulder or in a basket. In London Town the type of goods or services for sale was recognized by the peddler's cry, bell, or whistle. "Buy a Broom!"; "Milk Below"; Scissors to Grind"; "Mackerel!"; "Bow Pots! Two a Penny!"; "Umbrellas to Mend!"[2]

The traveling salesmen of early days carried woolen cloth, lace, gloves, combs, needles, brooms and brushes, mirrors, bangles, spices, brandy, etc. Source of supply were generally small artisans and handcraftsmen and cottage industries.

The Yankee peddler, forerunner of the American system of retailing, sold pots and pans, but also bibles, almanacs, primers, and magazines, calico, hair tonic, beeswax, axe-helves, and patent medicine.

He was also a carrier of news, news of the towns: politics, business trends, new modes and manners. Some of these peddlers became drummers, salesmen for manufacturers, wholesalers, or big stores.

Some peddlers, like the first John D. Rockefeller, who peddled kerosene from a pushcart, L. S. Ayres, the Rich brothers, Adam Gimbel, Elihu Sanger, and Richard Warren Sears, became tycoons of retailing. Rockefeller founded an oil empire; Ayres, the Riches,

[2] Luke Limner, (pseud.) John Leighton, *The Cries of London* (London, Circa 1845).

Gimbel, and Sanger founded great department stores; and Sears built a great mail order company and retail chain with the help of his partner Roebuck.

The ancient peddler brought the goods (and the news) to the people.

Then came the medieval fairs, Oriental bazaars, and trading posts where shrewd traders brought the people to the goods. Adam Gimbel had a trading post in Vincennes, Indiana, in 1842. Later he and his brothers moved to New York and opened a general store from which sprang the great Gimbel organization.

The trading post, usually at the headwater of a stream, or near a frontier, traded supplies for pelts. The posts lasted until 1850. Indeed, some still exist in the Arctic Circle.

These were crude beginnings and the changes that followed happened because someone had a better idea. The peddler bought a horse and wagon. It increased his cost of distribution, but it also increased his volume of business and expanded his territory. He sold more goods. The trader built a permanent shop. This increased his cost of distribution, but made it possible for him to sell more goods than the peddler.

Then came the department store, embracing many specialty shops under one roof. New services and new ideas for styling and promotion. The size and location further increased the *cost* of distribution, but also increased the distribution of goods.

With its branch stores springing up in Suburbia the modern department store is in effect bringing the goods to the people as of old. The story of retailing is a great unfinished chapter in the history of business which is intimately interwoven with the history of business journalism and closely fused with the history of mankind.

The general store, like the trading post, had no one-price system to begin with. The proprietor charged what traffic would bear, or he bartered with the customers. Rum, molasses, linen, wool, and hardware were the main lines, but local products, accepted in lieu of money, also were sold.

Specialty stores grew from the public demand for variety of lines of merchandise and for more complete assortments in each line from which to make selections, and for more personal attention.

Department stores, to render extra services to the customer (credit, delivery, advertising, display, and lower prices), assembled groups of specialty shops under one roof and one management. The department store, in 1880, firmly established the one-price system and the policy of the cash transaction.

In 1900, the growth of new types of retail outlets was rapid: mail order (selling from catalogs, mailed to consumers); chains (syndicates of stores); co-operatives (syndicates of consumers); supermarkets (self-service stores, dealing in foods and non-foods), and discount department stores selling national brands on a fast turnover system at very low margins of profit.

Having served for over a quarter century as chief editor of the oldest trade paper in the housewares industry, *Housewares Review*, the author's experience will serve to illustrate the great changes that have taken place in the distribution of consumer goods in terms of this one periodical.

Housewares (1958) is a business of about $4 billion a year and 10 per cent of that is in pots and pans. In Macy's basement in New York City, the largest retail housewares department in the world, only 5 per cent of the volume is pots and pans.

Twenty-five years ago pots and pans were the biggest volume category in housewares, and the readers of this trade paper (founded in 1892) were housewares manufacturers and jobbers, who sold mainly pots and pans, and department stores, who were their main customers.

In 1958 there were 32 different types of retailers and wholesalers buying housewares, as shown in the following breakdown of the readership of *Housewares Review*.

Retail buyers: drug stores, supermarkets, farmer's markets, consumer co-operatives, jewelry stores, discount houses, hardware retailers, housewares stores, mail order houses, stamp plan redemption centers, variety stores, furniture stores, premium buyers, club and party plan operators, house-to-house installment operators, buying syndicates, filling stations, appliance retailers, and department stores.

Wholesale buyers: housewares, hardware, and appliance distributors; automotive, jewelry, drug, carnival, variety, rack (supermarkets), and premium jobbers; stamp plan suppliers; catalog wholesalers, exporters and importers.

Producers: Materials used for housewares, once only wood or metal, today include chemicals, paper, plastics, synthetics, ceramics, glass, rubber, and textiles, and a completely new set of readers has been added from the primary fields.

Housewares, once mainly kitchen products, today include consumer goods for every room in the house, for the basement, and the garden: portable appliances, cook and bakeware, picnic and barbecue equipment, bar equipment, cleaning equipment and supplies, garden equipment and supplies, kitchen and garden furniture, power tools and other tools for the home workshop, hardware, plastic dinnerware, stainless steel cutlery, bath shop equipment, paper supplies, and pet shop equipment.

There were a number of significant changes in retailing after the turn of the century, such as:

1. The development of chain stores.
2. The introduction of the self-service grocery store in 1916.[3]
3. The opening of retail stores by the two leading mail-order houses in 1924—later to become the main sources of their sales.[4]
4. The introduction in the early 1930's of the supermarket, which was destined to become the prevailing kind of food store.
5. The adoption of self-service by variety stores, drug stores, and other kinds of stores to which it was applicable.
6. The rapid development of planned shopping centers after World War II to meet the need created by the population shift to the suburbs.

Chain store: perhaps the most fundamental of these changes was the spectacular growth of the chain store system of distribution in the first quarter of the century. By 1925 the leading chains in several major fields had already expanded to such an extent that the future of the chain store as a permanent and important feature of our distribution set-up seemed beyond question. What actually happened during the next 30 years is revealed by the U.S. Retail Census for 1954. It shows that of the total retail volume, which amounted that year to $170 billions, the chains accounted for $40 billions, or 23.7 per cent.

Returning to the situation existing in 1925, the need for a business-paper to serve the rapidly growing chain store field was clearly indicated. It was met by the establishment of *Chain Store Age,* a monthly publication conceived by Arnold D. Friedman and developed with the help of Godfrey Lebhar.[5]

[3] "Piggly Wiggly" store, Memphis, Tenn., was first self-service grocery, 1916.
[4] Sears Roebuck and Montgomery Ward.
[5] See Chap. V, section 33.

Originally *Chain Store Age* was designed to cover the problems of multiple store operation which were common to all chains. By 1928, however, the need for specialized publications for each of the major fields in which the chain stores were active was met by publishing separate editions of *Chain Store Age*. Separate editions were developed for the grocery chains, the variety store chains, the drug chains and the restaurant chains, besides a general edition for chains in other fields. Actually, two editions are issued for each of the major fields, one for executives at headquarters and the other for the store managers.

The editorial scope of *Chain Store Age* is broad enough to cover the specific merchandising problems in each field as well as the operational and general management problems common to all.[6]

Another well-known chain store businesspaper is *Variety Store Merchandiser*, covering the expanding $3,500,000 variety store market (1957) with a distribution of 30,000 copies a month.

Chain stores go back to ancient China (200 B.C.). Fugger operated chain stores in fifteenth-century Germany. The famous Mitsui chain store system began in Japan in 1643. In America the oldest chain store system was Hudson's Bay, begun in 1670, which also included trading posts and banks.

George Gilman, leather merchant, bought a shipload of tea in 1859 and opened a little tea store on Vesey Street in New York. He painted the store bright red and hired George Hartford as manager. Soon other bright red tea stores sprung up and so began one of the biggest retail chains of the twentieth century, The Great Atlantic & Pacific Tea Company.

Frank W. Woolworth, ten-dollar-a-week clerk in a store in Watertown, New York, a few years after Hartford began managing red tea stores, also had a vision of a chain of red store fronts. He assembled a stock of merchandise he could sell at retail for nickels and dimes and founded the Woolworth chain of five-and-ten-cent stores.

The chain store, as we know it, rudely shook up the smug and the complacent at the turn of the century. It challenged the sloppy, slovenly practices of independent retailers and the easy-going ways of wholesalers and manufacturers everywhere—and everyone benefited, competitors and consumers. The brightest role was played by the business press.

[6] From a memorandum to the author in 1958 by Godfrey Lebhar, distinguished chief editor and founder of *Chain Store Age*; see Chap. V.

Supermarket: more than 30 years ago, a grocer by the name of Michael Cullen began to preach the gospel of the supermarket. His gospel was an astonishing prophecy of the supermarket today. But no one listened to him. So in August, 1930, he opened his own supermarket with self-service in Jamaica, Long Island, and heralded himself as "King Kullen," the world's greatest price wrecker. While others were experimenting similarly elsewhere in our country, the opening of "King Kullen" provided the spark that set off the revolution in food distribution which has reverberated around the globe.

Michael Cullen set the pattern, although the evolution of self-service had been going on for a number of years before. In the past 25 years the supermarket has made international history. It is estimated that the system of self-service retailing in the quarter century period has sold America's consumers over $150 billion in foods and other merchandise at a possible saving of at least $15 billion, a contribution to the American economy which has been universally recognized.

Packaging—the self-service feature of the supermarket—has had a revolutionary impact. The supermarket, with its perfected technics of "sight and touch" selling, compelled the entire system of food retailing to meet its changes. New packaging had to be introduced, aiming to increase merchandise visibility and to facilitate handling. Hence the vast development in new package designs and, above all, in transparent packaging films.

Merchandising equipment and facilities to fit the needs of self-service, as well as to answer the demands for the best types of refrigeration, air conditioning, checkout modernization—all these have been radically changed for this mammoth system.

Before the war, supermarkets concentrated mainly on the sale of foods. However, during the war period, because of shortages of food items, supermarkets throughout the country began to feature non-food lines and to operate complete non-food departments, thus cushioning their volume and reenforcing their profit on higher profit products.

Their success and consumer acceptance influenced supermarkets to maintain these non-food features as a permanent part of their operation. This trend is still increasing through the country.

What about the supermarket's future? Are there goals beyond this, even greater diversification of merchandise, more services, more facets of appeal to attempt?

The answer may vary, depending on an individual operator's potential and vision. But this much may be said without qualification:

Until a better and more economical way to sell food and other merchandise is found, the supermarkets are here to stay and progress. From the start, these markets hit upon the correct formula for satisfying the mass market. With the years they learned how to do a better job at less cost and even greater satisfaction for their customers.

Possessing the key to mass appeal and recognized by consumers as proven, hard-and-fast economic selling units, the Supers are bound to interest more and more customers in ever widening circles of merchandise efforts. It is also clear that they will do so and keep high their standards of mass display, wide selectivity, ease of shopping, and low prices.[7]

More than 9 million people are engaged in the extraction, transformation, and distribution of food. Food industry management is one of the best informed of any industry. Except Alaska, each of the 49 states of our country has a retail grocers' association, and each association publishes a regional magazine, carrying the advertising of many food and beverage manufacturers anxious to get their products on and keep them on retail shelves.

Notable among these periodicals are *Food Merchants Advocate* (New York), *California Grocers Advocate, Colorado Grocer and Cleveland Grocer. Cooperative Merchandiser* is the official organ of the Cooperative Food Distributors of America and National Retailer-owned Grocers, Inc. It is published in Chicago and has a circulation of about 25,000 copies (1957). Other periodicals include *Progressive Grocer; Food Field Reporter; Meat and Food Merchandising; Food Mart News; Food Trade News; Food World; Frozen Food Age; Food Topics.*

The *I G A Grocerman,* official organ of the Independent Grocers Alliance of America (Chicago) has a circulation of 10,000 copies and *Nargus Bulletin,* official organ of the National Association of Retail Grocers (Chicago) has a circulation of nearly 67,000 (1957).

Fairchild Publications, a large multiple businesspaper publisher specializing in apparel and home-furnishings fields, entered the food field in 1955 with a weekly, in a newspaper format similar to other Fairchild dailies. It is called *Supermarket News* and in 1958 had a paid weekly circulation of 37,000. A seasoned business journalist, Julian Handler, was made editor. Full-time reporters in 30 Fairchild

[7] From a memorandum to the author in 1958 by the distinguished chief editor and founder of *Super Market Merchandising,* M. M. Zimmerman; see Chap. V.

news bureaus, 400 correspondents across the country, and the AP and UP wire service franchises give Mr. Handler an edge over many other food editors in covering this dynamic field of distribution.

So symbolic of a new era in the distribution of packaged consumer goods is the self-service operation that the U.S. Department of State began to employ the device abroad to help explain the American way of life. In the World's Fair in Rome in 1956 the American exhibit was "Supermercato USA," a life-size reproduction of an American supermarket. Again, in Zagreb, Jugoslavia, at the World's Fair in 1957, the United States pavilion was a "Supermarket USA," displaying $40,000 worth of typical foods and non-foods flown over for the occasion and afterward donated to various Jugoslav institutions and charities. Fair authorities reported that the exhibit was the most popular at this fair.

In 1957 there were about 18,000 supermarkets operating in more than 50 countries outside the U.S.[8]

Discount house—from pariah to prophet: "I am the creation of your copywriters," Stephen Masters, founder of one of the first discount department stores, told the Advertising Federation of America in 1955.[9]

What he meant was that national advertising had so heavily pre-sold the public on national brands, it had become easy to operate a department store *without sales personnel.*

United States advertising of brand names became a billion-dollar-a year expenditure in 1934 and reached $11 billion a year in 1958. To this huge sum must be added the unknown dollar value represented by pages of free publicity for national brands in magazines, newspapers, businesspapers, and by time on radio and television (give-away programs). A guess at the value of the free space and free time would be perhaps another $5 billion a year.

With the goods pre-sold, handed to the customer in the original factory carton or package, and eliminating costly services like credit, delivery, and the use of archaic ten-story structures with expensive escalators and vice presidents, the discount department store was able to operate on a markup of 11.9 per cent. Contrast this with the average markup of the typical department store, which is 36.6 per

[8] National Cash Register Company surveys.

[9] Stephen Masters, "Where Are We Heading in Distribution and Retailing?" paper read before the general session, Advertising Federation of America, June 8, 1955, Chicago.

cent. To put it another way, it costs a classical department store $36.60 to sell $100 worth of goods. It costs the discount department store $11.90 to sell $100 worth of goods. The average classical department store has four turns a year in its stock while the discount department store turns its stock from 8 to 14 times a year.

Masters' first store was a hole in the wall in New York in 1937, and he was looked upon as a pariah in the business community. In 1958, the U.S. Chamber of Commerce estimated there were more than 7,000 discount stores in this country doing business running into billions of dollars a year. Some have become chains. In 1958 Masters (nine stores) did $45 million; Two Guys From Harrison (16 stores) did $38 million; Polk Brothers (six stores) did $60 million; Korvette (seven stores) did $71 million; and Kleins-on-the-Square (three stores) $85 million. The public had cast its vote.

Now many orthodox stores are eliminating expensive services or charging for them; are putting in the cash-and-carry features of the mass retailers; are changing many sections to self-service. Or else they are becoming strictly class emporiums with snob appeal.

All the businesspapers covering the orthodox stores added the discount houses to their mailing lists and circulation statements, and most of the mass manufacturers and jobbers of consumer goods send their salesmen to call regularly on these high-velocity discount outlets.

The mass retailers have moved out (with the population) to Suburbia and Exurbia and set up branch stores where there is space to park a car or station wagon, and that brings us to the phenomenon of the shopping center, another mass retailing invention in the current revolution in distribution.

Shopping centers in Suburbia: an estimated $38 billion was spent in the nation's shopping centers in 1956.

Federal Reserve Bank of New York reported downtown department-store volume dropped an estimated 5 per cent since 1946 while suburban sales went from an estimated 12 per cent of total metropolitan volume to 27 per cent (1958).[10]

In the New York City area, alone, 110 department store suburban branches are now in operation, while within the city limits itself, four department-store giants folded (Loeser's, McCreery's, Wanamaker's, and Hearn's).

[10] "The Shopping Center," No. 1 in a series on new patterns in distribution, *Housewares Review*, January 1958, pp. 151-154.

An estimated 2,400 shopping centers with a total of 18,000 stores were in operaion, (1958) two thirds of them built since World War II.

In 1956, 50 per cent of all new variety stores were opened in shopping centers, 50 per cent of the new supermarkets, 77 per cent of the new drug stores.

According to a survey of 198 parent department and specialty stores in 40 major cities across the nation, the average chain store is now operating three suburban branch units.

The typical United States shopping center consumer has a better-than-average income (median is now up to $6,500, 70 per cent higher than the rest of the country); higher than the average home ownership; bigger than average home ownership; bigger than average families. She operates a home with as many push buttons as the family can afford, spends $19 million a year on food (one third spend over $25 a week and with emphasis on "convenience foods"). They are under heavy compulsion to earn and spend and buy many things on installments—housing, autos, TV sets, washing machines, etc.

Since 1934, the population of the suburbs has grown 75 per cent, while total population has grown 25 per cent.

Westchester Terminal Plaza, a 24-story, $41 million dollar shopping center, designed by Victor Gruen for New Rochelle, New York, in 1960, is a project inspired by the Gallerie Vittorio Emanuele in Milan, Italy, a four-story arcade erected almost a century ago. The Westchester Terminal Plaza will have 70 shops on its 24 floors, Macy's occupying the largest. It will contain a 15-story office building, a two-story, 100-room hotel, a 5,200 car garage, a bank, post office, auditorium, restaurants, and the railroad and thruway terminals. New Rochelle is a suburb of New York City.

Farmers' Market: descendant of the public markets of the Middle Ages, the more than 1,200 farmers' markets in our country alone are estimated to do a billion dolllars worth of consumer goods volume a year. Some fifty to a hundred merchants are housed in one operation renting space from a single management that owns the center. They are open only two or three days a week.

Their prices are lower than traditional retailers in the same area and they show net profits as high as 16 per cent before taxes compared to 3 or 4 per cent profit in the average retail operation. They advertise cooperatively in the local newspapers, and contribute to local charities. Pitchmen call out their wares, like a carnival, and a public address system is used to announce bargains. Often there are playrooms for children, lounges and game rooms and other attractions.

Premiums: Premium Advertising Association estimates this huge market device for the distribution of consumer goods at one and three-quarter billion dollars a year. It can be subdivided broadly into twelve branches of activity.

1. Self liquidator: This is the "box top plus some money, gets you a premium" type of promotion. The premiums desired here run from 10 cents to about $5 with $1 being the average. Anything that appeals to women or children is eligible.

2. Coupon redemption: Coupons that are affixed to merchandise are saved by the consumer and then exchanged for premium merchandise. Almost any kind of products that are desired by most men, women, or children are used, ranging in retail price from $1 to $15 or $20, with $5 being, roughly, the most popular price.

3. Trading stamp: Stamps are given for purchases in such retail establishments as supermarkets, hardware stores, filling stations, etc. Consumers accumulate and exchange stamps for selected premiums. Anything desired by a majority of people is used as a premium, ranging in price from $1 to $50, with the $5 to $15 bracket most popular. About 42 per cent of United States retail outlets have trading stamp programs. The stamp companies maintain over 1,600 stamp redemption or premium centers. In 1957 over $175 million worth of housewares were distributed by premium centers.

4. Giveaways: Here, premiums are given to consumers without charge, as an incentive for the consumer to perform some act, such as to open a new savings account in a bank, enter a store to watch a demonstration, buy one product rather than another which has no premium, provide a store with a sales lead, etc. Premiums with wide appeal are desired, ranging from a fraction of a cent to as much as $5 or $10, depending upon the application.

5. Sales incentive: These are sales contests in which salesmen receive premium merchandise for exceeding quotas. Almost any type of product that has broad appeal to men, women or children, or items for the home can be used as a premium ranging from a couple of dollars to an almost unlimited ceiling.

6. Dealer incentive: Premiums are given to dealers as incentive for them to perform some act, such as place a larger order, take on a

new line, put in a display, etc. The premiums used here are about the same as in sales incentives.

7. Party-plan: Premiums are offered to a housewife who will invite a number of her friends to her home to watch a demonstration of products sold by the party-plan firm. Premiums used generally are of appeal to women, or of use in the home, ranging from $1 to $25.

8. Tea and coffee wagon route: Premiums are given to housewife as incentive for her to buy staple groceries from truck salesman, and to continue being a customer. Items appealing to women, ranging from $5 to $25, are used.

9. Club plan: A selected housewife acts as a secretary-collector for a firm who sells products on installments. For her services, she receives premiums with woman-home appeal, ranging from $2 or $3 to $15.

10. House-to-house installment: This is similar to the club plan installment selling, except that actual salesmen call on the housewife to sell products to her on the installment plan. Premiums are used to get her to make the initial or subsequent purchases.

11. Advertising specialties: These commonly are business office, desk, or personal items which bear the donor's imprint, and are given as good-will builders. Included are pencils, pens, notebooks, calendars, etc., ranging from a few cents to $5 and up.

12. Business gifts: These are products of high appeal to men and women which are given to customers or clients for the purpose of building good will. These never bear imprints. Usually given at Christmas. Prices can range from $1 to $20 or more.

Serving the field are *Premium Practice,* a monthly started in 1905; *Premium Buyers' Guide,* a quarterly started in 1950; *Premium Merchandising,* a monthly founded in 1957.

Pay-as-you-go: credit financing moves big ticket goods like homes, automobiles, trips abroad, as well as furniture, appliances, kitchens, hotel and restaurant services. Low-income groups now enjoy higher standards of pay-as-you-go living; frozen foods, even completely cooked meals (frozen) are flown from other parts of the world to expand the distribution system to the smallest village store. An Iowa farmer can enjoy a meal prepared by Maxim's of Paris in a $3,000 electric kitchen on which he has thirty years to pay.

According to the National Association of House-to-House Installment Companies, New York City, seven out of ten married couples in the 18-44 age group with children under ten have installment debts (1958). John W. Johnson, executive secretary of the American Collectors Association, told the NAHHIC at their national trade show in the Hotel New Yorker, February 9, 1959: "In 1952 some 38 per cent of American families had installment debts compared to 45 per cent in 1956, and the percentage is still increasing. More and more people are realizing that through the wise use of installment buying, they have available the necessities and physical comfort on a grander scale than ever before possible." He also stated 98 per cent of the people were "basically honest."

Installment Retailing, official organ of the NAHHIC, has a sworn circulation of about 2,000 (1956). Another businesspaper in this field, *Salesman's Opportunity*, Chicago, claims direct selling is a $10 billion industry and that it reaches 300,000 independent salespeople, but no circulation statement is filed with SRDS. Another Chicago monthly covering this field is *Specialty Salesman Magazine*, which furnishes no circulation statement to SRDS.

Advertising: this force, as stated, has helped to bring about a revolution in the packaging and distribution of packaged, brand-name goods, and in redesigning the marketplace where the packages are displayed.

With the price of consumer goods usually appearing in the advertisement, price juggling and haggling between seller and customer ended early in this century. The consumer was protected by uniformity in price and quality. The brand name was generally backed up by a firm which was interested in protecting its reputation and holding its customers. These virtues, and the development of better packaging, more informative labeling, more compelling display at point-of-purchase, more intelligent sales training at the retail counter, and improvement in other marketing methods, gave merchants higher velocity, greater turnover, and enabled them to operate on a lower margin which was reflected in lower prices to the consumer. Newspaper advertising at the local level partly paid for by manufacturers (cooperative advertising) also helped.

The cracker barrel, burlap sack of coffee beans, sugar and tea bins, and the keg of molasses gave way to rows of brightly illuminated, self-filling shelves of attractively packaged, easily identifiable, branded merchandise.

Pre-selling through national brand advertising, neatness in display, good lighting, efficiency, self-service, low prices, and adequate parking space gradually brought on this revolution in the distribution of foods and non-foods.

Collaterally, the introduction of automation in wholesaling and retailing and the general improvements in market research enabled distribution to catch up with the outpouring of consumer goods from the production lines.

Government cooperated by establishing the first Census of Distribution in 1930 and by expanding the services of the Department of Commerce.

The advertising trade papers—*Advertising Age; Mediascope Advertising Requirements, American Press, Editor & Publisher, Printers' Ink, Industrial Marketing, Media Agencies Clients, Network,* and *Media*—service this dynamic and volatile field.

Automatic vending: Machines, unattended by humans, now move millions of units of goods in stores, plants, terminals, and elsewhere. Reputed to be a $2 billion market in 1958, the automatic merchandising machines sell 15 out of every 100 packs of cigarettes, 25 out of every 100 soft drinks, and 20 out of every 100 candy bars. In 1958 the mechanical robot machines dispensed $937 million worth of hot and cold foods and drinks alone. They also make change in subways and dispense stamps in post offices and terminals. Food processors and makers of robot vendors are working together to vend complete hot plate lunches. Packaged hot foods distributed automatically climbed from practically zero to $18.5 million in 1958. Business-papers serving this dynamic field include *Vend, The Coin Machine Journal, Coin Machine Review, The Cash Box,* and *Mass Vending.*

2. Two Common Markets Compared

Winston Churchill's dream of a "United States of Europe" passed its second milestone in January 1959, when six countries lowered or eliminated all trade barriers against each other and made their currencies convertible or freely exchangeable.[11] The countries are Belgium, The Netherlands, Luxembourg, France, Federal Republic of West Germany, and Italy. Together they have a population of 175 million—about the same as the population of the United States of America.

[11] At the same time Britain, Norway, Denmark, and Sweden took steps toward currency convertibility—a new degree of economic stability.

Three European countries already had several years of fruitful experience with economic union: Belgium, The Netherlands, Luxembourg, known as the Benelux countries. This new merger brings together the economic, atomic, coal and steel communities of all six countries, with vast potentials for expansion for each and higher living standards for all.

Described by the French as the *Assemblée Unique*, the Parliament of these six countries met in Strasbourg, France, a year earlier, to affect a merger of their economies—probably the most important event in Western Europe in this century (first milestone).

The United States of America has enjoyed a common market since the late eighteenth century. It has become so commonplace that the Americans give it little thought. A businesspaper columnist, William H. Grimes, made this comment in support of the European Common Market:

A man leaving his office at night dons a hat made in Connecticut, a top coat made in New York or Ohio. He rides a railroad car made in Illinois or an automobile made in Michigan. For dinner he has chicken from Delaware and peas from Wisconsin. Then he looks at television, the parts of which came from half a dozen states, meanwhile lighting a cigarette from North Carolina with a lighter made in Pennsylvania.

All the 170 million people [*of the U.S.*] *are a potential market for any producer. No barriers or restrictions are put between the producer and his customers. His principal worry is that competitors will find a better appeal to the market by making a product cheaper or designing it more attractively.*[12]

The European Common Market countries have traded with each other for centuries (when they were not fighting) but goods and capital have never moved freely between these six countries as it has for over 175 years between the states of the American Union.

In less than two centuries the United States common market has paid off in all kinds of wealth and growth, increased standards of living, vast purchasing power, and freedom to compete. The most important advantage of the European Common Market is that with mutual trust could come lasting peace for Europe, for it is an old axiom that where goods cannot cross borders soldiers will.

The traditional instruments used in Europe to meet the problems

[12] William H. Grimes, "Thinking Things Over," *The Wall Street Journal* October 16, 1956.

posed by neighboring countries were royal marriages, intrigue, assassination, and war. After the rise of republics and constitutional monarchies, only intrigue and murder were left. Intrigue often led to war—physical or economic. Neither pays any valuable dividends, often causes mutual bankruptcy.

When every producer is behind a high wall of protective tariffs shielding him from outside competition there is no strong incentive to find cheaper or better methods of production or to spend money in research and development of newer and better products and services. The consumer is the loser. And there is little need for a business press concerned with disbursing news and know-how of new technics for extraction, transformation, and distribution. In the small walled-in markets, producers either become members of small private clubs or cartels or are driven out of business.

The United States common market has encouraged the European Common Market for these reasons:

It is to no nation's advantage to have a world half prosperous and half poverty stricken.

Competition is the life of trade and trade is a universal word.

An economically strong Europe would be a politically strong Europe resisting any encroachment on the principles of the democratic process.

A strong, free Europe would be a fruitful source of scientific ideas and technological advancement—new inventions and discoveries.

Another advantage would be the growth of the world business press, already formidable in West Germany.

3. Market Reports and Credit

As we have said, markets thrive on confidence, which in turn is based on facts. Great confidence is placed in the accuracy and impartiality of the market reporters. The businesspaper is a *continuous* market reporter. Without the market reports of businesspapers, the movement of goods would soon slow down.

Another factor arising out of confidence that contributes to the movement of goods is *credit*.

Credit is a form of energy which gives its impulse to every step in the business process. Credit makes possible the purchase of equipment for the *extraction* of materials from the field, forest, mine, and well, from the ocean air and the ocean sea. *Transformation* of these materials into semi-finished and finished goods in the industrial plant depend on funds advanced by banks or investors. *Distribution* of materials and finished goods across the airways, seaways, and highways depends on credit as well as equipment; and ultimate use and enjoyment of goods and services by the public would not reach much volume without credit. The business process would slow down and stop were it not for credit and the available information on which credit is based.

Dun & Bradstreet: One of the great mercantile credit reporting agencies, Dun & Bradstreet, was established in 1841 and has become a world-wide fact-gathering facility, with its own businesspaper, *Dun's Review and Modern Industry*. The services of this organization revolve around the daily activities of 1,800 reporters who call on businessmen in every city, town, and village. Their reports are processed by a staff of 8,000 analysts and clerks in offices in every trade center in the United States and Canada and elsewhere in the world. Dun & Bradstreet write credit reports on business in all free nations of the world, their reporters working out of 70 overseas offices. A private, semi-automatic wire network connects 79 of their 142 offices. It transmits 65 words a minute.

Dun's Municipal Service Department furnishes credit surveys on states, countries, cities, school districts, and other government units for the use of banks, trust companies, insurance companies, private estates, and other investors in municipal and revenue bonds.

A huge business library in the Dun & Bradstreet building in New York is available to business journalism students, the working press, scholars, and business writers.

A staff of writers at Dun's provides articles for businesspapers and data for businesspaper editors.

4. Coinage—Confidence in a Trademark

"The distinctive thing about Ionia," says Lynn White, Jr., "the chief stimulus to the commercial prosperity which provided leisure for the atomistic philosophers, was the invention in Asia Minor of coinage."[13]

With the use of metal coins officially stamped and guaranteed to be of uniform weight (later with milled or raised edges to prevent

[13] "The Changing Past" in Lynn White, Jr. (Ed.), *Frontiers of Knowledge* (New York, Harper & Brothers, 1956), p. 75.

trimming) every commodity or service could be bought and sold through the medium of a trade mark in which the public had confidence—a coin of the realm. This did not end the age of barter, but it speeded up the processes of barter. The turnover was multiplied —and workers began to have freedom of movement, leisure to spend their money, freedom to change their possessions and locations.

One of the earliest standards of value was cattle. *Pecunia,* the Roman word for money, is derived from *pecus,* meaning cattle.

Before coins were invented traders of various countries used other things of value. Phoenicians used pearls as a unit of measure. Achaean islanders hammered tin, gold, and silver into small balls. Egyptians used gold, silver, and copper finger rings and bracelets. North American Indians used Wampum (strings of shell beads). Tobacco was legal tender in Colonial America and bottled gin was used as a medium in West Africa. Iron bars were used in ancient Britain.

Bars of precious metals often carried the stamp of either a temple or a deity—usually one of the market gods. Jehovah was the market god of the tribe of Levi. The Babylonian Shamash was another market god. Temples served as depositories, libraries, and banks for merchants. The Temple of Apollo at Delphi was a gold-depository and bank. Priests acted as judges in commercial disputes.

When you see Corinthian columns on security exchanges and modern bank buildings it is symbolic of Corinth, great trading and banking city of ancient Greece.

At the trade fair in Troyes in the time of Charlemagne (742-814) coin was offered in such a battered condition that it was sold by weight. The standard weight for dealing in coin became the standard for bullion everywhere in Europe and is known as Troy weight in our system of weights and measures, named after this city.

The Mediterranean port of Venice gave us the first gold ducat, minted in 1284, to remain famous for 600 years for its purity, weight, and fine quality. Today's Dutch guilder, a silver coin, goes back to the Dutch Guilds, which originally minted it.

Six years earlier (1278) bankers in Venice originated calculation by percentage instead of fractions.

No one really knows when or where money was first invented. The "sealed shekel" was a stamped piece of silver. King Croesus minted gold coins about 540 B.C. in Lydia. Today most money transactions are by check. Money is represented by demand deposits in banks represented by check and by currency (paper bank notes and stamped metal coins) issued by the government. Deposits are normally four or five times greater than currency.

"Gold began to go out of circulation as warehouse receipts came in many years ago," says Chase, "and now it is solemnly dug from a hole in South Africa and buried in another hole in the ground in Kentucky" (gold bars stored at Fort Knox).[14]

Now that we have a World Bank, farsighted men are thinking of a world currency. Certainly a universal currency, like a universal language, would be an ideal way to improve international trade on a planet that has so much else in common.

5. City—A News Clearing House

Communication lines and transportation lines converge on the City. The City is news-gatherer, news analyzer, news disseminator, and news creator.

The City *is* news, because it is the marketplace, the seat of church, government, legislature, court, bank, trade association, guild, academy, university, laboratory, arena, stadium, museum, depot, terminal airport, seaport, lakeport, riverport, warehouse, theater, morgue, night club, brothel, telegraph and broadcasting station, newspaper, businesspaper, magazine, and book.

The City is the nerve center.

"The City," says Mumford, "is the form and symbol of an integrated social relationship: it is the seat of the temple, the market, the hall of justice, the academy of learning. Here in the city the goods of civilization are multiplied and manifolded; here is where human experience is transferred into variable signs, symbols, patterns of conduct, systems of order."[15]

In the city the three most representative institutions of corporate life were the church, the guild, and the university. Curiously, the twelfth-century term for guilds was *Universitas:* the aim of the guild school was to prepare the student for the practice of a vocation or profession. The schools of theology, medicine, and law broke off from the guild school to lay the foundation for the university. The medical school was actually the first technical school. The walled village or town was sometimes encouraged by feudal lords, at other

[14] Stuart Chase, *Something Worth Knowing* (New York, Harper & Brothers, 1958), p. 183.

[15] Lewis Mumford, *The Culture of Cities* (New York, Harcourt Brace & Co., 1938), p. 3.

times opposed by them. Prior to the City, the monastery performed some of the city's functions. In the monasteries the written records were kept and multiplied. Certain technics of building, decoration, and manufacture were promoted, and markets were encouraged on the monastery grounds. In Germany (833) Lewis The Pious gave a monastery, which had provided a marketplace for merchants, permission to erect a mint. A cross in the center of the marketplace indicated to all traders that it was sacred ground. A court was set up to deal with merchants and traders at its fairs; weights and measures established; money coined; and market laws were promulgated.

Great trading cities flourished in the ancient world: Miletus, planned by Hippodamus along the rectangular lines of the Babylonian towns, Alexandria, Rhodes, Palmyra, Ephesus, Corinth, Carthage. *Mesion Pedion* was Main Street, built wide to accommodate commercial traffic.

> Three thousand years before Christ [writes Miriam Beard] the Mesopotamian merchant had a very considerable accumulation of technique and experience behind him; he was seasoned in affairs, wary in drawing up contracts, and stout in litigation. By 250 B.C., he was forming trading-companies for penetration of distant realms, he was trafficking in many kinds of wares, wool, spices, soda, silver, ointments and "fair-skinned slaves," bringing them by caravan or sailing ship to the cities of Ur, Uruk, Uma and other ancient centers of commerce, which are now being uncovered from the desert sands by the spades of excavators.[16]

The Etruscans, Italy's invaders, introduced the legal system, *disciplina etrusca,* which became the basis of Roman law, of city planning, and plumbing.

The Phoenician trading cities, Tyre, Sidon, Carthage, in Africa, were great trading cities when Rome was still in the barter stage. Carthage had a population of a million people. After the fall of Carthage in 146 B.C. there were no cities to equal it until The Hanse cities of the Middle Ages.[17]

The size of a city was defined by Plato as the number of people who could hear the voice of a single orator. It will not be long before that definition describes our planet.

Originally, the city was an invention of traders and merchants who

[16] Miriam Beard, *History of the Business Man* (New York, The Macmillan Co., 1938), pp. 11-17.

[17] H. G. Wells, *Outline of History* (New York, The Macmillan Co., 1920), Vol. 1, pp. 218-219.

wanted to provide a permanent market for goods and a clearing house for news intelligence. Political and military necessity, mechanization, the need for a monetary system, warehousing, transport, banking, contributed to town-making.

Towns became armed fortresses, and those not engaged in agriculture or mining were encouraged to live within the city walls and help in its permanent defense.

Cities became factories of human experience, transforming that experience, as Mumford says, "into variable signs, symbols, patterns of conduct, systems of order."

Eventually these business-news centers discovered their interdependence, the advantage of association and interchange of news information. Leagues of cities were formed: Rhenish League (1381), Swabian Cities (1376), Union of Cinque Ports in England. In fourteenth-century Italy there were more self-governing city states than in our entire twentieth-century world. The Swiss and Dutch were most successful in unifying their corporate towns.

The greatest city league was composed of the Hanse towns, usually known as the Hanseatic News League. Bruges, in Belgium, where many Hansa "merchant aristocrats" built their palatial homes on the banks of the canals, became the center of the fourteenth-century business world. (Today Bruges is a lace and linen center and tourist attraction.)

6. Hanseatic League—First Associated Press

When organized shipwrecking and piracy, highway robbery, and the plunder of peaceful communities were the professional pursuits of kings, princes, barons, and Knights Templar, a confederation of Germanic towns of the Baltic and North Sea was formed, in the thirteenth century. It became one of the most powerful and ruthless organizations of merchants in business history (*hansa*, a society of men), lasting 400 years. Historian Miriam Beard describes its integrated system of business news communication as the first "Associated Press." It is known in history as the Hanseatic News League.

From a few towns the Hanseatic News League grew to a group of 70 towns and soon to a league of 130 city-states, including many outposts in England, Norway, Sweden, Denmark, Holland, Flanders, Russia, and Italy.

Towns of the twelfth century, a form of life which had sprung from economic changes, as we have pointed out, were really quasi-independent, small republics. Trade in each town was regulated by the local guild or guilds of master craftsmen (see Chapter IV). Care of the poor was in the hands of the church. The town council took care of politics, protected the town walls, kept the municipal granaries filled, looked after the fire brigades, imposed tariffs, and maintained a local constabulary.

By 1370, the merchants of the Hanse towns had fought Waldemar III of Denmark to a standstill to prevent the abrogation of the herring fishing rights in the Baltic Sea, and concluded the Peace of Stralsund. The Hanseatic League was formally announced, backed by the great city-states of Lübeck, Hamburg, Bremen, Cologne, and Weimar. Many other city-states and towns soon sought the mutual security, trade privileges, and advantages of organized news intelligence which the league afforded.

The Hanse League coined its own money. The Western Hanse towns called the Baltic Hanseatic merchants the "Easterlings." English traders sold their wool for the coin of the Easterlings and thus it was that the pound of silver of the Ea-sterlings became the pound sterling of modern Great Britain.

Bergen, Norway, and Nijni Novgorod, Russia, became Hanse outposts. Bruges, hub of fourteenth-century commerce, became a Hanse town. Another was Antwerp, which became the most famous bourse of the sixteenth century. Other Hanse posts were established in Italy.

Goods of the Hanse merchants were accepted all over the world "as represented," whether it was herring, ship timber, salt, Russian furs, English wool, honey, rosaries, beer, hops, wax, or bacon.

The Hanse trading posts were sometimes called factories. In Venice such a one was located on the Grand Canal and contained 56 rooms. In London a Hanse factory was first known as The Guildhall of the Germans; then it was called Easterlings, and later the Steel Yard *(Stilliarde)*. In the Steel Yard was located the Great Scale of the City of London, where all exports and imports were weighed. With its huge buildings and markets it became a guarded city within a walled city. George Gieze was its Master. It was an important link in the first Teutonic *Kartelle* (Cartel).[18]

For four centuries the Hanse Cartellists enjoyed a monoply of materials and markets and distribution in most of Northern Europe.

[18] Miriam Beard, *History of The Business Man* (New York, The Macmillan Co., 1938).

They carefully avoided religious and political controversies, leaving these matters to temporal and spiritual lords.[19]

The Hanseatic News League was aided by the Knighthood of The Teutonic Order: Grand Master Hermann von Salza and the Knights of the Cross acted as the hired mercenaries of the Hanse merchants, subdued free competition with the sword, and built fortified trading posts for the cartellists on the shores of the Baltic. They subjugated the Prussians in the thirteenth century.[20]

But the fortunes of the Hanseatic News League reached a turning point. The Hanse were too smug behind their city walls. They were reading only their own news reports. They wasted their resources on internal dissension and external struggles to preserve their *Kartelle.* They did no research in new markets or better ways. Their mental isolationism left them unprepared for the shock of great events: the rise of the explorers, backed by the wealth of Spain, Portugal, and finally England and Holland; the discovery of new trade routes to India on the high seas; new uses of gun powder and cannon; new technics of trade and administration.

Soon the Italian Hanse towns and ports began to stagnate. The competition of Spanish, Portuguese, and later English and Dutch merchants in world markets was too much for the German cartellists. The Hanse merchants still traveled overland to India, paying heavy tribute to Turk and Arab gangsters for safe passage. Higher prices on their merchandise resulted in the loss of markets. Lack of a strong, well-financed central government, archaic stone walls instead of a powerful navy, these and other factors brought about the decline and fall of the great Hanseatic News League.[21]

In England, Sir Thomas Gresham II destroyed the power of the Steel Yard. The Thirty Years War completed the job. Merchant-aristocrats became paupers. The Fuggers and Welsers disappeared from the marketplaces and so did their news-letters.

After the Treaty of Westphalia, in 1648, only three out of 130 proud and free cities remained: Lübeck, Hamburg, and Bremen. In 1866 Lübeck surrendered her freedom. Bismarck took it away from Hamburg and Bremen in 1888.

[19] *Ibid.*

[20] Leon Koczy, *Baltic Policy of the Teutonic Order,* Baltic Countries, Vol. II, (Torun-Gdynia, Poland, Baltic Institute, 1936).

[21] H. G. Wells, *Outline of History.* In describing the downfall of the Hanse Towns, Wells suggests a link between the sixteenth-century and twentieth-century teutonic struggles for markets.

7. Religious Festival to Trade Fair

The ancient businessman's problem of reaching his widely scattered markets was solved by the social invention known as the fair (Italian, *feria;* French, *foire;* Latin, *ferie*—meaning festival, holiday, or day of rest). Many fairs were held under the auspices of the Church. The fairgrounds, being sacred, made it possible for merchants to trade in safety. The church got a commission on the business done. In some cases churches were banks, or repositories of gold. Priests were custodians of trade treaties and other documents for traders and provided a place for the "money-changers" to operate right in the temples, for a percentage of the profits.

Religious festivals were staged at the same time and attracted great numbers of traders. They came to worship, but also to barter. The Church guaranteed law and order. Businessmen in return provided financial support to the Church and its works.

The state also promulgated many of its laws at these trade fairs.

The Church often collected toll on the tents and booths displaying merchandise which were usually erected outside of the "holy circle." "Sacred marketplaces," as they were called, were held at stated intervals all over ancient and medieval Europe and Asia.

In 833 Lewis The Pious in Germany gave a monastery permission to mint money.

Otto II (A.D. 973-983) granted permission to the Widow Imma to found a cloister in Kärnten, "establish a market place, a *mint* and collect taxes." Many markets were supervised by the proprietors of monasteries. He who broke the peace and harmony was liable to fine or imprisonment. Traveling salesmen and merchant adventures arrived in caravans, armed to the teeth (in spite of the parchment treaties they carried in their saddle bags guaranteeing their political safety).

Charlemagne recognized the trade fair as a valuable social invention for the distribution of goods and the collection of information as well as tolls and taxes. Walford tells how this emperor encouraged trade fairs at Aquisgranum (Aix la Chapelle), Troyes, and Beaucaire (A.D. 742-814).[22]

France had many famous fairs in ancient days, those at Brie and Champagne were international.

[22] Cornelius Walford, F.S.A., *Fairs, Past and Present* (London, Elliot Stock, 1883).

In Belgium, the Earl of Flanders established a fair at Courtri which from the days of the Caesars has been a world linen center. There were fairs at Bruges, Mont Casel, and Torhout. Because of her fairs Antwerp became one of the world's great trading cities.

Unlike today, when merchants fly to fairs half way around the world in jet planes with their merchandise in flying box cars, to return home within two weeks, the merchants of ancient times would be gone many months or even years. The fairs themselves lasted several months. Bandits, weather, and terrain made the merchants' journeys to and from fairs an obstacle course. Merchants were accompanied often by troops of mercenaries and were lucky to arrive at the fair with half their goods, a good percentage of their personnel, and any of their soldiers. The rigors of the trip home still faced these merchant-adventurers.

Fairs were held in the streets of ancient Rome, in the marts of ancient Egypt, and in China thousands of years before the Christian era. These fairs became the rendezvous of traders and merchants from all parts of the known world. Not only did merchants bring their goods—they brought news: they brought ideas on merchandising and manufacture; they also brought ideas for political, social, and economic changes. Some of these changes they had the power to demand.

In the *Magna Charta* (A.D. 1215) King John was forced to agree: "Merchants shall have safety to go and come, buy and sell, without any evil tolls, but by ancient and honest custom."

The Romans who occupied the British Isles for 450 years introduced famous fairs in England. St. Giles at Winchester traded in slaves (chattels) as well as goods. The Mecklenberg Fair was a big slave market. One season 7,000 Danish slaves were exhibited. The males brough one mark (eight ounces of silver); attractive females brought three marks.

The Bartholomew Fair at Smithfield was another famous market, but the greatest of all English marketplaces of its time was Sturbridge Fair in Cambridge. Its market reporter was Daniel DeFoe, who wrote excitedly in 1723 of the traffic in the tents, booths, and shops: "of Goldsmiths, Braziers, Turners, Milliners, Haberdashers, Hatters, Mercers, Drapers, Puterers and Dudderies." Here you have the origin of the slang "Duds." *Dudde* meant cloth.

At Sturbridge, agents from the Houses of Fugger and Welser of

Augsburg mingled with agents of the Medici of Florence, with merchants of Venice, with Flemish traders from Courtrai and Bruges. Pekin merchants examined Toledo blades, French laces, Belgian linens, Morocco leather. They tasted wines from Portugal, priced pitch and tar from Norway, and bargained for furs and amber from Nijni Novgorod.

Another great international fair was held every year in the Tartar town of Nijni Novgorod, dating back as early as 1386. Monks of the Monastery of St. Macarius started its first fair as a religious festival and collected tolls every year up until 1751. During those four centuries Nijni Novgorod was *entrepot* for all Siberian caravans. Here the Volga and Oka riverboats converged, loaded with cases of caviar and sturgeon and mink and sable to be exchanged for ironware, leather, and tea. The Russians equal the British as tea drinkers. Agents of the great sedentary merchants and merchant adventurers from all over the world gathered at this famous marketplace. Silk shawls from Persia, soap of Kasan, chests of China tea were purchased here for English ladies. English silverware, cotton goods, and weapons were exchanged for rare gems and ivory. (In modern times this fair, held between July 15 and August 25, has accommodated as many as 400,000 traders).

The Old Fair of St. Germain was inaugurated in Paris in 1482 by Louis XI for the benefit of the Abbey of St. Germain-des-Prés and held annually until the Revolution. It played a very big part in financing the City of Paris, and after it was discontinued in 1790 the ground went to the City. In 1818 the area became a market and university center.

The ancient marketplace, as Mumford describes it in his *Culture of Cities*, was "the agora, the acropolis, theater, stadium, arena." It was also a press conference. Here were held the festivals, pageants, and plays, tournaments, military parades, religious and commercial processions, and magnificent exhibits of the arts and crafts of industry.

Here came the newsgatherers, the scribes and interpreters and the spies. The marketplace has always been the clearing house for news and gossip—local, national, international news. At the market men made their plans and schemes for future enterprise—sometimes bold, sometimes sinister.

"The great Fairs of the Middle Ages no doubt laid the foundation for the international capitalism of the 16th century, localized earlier in Florence and Augsburg and later in Antwerp and Amsterdam before it finally crossed in the 18th century to London," Mumford writes.[23]

Albrecht Dürer, famous early sixteenth-century engraver and scribe, describes a procession from the Church of Our Lady as he saw it in Antwerp:

All ranks and guilds had their signs, by which they might be known. . . . There were the Goldsmiths, the Painters, the Masons, the Broderers, the Sculptors, the Joiners, the Carpenters, the Sailors, the Fishermen, the Butchers, the Leatherers, the Clothmakers, the Bakers, the Tailors, the Cordwainers—indeed, workmen of all kinds and many craftsmen and dealers who work for their livelihood. Likewise the shopkeepers and merchants and their assistants of all kinds were there . . . , etc.

Read this fascinating description of the great trading port of Venice when Marco Polo was a young man.

You'd find cloves and nutmegs, mace and ebony from Moluccas that had come by way of Alexandria and the Syrian ports; sandalwood from Timor, in Asia; camphor from Bornes. Sumatra and Java sent benzoin to her markets. Cochin China sent bitter aloeswood. From China and Japan and Siam came gum, spices, silks, chessmen and curiosities for the parlor. Rubies from Peru, fine cloths from Coromandel, and finer still from Bengal. They got spikenard from Nepaul and Bhuton. Their diamonds were from Golconda. From Nirmul they purchased Damascus steel for their swords . . . You'd see pearls and sapphires, topaz and cinnamon from Ceylon; lac and agates, brocades and coral from Cambay; hammered vessels and inlaid weapons and embroidered shawls from Cashmere. As for spices . . . bdellium from Scinde, musk from Tibet, Galbanum from Korasan; from Afghanistan, asafetida; from Persia, sagapenum; ambergris and civet from Zanzibar, and from Zanzibar came ivory, too. And from Zeila, Berbera and Shehri came balsam and frankincense . . . and that was Venice.[24]

In the United States exhibits of consumer goods "for the trade" are held periodically in New York, Chicago, Boston, Pittsburgh, San Francisco, Los Angles, Grand Rapids, Dallas, St. Louis, Atlantic City and in other cities. Sometimes these trade shows are held in auditoriums like the one in Atlantic City and coliseums like the one in New York, or exhibit halls like Navy Pier on Lake Michigan or in

[23] Lewis Mumford, *Culture of Cities.*

[24] Donn Byrne, *Messer Marco Polo* (New York: Century Co., 1921), pp. 23-25.

the Stockyards Ampitheater in Chicago. Many are also held at hotels. There are huge "merchandise mart" buildings in a number of cities where manufacturers' permanent showrooms are housed all year around. These marts promote "market weeks" during the year.

Product and equipment shows are staged in connection with professional and industrial conventions, such as the American Medical Association, Supermarket Institute, Society of the Plastics Industry, or the meetings of engineering and chemical societies.

For example, exhibits of equipment are set up at international meetings of nuclear scientists.

At many trade and industry shows and exhibits, at conventions and other market events, the business press is active, gathering news, the editors often participating in panel discussions or acting as moderators at seminars and masters of ceremony at dinners. Businesspapers often set up facilities for the publication and distribution of daily show bulletins or newspapers as a service to those in attendance at fairs, shows, and conventions.

Months in advance of a market the businesspapers in that field will carry articles describing and previewing the program of the coming event, and in the weeks and months following trade shows the business press will report the event in detail for readers who attended and those who were unable to attend.

While many trade shows and expositions in the United States were started with the co-operation of businesspapers (who furnished the mailing lists and the publicity) independent businesspaper publishers in the United States have steered clear of operating or sponsoring trade shows themselves. On the other hand, National Trade Press, Ltd., of London, publishers of 26 businesspapers since World War II, has sponsored and actually operated many trade fairs in the industries covered by their businesspapers. NTP's subsidiary, Trade Fairs and Promotions, Ltd., in 1957 organized its first overseas fair, the "British Fashion and Textiles Fair," as a section of St. Eriks Fair in Stockholm.

Today more than 500 specialized international exhibitions, national industries fairs, and international trade fairs are held every year in some 40 countries, drawing more than 40 million people to them. Among the more notable are the fairs at Brussels, Cologne, New York, Paris, Liege, Antwerp, Milan, Vienna, Zagreb, Rome, London, Berlin, Leipzig, Montreal, Chicago, Valencia, Utrecht, Munich, Zurich, Düesseldorf, Copenhagen, Hamburg, Nuremberg, Frankfort, Hanover, Offenbach, Canton, the Karachi Fair in Pakistan, Levant Fair in Bari, Italy. There are toy fairs, leather fairs, housewares fairs, business machines fairs, horse fairs, and onion fairs.

It is estimated that about 165 international trade fairs are held every year: Belgium holds 9; France, 9; Austria, 5; Germany, 35; Britain, 27; the United States, 54; Italy, 13; Netherlands, 5; Switzerland, 4; Canada, 4.

The Soviet bloc participated in 150 such fairs in 1955 and between 1955 and 1958 Russia spent $22 million on their exhibits at fairs in 40 countries of the free world.

From 1954 to 1957 the United States participated in 47 international trade fairs, spent about $3 million a year.

8. The Exchange

Stock and commodity exchanges are the most sensitive primary markets. Their sensitivity is not always a barometer of what may be actually happening in business. Sometimes the exchange will reflect what *is* happening; sometimes it reflects what is *expected* to happen later on.

As a result, a business news industry flourishes in the financial community of every great city that has an "exchange." Information falls into two basic categories; bullish and bearish. The bulls are optimistic. The bears are pessimistic. When a great number of people decide it is a good time to buy, their buying action raises the average price of stocks. If the rise in price is big enough and lasts long enough it is called a bull market. The opposite is a bear market. Widespread selling sends the price of all stocks down. The ups and downs are recorded on a number of indexes. The best known are Dow Jones and Standard & Poor's Averages.

The largest volume of business-news information, statistical, analytical, and prophetical, comes from the stock brokerage houses who are members of the exchanges. Tons of analytical business information are distributed freely to customers and prospective customers who, on the basis of such news-information, may be expected to place orders to buy or sell securities or commodities. Theoretically, the brokers refrain from inducing anyone to speculate and are, therefore, not responsible for the profits or losses of their customers. In reality some brokers, since they only make money (commissions) when a customer buys or sells, give the customer what he wants and gear their news activity to day-to-day trading.

In addition to the brokers, news-information is distributed by other groups: investment bankers, security analysts, investment "services," banks, trust companies, etc. This news supplements the news services of newspapers and magazines of the financial community, such as (in the United States) *The Wall Street Journal, The Journal of Commerce, Forbes, Baron's, American Banker, Bond Buyer, Financial World, Investor's Future, Investment Dealer's Digest, Banking Journal of the American Bankers Association,* etc.

On its famous "big board" in the New York Stock Exchange are listed more than a thousand of our country's leading private, public, and quasi-public enterprises and the price of a share in any of those enterprises *at that moment.* Magnified ticker tape, annunciator boards, and electronic wall boards record the second-by-second aggregate transactions in securities as they change ownership all over the country. Simultaneously, the giant news strip from an automatic typewriter spells out the current events and news developments. There are over 2,600 tickers in 475 cities of the United States, Canada, and Cuba. Today, as ten thousand years ago, news controls markets, the difference being that the present moment is world-wide.

Fundamentally, the New York Stock Exchange, which is the feeder to about 650 brokerage houses located in more than 560 cities of the United States and 13 foreign countries, is a mechanism no different from the marketplace a housewife visits for meat or groceries. It is simply a trading post. As a matter of fact, it started as a trading post in 1792, under a buttonwood tree in front of what is now 68 Wall Street in Manhattan. Its first task in 1792 was to finance those private enterprises of our country which had buckled down to the postwar job of *paying off the debt* of the Revolution. The government had won the war and dropped the victory, as usual, into the laps of the businessmen to keep won! One winter under the sky was enough for the stock traders. In 1793 the exchange moved indoors, into the Tontine Coffee House, at the corner of Wall and William Streets. Like Lloyd's Coffee House in London, Tontine's in Manhattan was also a favorite news rendezvous of shippers and merchants, and therefore an important business information source. And like Lloyd's, which gave birth to one of England's oldest businesspapers, *Lloyd's List,* the Tontine gave birth to one of the first American businesspapers, *New York Prices-Current* (1795).

By means of this great primary market, private enterprise has been able to get money needed to build plants, equip those plants with machinery, hire labor, purchase other companies, buy raw materials, conduct research, design new and revised products, hire men to study markets, plan businesspaper and consumer advertising campaigns, train salesmen, set up better distributive systems, and move more goods.

The pattern of the modern stock and commodity exchange began about the twelfth century. The Paris Bourse in the twelfth century was conducted on a bridge over the Seine where money-changers made a market. The Royal Exchange in London brought traders from coffee houses to a palace in the sixteenth century.[25] Amsterdam's *Beurs* were set up at the turn of the seventeenth century. The London Stock Exchange was born in a coffee house in the eighteenth century. In Venice the Rialto was the street of the money-changers. *Rial* is an old form of *Royal* and means "a gold coin."

Today's exchanges are housed in great buildings modeled after the Roman and Grecian Temples. Paris Bourse resembles Rome's Temple of Vespasian. The original Royal Exchange in London (1567) was built by Sir Thomas Gresham with stone from his own estates and money from his coffers. It was destroyed in the great London fire. The pillars of the rotunda in the Antwerp Exchange have great depressions worn into the stone by the backs of countless thousands of traders who, since the sixteenth century, have leaned against them.

Parco buoi (cow pasture) is the name of the floor of the Milan Exchange, which has often been described as "a pen of raging bulls." Today the Milan Exchange is serene. A law in 1956 requiring brokers to furnish the government with the names of all buyers and sellers in every non-cash transaction has slowed down trading and turnover in Milan. Their identity revealed, Italian traders on the exchange would have to pay 22 per cent on their trading profits and their business affairs would be an open book for revenue collectors (as it is in the United States, Britain and elsewhere). This does not suit the Italian temperament.

Because there are no currency restrictions, the Zurich Exchange is the most cosmopolitan. Any investor with any kind of money anywhere in the world can trade securities in Switzerland. Because of

[25] See Chap. VII, section 2.

the international character of its exchange, Zurich is sensitive to any crisis anywhere in the world.

The stock and commodity exchanges from earliest times (Lübeck, Amsterdam, London) have always played the lead role in financing business expansion. In the United States the New York Stock Exchange financed the steamboats, turnpikes, and canals of the 1800's; the clipper ships and railroads of the 1830's; the steel mills of the 1840's; the cable and telegraph of the 1850's; the modern banking system of the 1860's; petroleum in the 1870's; the telephone in the 1880's; gold as money in the 1890's; mass production; the automotive and electrical appliance industries in the 1900's; movies, aviation, radio in the 1930's; television, air conditioning, plastics, frozen foods, wonder drugs, supermarkets in the 1940's; and jet propulsion, rockets and missiles, atomic submarines, automation, and communications engineering in the 1950's.

Through stock purchases almost 10 million people in the United States share directly in the ownership of the private enterprise system (1959) which led the Advertising Council to describe the United States as a "People's Capitalism." The repetition of this phrase "People's Capitalism" is said to disturb the Soviet Union more than any other piece of U.S. propaganda. Almost two-thirds of America's adult share owners had household incomes of less than $7,500 a year. This is an expression of faith in the private enterprise system by little people.[26] It does not mean, however, that the public controls the affairs of the companies in which it owns shares. The public, however, exerts a pressure by its decisions at cash registers, ballot boxes, and in stock brokers' offices.

The "Curb Exchange," which took over on the sidewalks when the New York Stock Exchange moved inside in 1793, eventually moved into its own building. A few years ago it changed its name to the American Exchange.

There is also an "Over The Counter" market of listings which are traded through brokerage houses.

The New York Mercantile Exchange, which trades in potato, platinum and butter futures and does "spot" trading in eggs, has four hundred memberships (1958).

About 30 commodity firms clear through the New York Mercantile Exchange and do business in stocks and bonds. In September

[26] Alfred Politz Research Study, 1956

1958 this Exchange announced it was considering stock and bond trading.[27] This would require that it register as a national securities exchange with the Securities and Exchange Commission, a federal government agency set up in the Franklin D. Roosevelt administration to protect the public (Securities Exchange Act of 1934) against fraud.

For a stock to qualify for original listing on the New York Stock Exchange, it has to be the certificate of a going concern with demontrated earning power of over $1 million annually under competitive conditions and after taxes and other charges. Such a company is usually required to have net tangible assets of over $8 million, with at least 400,000 common shares outstanding among not less than 1,500 shareholders.

To qualify for listing on the American Stock Exchange, a corporation must comply with the registration requirements of the Securities Exchange Act of 1934 and must submit detailed information on its qualifications, but the exchange has no stated rules as to size or demonstrated earnings ability. The firm must have 100,000 shares held publicly and 500 public shareholders.

Within the walls of the Chicago Board of Trade in Chicago, Illinois, nearly 90 per cent of the world's grain future business is transacted. All the lard futures and all the world's soy bean future business is transacted there. It is also the world's largest market for cash corn and soy beans. The total dollar volume in 1957 topped $25 billion.

The Chicago Board's first meeting was held in a room over the Gage & Haines Flour and Feed Store on what was then South Water Street (now corner of Clark Street and Wacker Drive), when Chicago was a village only 11 years old in 1848. Today's Chicago Board of Trade is housed in its own 45-story building, erected in 1930. Trading is done on the fourth floor. The Board's uniform standards are used by many other grain exchanges all over the world.

9. Eternal Middleman

Forty centuries before the advent of the Yankee peddler, traveling salesmen for the middlemen of Mesopotamia (2500 B.C.) were already carrying housewares, sickles, needles, weapons, wool, spices, ointments, and slaves through the Brenner Pass along the Danube and

[27] *The Wall Street Journal,* September 23, 1958, p. 8.

the Elbe, up into Scandinavian markets.[28] The Mesopotamian's caravans and galleys transported cargo to the ancient cities of Uruk and Ur—ancient before Rome was even built. Regulation of market prices, new laws for the conduct of business, and general news, as reported by the news gatherers of 44 centuries ago, were recorded on clay tablets. These tablets, "filed" in clay jars in the office vaults of buried towns, have been spaded up by modern archaeologists to testify to the antiquity of business journalism.

The middleman of today (see Chapter II, section 3) serve primary producers and ultimate consumers in a market position they have earned by countless centuries of toil and courage and merchandising genius. Now and then someone comes forward with a theory to eliminate the middleman as a "parasite," as though the distribution of the world's goods and services could be accomplished by a jinni produced by rubbing Aladdin's lamp. Goods, like ideas, have little value unless transported from where they are produced to where they can be used and consumed. Consumer demand has to be stimulated. Without the creative imagination and genius for style and design, for advertising and promotion, and the salesmanship employed by those in the fields of contribution and distribution, the primary producers would be in a bad way and so would the ultimate consumer. The mass production methods of our country require large plants and centralized manufacturing centers. Wholesalers perform a necessary function of assembling goods and distributing them to the enormous retail markets scattered from coast to coast. But these middlemen do more than distribute, as we saw in Chapter II. They create desire. They merchandise and promote. They sell and they train others to sell.

The manufacturer who transforms raw material into a finished product creates the *form* of goods. The wholesaler brings the goods to the *place* and at the *time* the goods are needed. The retailer moves the goods into final *ownership*. Time, place, and ownership are as important as form. Business journalists are familiar through long experience with the disorganized, chaotic market condition caused by efforts to eliminate the wholesaler. No change in the methods of distributing goods actually eliminates the basic wholesale function. Someone must perform the function.

[28] Miriam Beard, *History of the Business Man*, pp. 11-17.

The wholesaler keeps small manufacturers alive by giving them large enough bulk orders so that they can schedule production programs. He keeps small retailers alive by providing a single source—a stockpile or reservoir—from which they can quickly fill their merchandise needs. The everyday customer of a wholesaler would find it difficult and uneconomical to send to widely scattered factories for goods or to interview their thousands of salesmen. The manufacturer would find it uneconomical to ship small orders to widely scattered retail establishments or send salesmen to call on thousands of small retail stores. The same holds true for the industrial distributors for mines, oil wells, farms, the wholesalers of industrial machinery, equipment, and supplies. The strength of the wholesaler is his service to both manufacturer and retailer. That is what we mean when we say that organized mass distribution is as important to the whole economy as organized mass production.

The design of the marketplace would be incomplete without the free-wheeling middleman. Without him the logistics of distribution would be inconsistent. For example: one order from a retail druggist may involve 83 items from 68 suppliers in 35 cities in 20 states of the United States. If the pharmacy had to order direct from each manufacturer, the confusion, correspondence, and bookkeeping and the delay would put him out of business. In wartime or peacetime the wholesale drug house is "a stockpile against disaster." Something like 400 general line drug wholesalers in 180 cities channel the products of some 7,000 manufacturers to 51,000 drug stores and 6,000 hospitals. There are 170,000 different drug items. The average drug store has shelf space for 2,000. The wholesaler with a reserve of 12,000 pharmaceutical items is as close as the pharmacist's telephone —"the magic pipeline."[29]

From the Phoenicians, Mesopotamians, and Mercators, from the Hanse merchants, down the ages to the Yankee peddler of early New England days, and on to the contemporary distributor and wholesale jobber, exporter, and importer and manufacturer's representative, the middleman always has been the *key man*—the man to be reckoned with in all economic history. He is the fulcrum on which civilization can swing over from narrow nationalisms, leading to

[29] "The Pharmaceutical Story," *Medical Economics*, November 1956 to July 1957. Available in pamphlet form from Health News Institute, 60 East 42 Street, New York.

depressions and trade wars, to common markets and world trade. That is why the middleman is the eternal opponent of the doctrine of scarcity. He is the promoter of *abundance* in production because he wants to distribute ever-greater volume of goods in ever-wider markets of the world at ever-lower prices in order to give more people all over the world higher standards of living.

CHAPTER IV

HOW BUSINESS IS ORGANIZED

1. Trade and Professional Associations

TOCQUEVILLE could not get over his amazement, on a visit to the United States more than a century ago, at the penchant of Americans for joining associations ". . . to defend themselves against the despotic influence of the majority—or against the aggressions of regal power." He wrote:

Thus, the most democratic country on the face of the earth is that in which men have in our time carried to the highest perfection the art of pursuing the common object of their common desires, and have applied this new science to the greatest number of purposes.

Americans of all ages, all conditions and all dispositions constantly form associations. They have not only commercial and manufacturing companies, in which all take part, but associations of a thousand other kinds, religious, moral, serious, futile, general or restricted, enormous or diminutive. The Americans make associations to give entertainments, to found seminaries, to build inns, to construct churches, to diffuse books, to send missionaries to the antipodes; in this manner they found hospitals, prisons and schools. If it is proposed to inculcate some truth or to foster some feeling by the encouragement of a great example, they form a society.[1]

Tocqueville's classic definition of a trade association is widely quoted. J. Robert Oppenheimer quoted it in one of his lectures on the British Broadcasting System. The quotation appears in a booklet "Outline of Activities" of the American Association of Advertising Agencies:

[1] Alexis C.H.M.C. de Tocqueville, *Democracy in America* (original 2 vols., 1846) tr. Henry Reeve; edited with an introduction by Henry Steele Commager (New York and London, Oxford University Press, 1947), p. 320.

An association consists simply in the public assent which a number of individuals give to certain doctrines and in the engagement which they contract to promote in a certain manner the spread of these doctrines.

The right of associating in this manner almost merges with the freedom of the press, but societies thus formed possess more authority than the press. When an opinion is represented by a society, it necessarily assumes a more exact and explicit form. It numbers its partisans and engages them in its cause; they, on the other hand, become acquainted with one another, and their zeal is increased by their number.

An association unites into one channel the efforts of divergent minds and urges them vigorously toward the one end which it clearly points out.

The most natural privilege of man, next to the right of acting for himself, is that of combining his exertions with those of his fellow creatures and of acting in common with them."

The business press maintains a close contact with the trade and professional associations. These contemporary associations are important sources of news and statistical information for businesspapers. Conversely, the business press is itself utilized by trade association officials, both as a carrier and as a source of information. But more than this, the trade association provides the framework for industrial self-government, in which business journalists are deeply interested.

It is not uncommon for businesspaper publishers and chief editors to assume presidencies and directorships of trade and professional associations. Such associations are sometimes born in the offices of businesspapers.

The National Retail Merchants Association was created in the office of an editor of *Department Store Economist*; Linen Trade Association, dormant for 25 years, was revived in the editorial offices of *Linens & Domestics*; American Society of Mechanical Engineers was founded in the office of *American Machinist*; American Society of Chemical Engineers started in the office of the progenitor of *Chemical Engineering*.

Editors of businesspapers constantly participate in the programs of trade and professional associations, often serve as secretaries of trade associations.

2. Ancestor, The Guild

The trade association and chamber of commerce, often regarded as modern business inventions, are really old devices. Their prototypes were the Merchant Guilds (*Gilda Mercatoria*), Craft Guilds, and

Livery Companies of the Middle Ages (see Chapter III) which survived the first four centuries of modern times. These early trade associations were many things to their members. They were social clubs, labor unions, monopolies, pressure groups, often armed regiments. Most important, they were clearing houses of business news.

Like the clergy in their religious fraternities, and the aristocracy in the various Orders of Knighthood, the medieval merchant found protection and dignity in one or another of the powerful Guilds which arose in Germany, Austria, Belgium, Holland, Italy, Spain, Portugal, and England. He also found the answer to the important question: What's new? Merchant-adventurer members were the foreign correspondents (and often war correspondents) of the Guilds and Livery Companies whom they represented in foreign capitals at trade fairs and religious festivals.

Guilds of merchants can be traced back 36 centuries in business history, to China (the inevitable priority). During the Chang-Yu Dynasty (1686-1111 B.C.) a guild of Shang-kiu merchants was formed in Kweiteh fu, Honan, China. These Chinese merchant guilds, as early as 680 B.C. introduced coinage and standards of weight and measure.

Ancient Greek associations of merchants were called *Eranoi* or *Thiasoi*. The Romans had craft guilds. Plutarch described many in his books.

The word *gild* or *geld* is Anglo-Saxon, meaning a payment of dues, or contribution. The German and Danish word was *gilde;* Breton, *gouil;* Welsh, *guylad.*

Outside the church the Guild was the most important symbol of corporate life. There was a certain religious flavor to the Guilds. They, too, like the monastic orders, were brotherhoods. The Guild had its own chapels, schools, and endowed chantries. It maintained a theater and a court (wherein the Law Merchant had its origin.) They trained apprentices and journeymen. The Guilds were also health and old-age insurance societies.

Two famous medieval German guilds were the Weavers of Mainz (A.D. 1099) and the Fishermen of Worms (A.D. 1106). Even prostitutes in Hamburg and Wien formed guilds under municipal protection. Merchant Guilds controlled town life, regulated conditions of sale, protected the consumer against extortion, shielded the craft from "chiselers," and generally restrained free enterprise.

Guildhall (merchants), Cathedral (churchmen), Town Hall (politicians) and University (scholars and physicians) were the medieval city's four chief institutions.[2]

In some towns no merchant was admitted to the "freedom of the borough" unless he was a guild merchant. Guilds fixed prices, controlled imports and exports, made secret agreements, punished members who violated their laws, and had the power (sometimes abused) to seize and condemn goods not up to their standards. In their own courts they maintained absolute jurisdiction over trade disputes.

English Guilds are perhaps the best known of these famous institutions, having weathered the centuries into contemporary times, although no longer engaged in merchant-adventuring. The twelve great Livery Companies of London were the top ranking guilds of England.

The Mercers' Company was Number One. The Latin root *Merx* gives students interested in origins several basic business terms: *mercis,* merchandise; *merces,* reward or wager; *mercer,* merchant; *mercari,* to traffic; *mercatus,* to barter; *Mercury* (Roman divinity), messenger or intelligencer; *merceries,* originally, included not only cloth and apparel but all smallwares, toys, and even drugs; *mercenary,* now a term of disapproval, was once applied to soldiers of fortune whose allegiance depended on the amount of pay.

The second great guild was The Pepperers, later known as The Grocers' Company, which boasted of its antiquity among the traders in spices in ancient Rome.

The Drapers, incorporated in 1439, was the third greatest English Guild and became the guardian of the quality of apparel. The fifteenth-century Draper was a maker of cloth, not a retail shopkeeper as today in England.

English Guilds made their appearance in the seventh century and played important roles in political and social life for a thousand years. They counted Kings and Queens among their members, held sumptuous banquets and pageants in their great Guildhalls, proudly displayed their livery over their doorways and on the gowns they wore.

The French Guilds were destroyed in the Revolution of 1791, the Spanish and Portuguese Guilds in the Revolutions of 1833-1940. The German and Austrian Guilds and the Italian Guilds resisted until the

[2] See Chap. III, section 5.

Figure I
BUSINESS ORGANIZATION DOWN THE CENTURIES

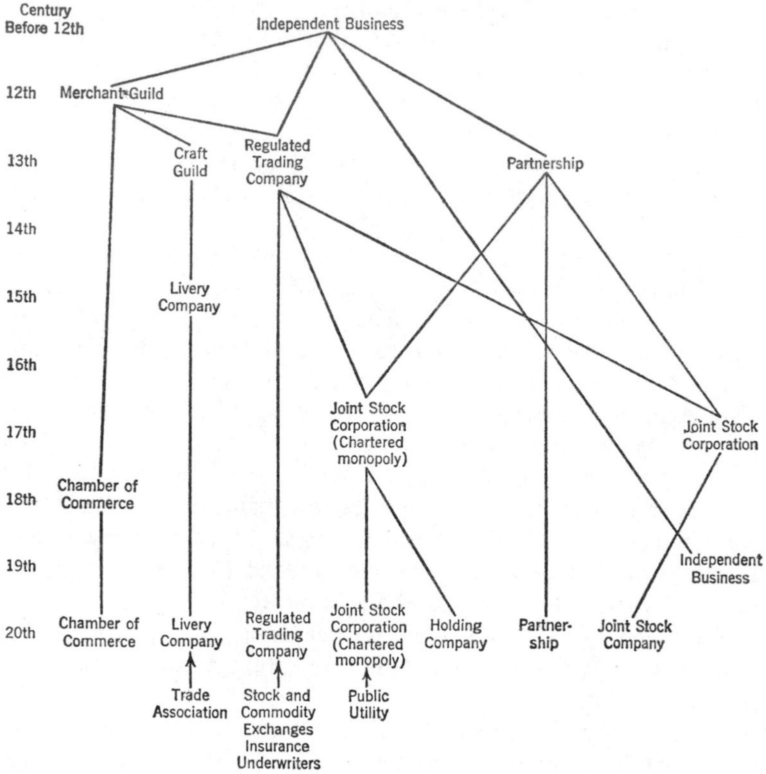

FROM *An Introduction to Business* BY MELVIN ANSHEN (NEW YORK, MACMILLAN, 1942); ADAPTED FROM CASEBOOK OF AMERICAN BUSINESS HISTORY BY N. S. B. GRAS (NEW YORK, F. S. CROFTS, 1939).

middle of the nineteenth century, then yielded to other types of monopoly.

Among the many reasons advanced for the downfall after the sixteenth century, of the guilds as well as the medieval cities which were the strongholds of the guilds, are these:

1. The rise of central authority, which gave security to the open country: more people began to live outside the walled cities; feudal

dues were converted into money payments; people moved more freely without taking on the status of serf or liegeman.

2. Growth of capitalism: sedentary merchants with capital farmed out work in the countryside and escaped guild regulations in wages and labor.

Figure II
TYPES OF BUSINESSMEN DOWN THE CENTURIES

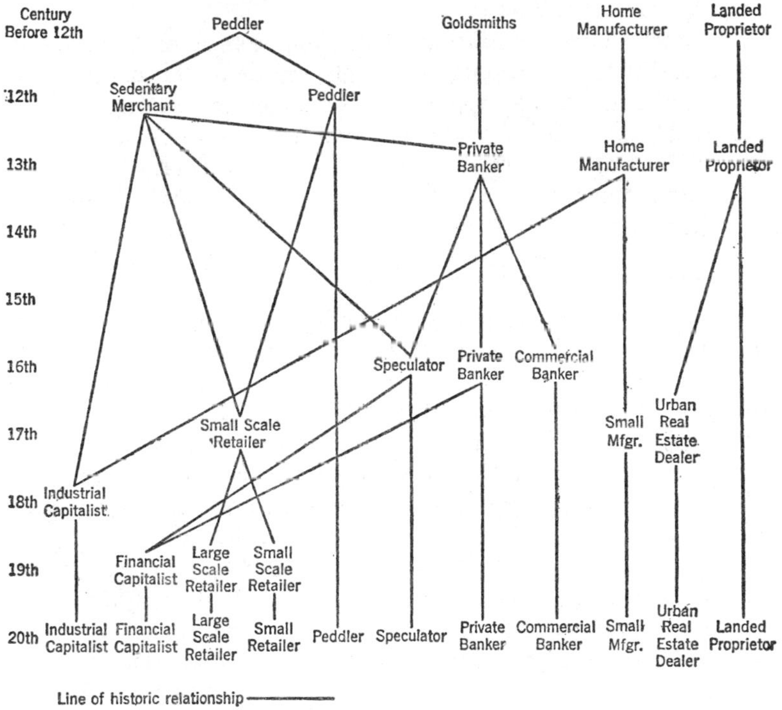

SOURCE: SEE FOOTNOTE TO FIGURE I.

3. Growth of international commerce, due to exploration and colonization which was financed by central powers.

4. Importation of gold and silver from the New World which increased the amount of money in Europe, raised prices, and led to the accumulation of money (capital) and the rise of such banking houses as Fugger and Welser.

5. Growth of jurisdictional disputes between craftsmen.

6. Growth of unskilled trades, such as dockers, porters, and navvies, and increases in the casual labor reserve.

7. Improvement in water transport, and growth of mining and other industries outside medieval cities.

8. Junction of cities with king against feudal aristocracies and princely dynasties.

9. Employment of gunpowder to propel cannon balls capable of knocking down stone walls.

The guilds taught businessmen the importance of organization and cooperation, of maintaining high standards in making and selling goods, of training apprentices for trades and professions, and of assembling, organizing, and distributing news-information. The folly of thinking they could survive without consideration for other groups and other interests and without progress was a lesson the guilds learned too late.

3. Self-Government of Business

Of the 4 million or more business enterprises in the United States the great majority hold membership in one or more of the 12,200 trade associations (1956). Of these, 1,700 were national and 10,500 were local-area organizations (1956).

You find most of these trade associations in transformative industry. Cost of membership in the national associations may be based on volume of business done, unit of product, number of employees, capital investment, credit rating, payroll, or by flat rate.

Many associations publish bulletins or directories carrying paid advertising or put on trade shows to supplement their income. *The trade association executives and their staff personnel are a government almost rivaling the federal government in functions and responsibilities.*

The National Retail Hardware Association, for example, consists of 37 state and regional hardware associations in the United States and Canada. NRHA conducts research studies and publishes manuals and handbooks on marketing and merchandising. It also publishes *Hardware Retailer*, a trade paper with 30,000 readers of which 25,000 are association subscriptions.

Then there is a National Wholesale Hardware Association, an American Hardware Manufacturers Association, and the National

Association of Sheet Metal Distributors which meets once a year with the other groups for a joint week-long convention in Atlantic City. Every problem and situation affecting the business life of a hardware dealer is given full consideration and study.

A trade association, as defined by Jay Judkins, Chief of the Trade Association Division, Office of Technical Services of the U.S. Department of Commerce, is "a non-profit cooperative organization of business competitors designed to assist its members and its industry in dealing with mutual business problems in such areas as accounting practices, business ethics, commercial and industrial research, standardization, statistics and trade promotion, and relations with government, employees and the general public."[3]

Among the largest trade associations, from the standpoint of membership, is the National Association of Retail Grocers, whose members own 111,000 food stores. It has a headquarters staff of 25 people. Foremost in size of staff is the Association of American Railroads, with 600.

Names of trade associations can be misleading. Many associations employ the use of the term national, although their influence is purely local or regional. The word national is no guarantee that an association is national in scope, or even the voice of its industry. The word association is no indication that an organization has more than a half dozen members, all that is required to incorporate an association. "National" and "Federal" and "American" are often propaganda words employed in the names taken by small pressure groups. Some full-purpose trade associations use such a word as "bureau," "institute," "conference," or even "guild," as part of their name. Some private companies use the word "association" or even "industries" for their purposes. The businesspaper editor must have no false illusions about any group he is dealing with or giving publicity to. He should *know* its size, structure, and objectives, its officers and *bona fides*.

Many changes in the structure of trade associations, in order to present a united front to the government, took place after the enactment of the National Industrial Recovery Act in 1933. The Federated Trade Association came into being to co-ordinate the functions of

[3] *Directory of National Trade Associations* (Washington, D.C., U.S. Department of Commerce, 1956). See also American Trade Association Executives, Washington, D.C.

numerous trade associations in the same industry, representing different geographical districts or different products.

The National Association of Retail Grocers is a horizontal federation of state associations. Each state grocers' association sends delegates to the national conclaves.

The National Lumber Dealers Association is another federation of state, regional, and metropolitan associations or groups of retail lumber dealers. Individual dealers are not eligible. This definition excludes such single-purpose associations as credit bureaus.

Some of the difficulties in drawing a line of demarcation between a trade association and a professional association, in certain cases, were discussed in the National Industrial Conference Board's Report.[4]

The Board pointed out:

> One of the distinguishing characteristics of a trade association is to be found in the fact that its membership is ordinarily limited to persons or firms engaged in a particular trade or industry—to the producers, or distributors, or both, of a particular product or generic class of products.
>
> On this basis, such "general business organizations" as the Chamber of Commerce of the United States or the National Association of Manufacturers, or corresponding local organizations, cannot be classified as trade associations. . . . On the other hand, those associated in the operation of commodity exchanges for the marketing of the staple products of agriculture which are subject to accurate grading may be deemed to be organized into a special type of trade association. Trade associations do not themselves produce, buy, or sell goods for profit. . . .

Professional organizations are not regarded by the National Industrial Conference Board as trade associations. "The professional societies are composed of *individuals*, united primarily by a common *intellectual* interest in a particular field." Trade associations, on the other hand, the Board holds, are "organizations of *business units*, which may be corporations, partnerships, or individual enterprises, and the common interest of the membership is primarily *economic* rather than intellectual."

Three of the oldest trade associations in the United States are the American Iron and Steel Institute (1855), The Writing Paper Manufacturers Association (1861), and The American Institute of Laundering (1886).

[4] "Trade Associations: Their Economic Significance and Legal Status," N.I.C.B., Washington, D.C., 1929.

Some of these associations are vertical, like the Better Vision Institute, Inc., which serves such groups as the Optical Manufacturers Association, Optical Wholesalers Association, and the Guild of Dispensing Opticians.

A typical horizontal association is the National Electrical Manufacturers Association, which has more than 100 "product" divisions.

The purpose in providing this association background material for students of business journalism is to show that a framework and pattern of experience exists for industrial self-government. As the antidote for bureaucracy in government, business journalists are constantly advocating that new fields of business develop a capacity for self-government.[5]

4. Chambers of Commerce

One of the earliest business associations in our country is the Chamber of Commerce of the State of New York, organized in 1768. Similar associations of traders were formed soon afterward in Boston and Philadelphia, and in 1773 a Chamber of Commerce was established in Charleston, South Carolina.

American chambers of commerce are corporations concerned with purely local or community affairs. They are represented in Washington by a federated association, called the Chamber of Commerce of the United States, which publishes a monthly news magazine, *Nation's Business.*

There are 4,000 chambers of commerce and other types of community development organizations in the United States (1959).

5. International Chamber of Commerce

Founded in 1919, the International Chamber (I.C.C.) has brought together all brackets of business in 59 countries in order to upgrade standards of practice. For example, in 1948, the following recommendations were made to businesspaper publishers of many countries in its "Code of Standards of Advertising Practice":

The purchaser of advertising in any publication or other media is entitled to know the number, general character and distribution of the persons likely to be reached by his advertisement and to receive genuine cooperation in this respect from media.

[5] Chap. V, section 17.

The Tokyo Congress of the I.C.C. in May 1955 went further and said in its "Code of Standards" that the advertiser was "entitled to receive proof of circulation figures and access to data regarding number and characteristics of readers and should be informed of the methods used to obtain such data."

6. United States Department of Commerce

The free world is a very hungry market for know-how. More than 30,000 copies of American businesspapers have been used to assemble trade promotion libraries sent to 23 foreign countries by the U.S. Department of Commerce. American trade missions found, according to a recent bulletin of the Commerce Department, that "contrary to general opinion, foreign businessmen did not consider tariffs, food and drug laws, export licensing and other such factors as major impediments to two-way trade." It was discovered that misunderstandings concerning methods of doing business in the United States were the real deterrents. "Thus the trade promotion libraries, containing businesspapers, trade and business directories, catalogs, statistical and marketing studies, technical manuals and other reference materials, have become an indispensable tool to the trade missions in providing specific information and guidance to foreign traders."

The Department of Commerce operates 42 field offices in the United States. Experienced marketing specialists and foreign trade analysts work with businessmen, trade associations, and businesspaper editors.

In each field office there is a reference library containing directories, official publications, periodicals, as well as various documents covering domestic and foreign commerce.

Four major offices serve the public: Office of Technical Services, which assembles, publishes, and distributes scientific and technical reports; Office of Distribution, which provides technical guidance in marketing; Office of Area Development, which provides expert counsel to groups in setting up programs of economic development; National Bureau of Standards, which tests materials and develops codes and specifications of physical standards.

Herbert Hoover, when he was the Secretary of Commerce, suggested that leading businesspaper editors of the United States come to Washington periodically to meet with him. That is how the

National Conference of Business Paper Editors came into existence. Being an engineer by profession, Mr. Hoover could appreciate the importance of organized and interrelated business intelligence, transmitted via the business press directly to industrial management. He also appreciated that the business press was a two-way carrier: it could bring information he needed to Washington as well as take away information. The many conferences were fruitful. Upon becoming President of the United States, Mr. Hoover wrote this message to businesspaper publishers:

The Business Press is probably the greatest force in making industrial opinion. The schools and colleges have an important place; the trade associations can do much in the fields of production and distribution; the government bureaus that keep in contact with business can help promote sound leadership in industrial and economic thinking. All have an important place, but the business and technical journals are in a unique position and have a unique opportunity. Your great group of journals cannot only recognize and support sound industrial leadership, but you can also initiate it. The field of your opportunity is practically limitless.

7. Trade Missions

Groups of industrial leaders (with an occasional businesspaper editor among them) are made up by the U.S. Department of Commerce to visit foreign countries, as guests of each country. The Missions tour the host country, visiting industrial installations and, as their visits usually coincide with a trade fair, the members of the Mission are stationed at the fair to answer questions about the United States market. The station where these men are available at foreign fairs is called the American Trade Information Center.

By the end of 1958 the Department of Commerce had organized and sponsored 59 missions to 38 countries and 470 cities.

More than 250,000 foreign businessmen have consulted with the members of these trade missions.

Traveling libraries of United States economic books, directories, catalogs and exhibits of 1,100 businesspapers accompany these Missions.

"By far the most conspicuous exhibit of each mission is the American business press," says E. Paul Hawk, Director Trade Missions Division, Office of Trade Promotion, Department of Commerce. "It is consulted constantly. It is read avidly. When the Mission goes home the library is left in the host country, either with the Chamber of Commerce, our Embassy or one of our consulates. There its utility goes on for years."

The opinion has been expressed by some career officials of the Department of Commerce that more businesspaper editors should make up the composition of these Trade Missions. Their training as journalists would enable them to present a clearer picture of our market to foreign traders and to take back home a better picture of the foreign market they have visited.

"Big shots who are included in trade delegations," one authority claims, "rarely get down to such elementary but vital matters as packaging, considerations of weight, sectional demands, methods of sampling before placing large orders, or the mechanics of reordering." "Businesspapers," Lewis L. Strauss says, "are performing one of our country's most vital tasks abroad."[6]

8. Patent System

The modern patent system was founded about 1623, the year the British public forced the "Statute of Monopolies" on King James I, in order to curb Crown monopolies which restricted private commercial enterprise and limited trade.

The King's grants of monopoly over existing trades and professions were outlawed by the Statute, but grants of "letters patent" for fourteen years or less were authorized.

In the first Article of the Constitution the founders of our republic granted power to Congress *"to promote the Progress of Science and useful Arts by securing for limited times to Authors and Inventors the exclusive right to their respective* Writings *and Discoveries."*

The first United States Patent Law was enacted April 10, 1790 and, although amended several times, remains basically the same.

9. Antitrust Laws—Charter of Economic Freedom

Perhaps it is not fair for any of us to assume, just because we enjoy citizenship in the United States, that other countries are eager to copy our system of business enterprise or our form of political government.

[6] "Thank You, Mr. Publisher!" A report on how businesspapers help U.S. Department of Commerce's Trade Mission Program throughout the world. Trade Missions Division, Office of Trade Promotion, U.S. Dept. of Commerce, Washington, D.C.

It is fairly certain, however, that other countries would like to enjoy the same kind of wealth we have, in the form of higher living standards for the majority, rather than the minority, of their citizens.

When they think of our wealth, most foreigners think of our natural endowments; metals, minerals, energy, waterways, geography, and so on.

Those natural resources were all here when the early American Indian had the place to himself. What did he do? Except for a little skill in handcrafts, his talents were for hunting, fighting, dancing, and procreating.

Within two generations, the Belgians transformed the Congo from a cannibalistic to an industrial economy, with modern towns, highways, airfields, railroads, utilities, industries, schools, hospitals; much of it administered by educated natives whose social and political status is put on a level with the white man's.

When all the Congolese were cannibals the same rich resources were at their disposal: waterpower, diamonds, uranium, gold. The most important resource was brought in by the Belgians—know-how. European *emigrés* brought America its most valuable resource: know-how. As we have said, America has no copyright on know-how. (See Chapter I.) But there is one kind of know-how that is peculiarly ours and that is the legal know-how embodied in the Sherman Act (1890); Clayton Act (1914); Federal Trade Commision Act (1914); and the Robinson-Patman Price Discrimination Act (1936), commonly referred to as the Antitrust Law.

It would be useless for any country to try to imitate the competitive enterprise system as we practice it in the United States without embodying in its own constitution and framework of law the principles of the free market and fair competition as written in our laws and decisions.

Long observation of business teaches business journalists that it is in the nature of some businessmen to be more aggressive than others. This may be in a spirit of good sportsmanship or it may be as ruthless as modern warfare. The ruthless seek unwarranted power in business, power to bend the will of others, power to destroy competition, to restrain trade, to control entire markets, power even to control governments or substitute private government for public government.

Ruthless was the word for many of the early business associations, the guilds, the league of Hanse merchants, the livery companies, the teutonic *kartelles*.

Knowing all this, our law makers set up legal inventions to keep the market free and open and the system of competitive enterprise competitive. The most notable of these inventions was the antitrust law. Under this law it is the duty of the lawyers and investigators of the Department of Justice to halt or break up any group activity which is deemed to be a combination in unreasonable restraint of trade, or which would lessen competition or create a monopoly in interstate commerce.

If such activities are discovered or brought to its attention, the Department of Justice, after careful investigation, files a civil or criminal antitrust suit against the alleged combination or trust in the federal courts in the name of the people of the United States. An adverse decision against businessmen or organizations so sued by the Department of Justice may be appealed to the highest federal court, the Supreme Court of the United States, whose decision is final.

The Department of Justice may proceed against a corporation after the commission of an act as in the order to DuPont to divest itself of a huge block of shares in General Motors Corporation. The court finally ruled, in 1959, that DuPont could not *vote* its stock at General Motors meetings.

The Supreme Court has held that advertising is an inseparable part of the flow of interstate commerce and thus, in 1955, the Department of Justice broke up an alleged price-fixing conspiracy in publishing circles (See Chapter V, section 22).

But it must be emphasized that restraint of trade, monopoly, or attempt to monopolize are not the only evils against which the antitrust division can proceed. In 1958 the Department of Justice brought action to enjoin Bethlehem Steel (second largest steel company) which wanted to merge with Youngstown Sheet & Tube Company (sixth largest integrated steel company). The federal court in which this case was tried held that such a proposed merger would substantially lessen competition, tend to create a monopoly by increasing concentration, and eliminate a substantial source of supply, and (in the language of the court) "result in the establishment of relationships between buyers and sellers which deprive their rivals of a fair opportunity to compete." This judicial opinion is based on Section 7, an amendment to the Clayton Act in 1950.

The original Clayton Antitrust Act (1914) declared that labor was not a commodity and organized labor was not to be suppressed in its legitimate activity. Competent opinion is currently divided on this point.

Exception to the anti-monopoly acts is the Webb Act, passed in 1918, which permits businessmen to form combinations in export trade to combat the tactics of foreign cartels, in competition for world markets.

In essence, the antitrust law is as essential to business competition as certain rules are to sports competition. They release energies essential to leadership, in technological development and high productivity. They open the door to skills and talents to embark on careers. Antitrust laws are an incentive, not a deterrent, to business activity.

10. Federal Trade Commission

Trade Practice Conference: The Federal Trade Commission Act, passed in 1914 and amended in 1938, set up the FTC as an agency to deal with competitive conditions in industry, to act to prevent unfair methods of competition and unfair practices in interstate commerce, and to protect the public interest. To do this, rules of fair trade practices are established under what is known as the *trade practice conference* procedure, a plan which has been in operation for more than thirty years. The FTC has conducted hundreds of conference proceedings and has established rules for fair enterprise in as many industries.

The "public interest" guides the FTC. Trade practice conference proceedings are authorized only when it appears that the public interest will be substantially served. The conference is initiated by application from industry itself, usually through a trade association which can show that its membership in annual volume of business, number of employees, and total capital investment is representative of that industry. Conferences are then held where interested parties, including representatives of the trade association, the industry, labor, and the consumer, participate with the commission in promulgating competitive standards of business practice. Harmful and unfair trade practices, as well as good practices, are defined and catalogued, and methods for eliminating the bad and sanctioning the good practices are provided.

The essence of the plan is to organize and encourage voluntary cooperative effort, or industrial self-government, to end unfair trade abuses, banish monopolistic practices which restrict private competitive enterprise, to create official, recognized standards, afford guidance respecting the requirements of the law, and to maintain the free and constructive functioning of the competitive economy.[7]

Voluntary Compliance: FTC Bureau of Stipulations, created in 1946, was made a division of the Bureau of Consultation in 1954. Here all violators of antitrust law except in cases having to do with foods, drugs, or cosmetics (dangerous to consumer) or industry-wide conspiracy, are given an opportunity to comply voluntarily with the law.

In fraudulent or deceptive advertising, misbranding or mislabeling of merchandise, etc., the businessman is generally given the benefit of the doubt by the FTC as to his ignorance of the law.

The stipulation procedure politely offers the alleged violator (after study by the Bureau of Investigation) an opportunity to comply voluntarily by signing a stipulation. The stipulation is an agreement that there has been a violation of the antitrust laws and that the practice will be corrected. With this signed stipulation the FTC says, in effect, that it will say no more about it and the firm agrees to cease and desist. This wraps up a great many cases quickly and cheaply. However, where a business concern feels it has not violated any laws, it may bring the matter into the courts. In that case the FTC field investigators go into action and make a thorough investigation to build up their case, calling on the firm's competitors for evidence. This formal procedure may involve months, even years.

11. Interstate Commerce Commission

The first of the Acts passed by the Congress to prevent industrial concentration and combination which might tend to undermine the system of competitive enterprise was the Interstate Commerce Act of 1887. This law forbade railway companies operating in interstate commerce from giving rebates to favored shippers and pooling freight. It also set up the Interstate Commerce Commission to regulate railways and terminals, express companies, pipe lines, sleeping car com-

[7] See Monograph No. 34, Report of the Federal Trade Commission to the Temporary National Economic Committee (Washington, D.C., U.S. Government Printing Office, 1941).

panies and to nullify rates found to be unreasonable or discriminatory among shippers.

12. Testing Laboratories

The American Council of Independent Laboratories lists 75 member-laboratories that test materials and products for business. The oldest and largest is United States Testing Company, of Hoboken, New Jersey. Others include Pittsburgh Testing Laboratory, Arthur D. Little, Foster D. Snell Inc., Materials Research Corporation, Stillwell & Gladding, and Froehling & Robertson.

The Underwriters' Laboratories, Inc. (founded in 1894), sponsored by the National Board of Fire Underwriters, is a non-profit organization operating laboratories to test systems, devices, and materials in relation to life, fire, and casualty hazards and crime prevention. Safety films, periodic lists of tests, booklets, and other services are available.

13. National Bureau of Standards

Working closely with these independent laboratories and all business is the National Bureau of Standards, a federal agency which sets up uniform standards to help science and industry operate more accurately and efficiently.

An Act of Congress set up the Bureau in 1901 "to provide standards of measurement . . . not to be obtained of sufficient accuracy elsewhere." Writes Ira Wolfert:

> The Bureau of Standards, plays a larger part in the daily lives of Americans than any other Government agency. You cannot bake a cake, mail a letter or drive an automobile without coming in contact with its work. The exact capacity of your measuring cup, the degree of stickiness on the back of the postage stamp, the octane rating of your gasoline were specified by the Bureau. The doctor who takes your blood count or temperature knows his instruments are accurate because they are calibrated against Bureau standards.[8]

Fifty years ago four different lengths were a legal 12 inches in Brooklyn and thirty years ago green was "stop" in some states and "go" in others.

Starting with $42,000 and a staff of 22, the Bureau in 58 years has

[8] Ira Wolfert, "Relentless Search for Precision," *Think*, publication of International Business Machines, October 1958, p. 12.

expanded until it now occupies 70 buildings, employs 3,000 people, and can spend $42,000 in one morning. It established the standard inch, ounce, pint, bushel, second, volt, watt, decibel, and candlepower —700 different standards, in fact, and faultless samples of 600 different kinds of basic materials.

As soon as an industry can afford to take over, the Bureau steps out of the picture. But it is always ready to step in. Today industry wants tolerances to a ten-millionth of an inch. In one of the Bureau's 100 laboratories and workshops such gauge blocks have been achieved.

14. National Science Foundation

Scientific societies have selected what they deem to be the leading Soviet publications and periodicals in their fields and these are now being translated into English from cover to cover by the National Science Foundation. This activity is being supported by the Atomic Energy Commission and the Office of Naval Research. More journals of the U.S.S.R. in other difficult languages than Russian and possibly journals of other countries will be added to the list, we are informed in a recent issue of *Special Libraries*.[9]

NSF also concerns itself with studies of communication practices and information requirements of scientists, classification and indexing systems, and projects of mechanized translation.[10]

NSF acts as a central clearing house for various data centers which compile, organize, correlate, standardize, and issue specific types of scientific data.

NSF also supports the National Federation of Science Abstracting and Indexing Services.

15. Arbitration—Clue to Peace

The National and Special panels of the American Arbitration Association are a body of about 15,000 business leaders and business journalists dedicated to the elimination of misunderstanding and discord from inter-American and Canadian-American trade. They work, except in special cases, without fee, as commercial and industrial peace officers.

In twenty years more than 30,000 disputes have been referred to

[9] *Special Libraries*, official organ of the Special Libraries Association, Vol. 49, No. 9, November 1958, p. 408.

[10] See also U.S.S.R. Business Press, Chap. VII, section 16.

the AAA. Each year several thousand cases are referred to arbitration in tribunals of the AAA. In all such referrals, the decision is binding on both parties and so recognized by the courts and police power.

In 1920 the first modern arbitration law was enacted, in New York State. In 1925 a United States Arbitration Law was enacted. A year later the American Arbitration Association was established as a non-profit corporation by Lucius R. Eastman and Felix M. Warburg. The three missionaries in this movement were Moses H. Grossman, founder of the Arbitration Society of America, Charles L. Bernheimer, organizer of the Arbitration Foundation and chairman of the Arbitration Committee of The Chamber of Commerce of New York, and R. Emerson Swart, later a president of the AAA.

Today arbitration procedure is embodied in many business contracts. The American Institute of Architects, for example, uses it in all standard building contracts. More than 500 firms in 60 major industries, insurance companies, hundreds of trade associations, the international labor unions, have all adopted AAA clauses. The AAA and the International Chamber of Commerce have joint clauses and facilities.

Long before the establishment of legal jurisprudence, men settled their business disputes by arbitration. It was common practice among Phoenician and Greek traders. Themistocles was the arbitrator of a dispute between Corcyra and Corinth for the possession of Leucas (480 B.C.).

Laws come into existence when enough people decide they want to live in an orderly society. The tendency is to have too many laws. Many students of the law believe people are best governed when they have the least laws.

The procedure in modern arbitration is rather informal. It is somewhat like a court of equity. There are lawyers present but the arbitrators themselves are businessmen. Common sense and fair play are the rules. Evidence is not ruled out on a technicality.

The ancient Saxon, Hammurabi, Mosaic, and Justinian codes laid the foundation for orderly procedure in a court of law or in society in general. The Brehon Code was a social design perfected by St. Patrick for the Celtic nation. The Brehon was an arbitrator and Brehonage was a pure system of arbitration in the fifth century. Ancient and medieval Ireland, without legislature, judiciary, or police power, lived under Brehonage for eleven centuries (A.D. 441 until the seventeenth century).[11]

It is probable that without commercial arbitration our courts would bog down hopelessly.[12] The arbitration clause in a business contract is the clue to political peace among civilized men, for more and more people seek accord and satisfaction by negotiation rather than by conflict.

All the 21 American republics are linked together by arbitration. The practice takes place in Inter-American Commercial Arbitration Tribunals and proves that people of different languages, traditions, creeds, and cultures, living far apart, can settle their disputes without force or bitter, drawn-out legal battles.

[11] A. M. Sullivan, "The Brehon—Ireland's Ancient Arbitration," *The Arbitration Journal*, Vol. 11, No. 1, 1956, p. 32.

[12] See Frances Kellor, *American Arbitration* (New York, Harper & Brothers, 1948), for complete history of the movement.

CHAPTER V

UNITED STATES BUSINESS PRESS

1. Size and Scope

FIVE specialized periodicals were published in the United States prior to the year 1800. The fields were commerce, agriculture, music, medicine, military and theology. (See Appendix I.)

By the year 1850 there were 88 starts and by 1900 there had been more than 580 starts. A dozen of these periodicals are in existence currently. Most of them lasted only a few years or decades. Many were regional.

After 1900, with the step-up in technology and invention, business periodicals began to spring up on a wide scale with national coverage as their objective. Currently there are over 2,000 businesspapers published within our definition (see Chapter I) in the United States (1958).

The Bureau of the Census for 1954 (the latest) listed 1,638 periodicals which fall within our definition.[1]

Standard Rate & Data Service, January 1957, placed the number of business periodicals at 2,238. The SRDS figure for 1958 was 2,093 (catalogs and annuals excluded). The *Printers' Ink* estimate for 1958 was 2160 titles.[2]

Circulation totals for the business press, reported by the Bureau of the Census and by sources cited within the business press, are at much greater variance. The Census Bureau placed the circulation per issue at 91,811,227 for 1,638 periodicals (1954). The other sources

[1] U. S. Bureau of the Census, *U. S. Census of Manufacturers: 1954,* Industry Bulletin MC-27 A, p. 18, Newspapers, Periodicals, Books and Miscellaneous Publishing, Washington, D. C., Government Printing Office.

[2] *Printers' Ink: Advertisers' Guide to Marketing for 1960,* p. 259.

cited placed the circulation figure for a period two years later at 37,984,885 (1956). The 1958 figure of SRDS is 40,837,000 distribution. *Printers' Ink* estimate for 1958 is 43,135,472.

Dr. H. P. Alspaugh, editorial director of *Standard Rate & Data Service*, suggests we deduct from the Census figures the sum of 19.6 million for Farm Publications; 28 million for Religious; and 4.6 million for Art, Music, Drama. These categories, Dr. Alspaugh claims, have the biggest circulation in consumer periodicals. Such deductions would bring the Census total down from 91.8 million to 39.6 million, which is more in line with the 37.9 million circulation figure given by sources within the organized business press, such as SRDS.

In short, the Bureau of Census classifications are very broad and difficult to interpret, as between business and consumer periodicals.

Another business press statistician, Angelo Venezian, vice president of McGraw-Hill Publishing Company, makes the following comment on the U.S. Census Table for U.S. Business Periodicals.

> I would say that the greatest reason for the difference is in the interpretation of businesspapers from the Census table and the type of publication listed in the businesspaper section of *Standard Rate & Data Service.* When the major portion of the advertising in the publication is not for the individual himself, but rather for his organization, then *Standard Rate & Data Service* is likely to consider it a business publication; otherwise, it is listed in one of the other sections.
>
> From the Census table, I have selected only five groups that seem to fit that requirement—the three groups under "Trade," the "Business and Finance" group and "type not specified." These total 1,242 periodicals with 31,647,000 circulation. Actually, in 1954, *Standard Rate & Data Service* listed 1,838 publications with 30,000,000 distribution; however, we understand that non-profit publications are not included in the Census figures; you have about 20 to 25 percent of business journals in this category, the great majority with small circulations. On this basis you come a little closer.
>
> I doubt if you can ever get these figures to argee because of differences in classifications. We just don't know what is in each of the Census groups.

Statistics of any kind depend on careful definition. Take, for example, *Business Week,* a McGraw-Hill periodical: it is listed in Business Publication directory of SRDS and also in the SRDS Farm Publication directory. *Fortune* is another example: its publishers regard it as a businesspaper—horizontal coverage and also depth—but a businesspaper. SRDS thinks so, too, for *Fortune* is listed in

SRDS business publication and farm directories—but *Fortune* is also listed in the SRDS consumer magazine directory. *Fortune* is taking no chances!

In addition to the more than 2,000 businesspapers (1958) there is a huge related press already referred to: 8,000 house organs; trade association bulletins and magazines; business reference books; manuals and handbooks; catalog files; incidental literature (so-called).

New York City is the largest center for the businesspaper publishing industry. Chicago ranks second. Some leading businesspapers are published in other key cities, generally in order to be close to the particular fields they serve. For example, there is the *Oil & Gas Journal* published in Tulsa, Oklahoma, and *National Provisioner* (meat packing) in Chicago; *Air Cargo* in Washington; *Cereal Chemistry* in St. Paul, Minnesota; *Commercial Fertilizer* in Atlanta, Georgia; *Automotive Chain Store*, Akron, Ohio; *Metal Progress* in Cleveland, Ohio; *Billboard*, Cincinnati, Ohio; *Driller*, Milwaukee, Wisconsin; *Jewelers' Circular-Keystone*, Philadelphia; *Life Insurance*, St. Louis, Missouri; *Architectural Products*, Beverly Hills, California; *Pulpwood Production*, Montgomery, Alabama; *Construction World*, San Francisco; *Fireman*, Boston; *Pacific Builder and Engineer*, Seattle; *Design News*, Englewood, Colorado; *Antiques Dealer*, Summit, New Jersey; *American Surgeon*, Baltimore, Maryland.

A recent study of 1566 businesspapers included this table to indicate where businesspapers are published:[3]

TABLE 3: U.S. BUSINESS PERIODICALS BY PLACE OF PUBLICATION

New York City	562
Chicago	247
Washington	97
Los Angeles	82
San Francisco	45
Philadelphia	43
Southern States	148
Canada	342
Total	1,566

Results of a BPEN survey published early in 1959 show that the average business periodical has a circulation of 17,203; 35 per cent of the periodicals are audited; the average periodical has been in business 25 years and 10 months; the average issue has 74 pages; the trim

[3] *Business Publication Editor's Newsletter*, Vol. 1, No. 1, Sept. 1, 1958, Jim Maroon, Editor and Publisher, 670 N. Michigan Ave., Chicago.

size is 8¼ × 11¼; the editor is 41 years and 4 months old; and is a male; he has been on this job 8 years and on his previous job 4 years; he worked on school publications; he has 3.3 people in his editorial department; 52 per cent of the editors had thought up new publications for the publisher; 72 per cent feel capable of starting a new publication themselves.[4]

2. Growth of Readership

The rapidly expanding scientific and technological community has stepped up the demand for specialists and for adult education with which to train specialists. It has also increased the demand for know-how for day-to-day decisions and long-range plans. This explains the steady increase in the number and variety of businesspapers and the growth of circulation figures since World War II.

In 1956 businesspaper distribution (paid and free circulation) had reached 37,984,855, as stated. This was an increase of 180 per cent from the 13,576,568 total in 1942.

The average rate of increase is about 1.25 million copies a year.

In 1958 the distribution was over 43 million.

From 1940 to 1959 the number of businesspapers grew from 1,700 to 2,093, a 25 per cent increase.

The editorial volume, in the same period, increased 84 per cent.

TABLE 4. BUSINESSPAPERS BY TYPE OF AUDIENCE

NUMBER BY TYPE	TOTAL		AUDITED		NOT AUDITED	
	No.	Per Cent of Total	No.	Per Cent of Total	No.	Per Cent of Total
Industrial	979	46.8	457	46.7	522	53.3
Merchandising	586	28.0	249	42.5	337	57.5
Export and import	62	3.0	28	45.2	34	54.8
Financial	110	5.2	32	29.1	78	70.9
Medical	228	10.9	29	12.7	199	87.3
Religious	15	0.7	2	13.3	13	86.7
Educational	64	3.1	13	20.3	51	79.7
Government	49	2.3	7	14.3	42	85.7
Total	2,093	100.0	817	39.0	1,276	61.0

[4] *Business Publication Editor's Newsletter*, Vol. 1, No. 12, Feb. 15, 1959. The survey is based on a 36 per cent return from questionnaires sent to 1,566 businesspapers. BPEN editor cautions that the "average publication" is a mythical one.

DISTRIBUTION BY TYPE	AUDITED		NOT AUDITED	
	Circulation	Per Cent of Total	Circulation	Per Cent of Total
Industrial	12,712,898	67.9	6,000,967	32.1
Merchandising	5,933,443	61.8	3,674,143	38.2
Export & import	1,703,425	68.0	801,642	32.0
Financial	881,348	53.8	756,286	46.2
Medical	1,571,516	43.2	2,062,174	56.8
Religious	228,690	29.5	546,776	70.5
Educational	579,491	24.7	1,765,020	75.3
Government	451,337	27.9	1,168,489	72.1
Total	24,062,148	58.9	16,775,497	41.1

SOURCE: *Printers' Ink*, "Advertisers Guide to Marketing for 1959," p. 259; *Standard Rate and Data Service*, January 1958.

3. Frequency of Publication

The increase in weekly, bi-weekly, and bi-monthly businesspapers since 1956 is a trend that bears watching, but monthly businesspapers are still the most popular (see Table 5).

In 1957 *Standard Rate & Data Service* listed 1,509 businesspapers in its April Business Paper Section (United States). These were grouped under 160 separate classifications.[5]

In its June 1958 issue, SRDS Business Publication Rates and Data contained 2,245 individual (non-duplicated) listings, under 173 actual classification titles.

TABLE 5. FREQUENCY OF PUBLICATION (21-YEAR COMPARISON)

	April 1937	January 1957	January 1958
Quarterly or three times a year	32	54	68
Monthly	1,062	1,519	1,557
Bi-monthly	45	56	148
Bi-weekly	30	58	120
Weekly	189	157	174
Daily (except convention dailies)	18	24	26
	1,509	2,238	2,093

[5] SRDS definition of a United States business publication: "Edited and published in the territorial United States; serving a specifically definable industrial, business or service/professional audience; carrying national advertising, and filing rate and circulation information with SRDS."

Of the 1937 total, 447 were organs of trade or professional associations; the 1957 total included 561 official organs of trade or professional associations.

TABLE 6. DISTRIBUTION BY FREQUENCY OF ISSUE

DISTRIBUTION BY FREQUENCY

	Total		Audited		Not audited	
	Circulation	*Per Cent of Total*	*Circulation*	*Per Cent of Total*	*Circulation*	*Per Cent of Total*
Daily	266,506	0.7	176,666	66.3	89,840	33.7
Weekly	3,660,252	9.0	2,748,401	75.1	911,851	24.9
Bi-weekly	3,362,408	8.2	2,454,917	73.0	907,491	27.0
Monthly	29,129,279	71.3	17,580,017	60.4	11,549,262	39.6
Bi-monthly	2,200,385	5.4	669,490	30.4	1,530,895	69.6
Quarterly	2,218,815	5.4	432,657	19.5	1,786,158	80.5
Total	40,837,645	100.0	24,062,148	58.9	16,775,497	41.1

NUMBER BY FREQUENCY

	Total		Audited		Not audited	
	No.	*Per Cent of Total*	*No.*	*Per Cent of Total*	*No.*	*Per Cent of Total*
Daily	26	1.3	6	23.1	20	76.9
Weekly	174	8.3	88	50.6	86	49.4
Bi-weekly	120	5.7	64	53.3	56	46.7
Monthly	1,557	74.4	632	40.6	925	59.4
Bi-monthly	148	7.1	20	13.5	128	86.5
Quarterly	68	3.2	7	10.3	61	89.7
Total	2,093	100.0	817	39.0	1,276	61.0

SOURCE: From *Printers' Ink*, "Advertisers Guide to Marketing for 1959," p. 259; *Standard Rate & Data Service*, January 1958.

4. Circulation Audits

In July 1944, *Standard Rate & Data Service* listed 1,610 United States businesspapers. Of these, 298 were members of the Audit Bureau of Circulations (paid subscriptions), 159 were members of the Controlled Circulation Audit (free but independently audited), 553 were paid circulation with publishers' sworn statements, 235 were distributed free with publishers' sworn statements, and 374 refused to furnish any circulation information.

In comparison, the total of 2,014 publications in June 22, 1958,

Standard Rate & Data's Business Publication Rates and Data included 222 ABC (Audit Bureau of Circulations) and 434 BPA (Business Publications Audit, Inc., succeeding Controlled Circulation Audit). Publishers' sworn paid circulation statements totaled 741 and 430 sworn controlled circulation.

"After three requests through mailings of Standard Rate & Data Service's sworn circulation statement forms," 231 did not submit sworn statements.

In addition VAC (Verified Audit Circulation Co.), operating principally on the West Coast but gradually extending eastward, showed 33 controlled audits in the June 1958 issue. Several publishers' sworn statements, which included both paid and controlled figures, were classified only by the larger of the two distribution figures.

Controlled audits by BPA (Business Publications Audit) replaced the former CCA (Controlled Circulation Audit). VAC (Verified Audit Circulation) is another circulation audit firm, of comparatively recent origin.

The 2,245 listings in Table 7 represent 2,443 publications in the SRDS Business Publication Rates and Data. Professional, State, County, or other groups (only four listings) account for the additional 198 publications, as follows: State Teachers Magazines, Inc., a single organization listing 44 publications; County Medical Society Magazine Group, with 106 publications; State Journal Group, of

TABLE 7. ANALYSIS OF UNITED STATES BUSINESSPAPER LISTINGS

	NUMBER		TOTAL CIRCULATION	
	Number	Per Cent	Copies	Per Cent
ABC and ABP Combined	154	7.65	3,052,638	7.29
ABC but not ABP	222	11.02	9,726,892	23.23
Sworn Paid Circulation	741	36.79	11,869,625	28.35
BPA	434	21.55	10,063,553	24.04
Sworn Controlled Circulation	430	21.35	6,655,519	15.90
VAC	33	1.64	499,357	1.19
	2,014	100.00	41,867,584	100.00
No Circulation Information	231			
Total Listings	2,245			

SOURCE: *Standard Rate & Data Service,* Business Publication Rates and Data, June 22, 1958.

TABLE 8. PERCENTAGE OF UNITED STATES BUSINESSPAPERS AUDITED

TOTALS			PAID Number	PAID Percent		CONTROLLED Number	CONTROLLED Percent
Audited	843	ABC	376	33.66	BPA & VAC*	467	52.06
Unaudited	1,402	Sworn	741	66.34	Sworn	430	47.94
	2,245		1,117	100.00		897	100.00

PERCENTAGE OF AUDITED PAPERS THAT BELONG TO AN ASSOCIATION

	ABP *Number*	ABP *Per Cent*	NBP *Number*	NBP *Per Cent*
Members	154	40.96	171	36.62
Non-Members	222	59.04	296	63.38
Total	376	100.00	467	100.00

* BPA and VAC audits some paid only, as well as controlled.
SOURCE: *Standard Rate & Data Service,* Business Publication Rates and Data, June 22, 1958.

official organs of State medical organizations, 33 publications; and the S.P.E.A. (State Pharmaceutical Editorial Association) Group, with 15 publications. Circulations for these 198 publications appear in the table as part of the Sworn Paid total, as given in the four Group listings named. In no case were the publishers' Guaranteed Circulation figures used. If the publisher's guaranteed figure was the only one given, the listing was counted as "No circulation information given." However, Government circulation figures were counted as sworn, since they must be notarized for acceptance by the Government.

In the Business Publications Audit 95 per cent of the list must be kept on stencils. Audits are made semi-annually. *Standard Rate & Data Service* publishes circulation reports of BPA member papers. In the June 1958 issue of Business Publication Rates and Data there were 434 listings showing BPA memberships, or about 52 per cent of the business publications listed as controlled circulation papers in SRDS.

The total number of controlled circulation papers in July 1944 was 395. CCA membership rose steadily in twelve years, from 37 in September 1932 to 170 in December 1944. Based on its July 1958 issue of Business Publication Rates and Data, SRDS listed 434 publications with membership in BPA, the successor of CCA. This growth of two and one third times within twelve years was also above the

395 figure for all businesspapers with controlled circulation at the end of 1944.

Besides those members of BPA, in the June 1958 issue there were 33 publications using the then recently organized VAC audit and 430 publications submitting publishers' sworn statements indicating controlled circulations (741 submitted paid statements). With the 434 BPA, this meant a total of 864 publications reporting a controlled circulation to SRDS, disregarding as duplications the very few which carried both paid and controlled audits.

5. Growth of Advertising

Despite the steady rise in advertising space rates, the number of pages of advertising in businesspapers continues to increase because it is still the cheapest buy to be found among all the media.

In 1940 businesspapers carried 415,000 pages of advertising.

Figure III
BUSINESS PUBLICATION ADVERTISING VOLUME (1945-1957)

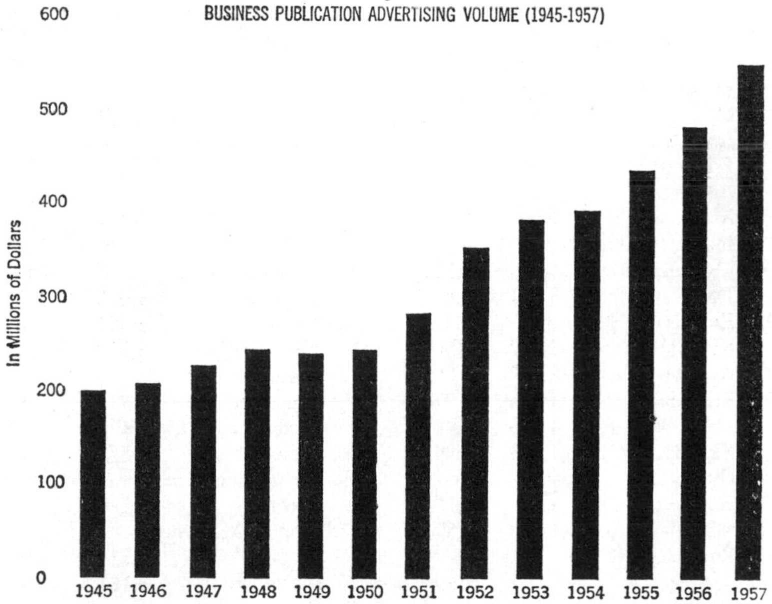

FROM *Printers' Ink* "ADVERTISERS' GUIDE TO MARKETING FOR 1959," P. 254. ESTIMATES PREPARED BY MCCANN-ERICKSON, INC.

In 1944 the figure climbed to 891,000. The postwar recession caused a dip in 1948 to 820,000 pages.

In 1952 the number of businesspaper advertising pages had reached 1,016,000.

In 1959 the total was 1,183,000 advertising pages.

Table 9. Advertising Page Volume of Top Fifty United States Periodicals 1956-1957

(General and business publications ranked by page volume)
Page totals include classified and display advertising except where otherwise noted.

Business magazines historically carry a larger physical volume of advertising than general magazines. As a matter of fact, the first general magazine in number of advertising pages is the New Yorker, which ranks 13th in the list of all magazines. In this list the first 12 magazines in advertising page volume were business publications and of the 50 leaders listed here only six (starred below) are not business papers.

1957 Rank	Publication	1957 Pages	1956 Pages
1.	Home Furnishings Daily	7,803	8,072
2.	Women's Wear Daily	7,665	7,923
3.	Oil & Gas Journal	7,552	7,441
4.	Steel	6,447	6,254
5.	Iron Age	6,220	6,069
6.	Business Week	6,117	5,932
7.	American Machinist	6,063	6,243
8.	Journal of Amer. Medical Assoc.	5,629	5,200
9.	Dail News Record	5,531	5,838
10.	Engineering News Record	5,227	4,801
11.	Aviation Week	5,057	4,885
12.	Electronics	4,994	4,919
13.	*New Yorker	4,984	4,937
14.	Electrical World	4,948	4,795
15.	Chemical Engineering	4,475	4,177
16.	Modern Medicine	4,397	3,875
17.	Product Engineering	4,249	4,393
18.	Florist's Review	4,242	4,352
19.	*Life	4,218	4,655
20.	Chemical Week	4,073	3,908
21.	Machine Design	3,832	3,240
22.	Southwest Builder & Contractor	3,823	3,657
23.	Chemical & Engineering News	3,798	3,539
24.	Advertising Age	3,696	3,656
25.	Machine & Tool Blue Book	3,684	3,306
26.	Design News	3,610	3,483
27.	Purchasing	3,565	3,217
28.	Hardware Age	3,491	3,743
29.	Billboard	3,406	3,323
30.	*Time	3,361	3,450
31.	*Newsweek	3,350	3,251
32.	*Saturday Evening Post	3,301	3,508
33.	Feedstuffs	3,292[a]	3,106[a]
34.	Factory	3,278	3,000
35.	Architectural Record	3,229	3,244
36.	Modern Machine Shop	3,224	3,104
37.	Machinery	3,181	3,132
38.	Electrical Manufacturing	3,162	3,108

TABLE 9. (Continued.)

1957 Rank Publication	1957 Pages	1956 Pages	1957 Rank Publication	1957 Pages	1956 Pages
39. Petroleum Engineering	3,098	2,983	46. Construction Bulletin	2,899	2,831
40. *U.S. News & World Report	3,084	3,205	47. Constructioneer	2,866	2,711
41. Automotive Industries	3,083	3,224	48. Industrial Distribution	2,826	2,798
42. Construction Digest	3,015	2,884	49. Medical Economics	2,816	2,340
43. Aviation Age	2,987	2,675	50. Mill & Factory	2,737	2,635
44. Jobber Topics	2,975	8,865[a]			
45. Western Builder	2,963	2,735			

* Not a business publication.
[a] Classified space not reported.

SOURCE: *Printers' Ink*, "Advertisers' Guide to Marketing for 1959," Oct. 31, 1958, p. 268.

Venezian's analyses of the gains made between 1948 and 1956 by businesspapers and consumer magazines show that 45.5 per cent of the dollar gains went to businesspapers. Consumer magazines had a 42.6 per cent gain. Comparing advertising page volume, 98.1 per cent of all the advertising pages gained went to businesspapers.

Referring to Table 9, it will be observed that the largest number of pages carried by any consumer magazine is carried by *The New Yorker*, with 4,984 pages in 1957. Next came *Life* with 4,218 pages in 1957.

Twelve businesspapers outstripped *The New Yorker* in number of advertising pages carried in 1957. The two businesspaper leaders were Fairchild periodicals, *Home Furnishings Daily* (7,803 pages) and *Women's Wear Daily* (7,665 pages).

Twenty-seven businesspapers outranked, in number of advertising pages carried in 1957, three consumer magazine giants: *Time*, *Newsweek*, and *The Saturday Evening Post.*

Since 1940, dollar volume gains by businesspapers have outstripped all other communications media except possibly television. In 1940 advertisers spent $64 million in businesspapers. In 1955 this sum had grown to $446,000,000 (including production costs). The expenditure by businesspaper advertisers in 1957 was $567,600,000; in 1958 it was $519,300,000 (for space only). For space plus production costs the sum spent for advertising in businesspapers in 1958 is estimated at $600,100,000. The long-term growth trend in dollar volume indicates that the business community's strong acceptance of businesspapers to do its basic marketing job will continue and increase.

Businesspaper space salesmen cannot sell "numbers" of readers the way the consumer magazine space salesmen sell. But in dollar purchasing power they have quite an edge on consumer magazine salesmen. Advertisers tap a market of $21 for every $1 of advertising bought in a consumer magazine. They tap a market of $372 for every dollar of advertising space bought in a businesspaper.

Businesspaper advertising estimates for 1957 were $1.08 out of every $1,000 of Gross National Product. In 1933 it was 57 cents per $1,000 of G.N.P.

Compared with national income the businesspaper figure for 1957 was $1.35 for every $1,000 of national income. The 1933 figure was 81 cents per $1,000 of national income.

Compared with capital expenditures for plant and equipment, the figure gives a different picture. The war year of 1944 showed a ratio of $28.65 per $1,000. The 1957 figure is $11.93 for businesspaper advertising per $1,000 of plant and equipment expenditure.

The industrial advertising budget for 1957 was $1.2 billion. McGraw-Hill estimated that businesspaper advertising accounted for 41 per cent. It is expected to reach 50 per cent by 1965.[6]

Total industrial (Extractive and Transformative) advertising investment for businesspapers, direct mail, catalogs, trade shows, merchandising, etc., for 1958, is estimated at $1.31 billion. Venezian arrives at this estimate by using the estimates of businesspaper advertising as a base, plus the proportions revealed by past budget studies of the Association of Industrial Advertisers (AIA).

Businesspaper advertising will reach $1 billion in 1965, according to *Industrial Marketing.*[7]

Industrial Marketing reported that "reliable experts" forecast a $2 billion expenditure for all industrial advertising in 1965, "with businesspapers accounting for half of the total."

[6] *Industrial Marketing,* Nov. 1957; June, 1958. Angelo R. Venezian, vice president and circulation coordinator, McGraw-Hill Publishing Co. *Printers' Ink* "Advertisers Guide to Marketing for 1958," August 23, 1957, by William D. Lanier, assistant to the director of advertising sales, McGraw-Hill Publishing Co. *Industrial Marketing,* Jan. 1958.

[7] 1959 Market Data and Directory Number, June 25, 1958, p. 31.

TABLE 10. PER CENT OF ADVERTISING DOLLAR VOLUME BY MEDIUM IN UNITED STATES

Medium	1935	1940	1945	1950	1955	1957
Consumer magazines	8.1	9.5	12.7	9.0	8.6	8.0
Newspapers	45.1	39.1	32.1	36.4	32.5	31.9
Television	—	—	—	3.0	11.2	12.6
Radio	6.7	10.3	14.8	10.6	5.9	6.2
Regional Farm and Businesspapers	3.2	3.9	7.5	4.8	5.3	5.4
Direct mail	16.7	16.0	10.1	14.1	14.1	14.4
All others	20.2	21.2	22.8	22.1	22.4	21.5

SOURCE: *Printers' Ink*, "How Magazines Can Survive: Get a Bigger Share of Advertising," May 2, 1958, p. 21.

TABLE 11. ANNUAL DOLLAR VOLUME OF ADVERTISING IN UNITED STATES
(Millions of Dollars)

Medium	1935	1957
Newspapers	762.1	3,283.3
Consumer Magazines	136.3	814.3
Television	—	1,290.9
Radio	112.6	622.5
Farm Periodicals	9.7	71.3
Direct mail	281.6	1,470.9
Businesspapers	51.0	567.6
Outdoor	31.1	206.1
Miscellaneous	311.8	2,021.3
Grand total	1,690.0	10,310.6

SOURCE: *Printers' Ink*, "Advertisers' Guide to Marketing for 1959," Oct. 31, 1958, p. 155.

6. Advertising Compared with Consumer Media

To move the United States Product ($358 billion in 1957), advertising managers and advertising agencies, taken together, spent most of the advertising dollar on consumer media: television, radio, consumer magazines, daily and weekly newspapers, direct mail, billboards, etc.

The businesspaper advertising page is seven times more efficient. Here is how it works out:

The total of all goods moved in 1957 in the United States was $358 billion.

It cost $9.1 billion of consumer advertising to move half of it.

It cost $1.2 billion of industrial advertising to move the other half.

Three studies afford the basis for these conclusions: (1) A study by Dr. H. T. Beckman, Ohio State University, estimated that 51.3 per cent of all goods are marketed and sold to industry, and 48.7 per cent are sold to consumers; (2) A study by the Twentieth Century Fund, which reported that the manufacturing industry purchased $47.2 billion as compared with annual consumer purchases of $48.7 billion; (3) A study by the Department of Commerce, on wholesale distribution of goods, which reported that 44.8 per cent goes to the industrial consumer, and 55.2 per cent goes to the home consumer.

Angelo Venezian splits the national income roughly fifty-fifty. Fifty per cent of the national income, which in 1957 totalled $358 billion, would be $179 billion for the consumer market and $179 billion for the industrial market.

Why, Venezian asks, is seven times as much advertising money required to move consumer goods?

The answers to that would vary: The consumer media have been more realistic in their advertising rates. The businesspaper audience is a higher intelligence level. The agency space buyer needs to be educated and sold on businesspaper values. Businesspaper advertising is prepared more intelligently.

7. Rising Costs of Publishing

Like all other types of private enterprise, the business press faces mounting costs. Some of these costs are self-imposed: expanding editorial and sales departments; expansion in research and development of product, services and markets. Other costs are unavoidable: higher prices for labor, printing, paper, ink, postage.

The Congress passed a bill in 1958 increasing airmail, first-class, postcard, and straight third-class rates. Rates on third-class bulk mail went up January 1, 1959. Publishers expect increases in second-class mailing privileges. All these increases will be eventually reflected in higher advertising and subscription rates.

Notwithstanding the high operating costs, businesspapers give the business community a better value today than twelve years ago.

A study of 574 comparable businesspapers listed in January 1940, SRDS, and January 1957, SRDS, show that while the 12- or 13-time advertising rate had increased 132.4 per cent since 1940, circulation

TABLE 12. BUSINESSPAPER COSTS (1951 vs. 1956)

Basic Operating Costs	1951 versus 1956	Prediction for 1960
Art work	up 10%	no estimate
Engravings and electrotypes	up 17%	no estimate
Paper	up 17%	up 18%
Letterpress printing	up 20%	up 15%
Wages	up 66%	up 25%
Editorial Costs	up 38%	no estimate
Postage rates	up 38%	no estimate
Traveling expenses	up 44%	up 25%

readers was up only 58 per cent. In other words, although advertising rates are up, advertisers reached many more prospects for their products and/or services.

Adjusted for 1940 prices, the actual cost per thousand in 1957 was 21 per cent lower than the 1940 cost per thousand. Determined by gains in this period were 47.2 per cent. As a result, cost per thousand the current buying potential of the businesspaper reader, and the improvement in editorial and advertising pages, the advertiser gets a better value for his investment in businesspapers than he got a decade ago.

Businesspapers in 1958 were delivering one-fourth more readers per dollar than in 1940. And the 1958 reader was a much heavier buyer and buying influence than the 1940 readers.

8. Rising Editorial Costs

In 1956 there were 718,266 editorial pages published in businesspapers, an increase of 73.5 per cent since 1940. Publishers' expenditures for editorial material was 512.6 per cent higher in 1956 than in 1940. The amount spent per page of editorial material in 1956 was up to an average of $100.14, or a 253 per cent increase over 1940.

About 20 per cent of the 50,000 people employed by the business press serve on the editorial staffs.

The vital information and new knowledge transmitted by the expanded, improved, and increased editorial pages, combined with the vital information contained in the increased volume of advertising pages, represent a major contribution to the growth and efficiency of the United States Plant. This is the view of industrialists of the caliber of Ralph Cordiner, board chairman of the General Electric

Company. Mr. Cordiner told an audience of businesspaper editors and publishers in 1957:

Only a greatly accelerated rate of appreciation of new knowledge to products, processes, services and materials can enable us to meet the multiple demands of our country's progress.

The objective of business is to apply new knowledge to the fulfillment of these needs as rapidly as possible. The businesspaper's objective is to make such knowledge available. Together, business publications and industry have an unprecedented opportunity to multiply United States progress, and to bring into being a new era of serving the public's needs.

9. Salary Structure

For several years Bernard Gallagher of New York, well-known circulation authority and negotiator for the purchase and sale of periodical properties, has published an annual survey of the salary structure of both consumer and business periodicals. The most recent appeared in February 1958.[8]

Respondents represented in this survey were only audited publications. Of 1076 questionnaires sent out, 235 publishers of ABC and BPA businesspapers and ABC consumer magazines responded (21.8 per cent).

QUESTIONS AND ANSWERS (C means Consumer, B means Businesspaper).

Q: Do you have a retirement or pension program?
C: yes, 67%; no, 33%
B: yes, 42%; no, 58%
Q: Do you have an incentive system for your employees?
C: yes, 62%; no, 38%
B: yes, 59%; no, 41%
Q: Do you have a management development program to replace retiring executives?
C: yes, 28%; no, 72%
B: yes, 26%; no, 74%

Personnel measurements: Interesting technics are currently used to measure the productivity of personnel in the various departments of a businesspaper publishing house. One of the yardsticks for measuring the efficiency is average billings per employee. Publishers with total billings up to a half million dollars annually show average

[8] Bernard P. Gallagher, *The Gallagher Report* (Fifth Annual Publisher's Forecast) Vol. VI, No. 4, February 1958.

TABLE 13. SALARIES ON BUSINESSPAPERS AND CONSUMER MAGAZINES COMPARED

	Average Salaries	
	Consumer	*Business*
Publisher	$30,750	$21,468
Top Editor	20,850	15,535
Writing Staff	8,550	7,273
Ad director	22,363	16,462
Promotion Manager	14,600	10,714
Circulation Director	13,140	8,140
Advertising salesmen	12,615	11,993

billings from $13,000 to $18,000 per employee. Where the total is half to a million dollars, the average per employee is $16,000 to $22,000; over one million a year in billings showed average billings per employee to be $17,000 to $30,000.

Advertising: On businesspapers in the extractive and transformative industries space salesmen produce more pages and more billing than salesmen on businesspapers serving distributive and contributive fields. As page rates increase the number of pages sold decline. In the extractive and transformative fields salesmen average 350 pages at $500 a page for an average net billing of $175,000. In the distributive and contributive fields salesmen sell 250 pages at $400 a page for an average net billing of $100,000. Less than fifty per cent of the houses have sales training programs or do advertising research. Compensation is in direct proportion to sales produced.

Editorial: Regardless of the size of a businesspaper publishing house or the field that is served, the number of pages of material handled per editor or writer seems to remain constant, at between 190 and 300 pages. The number of clerks varies with the number of editorial pages produced, whether a single or multiple publisher. From one to three thousand editorial pages, three to four clerks, or one clerk per one thousand editorial pages. In multiple publishing houses the practice of making one editor serve two or more publications is being abandoned. Where more than a thousand editorial pages are produced, there is a managing editor to ease the chief editor's workload and get him afield. Contributed material is purchased at 2¢ a word on a word basis; on a page basis the price runs from $25 to $100 or more, depending on both the periodical and the contributor. Where editorial pages are under 4,000, two persons in layout and production seem to suffice.

From 4,000 to 6,000 there will be three to six persons; over 6,000 pages, the staff may be from six to twelve. Compensation for editorial personnel varies with income. Income does not influence salaries in production.

Circulation: In computing the number of subscribers handled by this department as a whole (promotion and fulfillment), where outside fulfillment organizations are used, each $4,500 paid to an outside organization is assumed to be equivalent to one circulation employee. Where the average number of readers is under 20,000, the readership per circulation employee is 1,500–2,500. Between 20,000 and 30,000, the number per employee is 2,500–3,000. Over 30,000, it is 3,000–5,000. Total billings influence salaries in this division.

Administration: These people are measured against the total number of people in the company. For each 100 total employees there are a dozen to two dozen administrative employees.

Accounting: Where annual sales are under two million dollars, there are usually two to four accounting employees. Where sales are over two million there may be four to five. It averages two accounting employees per $1 million of sales.

TABLE 14. SALARIES ON ABC AND BPA BUSINESSPAPERS COMPARED

ACCORDING TO GROSS VOLUME OF ABC BUSINESS PUBLICATIONS

	to $250,000	$250,000-$500,000	$500,000-$1,000,000	Over $1,000,000
Publisher	$16,400	$20,333	$30,400	$32,000
Top editor	9,682	13,800	15,833	17,200
Writer	5,811	6,500	7,300	8,800
Ad director	7,960	12,666	15,166	17,833
Promotion manager	7,966	8,500	10,250	11,500
Circulation director	5,933	6,940	9,250	11,900
Advertising salesmen	8,125	10,080	12,500	16,650

ACCORDING TO GROSS VOLUME OF BPA PUBLICATIONS

	to $250,000	$250,000-$500,000	$500,000-$1,000,000	Over $1,000,000
Publisher	$13,000	$17,800	$28,887	$30,500
Top editor	8,800	12,428	14,800	18,500
Writer	5,485	7,166	7,337	8,400
Ad director	8,600	12,333	16,300	20,000
Promotion manager	7,800	7,855	10,000	11,300
Circulation director	5,500	6,000	7,400	10,500
Advertising salesmen	8,800	11,166	12,687	14,500

SOURCE: *The Gallagher Report*, February, 1959. Vol. VI, No. 18, September 1959 (170 replies).

In 1950, Lasser calculated editorial salaries should be "10 to 12 per cent of gross income."[9]

The 1959 Gallagher study indicates editorial salaries have not kept pace with the rising inflation in the economy. Editorial salaries do not reflect 12 per cent or even 10 per cent of the gross income of business periodicals.

Commenting on his own February 1958 study, Mr. Gallagher stated in his September 1958 Report:

> There should be proper recognition and incentive for the editor. Yet *The Gallagher Report* studies show editors are vastly underpaid. Average business magazine editor makes less than $16,000; his counterpart on consumer magazines less than $18,000. The editor is a key man; he should be treated as such in every respect.[10]

A J. K. Lasser confidential manpower study of 32 multiple business-paper publishing houses in 1959 revealed "a definite continuity of career from editorial assistant to full editor" in about thirty years time. The report said: "A capable college graduate entering a business publication house . . . in his early twenties could normally expect to be . . . managing or full editor sometime in his forties or early fifties."

10. United States Farm Periodicals

National, regional, state, and specialized farm periodicals suffered a temporary setback in 1957-58. In 1957 advertising revenue was down 10 per cent from 1956. Lineage was down again in 1957, but rate increases improved the revenue picture somewhat.

Farm media are paying the penalty while advertisers wait to see if farm prosperity is permanent, according to some observers. Also, the farm market is no longer isolated: farmers are exposed to radio, television, and general magazines.

The number of farms in the United States reached its peak in 1935 with 6,800,000. In 1950 this figure had shrunk to 5,400,000 and in 1957 to 4,855,800.[11] Two million farms disappeared in twenty years, but the land was absorbed by larger remaining farms. The rate of decrease is 130,000 farms a year. Little change has taken place in

[9] J. K. Lasser, C.P.A., "Fundamentals in Businesspaper Accounting," in *Businesspaper Publishing Practice* (New York, Harper & Brothers, 1952), p. 26.

[10] *The Gallagher Report*, Vol. VI, No. 18, September 1958.

[11] U.S. Department of Agriculture. See also *Industrial Marketing*, "1959 Market Data and Directory Number," Farm Markets, p. 523, June 25, 1958.

the total average of land since 1940. The average size of the farm has increased from 174 acres in 1940 to 252 acres in 1954. The farm population decreased from 30,500,000 people in 1940 to 21,900,000 in 1954—a drop of 28 per cent. Less people operating fewer, but larger, farms producing more with less man-hours. In 1900 one farm worker produced enough for himself and seven others. Today he produces enough for himself and 19 others. The investment per agricultural worker in 1940 was $3,430. In 1956 it was $15,000 (in terms of 1947-1949 dollars the increase was from $7,380 in 1940 to $12,760 in 1956). Total income of farmers in 1957 was $11.9 million.

Circulation in 1957 of the 39 farm publication-members of *Farm Publication Reports, Inc.*, was 12,750,000.

There are 36 monthly (some with regional editions) farm publications, 23 semi-monthly, 3 bi-weekly, 3 weekly, 4 daily publications—a total of 69 publications (not counting regional editions).

The figures in the 1954 Census (Bulletin MC27A-18) list 126 Agricultural and Farm Periodicals (general and specialized) with a circulation of 19,622,494, advertising revenue of $47,773,000, and a subscription and miscellaneous sales revenue of $8,575,000.

11. Trends and Predictions

"There is a distinct trend toward a more realistic rate base in this underpriced field," said *Printers' Ink*, referring to the business press.[12]

The trend over the long term, 1940 to 1958, for 557 comparable businesspapers showed the following: page rates up 137 per cent; circulation up 56 per cent; cost-per-thousand up 52 per cent.

Over the same period (1940-1958) the value of the dollar decreased 52 per cent so that 1958 cost-per-thousand is actually 27 per cent under 1940.[13]

There is a trend among manufacturers to use more advertising pages in the business press because it reaches prime decision-makers at a very cheap cost per reader. Completely factual and honest research is helping this trend.

The efficiency of businesspaper advertising, despite its low cost, is seven times greater than consumer advertising, according to studies cited which find that the distribution of goods in the United States

[12] *Printers' Ink*, "Advertisers' Guide to Marketing for 1959," Oct. 31, 1958, p. 259.

[13] *Ibid.*

is divided fifty-fifty between the consumer market and the business-paper (industrial) market (1958).[14]

To repeat: The total cost of all goods moved in the United States in 1957 was $358 billion.

It cost $9.1 billion of consumer advertising to move half of it—$179 billion of consumer goods—to homes.

It cost $1.2 billion of industrial advertising to move the other half—$179 billion of goods—to business.

There is a trend to decrease the volume of editorial pages.

In the period from 1940 to 1959 the editorial page volume of businesspapers increased 84 per cent. In the same period the advertising page volume increased 175 per cent.

In the next decade the percentage increase in readership will be much greater, due to the rapid technological advances and to the difficulty technicians and specialists will find in keeping up with new knowledge except by reading the continuous textbook of adult education which is the businesspaper.

With increased revenues from increased advertising and subscription sales, editorial budgets and the volume of editorial pages should increase and the editorial salary structure should be more in line with the Lasser formula: "10 to 12 per cent of gross income for editorial salaries."

Pensions or profit-sharing plans, show up as a trend among business-paper publishers.

Predictions: costs of salaries, postage, printing, and engraving will continue to rise; paper costs will level off; new printing and engraving methods will be adopted to combat mechanical costs; lighter weight paper will be used to offset postage increases; more publishing houses will streamline office procedure and work flow; rate increases for advertising space are inevitable but will be based on improved editorial content, improved services, and increased circulation; publishers serving growth industries will be in the best position to justify rate increases; demands and pressures for more accurate market studies and more scientific statistical surveys will increase; promotional effort will be "more factual and less frothy"; simpler, less costly promotional literature will be used; editors will be required to travel more extensively; there will be increased emphasis on professional journalism training.

[14] See this chapter, section 6.

"Fewer and fewer talented and well qualified editors are available," and "the supply of good salesmen is limited," were among the comments in a recent issue of *Printers' Ink* by experts in the field of businesspaper publishing.[15]

New markets are being explored by the business press: the $600 million field of automated office equipment; the multimillion dollar field of cybernetics; the one-and-a-quarter-billion-dollar field of assembly-and-fastening; the multimillion dollar fields of adhesives, aerosol propellants, petrochemicals, and instrumentation.

New businesspapers concentrate on recently matured or newly created markets while old businesspapers widen their coverage.

12. Rise of the Specialized Press

Printers' Ink twenty years ago described a significant transition period in the history of the business press of the United States:

> The old-time business man (prior to 1895) believed in maintaining a veil of secrecy over all his movements. He was extremely jealous of competitors and the idea of publishing news concerning the flow of business was not at all relished. The pioneer business publishers had no easy time.
>
> In the very earliest days the business periodical was represented by a handful of journals of broad editorial scope. A single paper, for example, would cover all phases of mechanical matters, another every type of manufacturing product. Lists of topics were comprehensive.
>
> Then came new papers which addressed themselves to some specific branch of business which seemed inadequately served by the more general publications. . . . The specialized businesspaper was the outgrowth of an endeavor of the "wholesale man," or manufacturer, to find his custormer in a more direct manner than was possible through the daily newspapers, and it took the rudimentary form of putting his wares under the customers' eyes in an advertising circular to which was attached a thread of reading matter on some subject that might interest the readers. In other words, it was simply a house organ.
>
> Some few newspaper men, usually of limited means and experience, took up the idea of publishing papers of their own. The conditions were not favorable for attraction of the best talent and the possibilities of the field were not recognized. Business journals were looked upon as a luxury and support was to be had only through cultivating the vanity of manufacturers. Facts were ignored in favor of windy write-ups given in return for advertising contracts. The businesspaper was still a house organ, though published by proxy.

[15] "I Predict for 1959," *Printers' Ink*, January 2, 1959, pp. 38-40.

Gradually these publishers, or wiser men who succeeded them, came to learn the practical disadvantages of servility and slowly the fawning clip-sheet gave way to the paper that stood on its own independent feet. It was seen that success depended upon *bona fide* circulation, which in turn rested with favoring the reader in terms of progressive and fearless news-gathering methods. Though the publisher who remained with his face turned toward the advertiser was still in the majority in 1890—and has not entirely disappeared to this day—the businesspaper which stood as the exponent of progress and guardian of sound practice in the trade it represented had made it mark.[16]

By 1880 there were nearly 500 specialized periodicals in the United States serving business: trades, industries, professions, education, medicine, etc. Everyone—writers, publishers, advertising men, and industrial advertisers—began to feel the urge to "unite into one channel the efforts of divergent minds," as Tocqueville put it.

13. Press Associations

In 1887, in Rochester, New York, 51 newspaper publishers met and established the American Newspaper Publishers Association (ANPA), primarily a newspaper trade organization, to adjust conflict of viewpoint and practice between advertiser, agent, and publisher.

In 1888, the Association of General Newspaper Agents was formed in New York, the first organized advertising group.

In 1890, the Business Writers Association was started in Detroit as a social group.

In 1894, the Agate Club was formed in Chicago by magazine advertising representatives and claims to be the oldest advertising club in the United States.

In 1895, 60 farm paper publishers, editors, and business managers formed the Agricultural Press League of Chicago.

In 1896, the Sphinx Club was formed in New York to bring together advertisers, agents, and publishers.

14. Federation of Trade Press Associations

Something else that had been holding up businesspaper growth was the unpeaceful state of affairs existing between agents and publishers [*Printers' Ink* reported]. The former complained of cut rates, uncertain circulation and lack of commissions. The large majority of papers paid no

[16] *Printers' Ink*, Fiftieth Anniversary Issue, July 28, 1938.

agent's commission. The publishers, on the other hand, resented the slight regard which the agents accorded the businesspaper as an advertising proposition and felt, often rightly, that the agent was unable to handle technical accounts intelligently.[17]

The first trade press associations were formed early in the twentieth century. About 550 businesspapers of all kinds were being published (see Appendix I). Four associations were formed, in New York, Philadelphia, St. Louis, and Chicago.

By 1906 they had joined forces as the Federation of Trade Press Associations, and the following year the Federation held its first conference in Washington, D.C., on postal matters.

In 1915, the Federation of Trade Press Associations adopted "standards of practice." Similar standards were adopted the same year by the Associated Advertising Clubs of the World.

The following businesspaper publishers served as officers of the Federation of Trade Press Associations in its first eventful decade:

John A. Hill (President 1906) Hill Publishing Co., New York

John Newton Nind (Vice President 1906, President 1907) President, Periodical Publishing Co., and publisher of *Grand Rapids Furniture Record*

Henry G. Lord (Secretary-Treasurer 1906; Vice President 1907, 1908; President 1909, 1910) *Textile World Record*

Emerson P. Harris (Secretary Treasurer 1907) *The Journal of Railway Appliances*

David Williams (President 1908) *Iron Age*

Charles V. Anderson (Vice President 1909)

John Clyde Oswald (Secretary-Treasurer 1908, Vice President 1913, President 1914-15) *American Printer*

P. H. Litchfield (Secretary-Treasurer 1909)

Evan Johnson (Vice President 1910) *Office Appliances*

Henry Lee (Secretary-Treasurer 1910-11); Vice-President, *Railway Age*

E. R. Shaw (President 1911) Technical Publishing Company, *Practical Engineer*

Wm. H. Taylor (Vice President 1911), McGraw-Hill Publishing Co.

H. M. Swetland (President 1912) United Publishers Corporation

E. C. Hole (Vice President 1912) *American Lumberman*

[17] *Ibid.*

F. D. PORTER (President 1913) Porter-Langtry Co. *Buildings and Building Management* (Chicago)

E. E. HAIGHT (Secretary-Treasurer 1913, President 1915-1916)

AINSLEY A. GRAY (Vice President 1914, President 1915-1916) *The Electrical Review and Western Electrician*

JAMES H. MCGRAW (McGraw Publishing Co.) served as "National Counsellor, representing the Federation in the Chamber of Commerce of the United States."

15. Associated Business Publications, Inc.

It was not until 1916 that the Federation of Trade Press Associations adopted a new constitution and the new name, Associated Business Papers, Inc. The purpose, as stated in its constitution and by-laws, was "to foster the best interests of the business press and to secure the proper solution of problems common to trade, class and technical papers."

In 1950 the name was changed to Associated Business Publications.

The ABP barred from membership "organs or mouthpieces of any house or combination of houses to further its or their special interest as against the joint interests of the trade."

The job faced by charter members of the Associated Business Papers was no small one. Through their efforts the businesspaper division of the Audit Bureau of Circulations was brought into existence. The charter members of ABP drew up standards of practice in 1916 in pursuance of a new theory: *that businesspapers should be edited for the reader, not the advertiser.* For many years this original code of 1916 stood as a publishing guide for every businesspaper member or non-member which operated to render a real service to subscribers and advertisers.

However, new business and publishing concepts developed during the next two decades. In 1939, the Associated Business Papers unanimously adopted a "Revised Code of Ethics and Standards of Practice." Each ABP member publication pledged itself to observe these high professional standards.

The membership of ABP in 1949 was limited to businesspapers with paid circulations which were also members of the Audit Bureau of Circulations.

In 1958 there were 167 members in the ABP. The address is 205 East 42nd Street, New York, N. Y.

16. Birth of Audited Circulation

The circulation liar began to worry honest publishers and advertisers as early as 1889. The California legislature in 1893, largely through the efforts of the *San Francisco Examiner*, finally passed a bill (introduced three years earlier) enabling an advertiser who had any reason to doubt the circulation of a periodical to bring the publisher into court and make him produce proof. This act had a sobering effect on circulation liars. So did the clamor for standardized and uniform advertising rates. The pressure of advertisers and advertising agents for lower rates put it up to the publisher to prove that he deserved his present or higher advertising space rates.

Another impetus to verified circulation statements was the publication directory. One of the earliest was issued in 1869, the *American Newspaper Directory*. By 1878 it was guaranteeing the accuracy of the circulation statements reported in its columns. George Presbury Rowell, pioneer advertising agent who was the publisher of this directory, invited publishers to submit "signed statements" of their circulations, on the theory that they would avoid appending their signatures to fraudulent figures. Rowell also offered $100 reward to anyone who could disprove the figures he published. (The reward was claimed and paid five times in one year.)[18]

Rowell's directory differed from Mitchell's *Directory of the Newspapers of Great Britain* in two ways. Mitchell's sold for a shilling and Rowell's for $5. Mitchell's was silent on circulation. "I was often told that it would not be allowed in England," Rowell says in his autobiography, ". . . an effort made in London about two years ago to bring out a directory on a plan so long in use by us was promptly squelched by the courts."

Other American advertising agents, N. W. Ayer and Lord & Thomas, for example, soon began publishing directories, and by 1890, 14 directories were being published.

A transition in the functions of the advertising agent are worth noting at this point. The advertising agent started out originally as the agent of the publisher, who paid his commission. His equipment included a list of good publications, a pretty accurate guess of their *actual* circulation figures, plus an aggressive bargaining power to get

[18] G. P. Rowell, *Forty Years an Advertising Agent* (New York, Franklin Publishing Co., 1926). Mr. Rowell was the founder of *Printers' Ink*.

the lowest possible rates (before rates were fixed and standardized) for an advertising prospect. Armed with this equipment the agent sallied forth to "pick up ads." He placed the orders, mailed the copy, and checked insertions for the advertiser. Whether the copy was right and what results the advertiser obtained were not the agent's problems. By 1900 the agent's loyalty was reversed—he had become, in effect, part of the advertiser's organization rather than the publisher's. Sometimes he received large fees from advertisers not only for preparing their copy but for setting up and training their sales organizations and even for analyzing markets for their products or services.

Guesses, estimates, and publisher's signed but still doubtful statements of circulation eventually became unacceptable to most advertisers and advertising agents. They wanted a more accurate measure of circulation. That meant one thing: the advent of the independent professional auditor of circulation.

In the spring of 1899 representatives of some 30 advertisers met in New York City and formed the Association of American Advertisers with Frederick L. Perine of Hall & Ruckel as first president. In three years the AAA (known as the 3-A's) audited 400 publications (chiefly consumer) and made "inspection reports" on 57 cities. Similar auditing work was started by a western organization, American Society of National Advertisers, headed by C. W. Post, which subsequently merged with the AAA.

The Association of American Advertisers, by 1912, had examined more than 1,000 separate circulation statements but never was able to get more than a handful of advertisers to underwrite the expense of this type of work. By 1913 things were pretty bad. Lawsuits were filed against publishers, demanding circulation rebates. In a speech that year one publisher said, "*Circulation liars humiliate honest publishers.*"[19]

Two new movements started in 1913 aimed at accomplishing what the 3-A's had failed to achieve. One was the Association of National Advertising Managers in New York, which had changed its name to the Association of National Advertisers. The other was Western Advertising Agents' Association, a Chicago group of advertisers and agency men, headed by C. Stanley Clague, a Chicago advertising agency executive, who had been backers of the 3-A movement.

[19] *Printers' Ink*, Fiftieth Anniversary Edition. July 28, 1938.

Finally, the same year (1913), an "Advertising Audit Association" was formed in the West, and a "Bureau of Verified Circulation" in the East, to tackle this problem of audited readership and forestall a threatened collapse of the entire advertising structure.

A proposal was made to President McChesney of the Association of National Advertising Managers by O. C. Harn. Mr. Harn was the advertising manager of the National Lead Co., New York. He proposed that the group organize a new auditing body admitting publishers to membership. The publishers would provide most of the income; the advertiser-members would hire and control the auditors. A "circulation audit committee" was appointed, with Mr. Harn as chairman, and L. B. Jones and G. B. Sharpe as members.

Invitations to a conference on April 22, 1913, at the Hardware Club, New York, brought together representatives of many publishing and advertising associations with businesspaper associations playing a dominant part. A permanent organization was recommended with three representatives from each of the following organizations: Federation of Trade Press Associations, Grocery and Allied Trade Press Association, Technical Publicity Association, Farm Press Association, American Newspaper Publishers Association, Quoin Club, Periodical Publishers Association, New York Advertising Agents' Association, Association of National Advertising Managers, and Association of American Advertisers. The Bureau of Verified Circulations was organized.

First organizations to adopt the plan were the Grocery and Allied Trade Press Association and the Association of New York Advertising Agents. Only the 3-A's openly opposed the plan. Their Mr. Bert M. Moses suggested merger with the 3-A's. This was rejected. That summer the 3-A's collapsed, owing several thousand dollars. The members blamed the Bureau of Verified Circulations in the East for their downfall and turned for help to Mr. Clague's Western Advertising Agents' Association of Chicago, which group had not been invited to the New York conference of April 22.

Mr. Clague drew up a new plan and an "Advertising Audit Association" was formed at the La Salle Hotel, Chicago, in September, 1913, headed by Clague, Colonel Emory Mapes (Cream of Wheat Co.), and Jason Rogers. This group paid off the indebtedness of the AAA. In October, 1913, the organizers of the Bureau of Verified Circulations went to work. On their board was F. R. Davis of

General Electric, representing Technical Publicity Association; A. W. Erickson, representing New York Association of Advertising Agents; O. C. Harn, Association of National Advertising Managers; M. C. Robbins of *Iron Age*, representing the Federation of Trade Press Associations of the United States; George M. Rogers of Cleveland *Plain Dealer* representing American Newspaper Publishers Association; George Von Utassy, of *Cosmopolitan* magazine representing Periodical Publishers Association, and Wm. H. Whitney, Farm Press Association.

After several meetings with representatives of both eastern and western groups, the bodies consolidated as the "Advertising Audit Association and Bureau of Verified Circulations"—headquarters in New York and Chicago.

On Aug. 21, 1914, the Audit Bureau of Circulations was duly incorporated, the first president being Louis Bruch of American Radiator Co., Chicago; Erickson and Davis were vice presidents. To A. W. Erickson, an advertising agency executive, acting as temporary chairman, must go credit for successfully engineering the merger of these two groups in 1914. Mr. Clague served as managing director for many years. His son, Stanley R. Clague, is secretary of Modern Hospital Publishing Co.

17. The Audit Bureau of Circulation

Know by the symbol "ABC" the merger in 1914, which we have described, brought together 400 advertisers, advertising agencies, and periodical publishers into the now internationally famous public accounting organization known as the Audit Bureau of Circulations.[20] Co-operative and nonprofit, the purpose of ABC is to collect and verify *paid* circulation data, establish uniform methods of auditing paid circulations, and disseminate information among its members by standardized reports. Its establishment provided the first adequate yardstick to measure the value of publication media. This yardstick of values is found in the standards and audits of the ABC. The ABC Publishers' Statements, sworn to by the publisher, are issued in printed

[20] By 1942, ABC membership embraced every leading periodical of paid circulation in the United States and Canada as well as the leading advertising agencies and the leading advertisers. The British ABC, founded in 1931, is the largest in Europe. The French ABC, founded in 1923, is the second largest. Belgium, Switzerland, Holland, Norway, Sweden, and Australia have similar Audit Bureaus of Circulation.

form every six months. Regularly employed, experienced ABC auditors are sent once each year to each publisher's office to make an exhaustive investigation and audit of the circulation. These findings are embodied in the ABC Audit Report, which is issued annually in mimeographed form (Chart 26). If the previously issued publisher's statement was in error, the Audit Report points it out.

It is noteworthy that, while the ABC is financed chiefly by sellers of space (the publisher), the control of its policy rests with the buyers of space (advertisers and their advertising agents).

The rules and regulations of member publications are the strictest and the severest with regard to methods of getting new subscriptions or receiving expirations.

In 1958 ABC's membership included about 4,000 advertisers, agencies and periodical publishers in the United States and Canada. It is governed by a tripartite board of directors on which advertisers and advertising agencies have a majority vote. Publisher membership is predicated upon 70 per cent of a publication's distribution qualifying as paid. Headquarters are 123 N. Wacker Drive, Chicago 6, Illinois, and 357 Bay Street, Toronto 1, Canada.

18. Business Publications Audit of Circulation, Inc.

During the depression following World War I, circulation managers of businesspapers discovered that even with the best-edited businesspapers it was economically impossible to sell much more than 50 per cent of the buying power in many industries. To get as much as 60 per cent of the buying power in some fields usually cost 1½ times the subscription price.

By 1930, high-pressure selling, according to some authorities, had become necessary in order to get circulation. Expensive mail effort was supplemented by the use of premiums and sheet writers. The sheet writer is an independent subscription solicitor who usually collects the full subscription price or more, as his fee. He sells groups of businesspapers. Sometimes, he gives away premiums as an inducement. Even with all this effort, it was impossible for some businesspapers to attain more than 50 or 60 per cent coverage of their buying power.

The Controlled Circulation Audit, Inc., was formed by Frank L. Avery in 1931 to supply verified information about businesspapers which were being circulated *free of charge* in widely scattered areas and in fields where it was claimed to be difficult to obtain paid subscriptions in large numbers. By 1930 the number of such free circulation papers had increased to about 100.

A few years ago the name was changed to Business Publications Audit of Circulation, Inc. In 1959 BPA had 479 publication members and 209 advertisers and advertising agency members. BPA Form A audit covers businesspapers which may be free or have some qualified paid circulation. BPA Form B paid and free controlled circulation are audited separately. Offices are 420 Lexington Ave., New York, 35 E. Wacker Drive, Chicago, and 6363 Wilshire Boulevard, Los Angeles.

19. Verified Audit Circulation Company

In 1952 the John B. Knight Company, a national market research organization, formed the VAC. It has a tripartite board of governors, consisting of nine members: three national advertisers, three national advertising agencies, three periodical publishers. VAC audits all types of circulation, paid, free, bulk, rotated, or controlled. Verification is mandatory and the VAC audit is made independently of the periodical. VAC states the percentage of copies actually received and those within the classifications claimed by the publisher. VAC also publishes a readership analysis giving the percentage of recipients who read the periodical and found the editorial and advertising content valuable. Offices: 1528½ N. Wilcox Ave., Hollywood 28, California.

20. Office of Certified Circulation, Inc.

OCC, established by the Inter-American Press Association, adopted its by-laws on June 6, 1958, and its rules of practice on May 25, 1958. OCC is set up to audit paid or controlled circulation print media below the Rio Grande in the Western Hemisphere the same as ABC and BPA in the United States. In 1958 Arthur A. Kron was president and headquarters office was in New York City, at 22 East 60th Street.

21. National Business Publications

In May 1949, a growing conflict of opinion on circulation philosophy and distribution practice came to a head at the annual convention of the ABP in the Homestead, Hot Springs, Virginia, and split the membership of ABP into two camps. More than thirty publishers, who had periodicals with free circulations as well as with paid circulations, resigned immediately and joined the National

Business Publications, an organization founded in 1940.

"All NBP publishers," stated an advertisement of this group in the January 22, 1957, *SRDS Directory*, "are dedicated to the proposition that one strong national organization can best serve the interests of readers, advertisers, agencies, publishers, business and industry, government and country."

NBP supports the principle of a single circulation audit for all businesspapers whether such circulations are paid, free, or part free and part paid, and includes in its ranks publishers of ABC, BPA, and "combined" periodicals.

Rex W. Wadman served as the first president of NBP in June 1940. In 1959 NBP had 205 members.

NBP is financed by membership dues based on a percentage of the net advertising income of each member publication. The association has non-voting members (college journalism professors and advertising agency members who pay no dues, have no vote, but are eligible for all services and facilities). NBP headquarters in Washington, D.C., are at 1913 Eye Street, N.W.

22. American Association of Advertising Agencies

Called the "4 A's" in publishing circles, this organization was an amalgamation, in 1917, of New York, New England, Philadelphia, Southern, and Western advertising agency associations.

Membership is by application and is open to agencies which are able to meet the Association's qualifications: independent ownership, adequate experience, proper staff and facilities, financial responsibility, ability to render complete agency service in reasonable conformity to the AAAA agency Service Standards and Standards of Practice.

AAAA is governed by an elected board of directors. Fifteen national committees deal with all aspects of the agency business. Geographically it is organized into four sectional regions and 19 local councils, each headed by boards of governors. At any one time, some 500 member agency people are serving in these national and local capacities.

Administering the activities is a staff of some fifty people, including twelve executive specialists, at AAAA headquarters, 420 Lexington Avenue, New York. A Western Region office is maintained in the Russ Building, San Francisco.

On behalf of the advertising agency business, AAAA promotes its standards and other "suggested practices," has developed copyrighted order blanks and contracts to facilitate the placing of advertising with media, works with other segments of advertising, and serves as general spokesman for advertising agencies.

On behalf of advertising as a whole, AAAA sponsors programs for the improvement of advertising personnel, advertising research, advertising content, and better understanding for advertising; some of these are joint enterprises, such as the Advertising Council, Advertising Research Foundation, and Traffic Audit Bureau.

In the field of member service, AAAA supplies numerous aids to help members be well managed, provides an information and bulletin service, committee aids to members, and sponsors periodic meetings.

Antitrust action: On May 12, 1955, the Department of Justice in the name of the people of the United States, filed an antitrust suit against the AAAA and five publishers' associations: Associated Business Publications (ABP); Periodical Publishers Association (PPA); Agricultural Publishers Association (APA); American Newspaper Publishers Association (ANPA); and Publishers Association of New York (PANY).

The government contended the system used to "recognize" advertising agencies, and thus make them eligible to receive the publisher's 15 per cent commission for advertising placed, was a penalty on direct advertisers who wanted to cut costs by placing their advertising direct with publishers. They also contended it was a boycott of agencies who had not been granted "recognition," including "house agencies," thus giving other agencies with "recognition" sanctuary from such competition. The government further contended that a ban by AAAA on speculative new business presentations lessened competition. Finally, they contended that a 15 per cent agency commission, with penalties for rebating any of the amount, was a "price-fixing conspiracy" between the media groups and the advertising agencies within the AAAA.

All the publishing groups involved, and the 4-A's, within a year after the government action began, signed "consent decrees," agreeing to abandon the practices attacked by the government: 15 per cent commission; ban on rebates and fee-splitting; prohibition of speculative presentations; sanctity of media rate cards; and agency "recognition" standards mentioned above.

The settlement of this case recalls the fact that a quarter century earlier, in 1930, the Federal Trade Commission dismissed a complaint involving many of the same issues.[21]

Frey Report on Agency Practice: Growing out of the successful antitrust action by the Government, the Association of National Advertisers (ANA) in 1956 commissioned two marketing professors, Dr. Albert Frey and Dr. Kenneth Davis, at the Tuck School of Business Administration, Dartmouth College, to make a study of the working relationship of advertiser-agency-media.

In October 1957, the 500-page "Frey Report" laid down a framework for modern advertising agency practice, in line with the antitrust law philosophy of fair competition. It spotlighted many weaknesses and listed its recommendations for better procedure.

Advertising expenditures in the United States in 1957 were well over $10.3 billion, almost matching corporate dividend payments which came to about $12 billion the same year.[22]

Business corporation advertising managers say they expect a more efficient job from advertising agencies in evaluating media and markets, as well as copy, in the future.

23. Association of Industrial Advertisers

For years the extractive and transformative industries had neglected or ignored the merchandising function in selling to other processing industries. As so-called "industrial" buying became more and more discriminating, these extractors and semi-finished goods manufacturers recognized the great need for better advertising and marketing technics and practices. Small groups which had met regularly in several cities, in 1922 established the National Industrial Advertisers Association (NIAA) with organization headquarters in Chicago, and district chapters in key industrial cities. The name was changed in 1959 to Association of Industrial Advertisers.

District chapters of AIA meet once or twice a month for clinical or round-table sessions or to listen to outside speakers. Annual conferences are held. Advertising and sales promotion managers, agency account executives, and businesspaper and service organization executives make up the membership. Investigations are conducted on advertising and marketing, budget procedure, standard records and

[21] *Lorraine Journal* v U.S. 342 U.S. 243, 152.
[22] Research Division, McCann-Erickson, Inc., New York.

contracts, direct mail and catalog practice, public relations, United States census activities, publishers' statements, and phases of distribution.

The "Publisher's Statement" of the AIA is an analytical form which, when filled with the requested information, provides a check list for users of businesspaper space. Another form is provided for users of catalogs and directories and for publications issued by charity and political enterprises. A bulletin, *How and Why to Use the AIA Publisher's Statement,* is also issued.

24. Association of National Advertisers

The Association of National Advertisers in 1958 represented over 612 national advertisers, many of whom were among the largest in the country. These advertisers included firms in virtually every classification of industry, from makers of food to makers of steel. Their individual advertising budgets range in size all the way from a few thousands to several millions of dollars. The word "National" here means advertisers in the national consumer press. The industrial press also gives national coverage.

In June 1912, advertising managers of 17 of the largest companies in the United States met in a hotel in Detroit to discuss their current problems. At that time there was no organization composed of, or acting in the interests of, buyers of advertising. These men decided that what they needed most was a forum where the problems of advertisers could be discussed intimately and impartially, a place where one could hear and profit from the experience of the others, an organization which would express the voice of them all and would become a power for protecting their mutual interests and increasing the efficiency of their advertising expenditures. So they founded the Association of National Advertising Managers, later to be changed to the Association of National Advertisers, Inc.

The association aims to eliminate experiment in the buying of service, space, printing and in the formulating of sales and merchandising plans, as much as possible. It fosters the practice of scientific principles in advertising, gathers fresh and accurate sales and advertising information, and cooperates with other organizations in the advertising and sales field.

Many of the organizations and facilities on which all advertisers now depend with confidence, and often take for granted, including the Audit Bureau of Circulations, the Advertising Research Foundation, the Co-operative Analysis of Broadcasting, the Traffic Audit Bureau and others, originated as activities of, or through the efforts of, the ANA.

25. Advertising Federation of America

Advertising, spark plug of business, began to think of itself nationally in 1905. In Chicago that year the various advertising clubs of key cities organized as the American Federation of Advertising Clubs, a year later changing their name to Associated Advertising Clubs of America. In 1911, the "Truth-in-Advertising" movement was launched. In 1914, the name was changed to Associated Advertising Clubs of the World and a year later the first educational program was launched. In 1916, the first Women's Advertising Club was founded. In 1912, a speakers' bureau began operating. In 1926, the name was again changed, to International Advertising Association, and in 1928 a bureau of research and education was established. In 1929, the present name was adopted. Advertising agents, journalists, publishers, radio broadcasters, publicity men, advertising managers for manufacturers, retail stores, utilities, and railroads, and trade association officials make up its board of directors. Prime objective of AFA is (quoting from one of their brochures):

"To help make advertising increasingly effective as an instrument of distribution" and "to preserve freedom of individual enterprise in America."

26. Round Tables and Workshops

In New York, Chicago, Toronto, and elsewhere businesspaper publication managers and sales, circulation, and production managers belong to luncheon clubs they attend regularly to discuss their problems or to hear outside speakers, such as agency executives, industrial advertisers, editors, and publishers. These clubs are variously named: round tables, clinics, forums, etc. One group of space salesmen call their's the "Dotted Line Club."

Workshops are conducted regularly by the editorial groups. One group of editors meets for several days, twice a year, at Arden House, Harriman, New York, which is a chateau used by Columbia University professors as a hide-away for intellectual discussions.

National Conference of Business Paper Editors: Organized in 1919, this was the leading organization of businesspaper editors in the United States for thirty years. When the publishers split into two groups (ABP and NBP) on circulation policy (see section 21, this chapter) many editors resigned and formed another group, the Society of Business Magazine Editors. The NCBPE lost its independence and was finally liquidated and replaced by the Editorial Division of ABP, at 205 East 42nd Street, New York.

Society of Business Magazine Editors: Paul Wooton, dean of Washington correspondents, founder and for many years president of the NCBPE, was one of the founders in 1949 of the SBME, which stresses in its Constitution (Article II), "This society shall be completely independent of any affiliation with any organization in the business publishing field." Applicants for membership are judged by their professional standing and the ethical standards of their periodical, without any reference to the manner in which it obtains its circulation. Headquarters are 1015 National Press Building, Washington, D.C.

New York Business Paper Editors Association: This association was founded in 1916 and is open to editors of independent business periodicals regardless of the publisher's circulation policies. This group is strictly business: workshop courses in basic editorial practice are conducted in the evenings, affording junior members practical knowhow in writing, interviewing, editing, production, and layout. The courses are available to non-members.

Monthly luncheon meetings are held, similar to the luncheon meetings of other editorial groups. An outside speaker or one of their own members discusses some problem or phase of editorial practice.

The American Association of Industrial Editors: Founded in 1937, this is one of the oldest of company editors' organizations. A significant special service for magazine educators was provided in 1956 by AAIE. Under the sponsorship of this association, the Remington Rand Corporation produced a movie entitled, *Management Looks at Externals.* The movie is 16 mm, sound, black and white. Extra prints, or the use of a print, may be secured through A. C. Hancock, Director of Publicity and Publications, Remington-Rand Corporation, 315 Fourth Avenue, New York 10, New York. Universities which are now members are Illinois, Maryland, Cornell, Oklahoma A. & M., and Southern California.[23]

[23] As reported by the Association for Education in Journalism, August 27, 1957.

The International Council of Industrial Editors: Many of the local groups within ICIE conduct active programs. The Dallas (Texas) Association of Industrial Editors staged a series of workshop evenings in 1956 at which well-known figures, such as Dr. Rudolph Flesch of New York University, made talks and led discussions. The workshops were held at Southern Methodist University and journalism teachers participated with the editors. A similar close working arrangement exists between most local industrial editors' organizations and nearby college and university schools of journalism, particularly Rutgers University in the East, the University of Georgia in the South, and Northwestern University in the Middle West.

At the national level, ICIE has been in flux due to mergers with other national industrial editors' groups. The death of Garth Bentley, chairman of the Education Committee in 1956, removed from the scene a distinguished leader in corporate journalism. ICIE headquarters mails reprints of articles on industrial journalism and related subjects to colleges.

Several local house organ editors' groups have established scholarships for journalism students in nearby universities.

"Operation Tapemeasure," published by ICIE, is a report of a survey of company publications in the United States, taken in 1956. Henry B. Bachrach (chairman of the Survey Committee) is with General Electric Company, 570 Lexington Avenue, New York 22, New York.

A national office was opened in 1957 for ICIE at 2108 Braewick Circle, Akron 13, Ohio.[24]

27. Publications of Editorial Associations

Many associations of magazine editors have their own publications which can be secured for journalism libraries. An incomplete list follows:

Action Report, published by the Magazine Publishers Association, 232 Madison Avenue, New York 16, New York.

Better Editing, published by the Editorial Division of the Associated Business Publications, Editor, Irene Pearson, 205 East 42nd Street, New York 17, New York.

Editor's Notebook, published by the American Association of Industrial Editors, c/o James Limner, 54 Fairfield Street, Montclair, New Jersey.

[24] See the 1957 Report, Association for Education in Journalism.

h m Eye, is a bulletin published for members of the House Magazine Institute, New York City.

Reporting is the official membership publication of the ICIE. Executive Secretary in 1958, Mrs. Ludel Sauvageot, 2108 Braewick Circle, Akron 13, Ohio.

National Business Publications, 1413 K Street, N.W., Washington 5, D.C. issue two news publications: *Week-End Report,* which carries bulletin reports on important news developments in the field of business journalism and within the association. *The NBP Round Table* is a multilithed publication, generally two to four sheets. A query on some common problem is submitted to several editors; the query and the responses are then reproduced in the *Round Table.*

Two other publications, independently published, are *The Gallagher Report,* by Bernard Gallagher, 500 Fifth Avenue, New York, N.Y., and *Magazine Industry Newsletter,* by Roy Quinlan, 40 East 46th Street, New York, N. Y.

28. Awards and Grants

The *Industrial Marketing* Award is given to business periodicals for excellence in editorial content and presentation by *Industrial Marketing* magazine.

The Jesse Neal Editorial Award, named after the first executive secretary of the ABP, Jesse H. Neal (1916-1926), is given to individual editors by ABP.

The advertising competition, originated by the Chicago Business Publications Association, was turned over in 1943 to ABP. The advertising awards are presented annually at meetings of various chapters of the Association of Industrial Advertisers.

Some businesspapers sponsor distinguished service awards to their own industries. *Factory* gives an annual award to the ten best new plants of the year. *Electrical World* gives an award to utilities. *Aviation Week* gives an award for flying safety. *Chemical Engineering* gives an award for achievement in its field.

A world-wide annual contest is sponsored by the International Council of Industrial Editors (ICIE) for the best corporate publications.

Raymond Bill Publication Corporation, on October 10, 1958, established the Raymond Bill Memorial Award ($400) in Journalism. It is given annually to a graduating senior in a school of journalism for graduate study and research in the businesspaper field.

Associated Business Publications make available annually maximum grants of $1,000 each to accredited schools of journalism to help finance specific projects, such as the Business Press Institute set up in 1958 at Northwestern University's Medill School of Journalism.

National Business Publications give "Silver Quill" awards each year to the person in the United States who has "done the most for business." Recipients have been: 1951, Paul Wooton, former President of the Society of Business Magazine Editors; 1952, Bernard C. Duffy, Vice Chairman, Batten, Barton, Durstine & Osborn; 1953, Richard M. Nixon, Vice President of the United States; 1954, Herbert Hoover, former President of the United States; 1955, Charles F. Kettering, former Director of Research, General Motors; 1956, Senator Harry Byrd, Chairman of the Committee of Finance. U.S. Senate; 1957, Benjamin Fairless, President, American Iron & Steel Institute; 1958, Hon. Sam Rayburn, Speaker of the House of Representatives and Hon. Joseph W. Martin, Jr., former Speaker of the House of Representatives; 1960, General James Doolittle.

The awards are presented at "State of the Nation" dinners in Washington which are attended by Cabinet members, distinguished government officials, Justices of the Supreme Court, ambassadors of foreign countries, high-ranking members of the military establishment, industrialists, and members of the business press of the United States and Canada.

The loan features of the National Defense Education Act (1958), although designed to step up the production of scientists, applies to students in all areas, including journalism. It provides loans of up to $1,000 a year per student, at 3 per cent interest, with repayment beginning a year after graduation. Although students prefer direct grants to loans, incoming freshmen and those already enrolled who are ambitious for careers in business journalism, if they need money, should be encouraged to apply for such loans under the new law. Applications can be made at any university's student loan office or to the Office of Education, Washington, D.C.

29. Placement Service

Every association of magazine editors and publishers provides aid for those seeking jobs. ICIE has thirteen area directors, each of whom serves informally as a clearing house between job seekers and job openings in the area. A national placement committee likewise functions in this regard. The Chicago Industrial Editors Association has a placement committee.

James Limner, executive secretary of AAIE, 24 Fairfield Street, Montclair, New Jersey, has been helpful in placing applicants in the field.

The National Business Publications, from its Washington headquarters, issues a weekly news letter called *Week-End Report.* One department, "Manpower Market," is utilized to present information about persons wanting positions in the business journalism field.

The Associated Business Publications, New York, has a placement service under the direction of Miss Irene Pearson.

30. Business Information Sources

Those preparing for careers and working business journalists should become familiar with a handbook by Marian Manley called *Business Information.* The book represents the culmination of thirty years experience by Miss Manley as the distinguished business librarian for the Public Library of Newark, which owes its world-wide fame to her and to its founder, John Cotton Dana (1904).[25]

It is as important to a business journalist as it is to a lawyer or doctor to know how to find information he needs.

Suppose you are assigned to interview an important man. Naturally you want to know all about him before you call on him. There is a set of *Who's Who* reference books: *Who's Who in America, Who's Who in Advertising, Who's Who in Commerce and Industry, Who's Who in New York, Who's Who in the East, Who's Who in the Catholic World, Who's Who in World Jewry,* and *Who Knows-And-What,* and an *International Who's Who.* There are the professional directories covering his particular specialty or activity. Is he a chemist, physicist, mechanical engineer? Is he a member of the American Medical Association? Fellow of the College of Surgeons? There are all kinds of directories, and directories about directories.[26] Reference books line the shelves of all big city libraries and many small town libraries.

If you want data on a corporation or business firm there is *Dun & Bradstreet, Thomas' Register, Kelley's Directory of Merchants, Manu-*

[25] Marian C. Manley, *Business Information, How to Find and Use It* (New York, Harper & Brothers, 1955), with annotated bibliography of sources.

[26] *Trade Directories of the World* (Queens Village, N. Y., Croner Publications).

facturers and Shippers, Standard & Poor. Dun (if you know a member, or if your own firm is a member) will draw you a report on almost any corporation in this country or in any other country (see Chapter III, section 3).

There are the Departments of Commerce and Chambers of Commerce, already cited, and Better Business Bureaus. Of course, the business press itself is a source.

Try the businesspaper in your man's particular field. Their morgue may yield data, or the local newspaper morgue may have it.

To learn about a firm, get its house organ. *Printers' Ink Directory of House Organs* lists them. Or try *Fortune* magazine index, or the trade association to which the firm belongs.

If you want data on a city, county, or state, there are, in addition to government bureaus, the local newspapers.

Interested in markets? The American Newspaper Publishers Association, Magazine Publishers Association, trade associations, and large publishing houses like Curtis, Time-Life-Fortune, Scripps-Howard, Hearst, and McGraw-Hill, make market studies of many kinds. Also basic material suppliers, such as DuPont, Dow, Union Carbide, American Cyanamid, United States Steel, International Nickel, and giant firms, such as General Motors, General Dynamics, General Foods, Standard Oil of New Jersey, and International Business Machines, make studies of markets. So do large advertising agencies—for example, J. Walter Thompson, McCann-Erickson, Young and Rubicam, Batten, Barton, Durstine & Osborn, and N. W. Ayer.

Securities brokerage houses—the big ones—make studies of corporations, industries, and markets. Such firms as Merrill, Lynch, Pierce, Fenner & Smith; Arthur Wiesenberger; Goodbody; and scores of others make studies of firms and industries.

In large cities there are numerous private libraries rich in source materials, such as the J. P. Morgan library, Dun & Bradstreet library. Many clubs, like the University Club in New York, have fabulous libraries to which access can be obtained. In New York City there is the Mercantile Library, an endowed lending library which charges members a nominal fee.

Most leading businesspaper publishers publish directories of their trades, have excellent morgues and fair libraries of their own.

There is *Standard Rate & Data Service* if you want data on any periodical, newspaper, businesspaper, or consumer magazine in the United States and Canada.

Standard Advertising Register tells you what firms advertise and who their advertising agents are. *Printers' Ink, Industrial Marketing,* and other sources will tell you how much the leaders spend and on what media. *Brad-Vern's* Reports (Woolford, Maryland), a "Blue Book of Businesspaper Advertisers"—750 pages—carries advertising schedules of about 10,000 companies.

Trade names? The *Trade Names Index* compiled by the Science-Technology Group of the Special Libraries Association contains more than 125,000 registered trade names, definitions of technical material, processes, and technical equipment, and a classified bibliography of sources of trade marks and brand names. Volume III of *Thomas' Register* lists brand names, too. Many businesspapers who publish directories of their field list trade marks among other things.

The *Public Relations Directory* lists all the leading publicity men, and there are directories of industrial designers, artists, photographers, and so on.

Most famous of all directories and, of course, the best known, is the "Yellow Pages" of the local telephone directory and, of course, the big city "Red Books," all published by the Reuben H. Donnelly Corporation, which also publishes nine businesspapers.

Other sources of business information are research organizations like Prentice-Hall, big banks, encyclopedias, annuals, maps, gazetteers, handbooks, manuals, annuals, catalogs, and indexes.

Industrial Arts Index is a monthly index to articles in several hundred periodicals in the fields of business, science, and technology, available in many libraries. There is *The New York Times Index* (by subjects) and *Public Affairs Information Service Bulletin* (New York) a weekly index to current books, pamphlets, government documents, and periodical articles in the fields of economics and public administration.

31. Directories and Data Yearbooks

Publishing directories has always been a basic function of businesspaper publishers. In 1667, A *Collection of the Names of Merchants* was published in London, one of the earliest known directories. Benjamin Franklin published a directory of Philadelphia in 1785. George P. Rowell, in 1869, issued *The American Newspaper Directory,* first attempt to list periodicals and give their circulation figures. In his directory there were just 56 publications listed under the headings "Commerce & Finance" and "Mechanics." Forty medical journals were listed.

Eleven years later, in 1880, the first edition of N. W. Ayer & Sons' *American Newspaper Annual* listed 323 periodicals under the heading Commercial, Financial and Trade; 110 under Fashion; 28 under Insurance; 38 under Legal; 18 under Real Estate; 53 under Mining; 32 under Music; 22 under Railroad; and 19 under Typographic; making 669 periodicals which, even at that time, were regarded as businesspapers. There were also listed about 1,000 professional and so-called class periodicals of various kinds: medical, educational, agricultural, religious, etc. There were nine foreign-language lists in 1880, and 19 secret society lists. Rowell's directory was merged with the N. W. Ayer directory in 1880.

The Annual Market Data & Directory Number of *Industrial Marketing* contains a wealth of valuable information regarding industrial and trade markets, as well as directory information on all business and professional publications in the United States and Canada. *Industrial Marketing* and its reference annual are published by Advertising Publications, Inc., Chicago, which also publishes *Advertising Age,* weekly advertising and marketing journal, and *Advertising Requirements,* workbook of advertising and sales promotion.

Printers' Ink publishes a most comprehensive *Advertisers' Guide to Marketing* every year. Statistics on all media in the United States and Canada are included and the status of the United States economy from a marketing viewpoint is given, with analyses of every trading area in the country.

Nine separate monthly directories are issued by Standard Rate & Data Service of Evanston, Illinois (SRDS). The tenth SRDS publication, A.B.C. *Weekly Rates and Data* is issued semi-annually. *Business Publication Rate and Data* (1264 pages), *Canadian Media Rates and Data* (248 pages), *Consumer Magazine and Farm Publication Rates and Data* (484 pages), *Films for Television* (116 pages), *Network Rates and Data* (84 pages), *Newspaper Rates and Data* (784 pages), *Spot Radio Rates and Data* (944 pages), *Spot Television Rates and Data* (554 pages), and *Transportation Advertising Rates and Data* (80 pages), totaled at least 4,558 pages a month in the full monthly service. Either the Business Publication or the Spot Radio book includes more pages than the entire service published twenty-five years earlier (SRDS was founded in 1919).

Development of its own patented "d.i.-Offset Process" has enabled SRDS to maintain accuracy at the increased pace which volume and costs demand, while holding to moderate rates for the services rendered to subscribers and advertisers alike. This "direct image" offset printing process eliminates all time-consuming and costly photomechanical steps by creating inexpensive grained aluminum foil offset plates direct from letterpress forms. Especially valuable where frequently used standing matter is subject to periodic scattered revision, the process has been made available to, and accepted by, more and more publishers and printers. The fact that the standing type receives no press wear has special quality and economy appeal.

32. Research Organizations

The term "research" applied to this activity sometimes falls far short of the scientific method employed by scientists. In fact, some research men get their hackles up when they see what the press or the advertising agencies describe as research.[27]

Independent research bureaus were employed by 78 businesspapers in 1958 to check 576 issues on readerships: to find out who they are, what they do, how they read, how much they buy, what they like and dislike in the businesspaper, etc. Among these research organizations are R. C. Eastman, Daniel Starch and Staff, Readex, Inc., John D. Fosdick Associates, Mills Shepard, Inc., Harvey Research Organizational Ad-Gage and Media Echo. Target Reports now deals only with advertisers.

Some businesspapers conduct their own research, especially multiple publishers who can afford to maintain their own research departments.

Research projects are also conducted by businesspaper publishers for advertising agencies and advertisers and other organizations.

Penton Publishing Co. (Cleveland) owns the Ad-Gage readership measurement service.

Media Echo is a service of the American Society of Mechanical Engineers (New York) for *Mechanical Engineering.*

"Reader Feedback" is the McGraw-Hill readership check on 18 of its own and one outside periodical.

In 1952, the National Industrial Advertisers Association (NIAA)

[27] See Chap. IX, section 6; see also section 11 in this chapter.

founded the Industrial Advertising Research Institute (IARI). The IARI, by studying industrial advertising, seeks to reduce the cost of selling and increase the effectiveness of the advertising. Five projects have been undertaken by IARI: Methods for Handling and Evaluating Inquiries; How to Establish the Budget for Advertising Individual Products; Yardsticks for Evaluating Industrial Advertising Research; Organizing and Controlling the Industrial Advertising Operation.

The Advertising Research Foundation conducts continuing study of media. They use three methods to measure the reactions of readers to advertising: (1) opinion studies, (2) data collected about the audience, (3) readership studies of editorial material and advertisements, item by item.

33. Distinguished Editors[28]

Paul Wooton, of The Chilton Company, currently dean of Washington correspondents, has been one of America's outstanding business journalists, for more than forty years.

When Herbert Hoover became Secretary of Commerce he asked Paul Wooton, then Washington correspondent for McGraw-Hill and the *Times-Picayune* of New Orleans, to organize a national group of businesspaper editors to act as liaison between the Department and private enterprise. Wooton and some of his colleagues in 1919 founded the National Conference of Business Paper Editors, which enjoyed the high esteem of official Washington for three decades (see Chapter V, section 26). Few, if any, other journalists can boast of being called by their first name by five Presidents of the United States: Coolidge, Hoover, Roosevelt, Truman, Eisenhower. In 1958 Wooton introduced Queen Elizabeth of England to the National Press Club in Washington over a nation-wide television hookup.

An incident serves to show the high regard people have for Paul Wooton. More than 90 businesspaper editors crowded around President Franklin Delano Roosevelt's desk at a White House conference one morning during the strenuous war days in June 1943. The President was in his shirt sleeves, puffing a cigarette in an ivory holder which jutted from the side of his mouth at a cocky angle. He was in fine fettle. News of the capture by the Allies of the island of Pantelleria in the Mediterranean, stepping-stone to Sicily and the continent

[28] See Chap. VI for names of many more distinguished American businesspaper editors.

of Europe, had just reached him. The president of the National Conference of Business Paper Editors, Paul Wooton, started his formal introductory remarks:

"Mr. President, there are so many of us this morning, we will dispense with the usual handshaking and introductions. Before you commence your off-the-record remarks I would like to say that the business press has done a pretty good job in the war effort to date and——"

President Roosevelt, interrupting, said, "Are you trying to sell me the business press, Paul? I'm sold. Go no further!"

Mr. Wooton, paling, said, "I simply wanted to say——"

The President, interrupting again, announced, "You are not going to say anything this time! *I'm* going to be the spokesman for the business press today! I'm going to tell you what they think of you and what I think of you! I have been waiting for this opportunity for years."

Chuckling to himself, Mr. Roosevelt reached in his desk drawer and brought out a leather case, which he opened. In it lay a watch. He read aloud the inscription: "Presented to Paul Wooton by President Franklin Delano Roosevelt, on behalf of the National Conference of Business Paper Editors."

For the one time in his career Paul Wooton was speechless.

History provides no other occasion when a President of the United States ever presented a gift to anyone on behalf of a private organization. This was the one and only time. The incident remains indelibly impressed on the minds of those who stood in the office of the Little White House on that June morning.

Mr. Wooton, still representing the *Times-Picayune,* is a former president of the National Press Club and the Gridiron Club of Washington, D.C. He is also a columnist for *Nation's Business.*

The pioneer authority of the supermarket movement is Editor M. M. Zimmerman. In 1930, with the opening of King Kullen's first market, he began to study this new type of mass retailing, which resulted in a series of ten articles in *Printer's Ink* in 1936, heralding the future of the industry. That same year he founded *Super Market Merchandising* which over the years has been the prophet of this industry. In 1937 he organized the Super Market Institute to establish the supermarket as an industry. The Institute today is one of the most powerful organizations in the food industry.

Mr. Zimmerman's periodical pioneered self-service throughout Europe, and in 1950 he organized the International Association of Food Distribution, with its first Congress in Paris that year. Subsequently, every third year Congresses have been held in Ostend, Belgium, in Rome, in Lausanne, Switzerland, in 1959.

Continuing his work in spreading the gospel of self-service, Mr. Zimmerman flew around the world, lecturing in such countries as Australia, Turkey, and other Far Eastern countries.

For his European work, three nations, France, Belgium, and Italy, honored him with decorations.

He is the author of *The Challenge of Chain Store Distribution* (Harper & Brothers); "Super Market—Spectacular Exponent of Mass Distribution" (Super Market Publishing Co.); *The Super Market Grows Up* (Super Market Publishing Co.); and *The Super Market: A Revolution in Distribution* (McGraw-Hill).[28]

An interesting phase of the service *Chain Store Age* has rendered its field embraces the activities of its first editor-in-chief, Godfrey M. Lebhar, outside of the columns of the periodical itself. From the early days of *Chain Store Age* (1925-1940), when efforts were constantly made to check chain store growth through the imposition of special chain store taxes, Mr. Lebhar took to the public platform, to legislative halls, to the courts and to the air to champion the chain store cause. His book, *Chain Stores in America, 1859-1950* (New York, Chain Store Publishing Corporation, 1952), is the definitive history of the chain store system in this country.

Lawyer, journalist, editor, and author, Mr. Lebhar was born in London, graduated from New York University Law School in 1904, was admitted to the New York bar and practiced law for five years. Together with Arnold Friedman, he established *Chain Store Age* in 1925. His first book, *Chain Store—Boon or Bane?* (Harper & Brothers, 1932) appeared when there was a wide division of opinion as to whether chain stores were here to stay. Mr. Lebhar believed they would survive.[29]

Few editors become publishers. One of the few was John H. Van Deventer who stepped from editor to publisher of *Iron Age*. Another editor, James G. Lyne, president of Simmons-Boardman Publishing Company and a former president of the Associated Business Publica-

[28] See Chapter III No. 1.
[29] See Chap. III, section 1.

tions, was for many years editor of *Railway Age.* Philip Salisbury, editor of *Sales Management* for many years, became the publisher in 1957. Eldridge Peterson, editor of *Printers' Ink,* became the publisher, retiring in 1958. He is the author of a new book on magazine advertising and a publishing consultant.

Sam Dunn, editor of *Railway Age,* became head of Simmons-Boardman Company. He was also president of ABP, and of NCBPE. John A. Hill, editor of *Locomotive Engineer,* became publisher of *American Machinist.* Editor Floyd Chalmers became president of MacLean-Hunter in Canada.

Philip Swain, who retired in 1954 and died in 1958, was editor of *Power* from 1934 to 1954. He joined the staff in 1921, after serving in World War I. In 1946 he was one of only two businesspaper editors to have the distinction of covering the historic atomic tests at Bikini atoll. The other was Sidney D. Kirkpatrick, then editor, now editorial director, of *Chemical Engineering.*

Top authority in the plastics industry is the distinguished chief editor of *Modern Plastics,* Hiram McCann, author and lecturer.

Harry Reimer, editor of the *Daily News Record,* retired in 1958 after serving that publication 41 years. He was assigned by General Brehon Sommervel to write the Fast East textile story of World War II. Reimer founded and served as president of the Textile Square Club for 22 years. In 1955 he made an eight-month air tour of the world's textile centers, covering a half-million miles. He received honorary degrees from Philadelphia Textile Institute and Lowell Institute of Technology.

Arthur D. Anderson, author of the *Shoe and Leather Lexicon,* served as editor of the *Boot & Shoe Recorder* for 27 years, was a former president of the National Conference of Business Paper Editors.

Carl Avery Werner for 46 years was editor of *The Tobacco Leaf,* as well as a poet, novelist, and short story writer. He started his career as a reporter on the *Watertown* (New York) *Daily Times* and entered the businesspaper field in 1899. He was an authority on the tobacco business and founded the New York Tobacco Table, a trade association. He died in 1944.

Roger Barton, editor of *American Printer* and later editor of *Advertising Agency,* in 1958 became the editor of a new businesspaper, *Mediascope.* He is the editor of *Advertising Handbook* (1950), and author of *Advertising Agency Operations and Management* (1955).

He is a former president of the National Conference of Business Paper Editors.

Clair B. Peck, retired editor of *Railway Locomotives and Cars,* who died in 1959, was a Fellow of the American Society of Mechanical Engineers and a leader in the railroad business. He was for many years one of the editors of *Railway Age.*

The consulting editor of *Power,* Fred A. Annett who also died in 1959, was the author of numerous technical text books on electrical equipment. He was a member of many distinguished engineering societies in the United States and Canada. He had served for 35 years as associate editor of *Power.*

Among the women who hold key editorial positions on leading current businesspapers are these award-winning editors: Wanda M. Jablonski, senior editor of *Petroleum Week;* Sarah Lee Gerrish, associate editor, *Printers' Ink;* Ruth Hahn, executive editor, *Sales Management;* Olga Gueft, editor of *Interiors;* Evelyn M. Dockstader, editor, *North Western Druggist;* Ruby Redford, editor, *Illuminating Engineering;* Jane Mitarachi, editor, *Industrial Design;* Florence Small, agency editor of *Broadcasting.*

34. Corporate Journalism

Private corporation periodicals or company magazines commonly known as house organs, in number of titles published and total distribution, are a huge industrial press in their own right.

In the United States the readership of house organs includes the literate portion of practically the entire labor force.

Private corporations publish two general types of company magazines for these purposes:

Internal periodicals, to communicate with employees: build up their morale, loyalty, pride, good will, encourage team work, give a sense of job security, announce changes in personnel, policy, and products, and, as an over-all objective to give the employee a feeling of complete identification with the company.

External periodicals, to communicate with suppliers, stockholders, customers, and the press, particularly the business press. The external house magazines discuss new products, equipment, services, research and development, finance, trends in the field, and, often, issues affecting the entire industry or business in general. The external magazine promotes the company's leadership in design, research, engineering, manufacture, public service, corrects misinformation, carries the annual financial statement, and is often used as a medium for attacking or praising government or labor policies.

Four popular formats for corporate periodicals are magazine, newspaper, newsletter, and community newspage (in the local press).

There were 575 house magazines published in the United States in the prosperous year of 1929. A study in 1952 by the International Council of Industrial Editors (editors of company magazines) revealed that 6,500 house periodicals were being published in the United States in that year with a combined monthly circulation of 70,728,860 readers. Two years later, in 1954, *Printers' Ink Directory of House Organs* listed 6,671 individual titles. By 1958 the total had reached 8,000 house periodicals, costing half a billion dollars a year to publish and distribute to about 80 million readers.[30]

In 1956 a study of company magazines in the United States, Hawaii, and Canada estimated the per issue combined circulation to be 300 million.[31]

Other countries have a growing company periodical press. The Federal Republic of Germany reports 264 corporation periodicals published (1957), and Britain reports 305 company periodicals (1957). Figures from other countries are not obtainable because no one as far as we can learn has tabulated them.

Company publication editors' salaries, shown in Table 15, represent the averages paid in 1956. The level represented an advance over the compensation level in 1951 when the previous survey was made. According to Henry B. Bachrach (Chairman of ICIE in 1958) salaries have risen some since late 1956.

People editing company magazines are well educated and possess wide experience. More than 70 per cent had college degrees (1956 survey) and 12 per cent graduate degrees. The largest percentage (345) come from newspaper work. Percentage from other fields: Advertising (25); Public Relations (22); Writing (22); Sales Promotion (18); Publicity (15); Other (25).

[30] National Chamber of Commerce of the United States, *Washington Report,* Vol. I, No. 11, Dec. 27, 1957.

[31] Operation Tapemeasure, Third Survey, prepared by International Council of Industrial Editors, Henry B. Bachrach, chairman, General Electric Co., N. Y., 1956. *Better Business Relations Through Employee Publications* (Washington, D.C., Chamber of Commerce of the United States, 1958), 47-page brochure.

TABLE 15. SALARIES OF COMPANY PUBLICATION EDITORS

	$300 or less	$301 $400	$401 $500	$501 $600	$601 $700	$701 $900	Over $900*
All Editors	6%	17%	23%	20%	12%	11%	5%
Under 30 years	13	32	34	13	3	1	0
30-39 years	5	14	26	27	12	9	3
40-49 years	2	10	14	22	19	17	9
Over 50 years	5	5	12	16	13	21	17
Durable goods	4	15	26	19	13	12	6
Non-durable	6	12	23	25	11	9	6
Transportation, communications, utilities	5	13	23	23	17	10	5
Wholesale & retail	12	18	23	17	8	10	6
Finance, insurance	9	30	17	19	10	8	5
Other	8	19	20	19	12	9	5
Northeast	6	14	21	20	13	11	7
South Central	7	17	26	19	12	9	5
South	7	22	20	21	12	10	4
West	6	16	23	21	13	12	5
Canada	6	13	23	32	0	6	0

SOURCE: "Operation Tapemeasure," report prepared by the Survey Committee, International Council of Industrial Editors, 1956, p. 7.

* A small percentage in each horizontal line did not report.

More mature people are being employed to edit company periodicals. Over 36 per cent are 40 or over. More than 70 per cent are between 30 and 60.

	per cent
21-29 years	24
30-39 years	39
40-49 years	23
50-59 years	10
60 and over	3
Not reporting	1

Only 24 per cent spent full time on their publications. About 76 per cent had other duties, which would suggest an even lower level of compensation than indicated in the salary chart.

The majority of the company publications (65 per cent) are of an internal nature and the majority (58 per cent) are monthlies. Only 5 per cent are weeklies and less than one per cent dailies. Magazine format is used by 63 per cent and newspaper format by 16 per cent. Others are special kinds of periodicals.

Most publications (62 per cent) are printed by letterpress with 31 percent using offset.

Only 38 per cent of those who responded to the 1956 survey stated they had "specific objectives" for their periodicals.

The 1956 ICIE survey observes: ". . . while much progress has been made by editors for themselves and their work over the past five years, there is still a long way to go."

The house organ is actually the ancestor of the businesspaper. Indeed, some contemporary businesspapers started as house organs. The court circular may be said to be the ancestor of the house organ.

The first court circular papers were published by feudal lords in China during the Han Dynasty (200 B.C.). In the Tang Dynasty (seventh century before the Christian era) they became official gazettes. The house organ flourished in Germany of the Middle Ages in the form of newsletters. *Neues Zeitungen* of the House of Fugger as well as the famous house organ of Lloyd's of London are described in Chapter VII.

Ben Franklin's Print Shop in eighteenth-century Philadelphia issued *Poor Richard's Almanack,* first house organ in North America and popularly but erroneously supposed to have been the ancestor of the *Saturday Evening Post.*[32]

Factory News, first published by National Cash Register Co., in June 1891, was one of the earliest house organs in the United States.

Many book publishers started house organs which eventually became independent consumer magazines, such as *Atlantic Monthly, Harper's* and *Scribner's.*

Printers' Ink was the house organ of the George P. Rowell Advertising Agency. *Scientific American* was the organ of a firm of patent attorneys, Messrs. Munn & Co. Southern Pacific Railway started *Sunset Magazine.*

The Travelers Protection (Travelers Insurance Co., 1865-1906) and *Locomotive* (Hartford Steam Boiler Inspection and Insurance Co. since 1867) are said to be the two oldest house organs published continuously in the United States. *Aetna* was published from 1868 to

[32] For the authentic history of the *Saturday Evening Post* see Mott's *A History of American Magazines* (Cambridge, Mass., Harvard University Press), in 4 volumes. (Last volume 1957.)

1908 and *Equitable Record* from 1871 to 1905 by those well-known insurance companies. *Sunnyside,* started in 1871 as the house organ of a casket maker, is the current businesspaper for funeral directors, *Casket and Sunnyside.*

Other notable corporation periodicals are *Dun's Review and Modern Industry* (Dun & Bradstreet) which carries advertising; *Sear's World* (Sears, Roebuck & Co.); *Think* (International Business Machines); *The Lamp* (Standard Oil of New Jersey); *Circle-News* (B. F. Goodrich); *Better Living* (DuPont); *News and Views* (Caterpillar); *Koppers News* (Koppers Co.); *Atlantic Magazine* (Atlantic Refining); *Arvin Folks* (Arvin Industries); *Kennescope* (Kennecott Copper); *Floor Plant Journal* (Armstrong Cork); *Trading Post* (Timken Roller Bearing); *Avisco News* (American Viscose); *Ohio Bell* (Ohio Bell Telephone).

Biggest house organ publisher in the United States is probably General Electric, which publishes two groups. (1) Internal papers for their own stockholders, firm members, and employees, such as *G-E Monogram,* 17,000 monthly, *General Electric Review,* 6,000, *Work News,* 175,000 weekly. (2) Numerous other magazines and newspapers for external distribution, to dealers, wholesalers, customers, and prospects, including the utilities: *G-E News Graphic* for the appliance field; *Light* for lighting engineers; *G-E News-Digest;* and *General Electric Review,* an ABC paper which disseminates information from its various laboratories and engineering departments to utilities, consulting organizations, colleges and trade schools, and electrical concerns.

Editors of *G-E Work News* have their offices in the largest G-E factories. A general manager in the Schenectady plant coordinates the work of eight editors and their staffs, syndicates various editorials, cartoons, and news on general company matters.

Industrial Marketing (June 1958, p. 126) reported that 25 per cent of corporations publishing house magazines in Great Britain sell these periodicals to their employes and encounter little resistance. The nominal charge (one penny to three pence) tends to avoid the stigma of "management propaganda" and employes are said to place more value on the publication because it cost money to get it. Among the larger British corporations selling their house magazines are Ford (autos), Shell (gasoline), Guinness (beer), Bata (shoes), Richard Thomas & Baldwin (Steel), and Marconi (Communications).

The editors of house magazines prefer to be called industrial editors and they have two associations: American Association of Industrial Editors, 24 Fairfield St., Montclair, New Jersey, and International Council of Industrial Editors. The president (1958) is Henry B. Bachrach of General Electric Co.

CHAPTER VI

EARLY UNITED STATES BUSINESSPAPERS

THE period after the Civil War was a period of confidence in the future of the United States. Printing and engraving processes improved and a general magazine boom started. Dr. Mott, historian of the American magazine press, estimates that between 1865 and 1885 almost 9,000 periodicals (not newspapers) had publishing starts.[1]

Tremendous gains in power conversion, mass production of iron and steel, the textile era, the railway age, the growth of science, and mechanical engineering, the electrical age marked the three decades preceding the opening of the twentieth century. These last 30 years of the nineteenth century were the formative period of the American business press. Until the Civil War (1861-1865) about 160 businesspapers came into existence covering such industries as iron and steel, gas, coachmaking, leather, telegraphy, photography, printing, dry goods, mining, meat packing, shipping, pharmacy, science, railroads, banking, medicine, dentistry, insurance. Some 30 of these pioneer businesspapers have survived to this day and in their time have absorbed other leading businesspapers.

The period known as *post bellum*, following the Civil War, was a flourishing one for specialized businesspapers. By the twentieth century there were few industries or professions which did not have at least one businesspaper.

1. Scientific Group

American interest in things scientific was stimulated by the startling discoveries and inventions here and abroad after the Civil War.

[1] Frank Luther Mott, *History of American Magazines* (Cambridge, Mass., Harvard University Press), Vol. III (1865-1885), p. 5.

Scientific journals sprang up everywhere. Business journalism was prolific on "mechanics." The Centennial Exposition in Philadelphia, in 1876, and the World's Fair in Vienna, in 1873, further stimulated scientific interest.

Rufus Porter, shoemaker's apprentice and house painter, started the *Scientific American* in 1845. He had been a peddler of a "revolving almanac" of his own invention and had many other devices to his credit: fire alarm, signal telegraph, fog whistle, camera obscura, washing machine, rotary plow, portable house, corn sheller, flying ship. In 1841 he was editing the *New York State Mechanic* and experimenting with electrotyping when he founded the *Scientific American*, "The Advocate of Industry and Journal of Mechanical and Other Improvements." It was bought in 1846 by Orson Desaix Munn (whose grandson, Orson D. Munn, died while publisher in 1958) and Alfred Ely Beach, son of Moses Y. Beach, editor and publisher of the *New York Sun*. These men were patent lawyers. To the *Scientific American* came A. B. Wilson with his model sewing machine and Thomas A. Edison with his talking machine, for "write-ups." Also to its editorial office came Samuel F. B. Morse, Elias Howe, Captain John Ericsson, Dr. R. J. Gatling, Peter Cooper Hewitt, Samuel P. Langley, and Glenn Curtiss. Its editorials fought fakers and quacks persistently. From a purely technical businesspaper it expanded into a popular consumer magazine about 1875.

First scientific journal in North America was *Medical Repository*, a New York quarterly (1797-1824). It had another distinction: it was the first technical magazine to live longer than eight years. Co-editors were Elihu Hubbard Smith, physician, Samuel Latham Mitchell, Professor of Chemistry at Columbia University and a physician, and Edward Miller, also a physician.

Dr. Mitchell was one of the first U.S. Senators from New York.

This was the era of the yellow fever epidemic. The year *Medical Reporting* was founded, Philadelphia was having a "great plague" which resulted in the death of 3,521 persons. Thus the magazine gave most of its attention to epidemics. Dr. Smith died of the yellow fever in 1798.

New England Journal of Medicine and Surgery was founded in 1812.

The first *Bulletin of the American Geographical Society* was published in 1852. The last issue appeared in 1857. G. P. Putnam, New

York, was the publisher and George Bancroft was president of the Society. After two years of irregular issue, it became a monthly and "Bulletin" was changed to "Journal." This publication lasted until 1915. Early volumes contained much information on polar and African exploration. In 1916 it became *Geographical Review* and in 1921 became a quarterly.

One of America's first specialized scientific periodicals was the *American Mineralogical Journal*, published by Collins & Co., in 1810. It survived four years. The editor was identified on the title page as "Archibald Bruce, M. D., Professor of Materia Medica and Mineralogy in the Medical Institution of the State of New York and Queen's College, N. J." He discovered the mineral, Brucite, named after him.

In 1818 a professor of chemistry and mineralogy at Yale became editor of *The American Journal of Science and Arts, More Especially of Mineralogy, Geology and Other Branches of Natural History, Including Also Agriculture and The Ornamental as Well as Useful Arts.* The publisher was not overlooking any bets. Indeed, contributions were solicited in the fields of music, sculpture, engraving, and "all fine and liberal as well as useful arts." Applications of science to navigation, meteorology, anatomy and physiology were also covered. In 1880 the magazine title was shortened to *American Journal of Science.*

The American Journal of Pharmacy (1825–current) claims to be the oldest pharmaceutical businesspaper in the English language. Founded in 1825 as *The Journal of the Philadelphia College of Pharmacy*, it changed to the current title in 1835. It is still sponsored by the Philadelphia College of Pharmacy and Science, which claims to be the oldest pharmaceutical college in the world. The first editor was a Quaker, Daniel B. Smith.

The Astronomical Journal started publication in Cambridge, Mass., in 1849, suspended in 1861, and resumed publication in 1886. The founder and first editor was Benjamin Apthorpe Gould, Jr. In 1908 Lewis Boss purchased the *Journal* and took it to Albany to publish in connection with the Dudley Observatory located there.

To indicate the diverse scientific disciplines demanded in a single field today, here are the titles of some of the contemporary technical and scientific journals one might observe in a chemical research laboratory such as that of the DuPont company: *Journal of Histochemistry and Cytochemistry, Journal of Polymer Science, Economic Geology,*

Journal of Mathematics and Physics, Journal of Experimental Botany, Journal of Animal Science, Applied Scientific Research, Journal of Organic Chemistry, Journal of Research, Chemical Abstracts, Biochemical Journal, Agriculture Chemicals, Aerosol Age, Analytical Chemistry, Cereal Science Today, Chemical Engineering, Chemical Processing, Petroleum Refiner, etc.

2. Medical Group

Dr. Oliver Wendell Holmes, serving as chairman of a committee on medical literature for the American Medical Society in 1861, said that the medical editors "sat in each other's laps." The editorial content, according to Dr. Holmes, showed little original material—mostly reports of epidemics, endemics, operations, case histories, book notices. *American Medical Times* said: "The subject of medical education is a trite and hackneyed theme . . . it would seem no new aspect of the subject could be presented." (Oct. 12, 1861.)

In 1869, Rowell's American Newspaper Directory listed 40 medical journals. This list had grown by 1885 to some 400. Seventeen "homeopathic" journals enjoyed brief existences.

Medical Repository, founded in 1797, was one of the two oldest specialized periodicals founded in the United States (see Appendix I).

New England Journal of Medicine & Surgery was founded in 1812.

The two oldest, according to Dr. Mott, were the *American Journal of the Medical Sciences,* founded and edited by Dr. Isaac Hays and the *Boston Medical and Surgical Journal.*

American Journal of The Medical Sciences (1827–current) was a successor to the *Philadelphia Journal of the Medical and Physical Sciences,* founded in 1820 by Dr. Nathaniel Chapman, first president of the American Medical Association, and Professor of The Theory and Practice of Medicine, University of Pennsylvania. In 1827, Dr. Isaac Hays became the editor and the name was changed by the publisher to *The American Journal of the Medical Sciences.*

The career of Dr. Morris Fishbein (Mr. Medicine) as chief editor of the *Journal of the American Medical Association* is probably one of the most exciting in modern business journalism. From the time he took over the post in 1924, until 1940, libel suits totaling $4,500,000 had piled up against the AMA as a result of his forthright editorials. Dr. Fishbein never faltered or wavered in his editorial war on frauds and nostrums, quacks and quackery. He attacked Brinkley the Goat Gland Man, "Painless" Parker the Exodontist, Ghadiali and his "Spectro Chrome Therapy" among many others. When he stepped down as editor, JAMA had 135,000 readers, more than all the other medical journals put together, and was publishing 150 pages a week of which half was paid advertising (which not only paid the expenses of the *Journal* but of the entire AMA).

"Medicine is the only profession," Lord Bryce once remarked, "that labors incessantly to destroy the reason for its existence."

3. Mechanical Engineering Group

The Journal of the Franklin Institute, The Scientific American, and *The American Artisan and Patent Record* (1864-1875) were devoted to mechanical inventions and patents.

American Mechanics Magazine started in 1825 when the average mechanic earned a dollar for a day's work. Thomas P. Jones, Professor of Mechanics, University of Pennsylvania, founded it on the lines of the *London Mechanics Magazine.* A year later it merged with the *Journal of the Franklin Institute* (1826–current), sponsored by The Franklin Institute for the Promotion of the Mechanic Arts. Jones became editor and held the position until 1846. He served at the same time as Superintendent of Patents, United States Patent Office, and his *Journal* published patent reports and digests of mechanical and scientific progress.[2] Jones' successor was Alexander Dallas Balche, president of Girard College and later Superintendent of the United States Coast and Geodetic Survey. A long list of distinguished editors followed Balche, most of them occupying chairs at the University of Pennsylvania.

A well-known contemporary consumer magazine of science and hobbies, *Popular Mechanics,* purchased in December 1959 by the Hearst Corporation, was founded by a businesspaper publisher. Two young men, Hiram J. Kenfield, a day clerk at the old Palmer House, Chicago, and W. H. Windsor, employed by the Chicago Railways Company, pooled their capital ($600) and launched *Street Railway Review* (1891-1898). The competitor in that field was *Street Railway Journal* published by James McGraw. Windsor wanted to make a separate periodical of a department called "Mechanical Shop Kinks."

[2] Mott, *A History of American Magazines,* Vol. I, pp. 557-558.

Kenfield thought the idea was crazy. Windsor resigned and started *Popular Mechanics* in 1902. Its volume in 1958 was $8 million.

4. Educational Group

Seventy-six educational journals were listed for the years 1850 to 1865. Twenty-five of the 36 states of the Union had one or more of them, most being sponsored by state teachers organizations.

One of the earliest in the field was *American Journal of Education* (1826-1839), published in Boston. Its editor, William Russell, was a native of Glasgow, Scotland, who came to the United States at the age of twenty-one to teach public speaking at Harvard. He also taught at Andover and in other schools and lectured at teacher's institutes. Dean Mott describes Russell's *Journal* as "the first really important American magazine in the field of education.[3]

Barnard's *American Journal of Education* (1855-1882) and *The Connecticut Common School Journal* (1838——) were outstanding publications. Henry Barnard, editor of both journals, was a Yale graduate at twenty. He was trained in law, served in the Connecticut legislature, and headed the common schools of Connecticut and Rhode Island.

Another outstanding magazine in this field was Horace Mann's *Common School Journal* (1838——), published in Boston.

5. Agricultural Group

McCormack's reaper in 1831 crowned King Wheat. In 1844, the *Price Current-Grain Reporter* appeared. Mechanized processes and steam power were applied throughout industry. Farming methods were transformed. Population in the United States jumped from 5 million in 1800 to 25 million in 1850. In the same period businesspapers increased from a single paper to 49. Population jumped from 25 million in 1850 to 75 million in 1900. Businesspapers increased to 800.[4]

In 1850 the value of the United States manufactured products was $1 billion. In 1900 it was $13 billion, several times the value of agricultural products. In 1929 the value of manufactured products was $70 billion; population neared 130 million, and businesspapers had multiplied to about 1,500.

[3] *Ibid.*, p. 543.
[4] *American Newspaper Directory*, 1900 edition.

In 1793 a publication called *New-Hampden Journal: or Farmer's Weekly Museum* was founded. It survived until 1810.

In 1810 the Reverend David Wiley brought out, at Georgetown, D.C., the first agricultural magazine in the United States, called *Agricultural Museum.* The magazine lasted until 1812. In 1819 John S. Skinner, postmaster at Baltimore, purchased a weekly newspaper called *American Farmer.* It had started publication in 1807. This lasted until 1897. Its later titles included *The Farmer and Gardener, Livestock Breeder and Manager,* and *The American Farmer and Rural Register.*

One of the oldest farm journals, *The New England Farmer,* was published weekly in Boston from 1822 to 1846. Daniel Webster was a contributor. The first publisher was Thomas W. Shepard. The first editor, Thomas Green Fessenden, lined up all the agricultural societies to send him reports of their proceedings. Foremost among these was the Massachusetts Society for the Promotion of Agriculture.

Farm journals sprang up all over the country: *American Farmer* (1833), *Farmer and Planter Monthly* (1850), *Farmer's Journal* (1852), *American Cotton Planter* (1853), *Pioneer Farmer* (1853), *Practical Farmer* (1855), *Journal of Agriculture* (1856), *Northwestern Farmer* (1856), *Oregon Farmer* (1858), *American Stock Journal* (1859), *Plantation* (1860), *American Bee Journal* (1861), *Western Farmer* (1862), *Kansas Farmer* (1863), *Maryland Farmer* (1864).

A. B. and R. L. Allen, two brothers in the livestock business in Buffalo, founded *The American Agriculturist* (1842–current). It was published as a monthly in New York City, where agricultural fairs were held in that period. It was designed as a business journal for the planter as well as the farmer and claimed a circulation of 10,000. The subscription fee was a dollar a year. In 1848 it acquired Josiah Tatum's *Farmer's Cabinet and American Herd Book* (Philadelphia). In 1852 the Allens went into the farm implement business and started *The Plow* and suspended (or merged) *The Agriculturist.* Late in 1853 *The Agriculturist* was resumed as a weekly with a young agricultural chemist, Orange Judd, as co-editor. Judd's fame as a writer on scientific farming brought him an offer to become *The New York Times* agricultural editor—an offer he accepted in 1855. In 1856 he became sole owner and editor of *The Agriculturist.* The circulation had dropped to 812 and the purchase price was $226. He changed it to a monthly, put out a German edition in 1858, and in 1859 had a "sworn circulation" of 45,125. He used as subscription premiums, seed, microscopes, sewing machines, melodeons, farm implements, and fancy livestock—even pieces of the broken first Atlantic Cable. In 1864 he claimed 100,000 circulation and increased the subscription to $1.50. The advertising ratio was 15 per cent and was censored by Judd. Judd was a man of many parts—founder of the sorghum industry, president of the New York & Flushing Railroad, active as a Wesleyan alumnus. In 1883 he withdrew to go to Chicago and manage *Prairie Farmer.*

There were, of course, many horticultural and floricultural magazines published in this period, as well as forestry, horse, hog, and sheep journals.[5]

6. Metals Group

In the middle nineteenth century most bloomeries, forges, and blast furnaces converting ore into iron were located in the country because the basic fuel was charcoal. The owner of the mill ran a country store. Workers were paid in truck. In the 1850's, with high tariffs reaching even 100 per cent *ad valorem,* our crude iron production was not large enough to fill domestic needs. Foreign ore and iron were imported. In 1826 there were seven rolling mills in the Pittsburgh area. The *Pittsburgh American Manufacturer* was started in 1838. *Iron Age* was started in 1855 as a three sheet paper. *Hardware Age* was started. Ironmasters did not erect their own blast furnaces in Pittsburgh until 1859. The Civil War really inaugurated the Iron Age of American industry. Orders for rails, armor plate, cannon, shot and shell, and other items poured in from the ordnance departments.

John A. Penton started *Foundry* in Detroit in 1892. The *Metallographist* was founded in 1898 in Boston by Albert Sauveru. In 1904 it was renamed *Iron and Steel* magazine; *American Metal Market* started in New York in 1882; *Tin and Terne and The Metal World* (1891) became in 1893 *The Metal World* (Pittsburgh) and merged with *Metal Market. Aluminum World* (1894)) absorbed *Brass Founder* (1902) and *Electroplater's Review.* In 1940 these became *Metal Finishing;* in 1902 *Iron and Machinery World* was founded in Chicago by the union of *Age of Steel* (St. Louis) and *Iron and Steel* (Chicago). In 1906 it was merged with *Iron Trade Review* (1888), which had already taken over *Industrial World and Iron Worker* (Pittsburgh). In 1930 the title became *Steel.*

[5] Mott, *A History of American Magazines,* Vol. I, pp. 728-732; Vol. III.

7. Food, Tobacco, and Spirits

Quartermasters of the Union Army during the Civil War sped up the integration of the meat and packing industry. Financed by government contracts, such groups of men as Nelson Morris, Jacob Dold, and Phil Armour began to assemble all the functions of slaughtering and packing under one roof. They set up stockyards and plants to utilize waste products. *The National Provisioner,* a businesspaper for the meat-packing industry, did not materialize, however, until 1889. A lapse of 81 years exists between the start of this paper and the other leading nineteenth-century meat publication, *Butcher's and Packer's Gazette* (1808).

Baker's Helper started as a house organ of Chapman & Smith, Chicago, in 1887. H. R. Clissold bought it and made it the first journal of the baking industry.

Kansas City Packer was founded in 1893. *Chicago Canner* began in 1895.

National Provisioner moved from New York to Chicago, to become the organ of the American Meat Institute.

American Creamery started in 1888 and ended nine years later in a merger with *Produce Review* (1895-1939) which, as *American Produce Review*, split into three weeklies: *Butter and Cheese Review, Milk Review* and *Egg and Poultry Review.*

Cheese Reporter started in 1876 as part of a newspaper and is still published in Sheboygan, Wisconsin, by the local newspaper. *Macaroni & Noodle Manufacturers' Journal* (1903-1919); *American Cheesemaker* (1886-1917); *Rice Industry* (1900-1911); *Oysterman* (1902-1916); and *American Brewers' Review* (1887-1918) are some of the early trade papers that folded.

Among the leading grocery businesspapers started in the eighties are *L. J. Callahan's Monthly* of New York (1897-1908), *Spice Mill* (1878–current), *Confectioner's Journal* (1873–current), *Retail Grocers' Advocate* (1896–current), *The Butchers' Advocate* (1879–current), *International Confectioner* (1892–current), *Grocers' Review* (1891-1917), and *Grocery World* (1887-1914). In 1901 the current *Tea and Coffee Trade Journal* was established.

Tobacco Leaf (1865–current) was edited in the nineteenth century by a songwriter and cigar-maker, Edward Burke. The songwriter-impresario, Oscar Hammerstein, once edited the *United States*

Tobacco Journal (1874–current). *Cigar and Tobacco* started in 1896 and is currently published.

Early beer and wine businesspapers were *American Wine Press* (1897-1918), *Midas Criterion of the Wholesale Whiskey and Wine Market* (1885-1917), *Wine and Spirit Gazette* (1887-1905), *Wine and Spirit Bulletin* (1886-1918), and *Brewer's Journal* (1876–current).

The *American Brewer* has been published without a break since 1868 (even during Prohibition). The current editor, Robert Schwarz, is the grandson of the founder, Anton Schwarz, and the journal has always been published by the Schwarz family.

8. Railroad Group

In January, 1832, when the *American Rail-Road Journal* (now *Railway Mechanical Engineer*) started to publish, canal expansion was over. "It is the object of this Journal to record the observations and suggestions of gentlemen of experience in the construction and use of railroads here; and to afford the whole at so cheap a rate, as to be within the reach of every person taking an interest in the subject" (from the January 2, 1832, issue). The railroad by 1850 was emerging as a long-distance contender instead of just a feeder for canal and waterway traffic. When the *Railway Gazette* (later *Railway Age*) started in 1856 there were little more than 9,000 miles of railroad. In 1860 there were 20,000 miles more. The Railway Era of America was destined to make the Iron Age a great one. It is not generally known that public, rather than private, capital played the pioneering role. According to Historian Hacker, The Baltimore & Ohio, first state-chartered railroad in America, in 1828, received $500,000 from Maryland, and in 1836 got an additional $3,200,000, which Maryland raised in the English money market. Massachusetts gave the Western Railway of Massachusetts $4,300,000 which had been raised in England. States gave public lands to private railroad companies. Cities built their terminals for them. In 1850, the federal government made generous grants from the public domain to the railroad promoters. For example, as a bonus for building the Illinois Central, the promoters received generous public land grants. It took six years and cost $16,500,000 to build its 700 miles of railroad. The same promoters realized $25,000,000 from the sale of these public lands. One can begin to understand what is meant when it is said that a public utility is affected with a "public interest."

From 1868 to 1872 railroads were the biggest customer of the extractive and transformative industries and founded the fortunes of several pioneer businesspaper publishers.

De Bow, president of the Tennessee Pacific Railway, in 1850 published *De Bow's Review,* which was promoting a southwestern route to the Pacific. *The Railroad Record* in Cincinnati (1853-1873), the *Western Railroad Gazette* in Chicago (1857-1908), and the *American Railway Times* in Boston (1849-1872) all plugged for a northern railway transcontinental to link the East with California.

Coaches were transformed into sleeping cars "instantly and while the cars are in full motion" by converting four seats into a bed, and there were visions of diners and better light and heat someday. Speed, meanwhile, was the dominant theme. "Lightning runs" were twenty-five miles an hour. The engine was characterized as an "Iron Ostrich" by *Putnam's Monthly,* "outstripping horses, antelopes and the wild ass, and running neck and neck with the tornado." Accidents were numerous, but the fast trains were the most popular.

James D. B. De Bow came back to Charleston, South Carolina, in 1845, from a commercial convention presided over by John C. Calhoun in Memphis, Tennessee, with a burning idea. Late that year he showed the prospectus of the *Commercial Review of the South and West* to friends. In 1846 *De Bow's Commercial Review* made its bow. On the first page was a quotation from Carlyle: "Commerce is King." Its purpose was to exploit the industrialization of the South and Southwest which lagged behind the North.

In 1860 the magazine called on the South to secede and form a great empire including Texas, Mexico, Central America, and Cuba. Secession was followed by war. De Bow became Cotton-Purchasing Agent for the Confederacy. In 1862 the magazine suspended and, except for a single number in July 1864, did not revive until 1866. De Bow received a pardon from President Johnson for his part in the Confederacy and became president of a projected railway to the West Coast called The Tennessee & Pacific. De Bow died in 1867. In 1884 the property was transferred to the *Agricultural Review* of New York. Both periodicals came to an end that same year.

E. A. Simmons, of the Simmons-Boardman Publications, left public school in 1889 to help support his mother, and started working in business at a salary of $1.50 a week at the bargain counter of A. D. Matthews' Sons Department Store in Brooklyn. In six months he was earning $5 a week reading exchanges for the *Railway Age-Gazette* (result of the merger, in 1908, of *Railway Age and Railway Gazette*), whose president was W. H. Boardman. In 1892 he took charge of their Chicago office and got married (on $12 a week). In 1894, when he was earning $20 a week as an advertising salesman, *American Engineer* offered him $40 "with regular increases and a quarter interest at the end of ten years." He submitted this proposition to Boardman, who countered by selling Simmons fifty shares at par in *Railway Gazette* for $5,000. Simmon's bank account had only $50 in it, but he borrowed the rest and bought into the business. In 1911, when Boardman was suddenly deprived of part of his faculties, Simmons paid a reputed quarter-million dollars for his holdings.

Simmons made Samuel O. Dunn chief editor. Mr. Dunn had specialized in railway journalism as an editorial writer on the Chicago *Tribune*. He joined the staff of *Railway Age* in 1907. In 1931 editor Dunn became chairman of the board of Simmons-Boardman, who are publishers of five leading contemporary railroad businesspapers. He is a past president of the Associated Business Papers and of the National Conference of Business Paper Editors.

Simmons-Boardman Co. bought the pioneer *American Railroad Journal* in 1911 and Roy V. Wright became its editor. In 1916 the title *Railway Mechanical Engineer* was adopted. Mr. Wright, an M.E., University of Minnesota, and Dr. Eng., Stevens Institute of Technology, had worked for two midwestern railroads. He was mechanical engineer of the Pittsburgh & Lake Erie Railroad when he became editor of *American Engineer and Railroad Journal* in 1904. A former president of the American Society of Mechanical Engineers, and editor of various editions of Cyclopedias in the locomotive- and car-building fields, he was a president of the Associated Business Papers and the National Conference of Business Paper Editors.

In the seventies, the *Railway Gazette*, singlehanded, pioneered the fight for a uniform width for railroad tracks. Some tracks were five feet apart and others only three and a half feet between rails. George Westinghouse came into this famous businesspaper's editorial offices with a model of the airbrake under his arm. One of its great editors, M. N. Forney, pioneered the adoption of standard threads for bolts and nuts. Consider what these three contributions alone meant to railroad progress.

Another editor, Colonel Prout, won a ten-year fight (1893-1903) for the Isthmian Canal to be cut across Panama instead of Nicaragua. The Nicaragua project, had it been successful, would not have been large enough for a modern cruiser, let alone a battleship, to pass through.

Horace M. Swetland, like James H. McGraw, Sr., was a schoolteacher who gave up that vocation for something he thought would pay better. He sold advertising space for the American Railway Publishing Co., later becoming manager of the firm, which published *Power*, *Street Railway Journal*, and *American Journal of Railway Appliances*. James Herbert McGraw, Sr., sold subscriptions for the same company during his summer vacations from schoolteaching. Later McGraw joined the firm as a full-time subscription solicitor and then became an advertising space salesman like Swetland.

Both Swetland and McGraw became part owners of the company. McGraw disagreed with some of his other publishing partners on the question whether motor power would supplant horses on street railways. McGraw and Swetland thought it would. The other partners are long since forgotten men.

The circulation of *Street Railway Journal* was partly to veterinarians and partly to engineers. Which readership to build up? That was the question. Baltimore, on August 28, 1830, witnessed a race between Tom Thumb, first locomotive built in the United States, and a horse and buggy. The horse was the winner. Advertisers of feed, wheelbarrows, and hay pressed for a decision. It was up to the editors to denounce the electric streetcar. The firm finally split up on which way the world would go, and McGraw got the two railway journals and the composing room.

Swetland got *Power*, which back in 1880 had been called *Steam*. For a time it was *Power-Steam* but in 1892 it was again *Power*. In 1908 it absorbed the *Chicago Engineer* and became *Power and the Engineer*. It absorbed nine or ten other papers and is currently *Power*.

McGraw, Sr., envisioned the electrical era, just as his four sons who succeeded him have envisioned the air era. *Street Railway Journal* was renamed *Electric Street Railway Journal*. The senior McGraw fought for electrified street railways, employed trained electrical engineers for his editorial staffs, and bought other electrical businesspapers. Swetland had faith in the automotive field. He sold *Power* to John A. Hill and bought automotive publications. When he wrote the first textbook on the business press he was president of United Publishers Corporation.[6]

John A. Hill, a fireman on the Denver & Rio Grande Railroad, started a daily newspaper in Pueblo, Colorado, in 1885, but sold it soon afterward to go back to the railroad. His correspondence for *Locomotive Engineering* brought him to the attention of the publishers, who gave him a place on the staff and eventually the editorship. Later he sold his half interest in that paper to become publisher of *American Machinist*. Hill built a large organization, publishing, in addition to the *Machinist, Coal Age, Engineering and Mining Journal*, and *Engineering News*. He acquired Swetland's *Power*.

After Hill's death in 1916, the McGraw and Hill publishing houses joined forces and the McGraw-Hill Publishing Co. was launched, with nine strong businesspapers. *Engineering Record* and *Engineering News* were combined. Expansion took place in many industries such as food, textiles, photography, aviation, electronics. *Power* became a McGraw-Hill paper.

Dr. Kimball Minor, part owner of the New York *American*, a daily, started the pioneer railroad businesspaper, as a weekly, in 1832. He called it the *American Rail-Road Journal* and gave the town wits quite a laugh. Why not a "Turnpike Commentator" or an "Aqueduct Chronicle"? they asked. Publisher Minor saw a vision: "iron roads superseding the canals" (*American Rail-Road Journal*, Jan. 2, 1832). There were half a dozen or more railroad journals in 1832 although the 12 railroads at that time had only 200 miles of road, and nine relied on horsepower. Only three had locomotives! Some of these journals were published in New York, Boston, Philadelphia, Cincinnati, Chicago. They all fought editorially for the transcontinental railroads to the Pacific. Minor moved the *Journal* to Philadelphia in 1846, but in 1848 it returned to New York as the property of John H. Schultz. Its new editor was Henry V. Poor. Poor, on the side, started a yearly reference work, *Poor's Manual*. In 1862, Poor resigned as editor to devote full time to the *Manual*, which was destined to become an institution in industry. Schultz took over as editor until 1879.

Van Nostrand's Electric Engineering Magazine (1869-1887) was merged with the *American Rail-Road Journal* in 1887.

[6] H. M. Swetland, *Industrial Publishing*, (New York, Business Publishers Association, Inc., 1923).

9. Mining Group

In August 1896 one of the world's richest gold strikes was made in the Klondike, causing a stampede to the gold fields of Alaska. A number of mining journals nourished by gold mine advertising and news of the gold fields had sprung up in the eighties.

Ayers Annual (1880) listed 53 mining businesspapers. Many of these were investment periodicals, or newspapers of the mining fields. A few were engineering businesspapers. After the strike more appeared. *Salt Lake Mining Review* (1899–current) became *Mining and Contracting Review* in 1934. *Pacific Coast Miner* began in 1897. When it folded in 1911 it was called *Mining Magazine. Black Diamond* started in Chicago (1885–current). *Mining Record* (1880–current) is published in Denver, where it started. P. A. Leonard's *Ores and Metals* (1891-1907) was a well-known mining journal published in Denver. *Mining Industry* was started in Denver, in 1886, but it folded in 1898 and was succeeded by *Mining Reporter* (1898-1918). *Ores and Metals* merged with *Mining Reporter* in 1907. *The Mining and Scientific Press* (1860-1922) was published in San Francisco for 62 years until it was absorbed by a New York periodical. *Pacific Index*, begun in 1864, became *American Mining Index* in New York in 1865 and lasted two years. *Mining Magazine* (1853-1861), New York *Mining Record* (1877-1892), and *American Mining Gazette and Geological Magazine* (1864-1868) were also New York mining businesspapers.

Edward A. Taft started the *Chicago Mining Review* in 1866. In the nineties its name was changed to *Mining Review and Metallurgist*. It lasted until 1907. The *American Journal of Mining* started in 1866 and in 1870 became *Engineering and Mining Journal*. It absorbed and merged many mining journals. Hill Publishing Company bought it in 1906 and it has been a McGraw-Hill businesspaper since 1917. G. F. Dawson was the first editor. *Coal Mining* (1899–current) is published in Pittsburgh. Its many absorptions included *Mining Review* (Chicago), *Mining Journal* (Michigan), *Mining & Scientific Press* (California), *Coal & Iron Record, Mining & Engineering World.*

10. Labor Union Group

More than 200 magazines and newspapers and hundreds of local periodicals make up the segment know as the "labor press." Samuel

Gompers, who was President of the American Federation of Labor for over half a century, started as a cigar maker. He was the editor and founder of the *Cigar Makers' Official Journal*, a union publication begun in 1876. *The Carpenter* started in 1879. The first labor publication was probably *Journeyman's Mechanics Advocate*, founded in 1827. The *Miners' Journal* started a year or so later. *Labor's Monthly Survey* is the publication of the American Federation of Labor and *Economic Outlook* is the publication of the Congress of Industrial Organizations. In 1949 the Labor Press Association was formed, serving as a cooperative newsgathering bureau owned by 185 labor weeklies with a combined circulation close to 15 million. The greatest public service performed by the labor press is the publishing of information which the daily press in some communities sees fit to suppress.

11. Religious Group

Of the journals devoted to the business of theology the most notable were *The Catholic World* (1865–current), *Methodist Review* (1818–current), *Baptist Review* (1879–1890), *American Presbyterian Review* (1837–1870), *Episcopal Recorder* (1822–current), *Congregationalist* (formerly *Boston Recorder*, 1816–current), *Christian Examiner* (Unitarian, 1824-1869), *Lutheran Church Review* (1882-1927), *American Hebrew* (1879–current), *Philosophical Journal* (Spiritualism, 1865-1905).

Many non-denominational and non-sectarian religious periodicals flourished in the nineteenth century. Churches were losing some of their influence. The mania for bicycling was one reason given. Mott lists a number of periodicals in this period which he classifies as "Acrimonious Weeklies," engaged in criticism of other religious groups and personalities. From 1865 to 1885 religious journals increased from 350 to 650. None of these had over 10,000 circulation.

12. Legal Group

More than a hundred legal journals appeared after the Civil War but few survived more than 20 years. Pioneers were *Legal Adviser*, Chicago, *Legal Journal*, Pittsburgh, and, in Philadelphia, *American Law Register and Review* and *Legal Intelligencer*.

The American Law Review was founded in Boston in 1866. Among its editors was Oliver Wendell Holmes, Jr. In 1803 publishing headquarters was moved to St. Louis, where publication continued until the 1930's.

In 1929 it was called *U.S. Law Review* and removed to New York (quarterly, 1866-1879; monthly, 1880-1882; bi-monthly, 1883–current.)

Three other well-known law journals were published in St. Louis: *Law Journal* (1880-1907), *Legal News* (1868-1925), a weekly, and *Central Law Journal* (1874-1927). *Albany Law Journal* (1870-1908) and *Maryland Law Record* (1878-1889) were well-known businesspapers of this era.

By 1900 American magazines were highly critical of the legal profession, charging among other things, low standards of ethical practice, low levels of education, and "the snail's pace of judicial procedure." The lawyers and judges had plenty of law journals, however, serving them usefully and advocating ethical practice.

Harvard Law Review began in 1887 and other ranking law schools started law journals in this period: *The Columbia Jurist* (1885-1887), *Yale Law Journal* (1891–current), etc. Some of the journals specializing in commercial law were *Banking Law Journal* (1889–current), New York, *Commercial Law Journal* (1888–current), and *Insurance Law Journal* (1871-1938).

The most important of the case reporters was *Syllabi*, founded in 1879 by West Publishing Company, St. Paul. Other case reporting magazines were added, and in 1887 it was called *North Western Reporter*. The entire country was covered by nine publications in the "National Reporter System," including one for Federal Cases and one for Supreme Court decisions. The West Publishing Company service, greatly amplified, is current.

13. Insurance Group

The great Chicago fire was both tragedy and blessing to the insurance business in New York. The total capital of New York companies was $10 million, while their income was $40 million and their risk $1.6 billion. The Chicago fire put 57 companies out of business (one third of the New York and three fourths of the Illinois companies), with a total loss of $85 million, far in excess of their aggregate capitalization.

The Spectator, a leading insurance journal, which had started in 1868, hailed the catastrophe: it made possible higher rates and a flood of business. *New York Underwriter* led in circulation, but many insurance businesspapers flourished in dozens of key cities. Twenty founded after the Civil War lasted half a century and about thirty are published currently. Several big insurance companies published powerful house organs in the 1870's.

The oldest insurance businesspaper currently published is *American Insurance Digest & Insurance Monitor*, which took over the old *Insurance Monitor* founded in 1853. Second oldest is *Weekly Underwriter* (1859). Other old-timers still being published are *The Standard* (1872), *Insurance Index* (1870), and *Rough Notes* (1853). By 1900 there were 75 insurance journals published, 20 of them in New York City.

14. Leather Group

In 1851 *Shoe and Leather Reporter* was started. *The Harness World* (1888) merged with *Harness and Spokesman* (1884) in 1922 and was called *Spokesman and Harness World*. In 1898 *Trunks and Leather Goods* was started and is currently *Luggage and Leather Goods*. *Hide and Leather* (1890) is currently *Leather and Shoes*. *Shoe Retailer* (1898-1929) and *Shoe Trade Journal* (1893-1910) started in New York and gave up their ghosts in Boston. *Weekly Bulletin of Leather and Shoe News* began in Boston in 1896 and is currently published in Manchester, New Hampshire.

William L. Terhune canvassed the leading shoe manufacturers and jobbers of Boston's famous market, in 1882, with his dummy for a proposed trade paper, to be called *Boot and Shoe Recorder*. Like Isbon Scott, first publisher of *Housewares Review*, and Warren Platt, founder of *National Petroleum News*, Mr. Terhune was an ex-newspaper journalist. After working on several Newark papers and the *Auburn (Maine) Herald*, Terhune had become editor of the *New Hampshire Independent*. In 1870, he was manager of a family magazine, *Merry's Museum*.

Terhune's first advertising order came from Goodyear & McKay Sewing Machine Co., for one inch of space, three insertions, at a cost of $4. *Boot and Shoe Recorder* had materialized. Everit B. Terhune, son of the founder, was succeeded as publisher by his son, Everit B. Terhune II, in 1958.

15. Grain, Feed, Coal, and Ice

Grain Dealers Journal (1891) became *Grain and Feed Journals Consolidated*. *Hay Trade Journal* started in 1892 and lasted until 1929.

In the coal business, *Coal Trade Review* (1896-1937) was the first; *Black Diamond* (1885) is current; *Coal and Coke* (1894-1911); *Coal Trade Bulletin* (1898-1926) are defunct.

H. S. Rice founded *Ice and Refrigeration* in 1891.

16. Building Group

The Bricklayer, founded in 1892, had by 1917 become a professional journal for architects and was renamed *Architectural Forum.* In April 1932, Henry Luce, publisher of *Time, Life,* and *Fortune,* bought it at the suggestion of a financier, Marriner Eccles. Both men saw building as the biggest single industry in the United States. The business magazine's editorial policy was broadened to include construction and in 1950 its name was changed to *The Magazine of Building.* In 1952 it split into two periodicals: *Architectural Forum* for heavy building industry and *House and Home,* edited for home builders and architects

Brick and Clay Record, started in 1892, is published currently in Chicago. *American Builder,* established in 1879, is published currently by Simmons-Boardman for over 100,000 paid subscribers.

American Lumberman & Building Products Merchandiser started in 1873 and is published currently.

17. Hotel Group

The first hotel periodicals were daily reporters, in the 1880's, but later hotel journals were issued weekly and monthly. *Chef and Steward* started in Chicago in 1891 and lasted for 29 years. *Hotel Monthly* began in 1893 in Chicago. *Caterer and Hotel Proprietor's Gazette* started in New York in 1893 and *Hotel Bulletin* in 1900. Today there are 35 or more businesspapers serving the group known as "Hotels, Motels, Tourist Courts, Clubs, and Resorts."

Destined to play a lead role for "Mine Host" in modern business journalism was Edward H. Ahrens, graduate of the A. W. Shaw Company, who founded The Ahrens Publishing Company in 1922. He was associated with Shaw for 12 years.

Undaunted by 35 competitors in the hotel publishing field at the time, Ahrens started *Hotel Management* in a small office in New York with two second-hand desks and a telephone. Three years later the company purchased a companion businesspaper, *Restaurant Management.*

In 1928 *Hotel World* (founded in 1875 by Henry J. Bohn in the West) was acquired. In 1930 its Eastern counterpart, *National Hotel Review,* was also acquired. These two periodicals were combined in 1931 as *Hotel World-Review.* The same year *Gehring Hotel Directory* was acquired, and in 1935 the name was changed to *Travel America. Restaurant Equipment Dealer* was successfully started in 1948 and *Frozen Food Age* (1952) was purchased in 1953. Don Nichols assumed direction as publisher on the death of Ahrens in 1947.

18. Textile Group

As late as 1830 household woolen production was greater than factory production in the United States, and did not become really negligible until 1870. Cotton textiles adopted the factory system earlier but it was about 1845 before it was going strong. Sam Slater used automatic machinery in 1791 at Pawtucket, Rhode Island, for spinning yarn (with child labor), but weaving was done by the parents in their own cottages. Wage payments were in truck (groceries) from the company-owned stores. At Waltham, Massachussets, in 1815, the first industrial community for cotton textiles started with automatic weaving and spinning machinery; the first complete factory system in our country. By 1868, when *Manufacturer's Review* and *Industrial Record* started, textiles had already piled up quite an industrial record. Textiles had become the backbone of the dry goods store, which in 1846 began reading its own businesspaper, *United States Economist and Dry Goods Reporter,* founded by W. B. Burroughs and Robert Boyd. Later it was called *Dry Goods Reporter & Commercial Glance.* Then *Dry Goods Economist* and now *Department Store Economist.* The National Retail Dry Goods Association was organized in the editor's office in 1911. William M. Thackeray, in a letter to Leigh Hunt, described a copy of the *Dry Goods Reporter* which he came across on a coffeehouse table in Glasgow.

Textile World was founded in Boston in 1888 by Henry G. Lord and Curtis Gould, as a monthly. In 1896 it absorbed *Textile Manufacturers' Review,* founded in 1868; then *Textile Manufacturers' Journal* (1894-1915). In 1915 it became a weekly and moved to New York. It was sold in 1928 to McGraw-Hill. Other veterans of the textile industry are *Textile Advance News* (1888-1920), *American Wool and Cotton Reporter* (1887–current), *Fibre and Fabric* (1885–current), *Textile American* (1904–current), *American Knit Goods*

Review (1898-1901), *Lace Maker* (1903-12), *Textile Colorist* (1879-1948), *Dyestuffs* (1898–current), *Cotton* (1899-1928), *Cotton Gin* (1889–current), *Cotton Trade Journal* (1901–current).

Chicago Apparel Gazette, founded in 1896, became *Men's Wear* in 1924. *Clothiers' and Haberdashers' Weekly,* begun in 1892, suspended in 1901. *American Furrier,* started in 1904 in New York, lasted 32 years.

19. Financial Group

In finance, one of the most notable businesspapers was *Thompson's Bank Note and Commercial Reporter,* founded in 1836. Later it was called *Thompson's American Bank Report* and in 1877 became *The American Banker.* Judge Thompson, the editor, laid the foundation of the current business magazine of banking by issuing a daily bulletin on rates of currency exchange. In 1863 he was the first man in New York to organize a national bank, the First National Bank, and in 1877 he founded the Chase National Bank, now the world's largest. Salmon P. Chase, after whom it was named, was Editor Thompson's close friend and co-worker. Charles Dow and Edward Jones founded *The Wall Street Journal* in 1882.

There were two other veteran financial businesspapers: *Banker's Magazine* and *Commercial and Financial Chronicle.* The latter was founded in 1865 by William B. Dana. It merged other financial periodicals over the years and in 1928 four of its supplements were spun off into separate periodicals: *Bank and Quotation Record, Railway Earnings Record* (monthly), *Railway and Industrial Compendium,* and *Municipal Compendium* (semi-annual).

Bradstreet's began as a semi-weekly in 1879, changed to a weekly in 1880, and in 1893 merged with *Dun's Review.* It was *Dun and Bradstreet's Review* from 1933 to 1936 and is currently *Dun's Review and Modern Industry.* Robert Graham Dun started *Dun's Review* as the house organ of his credit agency in 1893.

Rand, McNally & Company started *Bankers' Monthly* in 1884 in Chicago.

Banker and Tradesman was founded in Boston in 1872. In Chicago in 1895 *Banker's Encyclopedia* was started.

Bankers Magazine (1846-1849) was a leader in the field during its brief life. It was founded by I. Smith Homans in a period when

American currency was highly confused by the issuance of State bank notes.

Instantaneous distribution of news "without fear or favor" by means of an electric ticker was the revolutionary service introduced by the famous financial businesspaper, *The Wall Street Journal,* in 1897. Fifteen years before, in 1882, Charles H. Dow and Edward D. Jones, reporters for Kiernan News Agency, the leading financial news organization in Wall Street, set up their own agency, Dow, Jones & Co. They began publishing "Customers' Afternoon Letters" with a dozen subscribers. On July 8, 1889, Volume I, Number I of *The Wall Street Journal* appeared[7] under the Dow, Jones sponsorship. When its famous editor and publisher, Clarence W. Barron, who had bought *The Wall Street Journal* in 1902, died in 1928, his own tickers reeled off the news of his demise in 140 cities in the United States and Canada and in its Pacific Coast edition.

In addition to the New York paper, there is the *Philadelphia Financial Journal* and *Boston News Bureau,* owned by the same organization. The subscription rate to *The Wall Street Journal* is $18 a year. Dow Jones news ticker service costs stockholders, financiers, and other decision-making, policy-forming business executives $100 a month ($200 on Pacific Coast) in cities where Dow-Jones offices are located. This instantaneous news is gathered by special correspondents in 123 of the world's cities and is the largest of all news organizations serving news to business.

20. Foreign-Language Business Press

Many businesspapers are published for the export and import trade. The Business Publishers International Corp., through its affiliation with the Chilton Company and McGraw-Hill, publishes businesspapers in Spanish and Portuguese for Middle and South America. *American Exporter,* founded in 1877, is one of the largest export businesspapers. Its "Industrial Supplement" carries messages in English and Spanish. Claiming "a New Industrial Revolution, second in importance to the Industrial Revolution in 18th century England," the *American Exporter* published a brochure in 1943, showing the rapid industrialization of agriculture and pastoral countries such as

[7] A "Wall Street Journal," published as a weekly from 1852 to 1875 by John Hillyer, at 14 William Street, New York, is unrelated to the present journal.

Australia, New Zealand, India, South Africa, Middle and South America.

21. Automotive Group

The daily press had dubbed the automobile "horseless carriage," "motorcycle," "motor carriage," and "automobile vehicle." In 1895 the *Horseless Age* appeared and was destined to last until 1916. The year of its demise was the same year that saw the last issue of *Carriage Dealers' Journal* (1890-1916), organ of a national association. *The Motorcycle* also appeared in 1895 and published until 1900. *Automobile* (1899–current) was started in New York by M. G. Gillette and soon became a leading periodical of the field. Its name in 1902 was *Automotive Industries* and it was issued weekly. It merged two other auto journals, *Motor Vehicle Review* (1899-1902) and *Automobile Magazine* (1899-1907). *Auto Review* (1899-1908) Chicago, became *Motor Way* in 1905.

James Artman, head of the Trade Publishing Co., founded one of the oldest automobile businesspapers, originally called *Cycle Trade Journal,* in June 1896. In the next three years he was bitten by doubts whether the bicycle would be a serious rival of the horseless carriage in the twentieth century. In 1899, he was wisely calling his paper, *Cycle and Automobile Trade Journal.* That same year two men joined forces with Artman. They were George H. Buzby and C. A. Musselman. In 1901 the firm name was changed to Trade Advertising and Publishing Co., with Artman as president, Buzby as vice president, and Musselman as secretary-treasurer.

In 1907 the Chilton Printing Co., which printed the *Cycle and Automobile Trade Journal,* was purchased and the publishers took the name of Chilton for their company. It was not learned until 1913 where the name came from. It seems the owners of the Chilton Printing Co., Mr. Deputy and Mr. McFarlan, did not like each other's names, so they got a list of the families who came over on the *Mayflower.* One of the names was Chilton. They liked it. The source of the name was discovered when a Senator Chilton of North Carolina decided to look up his family tree. In December 1923 the Chilton Co., of Philadelphia and the Class Journal Co., of New York, which it already owned, were merged by the United Publishers Corp., who took over all the capital stock.

Messrs. Artman and Buzby retired from active business. H. M.

Swetland, founder of the Class Journal Co., remained as president of U.P.C. A. B. Swetland became vice-president of the Chilton Co. and remained as manager of the Class Journal Co. Upon the death of H. M. Swetland in 1924, C. A. Musselman became president and general manager of the subsidiary, Chilton Class Journal Co., with Joseph S. Hildreth as vice president. Some years later, the U.P.C., for purposes of simplification of title, changed its name to Chilton Co. and the Class Journal subsidiary became the automotive division of U.P.C. Mr. Hildreth headed up this division with Julian Chase and G. Carroll Buzby as vice presidents. In addition to publishing businesspapers in the steel, automotive, aviation, insurance, and consumers' goods industries, Chilton Co. own an equal interest with McGraw-Hill in Business Publishers International Corp., which publishers overseas editions.

In 1899 The *Cycle Age* publishers started *Motor Age* (1899–current), absorbing *Cycle Age* in 1902. *Cycle Track Journal* (1896-1940) became *Cycle and Automobile Trade Journal* in 1899 and *Automobile Trade Journal* (1912-1940).

Julian Chase was associated with the automotive industries from the turn of the century. Graduating from Brown in 1899, he engaged in designing, building, and selling automobiles as background for his first editorship, in 1906, of an automotive and marine businesspaper. In 1915 he was managing editor and part owner of *Horseless Age*, first automobile publication in this country, founded in 1895.

In 1899, the *Automobile and Motor Review* was started. In 1903, the *Automobile Horseless Age* was absorbed, and *Automotive Industries* became the foremost of Chilton businesspapers. Mr. Chase was on the War Department's General Staff, in 1918, organizing training centers for transport drivers. In 1933 he became directing editor of all Chilton automotive papers, which include *Automobile Trade Journal*, descendant of *Cycle Trade Journal* (1896). The "Cycle" was not dropped from the title until 1912.

William Randolph Hearst's first magazine was *Motor* (1903–current) inspired by seeing a copy of *Car* in London. For many years *Motor* was a consumer magazine concerned with races, tours, and motor shows. Currently it is described as "The How-To Magazine of Sales and Service for Dealers and Repair Shops," with a circulation of over 96,000.

22. Oil and Gas Group

The turbulent years of the first great oil rush at Titusville in the late 1850's are portrayed in a book by Miss Hildegarde Dolson.[8]

Professor Benjamin Silliman of Yale tested a greasy substance seeping from the ground near Titusville, Pennsylvania, and proclaimed that a lamp burning the substance gave as good light as anything else. The Seneca Indians had used the stuff as war paint and liniment; the medicine showmen peddled "Seneca Oil" for every known ailment. Colonel Edwin L. Drake drilled for it, and on August 28, 1859, the first "gusher" came in.

"Thus," says Samuel T. Williamson, in reviewing the Dolson book, "began an industry which sparked wars and the automotive and aviation ages, displaced the iron horse and thousands of coal miners, revolutionized home heating, paved roads, killed insects, aided low-calorie diets, brought us artificial rubber and fabrics and other synthetics, and turned the Middle East upside down and inside out."[9]

Among Miss Dolson's anecdotes is one of a thundering preacher who objected to oil drilling:

> *"He put that oil in the bowels of the earth to heat the fires of Hell. Would you thwart the Almighty and let sinners go unpunished?"*

Oil City, Pennsylvania, became a boom city of the 1860's. Here *Petroleum Monthly* started publication in 1870, to last two years, succeeded by *Monthly Petroleum Trade Report* (1873-1882) and *Oil City Derrick* (1871–current), now a local daily. *Petroleum Age* (1881-1888) was published in Bradford, Pennsylvania. *Harper's Monthly* (April, 1865) described Oil Creek, Pennsylvania, as "the richest oil producing region on earth."

In 1883 *Water-Gas Journal* started publication in New York, changed to *Progressive Age-Gas, Electricity, Water* in 1884, and served the gas, water, and electric utilities. In 1912 it became *Gas Age* and absorbed *Gas Record* of Chicago (1912-1921). In 1921 it became *Gas Age-Record*. Now *Gas Age*, it is published in New York by the Moore Publishing Company. It's first editor was E. C. Brown.

[8] Hildegarde Dolson, *The Great Oildorado* (New York, Random House, Inc., 1959).

[9] Samuel T. Williamson, "It All Began in Titusville," book review in *The New York Times*, February 22, 1959.

In the nineties there was an important business periodical called the *American Gas Light Journal,* published in New York by A. M. Callender for a decade. In 1897 *Petroleum Gazette* began publication in Titusville, Pennsylvania, and moved to Pittsburgh in 1918, where it was renamed *Along The Way. Light, Heat and Power* started in 1885 and lasted until 1894. *Acetylene Journal* started in Chicago (1899–current). *Compressed Air Magazine* started in 1896 and is currently published. *Light* (1901) became *Light, Heat and Power* in 1904 and, in 1910, *Gas Industry. Oil Investors Journal* started in Beaumont, Texas, in 1902; in 1910 the title changed to *Oil and Gas Journal,* with headquarters in Tulsa, Oklahoma, where it is currently published.

A twenty-five-year-old newspaper reporter, Warren C. Platt, in 1909, impressed by the antitrust suit against Standard Oil, started *National Petroleum News* in Cleveland by borrowing on his $2,500-insurance policy and "from a few oil friends." He became the crusader for the "Independents"—little oil men who were being forced out—when the government intervened under the power of the Sherman Act.

Platt was publisher, editor, advertising man, and circulation manager. He attacked John D. Rockefeller in his editorials and, when the Oil Trust was dissolved into more than thirty independent companies in 1911, *National Petroleum News* was on the map.

Throughout Platt's career as a crusading businesspaper editor, the businesspaper launched vigorous editorial campaigns, warned the readers of dangers, interpreted new developments, and served as "reporter and teacher, communicator and industry conscience."[10]

Approaching seventy, Platt sold NPN and his other publications to McGraw-Hill, on April 1, 1953, and the periodical was moved from Cleveland to New York.

23. Electrical Group

In April 1880, the *American Journal of Science* published a report by two physics professors who had visited the Wizard of Menlo Park. They had tested a light bulb perfected two years earlier by Edison and had found that it worked. They predicted the success of electric light. A story in *The New York Sun* in 1878, when Edison perfected the light bulb, told of the "panic in gas securities." In 1883

[10] *National Petroleum News,* Fiftieth Anniversary Issue, Feb. 1959, p. 90.

The New York Sun published an article stating that electric lighting was a commercial failure. *Electrical World* the same year ran a news item about the installation of 200 Edison Lamps in the offices of *The New York Sun.*

Nothing, except the talking machine, so stirred the nineteenth-century imagination as the electric light bulb. Seven years previous to the bulb, *Scientific American* (XXIX 352, Dec. 6, 1873) was publishing stories about the work being done on the electric dynamo by Siemens (German), Wheatstone (British), and Weston (American). It was the general belief that electric power could never be made cheap enough to compete with steam power.

The dynamo articles, however, inspired the creation of a dozen or more electrical businesspapers. Three leaders were *Electrical World, Electrical Engineer,* and *Electrical Review.*

Electrical World was founded January 6, 1883, by. W. J. Johnston, publisher of *The Operator* (1874-1885), a local telegrapher's periodical. He called it *Operator and Electrical World.* In April he separated it into two periodicals, and in 1885 he merged them again. In the years that followed, he merged half a dozen other periodicals. One was *American Electrician* (1882-1899) whose editor was F. L. Pope. In 1884 it was *Electrician and Electrical Engineer.* In 1888 when it merged with *Electrical World,* it was *Electrical Engineer.* W. D. Weaver, a former editor of *Electrical World,* gained world fame as editor of *Electrical Engineer.*

T. C. Martin succeeded Johnston as second editor (1889-1909); Weaver succeeded Martin as third editor in 1909.

Electrical World's editor in 1944, Samuel Baker Williams, had the distinction of being elected president of the Illuminating Engineering Society. He also served as Chairman of the New York Business Paper Editors in 1941.

Electrical Review started in 1882 as *Review of Telegraph and Telephone.* From 1883 to 1921 it was *Electrical Review;* from 1922 to 1931 it was *Industrial Engineering;* from 1931 to 1932 it was *Maintenance Engineering;* in 1928 McGraw-Hill bought *Factory* and issued *Factory Management and Maintenance.* (McGraw-Hill lists 1891 as founding date.) One of its great editors was Charles W. Price (1891-1921); another editor, Fred Feiker, became Dean of the School of Engineering, George Washington University. Another noted editor, L. S. Morrow, a former president of the National Conference of Business Paper Editors, serves currently as consultant on the periodical.

Journal of Electricity (1895–current) started in San Francisco. *Electrical Industries* started in December 1889. It gained national prominence in 1893, as a "World's Fair Supplement."

Electrician and Mechanic (1890-1915) represented a merger of several periodicals; *Electric Power* (1889-1896) was started in New York to promote power transmission; *Electricity* (1891-1906) started in Chicago but was moved to New York.

24. Aviation Group

Aeronautics (1893-1894) was the pioneer aviation trade journal, published by M. N. Forney, publisher of *American Engineering and Railroad Journal.* The next was *Aeronautical World* (1902-1903). The army journals in 1900 were stressing the military importance of aviation. *Electricity* wrote: "Few persons have confidence in any form of flying machine."

The author, on a visit with other businesspaper editors to the Smithsonian Institution in Washington several years ago, learned from the curator of the Wright and Langley collection that Langley had a better flying machine than the Wright Brothers and a better motor. Sam Langley was Curator of the Institution in 1891. In a paper that year he declared that man could fly. A mechanic's failure to connect a part on the launching pad brought Langley's 1903 attempt at flight to failure. Later the same year the Wright Brothers successfully flew at Kitty Hawk, but it was 1916 before businesspaper publishers began to take the "stunt" seriously.

The oldest business paper currently published in the field is McGraw-Hill's *Aviation Week*, established in 1916 and reaching over 63,000 paid subscribers in engineering and scientific management.

The publishing firm of Conover-Mast has played a lead role in the development of the aviation business press. Harvey Conover and Burdette P. Mast, Sr., entered the businesspaper field as partners in 1928, publishing that year the first issue of *Mill & Foundry*, one of the great businesspapers of the world. The men were only a year apart in age. Conover was born in Chicago in 1892; Mast in Plainview, Nebraska, a year earlier. In World War I, Conover was a fighter pilot, winning the *Croix De Guerre*, Distinguished Service Cross, and the Purple Heart.

Mast joined the businesspaper publishing house of H. P. Gould Co.,

Chicago, in 1915, leaving there in 1925 to join Engineering Magazine Company as vice president and Western manager.

In 1919, Conover joined the businesspaper publishing firm of A. W. Shaw, Chicago, publishers of *System* and *Factory*. From 1921 to 1927 he was successively Western manager and vice president and, when Mast joined as vice president, president of the company. In 1927 the company was sold to McGraw-Hill and Conover-Mast Publications, Inc., was founded.

In World War II, Harvey Conover went to England at the request of the War Production Board and the British Ministry of Production to work with Oliver Lyttelton, British Minister of Production, in promoting the exchange of war production information and technics between United States and British war industries.

In late 1944 and early 1945 he covered the Southwest Pacific theater under the sponsorship of the Naval Air Service, visiting advance aircraft air strips, and service bases, aircraft carriers, and service ships for the purpose of obtaining information on the work of the aviation ground and operating forces, later published in *Space/Aeronautics Magazine*, and given world-wide distribution by the Navy.

In 1948, Mr. Conover was sent to Germany by the Air Force to assemble facts covering the operation of the Berlin Airlift. These facts were later published in *Space/Aeronautics Magazine.*

Mr. Conover was a director of National Business Publications, Inc., a member of The Press Club, and an associate director of National Industrial Advertisers Association.

Harvey Conover remained president of Conover-Mast Publications from 1928 until his disappearance at sea in 1958. En route from Key West to Miami after a two-week holiday cruise on his prize-winning yawl, *Revonoc*, he was overtaken by a storm and perished with his wife, his son, Lawrence, and daughter-in-law, Lori Conover, in January of that year.

Aviation Maintenance was born in 1943, later changed to *Aviation Age*, and now known as *Space/Aeronautics.*

Business/Commercial Aviation, was started in January, 1958. The present number of Conover-Mast publications is nine—eight magazines and an industrial buying directory.

Western Aviation started publishing in Los Angeles in 1925.

Flight Magazine commenced publication in Dallas, Texas, in 1934.

One of the oldest names in United States aviation businesspaper publishing, *American Aviation* (founded in 1937) was changed in April 1959 to *Airlift.* To its more than 46,000 readers, of which nearly 38,000 are paid subscribers, it is the top authority on world air transportation. Wayne W. Parrish, president and publisher of American Aviation Publications, also publishes *Air Cargo, Armed Forces Management,* and *Missiles & Rockets.* An Italian version of the latter, *Missili E. Razzi,* began publication in Milan, Italy, in 1959, under the direction of the publisher, Dr. Giuseppe Stifani. It will be a monthly selection of articles from the weekly editions of *Missiles & Rockets.*

An early entrant in the field which is now described as an $11 billion market was *Aeronautical Engineering Review,* begun in 1934 by the Institute of the Aeronautical Sciences of New York. *Air Facts* started in 1938.

In August 1957, the American Rocket Society established *Astronautics,* to cover the guided missile and rocket field, which grew from a $21 million research effort to a $2 billion industry in six years. This Society started *Jet Propulsion* in 1930.

25. Printing, Publishing, Advertising Group

After the Civil War many printers' journals were born. R. S. Menamin started *Printers' Circular* (1866-1890) in Philadelphia, and, in Cleveland, *The Printing Gazette* (1866-1875) offered some competition. San Francisco had *Pacific Printer* (1877-1891).

The Inland Printer, founded in 1883, and the *American Printer,* founded in 1885 and later called *American Printer and Lithographer* were merged in 1958 as *The Inland and American Printer and Lithographer.*

H. Craig Dare started *Newspaperdom* (1888-1925). In 1925, James W. Brown, publisher of *Editor & Publisher,* purchased and absorbed it.

Editor & Publisher started as *The Journalist* in 1884, absorbed *Fourth Estate* in 1894.

The Journalist, founded in 1884, was the first businesspaper to gain a foothold in the field of United States journalism. In 1907 it was purchased from its founders and the name changed to *Editor & Publisher.* It became the leading professional service paper edited for newspapers. In 1912 the late James Wright Brown, Sr., purchased a controlling interest. In 1925 he purchased *Newspaperdom,* which had started in 1888, and *Advertising*. Both papers were consolidated with *Editor & Publisher*. *The Fourth Estate*, founded in 1894, was purchased and merged a year later.

Issued weekly, *Editor & Publisher* today specializes in serving the newspaper field in all its phases. A monthly section, Equipment Review, is devoted to the mechanics of newspaper production.

James Wright Brown, Sr., died in 1958. He was 85. A stout fighter for the loftiest principles of the free press, he once said: "Publicity is a blatant fraud upon the public, and the publicity agent commits an outrage when he colors the news to suit his client's wishes."

Two sons survive, Robert U. Brown, publisher, and James W. Brown, Jr., general manager of *Editor & Publisher*.

The *Editor & Publisher*, in 1912, advocated uniform sworn, audited statements of newspaper circulation. In October of the same year the Bourne law was passed, establishing the practice of publishing semi-annual statements of ownership and circulation in newspapers. This practice is now required, under the postal regulations, of all periodical publishers.

George Presbury Rowell established *Advertisers Gazette* in 1888. The *Gazette* changed its name in 1891 to the *American Newspaper Reporter*, which functioned chiefly as a house organ for Mr. Rowell's advertising agency business. This journal merged with N. W. Ayer's house organ, *Printers' Ink*, which, for more than half a century was the familiar pocket-size bible of the advertising profession.

The editorial content of *Printers' Ink*, Rowell's new name for the publication, was designed "to serve, without fear or favor," the best interests of the advertising profession and the men who used advertising to promote their business interests. Its publishers describe it today as "an open forum of interchange of method and experience among business concerns, together with editorial guidance on moving merchandise more effectively from factory to consumer." Many papers were launched in imitation of *Printers' Ink*, but few survived. The same editorial formula, however, adopted by businesspapers in other branches of industry helped those papers to survive the decades.

John Irving Romer (editor in 1908 and later president) was stirred by the epidemic of fraudulent advertising. He engaged the services of a well-known corporation lawyer, Harry D. Nims who drew up a *Printers' Ink* Model Statute on false advertising. Romer began to plug this statute in his editorials and eventually put it over. Today, 25 or more states have incorporated the *Printers' Ink* Statute into their laws. Enforcement of this statute by district attorneys and Better Business Bureaus has saved literally millions of dollars a year previously lost by the public through fake advertising.

In 1919, *Printers' Ink Monthly* was started, to deal with "human interest phases" of marketing, employing what the promotion manager called "a dramatic format," the larger page size. Twenty-three years later, in 1942, the familiar pocket-size weekly disappeared and *Printers' Ink* was issued every week in regular magazine size, combining both publications.

Printers' Ink, in 1957, was sold to Vision, Inc., by Richard W. Lawrence, who had been Romer's partner. William E. Barlow, head of *Vision,* became president, and Lawrence, board chairman of *Printers' Ink.*

In 1959 *Printers' Ink* absorbed *Tide,* which had also passed through many hands in its 38 year career as a competitor of P.I. *Tide* started as a house organ for Time, Inc., in 1921. It was sold to Raymond Rubicam, advertising man, in 1947, for a reported $10,000. Rubicam sold the majority interest to the staff members a year later. In 1951 *Tide* was bought by Magazines of Industry, Inc., and later by Billboard Publishing Company, which in 1956 sold the periodical to Bill Bros. Publishing Company. Bill Bros., according to a story in *Advertising Age*[11] got $75,000 for it.

26. Consumer Goods Group

Even to mention only the oldest periodical in each subdivision of this vast group would require more space than is available. Hundreds of specialized businesspapers served the consumer goods fields in the latter half of the nineteenth century. Publishing centers were New York, Philadelphia, Boston, Chicago, and St. Louis. Many of these trade journals spanned a decade before they folded. Some are current. By studying the list in Appendix I the geometrical progression of the consumer goods business press after 1850 will be noted.

A veteran publisher in the consumer goods field was Edmund W. Fairchild, who started in business as a grocery and yeast salesman in Chicago during the nineties. On the side he picked up news items for a friend who ran a grocery trade paper. In this way Fairchild became acquainted with the printer of this grocery paper. One

[11] *Advertising Age,* Feb. 23, 1959.

day the printer found himself the owner of an apparel trade paper he printed, called *Chicago Herald Gazette;* the owner, John B. Waldo, could not pay his printing bills. He promptly sold the *Gazette* to Fairchild. The name was changed to *Chicago Apparel Gazette,* and in 1890 Fairchild entered the businesspaper field as a publisher with his brother, Louis. In 1896 an eastern edition was issued as *Men's Wear* and soon the western edition adopted the same name. *Men's Wear* has since become one of the apparel industry's leading businesspapers.

At the Chicago World's Fair in 1892, Fairchild distributed a mimeographed daily news bulletin for visiting textile buyers. In the Panic of 1893 this news sheet carried the only national news in Chicago. First called the *Daily Trade Record,* its title was changed to *Daily News Record.*

During the great ladies' garment strike in New York, in 1910, the *Daily News Record* published a special page covering news of union attempts to organize that industry. Special reprints of this page were distributed free in the garment center. Out of these daily pages *Women's Wear Daily* evolved in 1910.

In 1929, *Retailing-Executive,* a section of *Women's Wear Daily,* was started as a weekly (suspended in 1941) and in 1931 *Retailing-Home Furnishings* commenced publication. It is now called *Home Furnishings Daily* and leads all periodicals in the United States (1958) in volume of advertising pages. Other Fairchild periodicals are *Footwear News, Supermarket News,* and *Electronic News.* Edmund Fairchild died in 1949 and Louis in 1950. Edmund's son, Louis, was president in 1958, and the senior Louis Fairchild's son, Edgar, was vice president and treasurer. The Fairchilds spend $4 million a year on 405 correspondents and stringers, on a network of 25 United States and seven foreign news bureaus, and on their Associated Press franchise.

On every floor of the 12-story Fairchild Building on 12th Street in New York City there hangs Founder Edmund Waldo Fairchild's motto:

"Our salvation depends on printing the news."

During the 57 years of his publishing life, to the time of his death, important advertisers who tried, whether by dire threat or sweet promise, to get "EW" to kill a news story because it might hurt a man, a company, or an industry, got a stock answer: The situation is sad. We don't want to hurt anyone or anything. If the story is true it would be unfair to the subscribers to withhold it. The story goes in.

Some advertisers canceled, but they always came back. They needed the Fairchild Publications more than "EW" needed them.

Currently, Fairchild Publications gross $20 million annually with three daily trade newspapers, three weeklies, and a semi-monthly magazine (*Men's Wear*). The firm employs 1,000 people in the New York offices.[12]

No editorial opinion is expressed in Fairchild businesspapers. "Let the reader make his own decisions," they say. There is no editorial page. Editors are simply senior reporters who express editorial opinion in the weight given to a news story, the size, location, and position on the page of the story, the size of the headline, and, perhaps, in the selection of the people interviewed on a current problem or controversy. Columnists are employed who express their own opinions with the sanction of the publishers.

Another veteran multiple-publisher in the consumer goods field was Andrew J. Haire, descendant of three generations of dry goods merchants. Fifty years earlier his father had operated one of the first chains of stores (four units) in Connecticut. Eighteen years later, Mr. Haire's son, A. P., started the Haire Publishing Co. A. P. Haire died in 1920. Andrew J. Haire who had joined A. P., acquired and started a number of businesspapers in the succeeding three decades. Many were consolidated. The company currently publishes 11 monthlies and one quarterly. Andrew J. Haire, on his death in 1956, was succeeded by his sons, Thomas B. Haire (as president) and Andrew J. Haire, Jr. (as vice president and treasurer). Executive vice president is John J. Whelan, oldest employe in the firm.

The three oldest Haire periodicals are *Crockery & Glass Journal* (1874), *Furniture Retailer*, formerly *Decorative Furnisher* (1878), and *Housewares Review* (1892), each representing several mergers. Arthur I. Mellin was Haire's senior editor. He left Textile World in 1921 to join the company. He was editor of *Notion & Novelty Review* and secretary of the National Notion Association. He retired in 1959.

Isbon B. Scott, who died at the age of ninety in August 1944, had served on the *U.S.S. Constitution* as a boy. As a young man he worked on the old *New York Post*. He joined Clifford & Lawton, a business-

[12] See "The Fairchilds of 12th Street," *Printers' Ink*, Jan. 23, 1959, pp. 52-54.

paper publishing house, in 1891. Under the name Clifford, Scott & Lawton, this firm published the *Upholsterer, Wall Paper News,* and *Shoe & Leather Review.* In 1892, Scott sold out his interest and started *House Furnishing Review* in Philadelphia as an independent venture. At that time "house furnishing goods" was scattered on every floor of a department store. To 75 department store owners of that era whom he had contacted, Scott promised that he would cover the entire field for news and new products if they would put all the miscellaneous "house furnishing" merchandise on one floor under one buyer and subscribe to his magazine. Thus was born the housewares department, which now flourishes in thousands of department stores, supermarkets, and other types of outlets. In 1909, Scott sold *House Furnishing Review* to the Trade Magazine Association. In 1927 it was acquired by Simmons-Boardman Co., who sold it, in 1932, to the Haire organization. Several years later the name was changed to *Housewares Review.*

27. Miscellaneous

William O. Allison founded *Oil, Paint and Drug Reporter* (1871–current) and *The Painters' Magazine* (1874-1933).

A manufacturer of caskets, H. E. Taylor, founded *Sunnyside* in 1871 in New York, as a free house organ. A newspaperman, Frank H. Chase, took it over several years later and made a trade journal out of it. In 1914 a journal called *Casket,* founded in 1876 by Albert H. Nordlinger in Rochester, and published by his widow and stepson, Simeon Wile, until 1914, was placed under the same editorship as *Sunnyside.* In 1925 they were merged as *Casket and Sunnyside.*

India Rubber World was founded in New York in 1889 by Arthur Clemens Pearson, who retired as editor and publisher in 1928. *India Rubber Review* of Akron, Ohio, was moved to Chicago and became *Tire Review* in 1934.

Glass and Pottery World (1893) merged with another periodical and is now *Pottery and Glass Salesman.*

Box-Maker (1892-1917), *Shears* (1892–current), *Barrel and Box* (1895) later *Barrel, Box and Packages,* absorbing *Packages* (1898-1929), and *National Coopers Journal* (1885–current) were all veterans in the packaging trade.

Humphrey's Journal of Photography (1850-1870) began as *The Daguerrian Journal.*

Pen and Pencil started in Cincinnati in 1853 and lasted a year.

Western Art Journal, edited by W. P. Strickland, Cincinnati, started in 1855 and lasted a year.

One early horizontal businesspaper that has survived is the current *Manufacturers' Record,* published in Atlanta since 1882.

Henry Bridgman, apothecary and druggist, in 1857 founded and edited the *Druggists Circular and Chemical Gazette.* He was a courageous enemy of nostrums, adulteration, and quackeries. The *Circular* published annual trade directories for forty years.

The *American Miller* (1873–current), an amalgamation of eight other milling businesspapers, is the oldest in that industry, founded by Samuel S. Chisholm in Chicago. Its circulation is international.

The *U.S. Army and Navy Journal and Gazette of the Regular Volunteer Forces,* like its name, has had a long record of service in a field which some regard as a business and others as a profession. Founded in 1863, it became *Gazette of the Land, Sea and Air* in 1926, and today is the *Army and Navy Journal.* A young soldier who fought with "War-is-hell" Sherman, Captain William C. Church, was the first editor and co-owner with Silas Casey. Church and his brother Francis, also an owner, were sons of a Baptist preacher, the Reverend Pharcellus Church, who ran a sectarian newspaper, New York *Chronicle.*

CHAPTER VII

ORIGINS AND GROWTH OF WORLD BUSINESS JOURNALISM

1. First Great Businesspaper Publisher

Neues Zeitungen, "News Tidings" of the House of Fugger, was a business journal well known to merchants during the fifteenth and sixteenth centuries. The mercantile House of Fugger, at its peak, lavishly supplied the exchequer of the Holy Roman Empire, shaped the policies of the Hapsburgs, financed foreign kings, worked intimately with princes and popes, owned and operated mines, banks, chain stores, and its own business news service. In a world without multiple printing or electrical communication, the Fuggers devised an elaborate chain news letter system, organized their own news-gathering services, and kept their world-wide clientele remarkably well informed on trade and politics, both local and international.

Jacob Fugger the Rich[1] operated his vast industrial empire from his countinghouse in Augsburg, Germany.

Scribes sent daily news letters about German business conditions to all Fugger branches even in China and South America. Others translated daily news letters as they arrived from Fugger foreign offices, and in turn sent copies to other branches, written in the language of each country. Thus the *Zeitungen* chain brought Jacob Fugger news information gleaned from all the world's marketplaces. They also kept him informed of the activities of his chief competitors, the Welsers. As this news information was organized and analyzed, Jacob Fugger made his *decisions.* Those decisions set into motion a dozen important functions practiced by this sedentary merchant-capitalist.

[1] *Fugger,* Victor von Klarwill (Ed.) (London, John Lane, The Bodley Head, Ltd., 1924), 2 vols.

1. Importing
2. Exporting
3. Manufacturing
4. Wholesaling
5. Retailing
6. Warehousing
7. Communication
8. Transportation
9. Banking (or Pawnbroking)
10. Insurance
11. Investment management
12. Administration

2. First Great Business Editor

Thomas Gresham III, born in Norfolk in 1519, became the greatest of the line of Gresham merchant-adventurers and the most famous of all English merchants. At twenty-four he was admitted to the freedom of the Mercers' Company and started his own career as a merchant-adventurer. He immediately went to the great Bourse at Antwerp where the Gresham tradition was already well established. Here he met the Fugger and Welser agents and merchant-adventurers of every country. He listened to the latest news information on markets, the state of royal exchequers, condition of roads, the size of armies and navies. He became the best-informed business consultant, as well as the greatest newsgatherer of his times, maintaining an army of reporters and spies in lesser marketplaces who reported to him via courier and sailing ship.

His news analysis made it possible for English merchants to outcompete the rest of the business world. His singular service to his country over a period of twenty years in the great news hub of Antwerp was largely responsible for the shift in the commercial center of the world from that Flemish city to the City of London. One might say the British Empire reached a top position in sixteenth-century world affairs because one man, in that critical period of history, appreciated the importance of organized business intelligence, gathered at its source, and consistently transmitted to the point where it would do the most good.

Sir Thomas Gresham III built a great personal fortune out of his ability to recognize and analyze news events and forecast trends. One of his monuments[2] is the Royal Exchange (1569), where, as

[2] Another is "Gresham's law," that bad money will drive good money out of circulation.

Gresham explained, "merchants could meet and trade instead of walking in the rain when it raineth, more like pedlars than merchants." He induced a group of 750 leading London businessmen to subscribe £4,000 sterling, which paid for the ground. Out of his own personal funds Sir Thomas built the Royal Exchange on this land.

Miriam Beard says of Gresham: ". . . he united in his single person functions which we today distribute over a variety of agencies: the Associated Press; the Diplomatic and Consular service; the Secret Service; the Board of Estimates. He was spy, ambassador, consul and councillor . . ."[3]

3. First Great Market Analyst

"First notable recognition," said Jesse Neal, "that there was anything in business worthy of public discussion was the publication by Adam Smith of *The Wealth of Nations*."[4] Like Gresham, this Scottish professor of economics was one of the great business investigators of his day, and the modern world's first great market analyst.

Adam Smith attacked the mercantilism of his times: the theory that the producer is more important than the consumer. He advanced the counter theory that competition works only where there is an approximate equality of *bargaining power*. He challenged the isolationist idea that a nation gained by a favorable balance of trade (excess of exports over imports) either (1) by exploiting its own colonies as suppliers of raw materials and purchasers of finished goods or (2) by exploiting other foreign markets. "Consumption," Smith wrote, "is the sole end and purpose of all production . . . but in the mercantile system the interest of the consumer is almost constantly sacrificed to that of the producer."[5]

The American Revolution was, in a way, a revolt against the British mercantilism expressed by such tyrannical directives as the Stamp, Sugar, Molasses, and Navigation Acts. In England, the elder

[3] Miriam Beard, *History of the Business Man* (New York, The Macmillan Co., 1938). Miss Beard describes Pliny and Plato as the ancient world's great market authorities.

[4] "A Review of Business Press History," by Jesse H. Neal, executive secretary, the Associated Business Papers, Inc., in N. W. *Ayer's Newspaper Annual & Directory* for 1922.

[5] Adam Smith, LLD., F.R.S., *An Inquiry Into the Nature and Causes of the Wealth of Nations* (London, Strahan and Cabell, 1776).

Pitt and other Whigs led the revolt against mercantilism, which Adam Smith had precipitated. These movements were part of a greater development: the Industrial Revolution, the beginning of the struggle for wider and freer markets in which to sell the increased production of factory labor and steam power. Adam Smith's *Wealth of Nations* is a good handbook for every student of business journalism. It will prepare him for a better understanding of the industrial and mechanical revolutions, which gave birth to the modern business press.

Nourished in the soil of the free market and supported by competitive private enterprise, the business press owes something to Messrs. Fugger, Gresham, and Smith. They taught three basic rules of business journalism: (1) gather news information at its sources, methodically and meticulously; (2) sift, organize, and interpret it carefully; (3) purvey it directly to the points where it is needed and show readers how to use this news for profit.

4. West German Business Press

The impetus given to wider communication by Johannes Gutenberg at his press in Mainz, in 1450, resulted in the outcropping of scores of printing presses throughout fifteenth-century Germany. Hundreds more improved presses appeared everywhere in the sixteenth and seventeenth centuries. The products of these presses—books, magazines, newspapers, and businesspapers—provided a great stimulus to industry and to scientific research.

The success of the Fugger news letter system, described at the beginning of this chapter, led to the founding of a weekly business publication, *Avisa, Relation, oder Zeitung,* in Augsburg, Germany, in 1609—almost a hundred years before the appearance of London's first daily newspaper, *The Daily Courant* (*Ca.* 1700). By the nineteenth century, German technology was of a high order and her business press (*fachpress*) was expanding greatly.

In 1837, Germany had about 200 businesspapers (*fachzeitschriften*); in 1888, about 2,725; in 1907, about 5,715; and by 1931, the German business press had reached its peak, with 7,475 specialized businesspapers being published.

By 1937, the Nazi program of confiscation and concentration of ownership, as well as state control of the press, had cut down the businesspaper total in Germany to 5,800. Of this total, the largest field in number of papers, strangely enough, was theology, with a total of 640 publications. Medicine came next, with 330; "technic" papers, 500. In 1907, there were 71 military trade journals, in 1937, there were 58. By comparison, there were published, in 1937, only a dozen businesspapers in the United States for the military profession.

By 1940, the German business press had become a small, unknown quantity to the outside world, tightly controlled by Propaganda Minister Goebbels, permitted to print nothing except what the military censors or the propaganda bureau ordered or approved.

At the end of World War II the entire German business press had ceased to exist.

A new start was made under supervision of the Allied Occupation Authorities. A licensing system secured the exclusion of all publishers and journalists who had supported the Nazi regime. In the Soviet Zone of Germany, the self-styled DDR—(German Democratic Republic), the press is still as regimented as it was under the Nazis.

In Western Germany, however, complete freedom was restored in 1949. This led to an astonishing development of the press in general and particularly of the business press. Detailed statistics are contained in *Die Deutsche Presse 1956*, published by the Institute of Journalism of the Free University of Berlin, and in *Der Leitfaden 1958*, published by W. Stamm in Essen, Germany.[6]

According to figures for 1957, compiled by *Advertising Age* (May 12, 1958, p. 88) there were 2,656 "trade, technical and business magazines" published in West Germany, all of which take advertising. The total circulation was placed "around 40 million" readers, and the advertising revenue $232,700,000.

In 1958, West Germany published 1,703 businesspapers carrying paid advertising, according to Messrs. Mangele and Dehmel of Carl Gabler Werbegesellschaft MBH in Munich, one of the new republic's largest advertising agencies. The total circulation was 23,069,800 readers.

West German corporations publish 600 house organs (*werkzeitschriften*) of which 264 are external house organs (*kundenzeitschriften*).

[6] From a report to the author by H. A. Kluthe, president, and Arnold Miethe, *Verband Deutscher Zeitschriftenverleger e.V.* (Association of German Magazine Publishers) *Frankfurt Am Main*, Germany, 1958.

The agricultural press of West Germany has the largest circulation of any businesspaper group: 6.7 million readers.

The circulation (*auflage*) audit bureau of West Germany is known as IVW (*Informationsgememeinschaft zur Festellung der Verbreitung von Werbertragern*). This is an independent bureau supported by the advertising associations. About 21 per cent of all West German businesspapers (having about 65 per cent of the total businesspaper circulation) are members of IVW, as well as 22 per cent of all consumer magazines (with 58 per cent of the total consumer magazine circulation).

One of Germany's oldest businesspapers of modern times—*Physikalisch-Oekonomische Wochenschrift* (Physical-Economic Weekly) —was founded in 1749; it is published at Stuttgart. The oldest businesspaper in existence until the Nazi regime came in (1937), according to Dr. Leo Lion,[7] was *Dingler's Polytechniches Journal*, established in 1820 in Berlin.

Publishers of West Germany business publications today form a special group within the Verband Deutscher Zeitschriftenverleger, Frankfurt am Main, Grober Hirschgraben 26, which is affiliated to the International Federation of the Periodical Press (FIPP) Paris 16e, 65, Avenue d'Jena. It also works in close harmony with the association of newspaper publishers and publishes with them *Zeitungs-Verlag und Zeitschriften-Verlag* (Bad Godesberg, Wurzerstr, 46), an organ which appears twice a month and deals comprehensively with all matters concerning the press.

Journalists are organized in the Deutscher Journalisten-Verband, Bonn Münsterplatz 20 and in the Berufsgruppe der Journalisten in IG Druck and Papier (affiliated to the Printers' Union). There are smaller groups, comprising motor journalism, agrarian journalism, etc.

5. British Business Press

In 1845 there were 24 British businesspapers. In 1937 the number had increased to more than 600.

In 1957 there were 1,580 businesspapers listed under the heading

[7] Dr. Leo Lion is former head of the businesspaper division of the House of Ullstein. For the story of this great publishing house destroyed by the Nazis, see *The Rise and Fall of the House of Ullstein*, by Herman Ullstein (New York, Simon and Schuster, Inc., 1942). Ullstein had a large businesspaper division issuing many technical periodicals in Germany.

"trade and technical," about 700 "religious and educational," or a total of 2,280 titles. In addition, there were 305 house magazines, 1,000 reference books, yearbooks, and directories. The majority of the business periodicals are monthly magazines. About 20 per cent are published weekly, twice as many as in the United States.

From 1951 to 1957 the percentage increase on the number of British businesspapers was over 30 per cent, while consumer magazines dropped more than 10 per cent, daily and Sunday newspapers dropped 5 per cent, and weekly newspapers fell almost 3 per cent in numbers.

In common with other branches of the press, advertising space rates in businesspapers have increased several times since the war. "On an average, taken over a number of leading technical journals, rates have increased by 50 per cent," according to Jowett in *The Financial Times* (London, April 24, 1957).

The readership of the British business press (1957) is estimated at 25 million. *Advertising Age* (May 12, 1958, p. 83) in its estimates of British advertising expenditures, put the British "trade and technical press" advertising revenue for 1957 at $108,600,000, a 14 per cent increase over 1956. This expenditure exceeded the British consumer magazine press advertising revenue by $4 million (1957) according to *Advertising Age.*

With the emphasis on export and the European Common Market, the British business press has been driving for overseas subscriptions and advertising revenue. Some of the more technical British businesspapers today include a *précis* of the main articles in three or four foreign languages.

A *Collection for the Improvement of Husbandry and Trade* is believed to be one of the earliest business magazines published in England. Many copies are preserved in the Sell collection (Sells Limited, London). No. 182, dated January 24, 1694, specialized in the corn market and contained miscellaneous shipping reports.

One of the earliest house publications in England (one of its most important today) is *Lloyd's List,* which was started as *Lloyd's News* (1696–current), published by Edward Lloyd. Instead of going out to its readers at first, the readers came to it: *Lloyd's News* was posted in Lloyd's Coffee House on Lombard Street in London. The bulletin reported shipping intelligence, war news, and other items having a bearing on the business of merchants who frequented this coffee house. Many coffee houses became similar news centers, just as barbershops once were news centers. Lloyd's had become, in 1700, the central clearing house for business news information of all kinds in London.

In 1728, Mr. Thomas Jemson organized a syndicate of coffee men to pool the news they collected at their respective coffee houses and issue a morning and evening paper. Nothing came of this project, but it is supposed to have given Mr. Jemson or his associates the idea of a specialized news sheet or businesspaper. Mr. Jemson died in February of 1734, and *Lloyd's List* appeared the following April as a weekly. In 1737 it was published bi-weekly.

Subscribers paid 3 shillings a quarter at the bar of Lloyd's Coffee House. Many of the subscribers were underwriters. *Lloyd's List* maintained correspondents at all the ports and paid an annual gratuity to the post officials for prompt delivery of shipping lists to their messengers and for exemption from postal charges, which were a much heavier item in those days than they are now.

Today *Lloyd's List* covers the fields of transportation, commodity markets, money and stocks, coal and fuel oil trades, aircraft, wireless, maritime, and commercial law.

Other well-known eighteenth century British businesspapers were the *Public Ledger* (1759), a daily, covering agricultural products; *Morning Advertiser* (1794), which was the daily businesspaper of the "Friendly Society of Licensed Victuallers"; *Bells Weekly Messenger* (1796), an agricultural paper; and, at the turn of the nineteenth century, a paper for the book trade, *Bent's Literary Advertiser* (1802), and *The Lancet* (1823).

The Lancet, in the fall of 1844, issued this warning to medical students:

> To those who have already spent a year in town, the routine of the life of a medical student is well known. They have made their choice and are either diligent and attentive to their studies, thus paving the way for future prosperity; or otherwise they have fallen, and become the prey to dissipation, thus preparing themselves for a career of imposture, not to say crime."

Other well-known trade papers (all over 80 years old) include the following, together with present circulations if published: 1825, *Journal of Commerce*; 1832, *British Medical Journal* (circulation

78,000); 1835, *Mining Journal* (2,560) and *Railway Gazette;* 1837, *Publishers Circular;* 1839, *Medical Press;* 1838, *Pawnbrokers Gazette;* 1842, *The Builders* (18,000); 1843, *Farmers & Stockbreeders* (125,-000); 1849, *Gas Journal;* 1853, *Photographic Journal* (7,700); 1854, *Architect & Building News;* 1856, *Engineer;* 1858, *Estates Gazette, Colliery Guardian,* and *The Bookseller* (9,950); 1859, *Chemist & Druggist* (11,000) and *Ironmonger* (10,500); 1861, *Grocer* (50,373), *Electrical Journal;* 1863, *British Trade Journal;* 1865, *Brewers Wine and Spirit Trades Review Journal;* 1866, *Engineering* (8,655), *Iron & Coal Trades Review, Hair & Beauty, Tailor & Cutter* (12,500); 1867, *Leather Trades Review;* 1868, *Tobacconist & Confectioner, Practitioner;* 1869, *International Sugar Journal;* 1870, *Coal & Appliances;* 1871, *Brewers Guardian;* 1872, *Furniture Record;* 1873, *Timber Trades Journal, Jeweller & Metal Worker, Mineral Water Trade Review;* 1874, *Poultry World, Municipal Engineering, Perambulator Gazette, Hardware Trade Gazette, Accountant;* 1875, *Watchmaker, Jeweller & Silversmith, Pottery Gazette, Textile Manufacturer;* 1876, *Dairy Engineering, Mechanical World, Hatters Gazette;* 1877, *The Baker, Music Trade Review.*

The Cabinet Maker, first published in 1880, started the firm of Benn Brothers, Ltd., famous contemporary publishers of British businesspapers. Nine others of Benn's many businesspapers also were started in the nineteenth century: *Hardware Trade Journal* 1874; (*Ironmongery* was merged in 1900); the *Electrician,* 1861; the *Gas World,* 1886 (in the seventies it was called *Lights* and in 1884, *Gas and Water*); *Fruit Grower,* 1895 (originally *Green Grocer, Fruiterer and Market Gardener*); *Timber Trades Journal and Export World,* 1863 (editions in Portuguese, Dutch, Italian, Chinese, Russian). *British Trade Journal* incorporates *Aeronautics,* founded in 1907, and *Commercial Intelligence.*

The international character of many of the Benn business publications was due to the British policy of extending its markets. Sir Ernest Benn, widely traveled himself, followed a wise policy of requiring all his editors, advertising sales managers, and the heads of departments to refresh their minds and methods by periodic visits to countries overseas. His oldest son, John Benn, studied at Princeton, in New Jersey, and his second son, Glenville Benn, worked on *New York Times* in Manhattan.

King George V sent his congratulations in 1930 to Sir Ernest

Benn, chairman of Benn Brothers, Ltd., on the occasion of the publisher's Golden Jubilee. The King's message expressed "the hope that every success may attend the efforts of your publishing house for the development of British trade." The British business press hailed this statement as a royal sanction of the businesspaper's claim to national status. It was a landmark in the history of British trade journalism.

The Benns, incidentally, have played important roles in the social, artistic, political, and military life of England. John William Benn was chairman of the London County Council, knighted in 1905. Sir Ernest Benn was created a baronet in 1914. Captain Oliver Benn died in action at Gallipoli in 1915. In 1929, the Right Honorable Wedgwood Benn, D.S.O., member of Parliament, became Secretary of State for India. Benn businesspapers, in World War II, wrote glorious chapters in businesspaper history in behalf of their country's war effort.

When the first edition of this book went to press in 1945 publishers of established British trade and technical businesspapers were working under wartime conditions—shortage of staffs and paper and curtailment by government restrictions. With the exception of a few export journals no new papers were allowed to be published during the war and during paper rationing. Restrictions for periodicals were lifted from March 1, 1950, and for a time the extra supplies of paper were used to increase the size of pages. Most of the pocket size editions returned to their prewar dimensions.

Today the four most popular page sizes for business publications are 8½"×5½", 11"×8½", 10¼"×7½", and 9"×6".

As wartime conditions in manufacturing as well as publishing eased, an intense struggle developed to find gaps in the trade paper field. The newer industries such as electronics, atomics, self-service supermarkets, chemical engineering, nuclear energy, plastics, etc., soon had new journals or developments of older ones; and, in addition, established trades were catered for by new journals appealing to specialized sections of a trade. For instance, where one or two trade papers formerly covered the whole of the drapery and fashion trades, there are now periodicals entitled and concentrating upon corsets, underwear, hosiery, millinery, handkerchiefs and scarves, costume jewelry, children's wear, coats and suits, and pins and needles. In fact, a drapery store has a choice of 40 businesspapers.

The turn of the half-century has also seen the advent and growth of the controlled circulation trade journal by the larger publishing groups. These are mainly sixteen page news sheets (page area 15″ × 10″). Trades already covered include food, building materials, hospital requirements, and factory equipment. Another tendency arousing wide interest is that of devoting a whole issue to one particular theme. An example of this was an issue of *The Architectural Review* dealing with "Inside the Pub." Most of the advertisements also tied up with this subject.

Despite rising costs of paper, wages, overhead, and increased taxation, publishers of trade and technical papers have continued to prosper and expand, especially the larger groups.

The Associated Iliffe Press, with 34 journals, claims to be the largest British publisher in this sphere, but some of their journals such as *Autocar, Amateur Photography, Yachting* are of more general appeal.

When *The Autocar* was first published in 1895 the law required that motor cars should be preceded by a man with a red flag. The first crusade of this British businesspaper was to have the red flag abolished and to encourage the growth of the automotive industry in the face of strenuous and widespread opposition.[8]

Hundreds of independent technical papers cover the fields of British industrial enterprise. The textile field has some 35 businesspapers, among its leaders being the *Draper's Record* which boasts the largest businesspaper circulation in the world; transport has 31; shipping, 16; liquor, eight; machinery, nine; printing, 17; engineering, 47; building, 25; commerce, 23; publishing and financial, 13 papers.

Odhams Press, with its latest acquisition of 13 specialized publications belonging to Tothill Press, are making headway, but here again many of its papers appeal to the general public.

Also in the first three must be included The National Trade Press. In recent years it has secured control of *The Textile Weekly, Packaging Review, Textile Recorder, Man Made Textiles,* and *Commercial Vehicles.* It has also founded *Children's Wear, Household Textiles, British Chemical Engineering,* and *British Communications & Electronics,* in addition to two controlled circulation fortnightlies. This organization has also developed an extensive book publishing section

[8] "Trade and Technical Press," by C. E. Wallis, managing director, Associated Iliffe Press, *The Newspaper World,* London, Golden Jubilee Issue, 1948.

and a trade exhibition department. Recent exhibition promotions have covered such industries as men's and boys' wear, household textiles, carpets, British cloths, nylon, footwear, jewelry and watches, British fashions, hosiery, machinery, etc. It has also organized a British Fashion, Footwear & Textiles Fair in Stockholm, Sweden, from August 31st to September 15th.

Apart from revenue from the letting of stands and space sold in catalogs, these exhibitions spell increased advertising in journals covering the specialized industries—N.T.P. businesspapers and rival papers—and they help promote friendlier feeling among all publishers. N.T.P. advertise fairs extensively in other suitable trade papers and these rival papers find it good policy to take space in the exhibitions.

National Trade Press, Limited, was privately organized in 1917 to acquire the *Organizer*, a general trade publication. It was discovered later, however, that there was little or no effective support from business for the general business publications, that specialization was essential to success. The *Organizer* was discontinued. Specialized papers were promoted, such as the *Drapers' Organizer*, *Footwear Organizer*, *Furnishing Trades Organizer*, *Styles For Men*, *British Shoeman*, and *Laundry Journal*. These were successful.

This firm also acquired five papers which had been founded in the nineteenth century: *Confectionery News*, 1887; *Dyer and Textile Printer*, 1879; *Cigar and Tobacco World*, 1888; *Laundry Record*, 1890; *Watchmaker, Jeweler and Silversmith*, 1875. A number of yearbooks and trade directories also are published as services to their trades.

N.T.P. has achieved notable leadership in all the various fields covered by its papers. The *Drapers' Organizer* inaugurated the first artificial silk exhibition ever held in any country, at Holland Park Hall, London, in 1926. The exhibit ran five years, until it merged with the British Industries Fair. This was also the first British businesspaper to issue fashion shade cards to its readers, which resulted in the formation of the British Colour Council. Fashion parades were staged under its sponsorship at the May Fair Hotel.

Several N.T.P. publications inaugurated well-known design competitions. The *Funrishing Trades Organizer* in 1927 organized a competition for "modernist" furniture which was then little known in England: £500 was distributed in prizes.[9]

[9] Much of the information on the British business press has been furnished by T. Ward Grice, retired chief editor of National Trade Press, Ltd.

Another British businesspaper known the world over is *International Textiles,* published by I. T. Publishers, Ltd.

Industrial Newspapers, Limited, another British publishing firm, counts among its publications such well-known British businesspapers as *Iron and Coal Trades Review, Foundry Trade Journal, Coal Merchant and Shipper, Fish Trades Gazette, Tobacco, Metal Treatment, Ryland's Directory, Tobacco Trade Year Book and Diary, Smoker's Handbook* (Retail Prices), *Decorator's Trade Reference Book & Diary.*

A famous nineteenth-century British businesspaper which enjoys an international circulation is the *Linen Trade Circular* of Belfast, Ireland, founded in 1851, now published by H. R. Carter & Son. It is a direct descendant of the personal news letters of the seventeenth and eighteenth centuries. Sir Robert Baird set the paper's type by hand in his youth, as a printer's apprentice. Great-grandfathers of the present Irish linen generation used to call for the *Circular* in person every Monday, after dining at their favorite tavern nearby. In the same year *Dundee Prices Current,* a jute paper, was founded. Other important British businesspaper publishers include Temple Press, W. Reed, Ltd., Morgan Bros., Ltd., the Nema and St. Margarets Press.

Temple Press, Ltd., has nine specialized monthly periodicals and five weeklies (1958). *British Rate & Data* in its "Trade Technical and Professional Periodical" section (February—March 1958) carried an advertisement for *Atom Industry,* "First Newspaper for the International Atom Industry," claiming a circulation of 14,864 in 100 foreign countries.

In an article in *The Financial Times* of London (April 29, 1957), H. R. Jowett, media manager, Technical and General Advertising Agency, Ltd., attributed the expansion in the number of British businesspapers to three factors: (1) rapid technological development, (2) growth and acceptance of free circulation businesspapers, (3) reluctance of British businesspaper publishers to disclose vital information on readership and markets.

The first reason related to the increase in the number of specialized fields, such as in engineering, chemistry, electronics, nucleonics, automation, and applied science generally, requiring more detailed, continuous, new work knowledge.

The second reason for expansion was the advent of the first controlled or free circulation businesspaper in 1951. By 1957 there were 35 British free circulation businesspapers that ranked with the best paid circulation businesspapers in readership, content, and prestige.

The third reason for rapid expansion of the British business press is a curious one: as Mr. Jowett explains, it is a negative reason: "... the unprogressive outlook of a majority of publishers ... the cloak of secrecy assumed by so many media owners in this section of the press has unwittingly provided an excellent cover under which the doubtful and the dubious are able to operate."

Mr. Jowett noted, however, that the British business press was "moving away from its complacent and apathetic posture" by greater use of audited circulation machinery to provide authentic material for space salesmen and space buyers.

The Periodical Trade Press and Weekly Newspaper Proprietors Association Ltd., London (P.T.P. & W.N.P.A.) is the leading British businesspaper association.

6. Dutch Business Press

Among the members of the representative professional association, the Netherlands Organization of Periodical Publishers (N.O.T.U.), the uncontested senior in the field of businesspapers is the *Nieuwsblad voor de Boekhandel* (The Bookseller's Bulletin), a weekly founded in 1834. *Cobouw*, a leading weekly for the building industry, dating from 1857, shares its venerable age with the *Nederlands Tijdschrift voor Geneeskunde*, an authoritative medical journal of international repute.[10]

Runners-up, all of them between 75 and 100 years of age, are the *Pharmaceutisch Weekblad* (Pharmaceutical Weekly) of 1865, the *Weekblad voor Fiscaal Recht* (Weekly Review of Fiscal Law) of 1871, *Het Gas* (Gas Technique) of 1880, the *Recueil des Travaus Chimiques des Pays Bas* (collection of papers in the field of chemicals) also dating from 1880, and the *Bouwkundig Weekblad* (Architectural Weekly) of 1882.

Six businesspapers, covering nursing of the sick, reclamation of soil, dentistry, trade administration, bakery, and the supply and demand of commodities and implements in the technical sphere, made their

[10] This report was written by W. H. van Baarle, former president of N.O.T.U., an international authority on advertising practice. He is president of the Dutch section of the International Federation of the Periodical Press, The Hague, Netherlands.

start between 60 and 70 years ago, and an equal number, catering for those professionally interested in the stock market, agriculture, druggist's shops, chemical industries and interior decoration, are only about ten years their juniors.

Number and breakdown of titles: The number of titles published on May 1, 1958, amounted to 576. Here is the breakdown of the Dutch business press for 1955:[11]

	Number of Periodicals	Number of Copies Distributed
1. Commerce	106	474,000
2. Industry and construction	71	388,000
3. Traffic	37	225,000
4. Craft	41	170,000
5. Agriculture	86	885,000
6. Education and tuition	52	173,000
7. Independent professions	88	320,000
8. Government and community	16	120,000
9. Economy	67	325,000
Totals	564	3,080,000

In 1958 the total distribution of the Dutch businesspapers was approaching three-and-a-quarter-million copies, thus offering a very fair coverage of the professional sectors of the Dutch population now numbering 11,000,000, representing about 2,900,000 households and people living on their own.

Paid and controlled circulation: In order to evaluate this circulation from an advertisers' point of view and to be able to gauge editorial influence, one should, first of all, look into its breakdown as to paid and free copies. From a sample analyzed to this end and consisting of a representative number of businesspapers having provided reliable data in late 1957 and early 1958, the following facts could be established:

The 136 businesspapers concerned appeared to have registered 272,065 individual paying subscribers, and were, furthermore, delivering 125,566 copies on the basis of collective subscriptions booked by various enterprises, institutions, and organizations, bringing the total of paid subscriptions up to 400,000

Apart from these, 78,194 copies per issue were regularly supplied

[11] W. H. van Baarle, *Reclamekunde en Reclameleer* (Advertising Know-how and Theory) (Holland, Leyden, 1956).

to members of professional organizations for whom the subscription rates are included in their membership fees. So, one way or another, about 480,000 copies distributed by 136 of the 576 Dutch businesspapers are paid for, an average of 5.790 copies being furthermore sold to non-subscribers.

On the total print-order of these 136 periodicals, amounting to 615,000 copies, two items remain to be accounted for. About 12,000 copies are used for filing and for the supply of back numbers; over 120,000 copies for "free distribution." The majority of this latter part of the circulation, however, is entitled to the American denomination "controlled circulation." To cite just one example: the monthly *Bulletin* of the Netherlands Organization of Periodical Publishers, on a print order of 600 copies, is sending more than half of them free of charge to authorities concerned with the press, to members of the State Press Council, to prominent advertisers, to all recognized advertising agents, and to other interested people who would probably buy the *Bulletin* if it was not offered to them free to cultivate public relations.

So the sample shows that 78.5 per cent of all copies are paid for and that the non-paid 20 per cent of the total circulation for a considerable part may be put on a par with paid copies. There is no reason to assume that the position of the businesspapers not belonging to the sample would be entirely different.

It may be remarked in passing that a hundred highly scientific magazines with a total circulation of about 180,000 are not considered "businesspapers" according to Dutch standards and, consequently, were not taken into consideration here.

Auditing of circulation: In contrast with the publishers of daily newspapers and mass magazines (illustrated weeklies, women's magazines, broadcasting programme papers, and the like), many among their colleagues of the business press up till a few years ago hesitated to publish their circulation figures and to give proof of them through auditor's reports. Many advertisers and even advertising agencies were inclined to compare the relatively restricted distribution of the trade and technical and other professional papers with that of the mass magazines. Thanks to a close collaboration that has been established between the national associations of advertisers, advertising agencies, and periodical publishers, the business press is now experiencing a better understanding of its value as an advertising medium. On the other hand, an increasing number of businesspapers have their circulation audited, or at least throw their books open to those advertisers wishing to have them audited for their own account.

Audience of the business press: So much for the number of copies distributed, totaling about three and a quarter million, a figure which it might be interesting to compare with the paid distribution of all Dutch daily newspapers—nationals, regionals and locals—which in May 1958 stood at 2,906,000, or approximately the number of households.

The audience of the Dutch business press is, of course, much bigger. No recent statistics on its size being available, reference may be made to the biggest Dutch investigation undertaken in this respect.

In 1949, voluntary contributions of 28 members of the N.O.T.U. enabled this association to charge the Netherlands Institute for Public Opinion Polling (N.I.P.O.)—the Dutch Gallup associates—to carry through an extensive quantitative and qualitative analysis of the circulation of mass magazines and businesspapers. As for the latter category 206 field workers interviewed 2,291 subscribers at their offices, plants, or homes. Among these interviewees were farmers and engineers, chemists and caterers, doctors, brokers, and lawyers, as well as butchers, greengrocers, and—most difficult to locate—millers.

In their final report the polling experts stated that from every 100 copies of paid-for-businesspapers, 57 were read solely by the subscribers concerned, while 43 were passed on by them to one or more other people.

The average number of extra readers per subscription appeared to be 4, the over-all average number of readers per copy 2.7, the latter figure representing an audience of about 8,775,000 copies.

Confirmation of the results of the aforementioned national survey was obtained in 1952, when the weekly *Cobouw*, covering all building and construction activities, set an example to the other businesspapers by commissioning the Nederlandse Stichting voor Statistiek to poll an extensive random sample of its subscribers. We don't need to go into details as *Cobouw*, in 1957, by way of celebrating its centenary, had the investigation repeated by the same research institute, a member of E.S.O.M.A.R. and W.A.P.O.R., which, this time, interviewed a representative sample consisting of 796 of the 13,633 subscribers, chosen at random. On this occasion the total number of regular readers per 100 paid copies proved to be 255, thus showing a slightly smaller average of 2.55 (against 2.7 for the national survey). When computing the present audience of the business press on the basis of this lower average and of the distribution increased since then, we again arrive at a figure amply exceeding 8 million.

Readership: Quoting once more from the report on the 1949 national survey of the Dutch business press, "We also find satisfactory proof of readership as it has been defined by our distinguished American colleague, Julien Elfenbein, *viz.*, the use readers make of a paper."

Out of every 100 subscribers interviewed, 13 considered their businesspaper indispensable, 43 very useful, 29 fairly useful, and 12 not very useful. 53 per cent of those interviewed were completely satisfied with its editorial contents; 74 per cent agreed with the frequency of appearance; and 57 per cent preferred the size over any other format.

Seventy-five per cent of the interviewees were in the habit of filing their businesspaper for later reference, and nearly two thirds stated that they were actually consulting copies after filing.

In 47 per cent of all cases investigated one to five persons per subscription stated the businesspaper exerted considerable influence on purchasing for their trade or other business. Seventy-five per cent of those interviewed appeared to belong to the upper and middle classes.

Again the *Cobouw* survey of 1957 offers confirmation of the aforementioned findings as to the high level of reader-interest the businesspapers have acquired and have been able to maintain, notwithstanding heavy competition in the field of newspapers and other means of mass communications, television included.

Advertising revenue: As is the case for most other countries outside the United States, The Netherlands are not yet able to produce complete and reliable figures on advertising expenditures. However, a recent conservative estimate by experts puts the annual advertisement turnover of the Dutch business press for 1957 at $16 million.

To this turnover, which is increasing year by year, quite a few magazines among the 576 professional businesspapers are not contributing at all, as they do not accept advertising. Those who do, have been and are fundamental in developing business and industry at home as well as in furthering export trade.

7. Swiss Business Press

In the 1947 edition of this volume the number of businesspapers published in Switzerland was placed at 847, with a circulation of 8,484,585 readers. Vice Consul Rudolf M. Neeser of the Consulate General of Switzerland, in New York City, in March 1958 placed the figure at about 700 "trade and technical" periodicals now published in Switzerland.

Charles G. Keel, in a paper he read at the 12th International Congress of the Periodical Press in Copenhagen, in May 1956, placed the total in the neighborhood of 900 with 6 million circulation.[12]

The Swiss market, according to information furnished by Neeser, is at once national and international. The advertiser in Swiss periodicals must adapt his appeal to the language, psychology, and buying habits of three different regions—German, French, and Italian. The market is highly competitive. Supplies from foreign trade are practically unlimited. Switzerland has had no wars in the last 150 years and its economic system is sound. Advertising practices differ here from American methods. Television is so far nonexistent. Advertising is excluded from the government-controlled Swiss broadcasting system. Today (1958) there are about 700 trade and technical periodicals published in Switzerland. Foreign publications are widely read. In such fields as radio, radar, nuclear physics, etc., United States businesspapers have relatively important circulations. "It has been noticed," says the Consulate, "that German technical and trade publications are coming back more and more in Switzerland."

It is interesting to note that Switzerland, in proportion to population, has more newspapers than any country in the world. There are over 500 political newspapers with a total circulation of 3 million readers. The Association of Swiss Advertising Agencies publishes a *Catalog of Swiss Newspapers and Periodicals* and a list of Advertising Consultants and their accounts (*Bund Schweizerischer Reklameberater*) which is available from Dr. Hans Duttweiler, secretary, Pelikanstrasse 3, Zurich.

The *Schweizerischer Zeitschriften-Katalog,* Schweizerisches Vereinssortment Olten, Switzerland, lists Swiss businesspapers, giving

[12] Charles G. Keel, "La Structure de la Press Technique et Professionnelle en Suisse et les Problèmes Relatifs a sa Redaction," *Proceedings of the 12th Congress,* International de la Presse Periodique, Copenhagen, May 11, 1956, p. 68.

the year founded. Publishers Associations are Schweiz, Fachpresse-Verband, Postfach (Box) 285, Zurich 32, and Schweiz, Zeitungsverleger-Verband, Routgenstr. 16, Zurich 5. The directories give no details on paid or unpaid circulations or the advertising revenue of the Swiss business press. There are no schools of journalism, but lectures in journalism are given at Federal Polytechnic School in Zurich and at leading Swiss Universities.

8. Swedish Business Press

The oldest Swedish businesspaper is *Kungl Krigsvetenskapsakademiens Handlingar Och Tidskrift* (Proceedings and Journal of the Royal Academy of War); this was established in 1796. *Jernkontorets Annaler* (Annals of the Swedish Ironmasters Association) was established in 1816; *Jtidskrift I Sjoevaesendet* (Navy Journal), in 1838; and *Svensk Bokhandelstidning* (Swedish Book Dealers Journal), in 1860.

Foreningen Svensk Fackpress is the Association of Swedish Trade Journals. There is a journalists' trade union called "Svenska Journalistforbundet" in Stockholm

Sweden had about 350 trade and technical journals in 1946. The total circulation of 230 of these was 1,628,600, but the circulation figures of the rest were unknown. The total income from revenue is also unknown.

From A. Hornquist of Tidningsstatistik Aktiebolag TS (The Swedish Audit Bureau of Circulations) advices were received in July 1958 that the business press in Sweden "is not so well penetrated as the others: dailies and weekly papers."

The new edition (1958) of *TS Fackpressbok* (Business Press Guide) contains information on 371 business publications which carry advertising. The total circulation is 1,437,900. There are 204,600 paid subscribers.

In 1959, titles were 1500, circulation 6,500,000, and revenue $7,150,000, according to Gunnar Hambraeus.

9. Danish Business Press

Danmarks Blad-og Bogverden (The World of Papers and Books in Denmark), edited by Folmer Christensen and published by Politikens Forlag, Copenhagen, 1955 (fourth edition), provides a list of 452

"professional and trade journals" published in Denmark. These publications announced circulation figures which total 1,928,036 readers (1955). Many Danish technical journals, including most of the medical journals, publish no circulation figures, so the actual readership of the Danish business press is much larger. How much, no one knows.

Some of the categories listed in the directory cited above are: book trade; press; religion; military; education; broadcasting; technology; medical science; heating, refrigeration, and electrical engineering; agriculture and forestry; domestic animals, veterinary medicine; commerce, advertising, accountancy; communications, shipping, philately; metal works; textile industry.

Among the early nineteenth-century businesspapers still published are *Ugeskrift for Laeger* (1839), with 7,000 readers; *Tidsskrift for Sovaesen* (1827), with 550 readers; *Tidsskrift for Industri* (1838), with 5,350 readers.

The Danish professional press association was headed in 1958 by Paul Pii Johannessen and A. Truelsen. Mr. Johannessen, as president of the Danish Section of the International Federation of the Periodical Press, was host at the 12th Congress in Copenhagen in 1956.

Denmark's trade union of journalists is Danske Journalisters Fällerepräsentation, in Copenhagen. The association of publishers of business magazines, also in Copenhagen, is Foreningen af Danske Ugeblade, Fagblade og Tidsskrifter.

10. Norwegian Business Press

About 125 businesspaper titles were published in Norway in 1957. Of this number, 80 were "professional, scientific and technical" association periodicals.

One of Norway's oldest specialized journals is a military periodical, *Norsk Militaert Tidsskrift*, founded in 1830. A journal for lawyers, *Norsk Retskidende*, was founded in 1835.

The total readership of the Norwegian business press, in 1957, according to the Norwegian Information Service of the Embassy of Norway in New York City, was estimated at 650,000. There are no reliable statistics on paid and free circulation or advertising revenue.

Categories are general: religion, social sciences, sociology, law, military, science, education, commerce, applied science, forestry, hunting and fishing, shipping industry, engineering, manufactures, business methods.

Businesspaper publishers in Norway have an organization in Oslo called Den Norske Fagpresses Forening. The trade union of journalists, also in Oslo, is Norsk Journalistlag.

Norwegian terms and their meanings: *bedrifts*—business, *handel*—trade, *tidskrift*—journal or review, *tidende*—journal, *teknisk*—technical, *fagpress*—businesspaper, *forening*—association.

11. French Business Press

Urbain J. Thuau, general secretary-founder of the Federation Internationale de la Presse Periodique, estimated in 1958 there were 2,000 "trade, technical and professional" periodicals published in France with "between four and five million readers." There are about 70 "syndicates" or associations of professional publications of which some fifteen are concerned with the French technical press.[13]

A former teacher of marketing at Columbia University, New York City, Dr. Francis Elvinger heads one of the leading European advertising agencies, with headquarters in Paris. From Mme. M. Th. Louveau, director of the Media Department of Elvinger, we received, in July-August, 1958, information that France had 317 leading businesspapers in the following categories: commerce (14); industry (13); sciences (13); agriculture (52); medicine (178); jurisprudence (45).

Some of these leaders furnished circulation figures. The total claimed was 3,092,543 (1957).

In 1957 it was estimated that the French Press included 178 daily newspapers with a circulation of 11,500,000, 1,000 weeklies with a circulation of 33,000,000, 6,149 periodicals (including the business press) with a monthly circulation of 55,000,000.

No information on advertising revenue is available and few advertising agencies reveal their billings.

12. Czechoslovakian Business Press

In July 1958 we received a study of the situation of the Czechoslovak Periodical Press from the Czechoslovak Foreign Institute in Exile.[14] It describes the periodical press prior to the communist

[13] *Annuaire de la Presse*, 1957, Paris.

[14] *Studies of the Czechoslovak Foreign Institute in Exile*, March 1955, P. O. Box 934, Chicago 90, Ill., U.S.A.; Postbox 91, Leiden, Holland.

coup d'état of February, 1948, and analyzes the Russian monopoly of mass communication in Czechoslovakia since 1948.

In the introduction to this study it is stated:

The Communist Party control over a state is based on five monopolies:
1) *The monopoly of mass communication media;*
2) *The monopoly of intellectual leadership;*
3) *The monopoly of organization;*
4) *The monopoly of arms;*
5) *The monopoly of the means of production.*

The Soviet purge of the Czechoslovak business press followed the same pattern as the Nazi purge of the German business press. Today there are about 131 technical monthlies and a dozen technical weeklies published in Czechoslovakia with an estimated readership of over a million. To mention a few by title: *Casopis Csl. lekarnictva* (Apothecary Magazine), *Drevarske hospodarstvi* (Forest Economy), *Cukrovarnicke listy* (Sugar Industry News), *Prehled technicke literatury* (Review of Technical Literature), *Lucebnik* (The Chemist), *Mlekarske listy* (Dairy Magazine), *Stavebnik* (The Builder), *Svet motoru* (The World of Motors), *Elektrotechnicky obzor* (Electrotechnical Horizon), *Hospodarsky obzor* (Economy), *Lekarske listy* (Medical Bulletin), *Strojnicky obzor* (Engineering News).

The following are monthlies: *Chemicke listy* (Chemical News), *Chemicky obzor* (Chemical Horizon), *Architekt* (The Architect), *Automoto* (Automobile Review), *Danova a bilancni revue* (Accounting and Tax Review), *Druzstevni revue* (Co-op Review), *Hospodarske rozhledy* (Economy Review), *Chemic* (Chemistry), *Nase veda* (Our Science), *Obchodni rozhledy* (Business Review), *Architektura CSR* (Czechoslovak Architecture), *Bansky obzor* (Mining), *Civilni letectvi* (Civil Aeronautics), *Doprava* (Traffic Magazine), *Elektrotechnicky prehled* (Electrotechnical Review), *Mlady technik* (Young Technician), *Patentni vestnik* (Bulletin of Cz. Patent Office), *Planovane hospodarstvi* (Planned Economy), *Sklo* (Glass News), *Statisticky zpravodaj* (Review of Statistics), *Technicky obzor* (Technical Horizon), *Textilni obzor* (Textile News), *Prirodovedecky obzor* (Magazine of Natural History), *Biologicke listy* (Biological News), *Energie* (Energy), *Pravni obzor* (Law review), *Casopis matematiky a fysiky* (Magazine of Mathematics and Physics).

13. Japanese Business Press

"The information we possess on the trade sheets (*sic*) and journals of Japan is very sketchy," declares Seiji Chihara, manager of the International Advertising Department of Japan's foremost advertising agency, Dentsu of Tokyo. Dentsu, which controls an important percentage of Japan's billings, maintains branch offices in Osaka, Nagoya, Fukuoka Sappora, Yokohama, Kyoto, Kobe, and Hiroshima. In his letter to the author on June 27, 1958, Mr. Chihara adds: "The standing of trade sheets and journals in this country is quite low, and very few, if any, advertising agencies have considered it necessary to recommend these publications to their clients."

1957 expenditures for advertising in Japan are sizable and broken down as follows (in thousands of dollars):

Newspapers	141,666	54.2%
Magazines	13,888	5.3%
Radio	41,666	16.0%
Television	16,666	6.4%
Outdoor and others	47,222	18.1%
	$261,111,000	100.0%

There are 221 trade newspapers. Of these, 46 are dailies and 175 "non-dailies" (Japan Newspaper's Association).

There are 718 magazines of a technical nature: law (36), economical, financial, administrative (78), labor (24), education (118), medical science, hygiene, drugs (76), industrial science, engineering (114), home economics (30), agriculture and forestry, fishing, live stock (52), commerce (41), transportation and communication (42), arts (48), motion pictures, dramatics (38), music (12), sports (29).

Advertising expenditures in all Japanese magazines is reported for 1957 as 5,098,037 (in 1,000 yen) as against 51,144,342 (in 1,000 yen) in newspapers. There was no breakdown to indicate what portion of the magazine expenditure went for the business press.

14. Belgian Business Press

Belgium seems to rely on the periodicals published by associations, syndicates, chambers of commerce, and banks as much as on the periodicals of individual, independent publishers. One directory listing many Belgian *revues* is *Indicateur Publicitaire*, published by the Federation of Advertising Cy, 112 rue de Treves, Brussels.

Some of the titles picked at random from a list of 93 business periodicals to which the Belgian Office of Foreign Trade subscribes for their own library are *Belgique Automobile, Bruxelles Medical, Bulletin Horticole, Chronique des Transports, Le Courrier Metallurgique, Elektron, Energie, Industrie Chimique Belge, La Marine, Revue Bege des Vins et Spiritueux, Technica, Textile, Le Technicien Droguiste,* etc.

This list was supplied by Robert Bodson, former public relations director of the Belgian Linen Industry, Brussels, Belgium.

Dr. Jan Albert Goris, Belgian Commissioner of Information, Belgian Government Information Center, N. Y., estimates there are only "about 40 independent businesspapers published in Belgium."

From the Belgian offices of J. Walter Thompson Company, through the courtesy of Lubertus Smilde of J. Walter Thompson Company, New York, a list of 335 business periodicals of Belgium was prepared for the author (July 1958) with a total of 2,614,918 readers. Eighty of the periodicals on this list, chiefly in the fields of education, religion, medicine, and hygiene, furnished no circulation figures. If available, our guess is the total business press circulation of Belgium would be in the neighborhood of 3 million readers.

The brackets with ten or more titles are automotive (23), chemicals (10), architecture (12), food (12), agriculture (23), construction (11), electrical (10), stock breeding (11), engineering (13), general industry (10), metals (11), textiles (11), transport and communications (15), medicine and hygiene (42), religion (17), education (11).

15. Australian Business Press

"In a country," writes Oswald Mingay, "with only ten million people covering an area the same size as the United States, one trade periodical has to serve several fields." The Australian Advertising Rate & Data Service (AARDS) of which Mr. Mingay is the managing director, is very similar to the Standard Rate & Data Service (SRDS) of the United States. Copies of GAARDS, General Media Australian Rate & Data Service, are available for inspection in the New York offices of SRDS and the New York offices of the Four A's. (It also covers New Zealand.)

From the 1957-1958 edition of GAARDS we find the business periodical press of Australia is classified as *Trade,* in 80 separate categories from accounting (5), advertising (8), and architecture (12), to timber (2), transport (5), veterinary (1), and watchmakers (1). In some categories no circulation figures are available. In other categories figures are available in some cases. For example, in advertising there are 8 periodicals. Three furnish circulation figures which total 3,546.

Under this general heading of *Trade*, Section 3 of GAARDS includes such categories as medical, legal, science, local government, educational, dental, veterinary, hospital, horticulture, nursing, mining, to mention a few, so it is evident that Trade as a label for Section 3 actually embraces the business periodical press as contrasted to the consumer periodical press. There are 360 businesspapers listed in the 1956-1958 edition of AARDS.

On the basis of the circulation figures furnished (by less than half the periodicals represented) the combined circulation is 420,224. A guess at the total circulation of Australian businesspapers, listed and unlisted, including those who failed to furnish circulation data, would be close to a million readers.

Quite a few of the periodicals are published by associations, such as *Bedding* (Bedding Manufacturers Association) with no circulation given; *The Australian Grocer* (Grocer's Association of Victoria) with 4,356 readers; *The Journal of the Retail Traders Association* with 1,536 readers; *Hardware* (Victorian Hardware Club) with 6,720 readers.

The categories with ten or more titles are: architecture (12), building (18), baking, catering, confectionery (11), business general (13), electrical (12), engineering (15), food (12), groceries and small goods (12), machinery (13), medical (19), motor (16), retail traders general (11), shipping (10).

16. U.S.S.R. Business Press

The Embassy of the Union of Soviet Socialist Republics, in Washington, D. C., provides the okay for one to receive a small catalog printed in English (1958) listing newspapers, general and technical magazines of the Soviet Union. While it reveals no vital information on readership or revenue, this catalog does paint a more comprehensive image of publishing in the Soviet Union than most Americans or Europeans carried around in their heads before Sputnik.[15]

[15] *Newspapers and Magazines of the U.S.S.R. for 1958* V/O Mezhdunarodnaya Kniga, Moscow, Russia.

Our copy of the catalog came from Moscow at the direction of Mr. V. Alkhimov, Commercial Counsellor of the Embassy.

Publishing for the Soviet Union is no simple matter, we discovered. Many of its magazines are printed, in addition to Russian, in Chinese, English, French, German, Polish, Korean, Sero-Croatian, Hindi, Urdu, Japanese, Finnish, Spanish, Swedish, and Arabic.

Preponderance of the subject matter is technical, scientific, and educational.

The output of the Soviet Union's publishing industry can be inspected in New York City at the Four Continents Corporation book store at 822 Broadway, or at three other stores in New York City, one in Washington D. C., and one in North Cohocton, New York. Nine firms in Canada also act as distributors on the North American Continent for Soviet technical magazines.

As far as we can estimate, there are 561 businesspapers published in the U.S.S.R. for technical and professional people. They cover all the fields which are covered by the business press of any other country outside the iron curtain. Presumably, each periodical is controlled to some degree by the particular Commissariat in control of that industry or profession which the periodical covers. The magazines carry no advertising. The readership runs to five million.

The Soviet business press in the Russian language is divided into seven sections. The number of titles in each section appear in parenthesis: economics, sociology, politics (74), scientific (112), national economy, industry, transport, communications, trade, finances (*sic*), architecture (12), educational and pedagogical (17).

The catalog then lists a second group of magazines (in which we have checked 61 periodicals) which could be described as businesspapers. These are printed in other languages of the Soviet Union—Latvian, Lithuanian, Moldavian, Tajik, Turkman, Uzbek, Ukranian, Estonian.

These are the titles most frequently observed in exhibits of the Soviet technical press: *Journal of Physics, Journal of Chemistry, Journal of Mathematics, Applied Mechanics, Journal of the Academy of Sciences, Geological Sciences, Biological and Agricultural Sciences, Biophysics, Geophysics, Astronomical Journal, Magazine of Atomic Energy, Automatics and Telemechanics, Oil Geology, Meteorology and Hydrology, Optics and Spectroscopy.*

Every phase of engineering has a specialized periodical.

The sociological, philosophical, economic, political, and cultural aspects of Russian activity, however, are not overlooked by Russian magazine publishers. Among the many fields covered are sports, youth, literature, ballet, art, history, education, economics, world news, gardening, viticulture and winemaking, building, architecture, automatic welding, husbandry, languages, health services, trade, finance, medicine, transport, communications, etc.

If a Russian technical journal is published on rockets and missiles it was not included in the directory.

Returning from a visit to Russia in 1959, Elmer J. Tangerman, editor of *Product Engineering,* told a group of editors and publishers that United States businesspapers were the "best sellers" in Russia, being obtained by subterfuge from other parts of free Europe by Soviet technicians. He said the Academy of Sciences employed 2,400 translators and issued over half a million abstracts of American businesspapers a year to Russian engineers. Twenty five per cent of the Russian engineers, incidentally, are women. Within four weeks the Russians know everything published in United States businesspapers in which they are interested. A Soviet Science and Technical Commission, reproducing by offset, distributes American business paper articles and materials to several thousand plants in the U.S.S.R.[16]

17. Italian Business Press

Italy has about 2,000 businesspapers and trade directories.[17]

Of this total, 160 are farm and forest periodicals (*agricultura e foreste*). We have eliminated 100 of these as probably not strictly technical.

The remainder of Italy's technical press fall into categories similar to those of most other countries. There are 45 classifications in the *Annuario.*

Among the classifications with the largest number of periodicals are *religioni, attiva missionarie,* (religious) 260, *guirisprudenza* (law) 164, *insegnamento pedagogia, notiziari, scolastici* (educational) 107, *medicina e chirurgia* (medicine) 353, *scienze, fisiche, matematiche, e*

[16] "What The Communist Countries Think of American Business Publications," Annual Eastern Conference of A.B.P. New York, Feb. 26, 1959.

[17] *Annuario Della Stampa Italiana,* Acura Della Federazione Nazionale Della Stampa Italiana, Fratelli Bocca-Editori, Milano-Roma (latest available at Public Library, New York City, is 1954-1955, Part 1 to 7, p. 641 *et seq.*).

naturali (sciences) 79, *caccia e pesca* (fisheries) 20, *chimica pura industriale* (chemicals) 17, *automobilismo, motorismo, ciclismo* (automobiles and bicycles) 43, *industria* (industry) 42, *ingegneria* (engineering) 46, *metalli, metallurgia* (metals and metallurgy) 15, *tecnologie* (technical) 33, etc. There are 10 million readers.

". . . The Italian advertising business," according to *Advertising Age*,[18] "is beset with near and complete monopolies on media and sometimes with practices which amount to fraud being practiced on advertisers and their agencies."

Leading Italian businesspaper publishers and advertising agencies are fighting a protracted battle to establish ethical standards of practice, according to officials of the International Federation of the Periodical Press.

Two space brokerage houses (according to *Advertising Age*), Societa per la Pubblicita in Italia (SPI) and Manzoni, control advertising space in 89 of Italy's daily newspapers. Manzoni controls space in 123 periodicals.

The largest space broker, Societa Italiana Pubblicita per Azioni (SIPRA), controls all space bookings in television, radio, and most of cinema.

SIPRA and SPI and Compagnia Internazionale Pubblicita Periodici (CIPP) control advertising space in 31 periodicals jointly. SPI controls space in 69 periodicals and 66 newspapers and owns the largest advertising agency in Rome, APPIA.

Almost two thirds of Italian press advertising appear in its periodical press, indicating the popularity of magazines.

No circulation figures are given in this directory nor are they obtainable from the Office of the Commercial Counselor, in the Italian Embassy, Washington. No figures on advertising expenditures in the Italian business press are available.

Italy's magazines and periodicals bulked together received $28.8 million in 1957, a greater sum than was spent on newspapers, which is the next largest medium. The total advertising expenditure in Italy in 1957 was $108 million, a 200 per cent increase in six years.

18. Canadian Business Press

Canadian businesspapers listed in 1946 numbered 271. Included in this category were businesspapers covering over 75 different special-

[18] *Advertising Age*, May 12, 1958, p. 120.

ized fields of professional and business activity. Their combined circulation was upwards of 850,000. Their advertising revenue in 1946 had increased to a total of $7,400,000.

By 1957 Canadian businesspaper titles had increased to 372, with 159 categories in *Standard Rate & Data Service* and 114 categories in *Canadian Advertising.*

In 1957 advertising revenues were estimated by the Business Newspapers Association of Canada at $23,045,125. These figures are net (less agency commission and cash discounts). BNAC calculates the addition of 12½ per cent would give a fairly accurate gross figure of $25,926,328.

Total businesspaper circulation, exclusive of farm journals, was over 2,500,000 in 1957. Canadian farm periodicals (51) had a net advertising revenue in 1956 (last BNAC figures) of $4,800,000. Religion, school, fraternal, juvenile, almanacs, etc., received $2,600,000 net in advertising revenue.

The farm press, with 51 periodicals and 2.5 million readers, is an important segment of the Canadian technical press. Among the largest are *Free Press Weekly Prairie Farmer* (381,021), *Country Guide* (300,688), and *Family Herald* (393,912). These, of course, have popular appeal as well.

In 1957 the Canadian businesspaper net advertising revenue (trade, technical, professional and farm) was $27,845,625 against a total of $240,400,000 net advertising revenue in 1957 for all Canadian print media. The share of the Canadian business press was 11.6 cents of every Canadian advertising dollar.[19]

The Canadian Circulation Audit Board, Inc. (CCAB) is like the BPA in the United States. It has 216 businesspapers in its membership. CCAB, while including periodicals with 100 per cent paid circulation, also provides figures on the average controlled (free) circulation of a periodical consecutively mailed and individually addressed. CCAB headquarters is Toronto, Ontario.

Business Newspapers Association of Canada (founded in 1919) has 122 businesspaper members. They must have an independent circulation audit, be owned by Canadians, and be published at least quarterly. Headquarters is Toronto, 137 Wellington Street, West, Ontario.

Businesspapers of the present type were not known in Canada

[19] "The Printing Trades" Bulletin No. 5704, BNAC (1957).

prior to 1850. Some of the earliest known Canadian trade journals were *Sapper and Miner*, published in York (now Toronto) in 1832, *The Artizan, Farmer and Mechanic*, and several others published in various centers (*ca.* 1800) throughout upper and lower Canada. None of these early journals is known to have survived. Records of the Royal Society prior to 1800 describe this type of trade journal, but the early Canadian journals were not widely distributed.

With the opening up of many new areas of hitherto untouched country, and with the tremendous development of industry and commerce, a new type of businesspaper commenced to appear shortly before 1850. Concurrent with the confederation of the independent governments of the various geographical regions into what is now eastern Canada, the *Monetary Times and Insurance Chronicle* was founded in 1867. The following year the *Canadian Pharmaceutical Journal* was first published. *The Trader and Canadian Jeweller* appeared in 1878. These papers, which still survive, were the forerunners of the present flourishing businesspaper publishing industry in Canada.

Several specialized journals published around the last quarter of the nineteenth century include *Canadian Entomologist*, 1865, and *Canadian Sportsman*, 1870. Among other early Canadian business publications were *Canadian Journal of Commerce*, 1875, *Shareholder and Insurance Gazette*, 1879, *Canada Lumberman*, 1880, *Merchants', Manufacturers' and Millers' Gazette*, 1880, *Canadian Manufacturer and Industrial World*, 1882, *Dominion Dry Goods Report* (now *Canadian Textile Journal*), 1883, *Books & Notions*, 1883, *Canadian Bee Journal*, 1884, and *Merchant*, 1885.

Sensing the need for publications which would give particular business fields detailed independent market information and provide a medium for the exchange of ideas and "know how" for the betterment of all branches of business, John Bayne Maclean, a commercial page reporter for a Toronto daily newspaper, and Hugh C. MacLean, his younger brother and a practical printer, founded the *Canadian Grocer* in 1886. Shortly afterwards, although Canada was experiencing a depression, they started *Hardware and Metal* and other publications.

These were the original units of what is now a string of 30 businesspapers covering a variety of fields, which make their publishers, Maclean-Hunter Publishing Company, the largest businesspaper publishing house in Canada and one of the largest in the British Commonwealth and Empire. The company also publishes four national consumer magazines. It publishes what the company calls "business newspapers" in both English and French, the two commercial languages of Canada.

Horace T. Hunter, now chairman of the board, started as an advertising representative on the hardware paper and rapidly assumed additional responsibilities as the organization developed. The company has offices in Toronto, Montreal, New York, Chicago, and London, and also publishes four businesspapers in the United States and one in the United Kingdom.

Many of the company's newer publications are the result of adapting former publications to newer conditions. Out of *Hardware and Metal* were developed the *Canadian Paint and Varnish Magazine,* serving the paint industry, and the *Painting and Decorating Contractor,* circulated among paint stores and decorating firms. The *Bookseller and Stationer* has today become two publications, the *Canadian Bookseller* and the *Canadian Stationer.* The *Dry Goods Review* has become *Style,* serving the women's wear field, and *Men's Wear Merchandising,* serving the men's wear trade. Other Maclean-Hunter trade papers are *Drug Merchandising, General Merchant of Canada, Sanitary Engineer, Plumber and Steamfitter,* and *Canadian Hotel Review and Restaurant*—whose fields are suggested by their titles.

The company's two French-language trade newspapers are *Le Prix Courant* in the general store field and *L'Epicier* in the grocery trade.

In addition to its trade papers or "merchandising newspapers," Maclean-Hunter has a number of industrial papers. The oldest is the *Canadian Machinery and Manufacturing News,* established in 1905, which was widely acclaimed in both world wars for its educational work in showing manufacturers how to produce shells, guns, and other armaments. *Canadian Aviation, Canadian Shipping and Marine Engineering News,* and *Modern Power and Engineering* have widely established reputations.

The company's *Canadian Printer and Publisher* (founded in 1891) is one of Canada's oldest businesspapers; and *Industrial Progress,* an export publication circulating in 30 countries, is one of the newest (founded in 1945).

In the automotive industry, the company publishes *Canadian Automotive Trade* for retail salesrooms and garages and *Bus and Truck Transport* for highway transport and coach operators.

The company has two publications aimed at the executive group. *The Financial Post,* founded in 1907, covers all phases of business, investment, and national affairs in the economic field. A publication of great influence, it has a circulation greater than that of most of the financial newspapers in countries of much larger populations. Its campaigns for honest public administration and its exposés of crooked mining and other promoters have often caused national sensations, landed wealthy men in prison, or brought about drastic reforms in the laws of the land. It is the most quoted publication of any kind in Canada; for each issue an average of about 100 references to its editorials is made in Canadian daily and weekly newspapers. Floyd S. Chalmers, who was its editor from 1925 to 1942, is now president of Maclean-Hunter; he is one of many examples of Canadian businesspaper editors emerging as publishers. Another Maclean-Hunter senior publication manager who started his career in editorial work is Herbert L. Southall, chief of the company's merchandising newspapers division.

The other "horizontal" publication reaching the executive group is *Plant Administration,* edited for industrial management. The company also publishes *Canadian Advertising,* a quarterly listing all Canadian advertising media and rates.

In addition, Maclean-Hunter has a group of annual publications that supplement the services of the businesspapers.

Hugh C. MacLean Publications, Ltd., Toronto, is another great Canadian businesspaper publishing enterprise. At first Hugh C. MacLean was general manager of the J. B. Maclean Publishing Company, Ltd. (later the Maclean Publishing Company and again later Maclean-Hunter Publishing Company) for a period of 11 years (1886-1897). He sold his shares and went to Winnipeg, where he owned and operated the *Winnipeg Commercial* and also the *Western Lumberman.* In 1907 he returned to Toronto and acquired the publishing interests of the C. H. Mortimer Publishing Company. These included the *Dominion Mechanical and Milling News,* now known as *Electrical News and Engineering,* and also the *Canada Lumberman.* Other publications were added in the belief that businessmen wanted to have the news and know-how of their trades or industry in the most accessible and specialized form.

In 1886 there were still few businesspapers in existence in Canada. The name *Dominion Mechanical and Milling News* was changed to *Electrical, Mechanical, and Milling News* and so continued until the early nineties, when, because of further important developments in the field of electrical science, it was again changed to *Electrical News and Steam Engineering Journal* and later to its present name, *Electrical News and Engineering.* In 1892 the *Maritime Merchant* was founded in Halifax, Nova Scotia, and still serves the maritime province trade.

The *Canada Lumberman,* founded in 1880, was purchased by Hugh MacLean. The *Canadian Architect and Builder,* with a weekly edition called the *Contract Record,* was established. This publication is now known as *Engineering and Contract Record* and its weekly edition as *Engineering News-Week.*

Other Hugh C. MacLean publications include *Shoe and Leather Journal,* established in 1888, *Canadian Woodworker,* 1900, *Furniture and Furnishings,* 1910, *Boating Magazine,* 1921, *Radio Trade-Builder,* 1924, *Electrical Appliances and Contracting,* 1925, *MacLean Building Catalogue* (Ontario Edition), 1923, *MacLean Building Catalogue* (Quebec Edition), 1923, and *Building Reporter,* 1945. The publishers also issue *MacLean Building Reports,* a daily service covering engineering and construction projects throughout Canada. Established in 1911, this service is issued from three offices: Toronto, Montreal, and Winnipeg.

John B. Maclean died in 1950. He had sold his majority interest in his company to Horace T. Hunter and Floyd S. Chalmers a few years before. Hugh C. MacLean died in 1949. He had transferred his holdings to his son, Andrew D. MacLean, who is currently board chairman of Hugh C. MacLean Publications, Ltd., Hugh A. MacLean, grandson of the founder, is active in the business.

Andrew D. MacLean served as president of the Periodical Publishers Association.

The MacLean and Maclean companies have the longest records in Canada as publishers under the same continuous management. Their histories are cited to show that the development of the business press in Canada has paced the swift growth of business and industry.[20]

Many businesspapers and publishing houses have changed owner-

[20] Hugh C. MacLean Company use a capital L in their name.

ship, amalgamated, or divided, and there have been a few failures. New businesspapers have been started to meet new needs, such as those created by the rise of the electrical and automotive industries. Among the newer Canadian business newspapers are those serving the plastics industry, as well as several in the export field.

Businesspapers have changed along with the fields they served.

Among the large Canadian businesspaper publishing houses are National Business Publications, Ltd., Gardenvale, Quebec, and the Consolidated Press Ltd., Toronto, founded in 1894 by H. C. Gagnier. Several French businesspapers are published by French Commercial Publications, Montreal.

National Business Publications, Ltd., Gardenvale, Quebec, was formed in 1929 by a group of editors and business managers under the presidency of the late A. S. Christie. It publishes three periodicals: *Canadian Mining Journal, Pulp and Paper Magazine,* and *Canadian Fisherman.* There is also one annual publication, *The Canadian Mining Manual.* All four are well established and have long and honorable records.

The *Canadian Mining Journal,* one of the early technical publications of Canada, was founded in 1879 as the *Canadian Mining Review.* The founder, W. Allan, of Ottawa, sold the paper in 1882 to B. T. A. Bell, also of Ottawa. At that time mining in Canada was a very small affair, and the *Canadian Mining Review* grew up with the industry under the farsighted management of Bell. This businesspaper took a prominent part in the founding of the Canadian Institute of Mining and Metallurgy. In 1907, the *Canadian Mining Review* was acquired by J. J. Harpell and renamed *Canadian Mining Journal.* Mr. Harpell sold it to the present company. Under the editorship of J. C. Murray, the *Canadian Mining Journal* took an aggressive part in cleaning up some of the promotional abuses which attended the development of the great silver camp. These were the days of Cobalt and the real beginning of mining history in Canada—days of rapid technical development and spectacular discoveries.

The *Pulp and Paper Magazine,* founded in 1903, was acquired by Harpell in 1912. It, like others in their respective fields, has grown with the pulp and paper industry, which is one of Canada's greatest industries. This magazine assisted in the establishment of the Forest Products Laboratories of Canada in 1913 and of the Canadian Pulp and Paper Association in the same year, as well as in the production of the industry's five-volume textbook on paper making.

The *Canadian Fisherman* was founded in 1914, at a time when Canada's commercial fisheries were laboring under handicaps. Through the efforts of this businesspaper, the Canadian Fisheries Association was organized in 1915. The *Canadian Fisherman* became the official organ of the association. Its editor, F. W. Wallace, was secretary for many terms, then executive vice president, and later president. On the re-organization of the association as the Fisheries Council of Canada in 1945, at Ottawa, he was elected honorary president.

In spite of the fact that the early 1930's were years of serious economic depression, National Business Publications at that time entered upon policies of aggressive development. In 1930 the *Canadian Food Packer* was established through a subsidiary company and first appeared as the *Canadian Canner and Preserver*. From its inception, editorial attention was given to organizing the canning industry on a national basis. At a meeting called by the editor of the magazine, the first association in the canning industry of Canada was formed in February 1931. From this original association evolved the present Canned Foods Association of Ontario. In 1936 the Canned Foods Association of British Columbia was formed. In 1942 the subsidiary company, Federal Publications Limited, which publishes this businesspaper, became a wholly owned subsidiary of National Business Publications. In 1935 the *Refrigeration Journal of Canada* was established to fill the needs of another rapidly growing Canadian industry.

In the same year, 1935, *The Canadian Doctor* was founded. Described as a "Business Journal of the Medical Profession," it was projected to fill a need in Canada for an organ to cater to the other-than-professional side of life of the Canadian practitioner. Its objective was to serve his economic interests both as an individual and as a member of society.

In 1937 *The Canadian Journal of Comparative Medicine* was established in the interests of pure veterinary science in Canada. Its editorial policy has been governed by an editorial board of leading scientists in this field.

The *Canadian Industrial Equipment News* was the first Canadian businesspaper to give its readers news exclusively on industrial equipment, parts, and materials and to offer a reader service on the contents of each issue. It was first published in July 1940, under the title *Canadian Industry*, and an editorial arrangement was subsequently made with the *Industrial Equipment News*, published by the Thomas Publishing of New York City, whereby editorial material of the New York publication became available to the Canadian businesspaper. In November 1940, the name of the latter was changed to *Canadian Industrial Equipment News* to take advantage of the reciprocal association formed with the older paper. This Canadian businesspaper, however, is entirely a Canadian entity from every standpoint.

During 1942 *Shop* was founded, to bring to Canadian industry information on supply sources for secondhand equipment.

A Spanish language paper, *Revista de Comercio*, which had been established and for many years operated by Señor Gonzales as an export paper, was acquired on his death by National Business Publications. War conditions caused its suspension until 1945, when it went into active operation again, with a completely redesigned format. The purpose of the paper is to bring before the buyers of Latin-American countries Canadian products available for export.

Locker Plants and Frosted Foods was started, also in 1945, to serve the rapidly growing field indicated by its title.

In addition to the many businesspapers it publishes, the company issues the following annual publications: *Pulp and Paper Manual, National Directory of the Pulp and Paper Industry, Ports and Shipping Directory, Industrial Equipment Handbook, Fisheries Manual, Marine Catalogue,* and *Canadian Mining Manual.* The various periodicals of the company have a circulation of well over 130,000 per month, and all circulations are audited by either the ABC or the CCAB. The publishers have been pioneers in the removal of advertising from front covers.

Canadian Transportation was founded in Toronto in 1898 as the *Railway and Shipping World.* Its name was subsequently changed to *Canadian Railway* and *Marine World* and later, in 1937, to the present title. It serves the entire Canadian transportation industry, which has played such a prominent part in the development of the country. Acton Burrows, who founded the paper and was its active editor for 37 years, in 1946 was still its president at the age of ninety-three. He went to the Canadian West in the late seventies and spent many years there during the construction of the Canadian Pacific Railway. Aubrey Acton Burrows, the vice president, commenced his publishing career with the paper in 1909 and since then has served it continuously in various capacities. At present he is the publisher.

Consolidated Press, Ltd., Toronto, was incorporated in 1929. The business had been operated under the ownership of H. C. Gagnier and after his death in 1922 by the executors of his estate. Business publications now operated by the Consolidated Press are *The Canadian Cigar and Tobacco Journal,* founded by Mr. Gagnier in 1894; *Canadian Trader and Jeweller,* founded by Col. W. K. McNaught in 1879 and acquired by the company in 1905; *Motor Magazine,* founded under the name of *Motor Trade* in 1910 by Mr. Gagnier; *Manufacturing and Industrial Engineering,* founded in 1922 by Gordon C. Keith and purchased in 1941 from the Keith Publishing Co.; *The Canadian Baker,* founded by the Action Publishing Company in 1888 and acquired in 1923; *Food in Canada,* established by the company in 1940; and the *Motor Wholesaler,* a digest-size magazine founded in 1945 for the Canadian wholesale automotive business.

The *Western Miner,* Vancouver, was established in 1928 as the *B.C.* (British Columbia) *Miner.* Rapid development and expansion of the mineral industry and other allied industries throughout the Canadian West produced a demand for an increase in scope to include all the metallic, non-metallic, oil, and coal-mining industries of the western provinces, the Yukon, and the northwest territories. The *Western Miner,* since its inception, has had the advantage of the editorial guidance of H. Mortimer-Lamb, a veteran mining business journalist with an outstanding reputation. He is secretary emeritus of the Canadian Institute of Mining and Metallurgy, and until the present year has been secretary of the Mining Association of British Columbia and secretary of the British Columbia Division of C.I.M.

French Commercial Publications Ltd., Montreal, was founded in 1927, as publisher of a general businesspaper known as *Le Detaillant.* In 1935 it was decided that the paper should specialize by concentrating exclusively on the grocery trade, and the words *Produits Alimentaires* were added to the title. In 1936 a second trade paper, *Le Detaillant en Quincaillérie,* was published; this was devoted to the hardware trade. In 1937 *Le Detaillant en Plombérie et Chauffage* was added, and in 1939 an automotive trade paper known as *L'automobile.*

Home Publishing Co., Winnipeg, produces the Stovel Publications, a group of six businesspapers. Stovel Company, Ltd., founded in 1889, was a printshop partnership of three brothers, John, Augustus

B., and Chester D. Stovel. As the little printing house grew in size along with the metropolis where it was established, the Stovel brothers became interested in the publishing business. They took over production of *The Nor'-West Farmer,* a pioneer farm journal of Western Canada, in the early nineties. Later, in 1899, *The Western Home Monthly,* now *The National Home Monthly,* was launched as a Canadian family periodical.

The businesspaper field was seriously entered by the company in 1910 with *Canadian Finance,* introduced as a semi-monthly journal of comment and review for business executives. In 1918 two more publications, *Canadian Farm Implements* and the *Canadian Blacksmith,* were acquired. The former paper, established in 1904, was for over forty years the only farm implement publication produced in Canada. It has always been an influential supporter of the Canadian farm equipment industry. *Canadian Welder, Blacksmith, and Repairman* is the present name of the former *Canadian Blacksmith,* which was founded in 1909. *Motor in Canada,* originally established in 1914, was taken over in 1922. Three more papers were added to the Stovel group in 1928 through acquisition, from another publishing house, of the *Winnipeg Commercial,* founded in 1882; the *Western Canada Coal Review,* established in 1918; and the *Western Canada Contractor and Builder,* started in 1905. The name of the *Winnipeg Commercial* has since been changed to *The Prairie Grocer and Provisioner,* to indicate the present-day service of that businesspaper to the food trade generally in Western Canada.

The Precambrian, founded in 1927, is published in Winnipeg by the Manitoba Chamber of Mines. Its editorial material relates to the geology of the territory and the current happenings and progress of the mining industry there.

Industrial Canada was established by the Canadian Manufacturers' Association in Toronto, in 1900, to provide information regarding progress of the manufacturing industry in Canada.

Pilot Publishing Co. Ltd., Vancouver, publishes the *Commercial Fishermen's Weekly,* which first appeared in 1935. In its early days it was published in newspaper form and was known as the *Pacific Coast News, the B. C. Fishermen's Weekly.* In 1940 the format was changed to its present magazine style. This businesspaper covers an industry whose members are scattered in the ports, harbors, and villages of a 7,000-mile coastline with Vancouver as operational headquarters. The publication has followed the fleets into a great number of settlements along the coast. Perhaps no other industry but the fisheries could make possible such a wide individual distribution of a businesspaper within the boundaries of that industry.

The *Canadian Textile Journal*, of Montreal, and its affiliated annual review volume, *Manual of the Textile Industry of Canada*, are the sole Canadian businesspapers exclusively devoted to the textile manufacturing field of the country. The original conception of these publications occurred in the year 1883, with the establishment of a monthly trade news and technical magazine called the *Dominion Dry Goods Report;* in 1886 the name was changed to *Canadian Journal of Fabrics*. The present title was substituted in the year 1908, and with no further change in the name the journal has since been continued without stoppage in publication. Present ownership in this publication was established in 1928, when the first edition of the *Manual* was published.

This record of continuous publication covers almost the entire history of the textile manufacturing industries in Canada, which in 1943 represented an invested capital of $445 million, covering nearly 700 separate plants in the primary and nearly 1,700 separate plants in the secondary, or converting, divisions of the industry.

With little or no textile processing machinery and equipment produced in Canada, much of the advertising through the years has been drawn from United States, British, and foreign machine builders and engineers. A steadily increasing volume of Canadian advertising, drawn from the equipment and chemical fields, has been a marked development in recent years.

Western Business and Industry, a monthly featuring Western Canadian developments, started in 1928 as *The Financial News*. Its name was changed in 1943. It is published in Vancouver.

Fraser's Trade Directories are published by George E. Fraser, who, in 1913, started the *Women's Wear* and *Men's Wear Canadian Directories*, each issued twice a year. The two were combined in 1917. The spring issues of each pocket-size book were combined in 1917 to form *Fraser's Canadian Textile, Apparel, and Fur Trade Directory*. In 1917 *Fraser's Canadian Leather Directory* was also started, and in 1918 *Fraser's Metal Products Directory*, as well as *Fraser's Wood Products Directory*. The metal and wood books were combined and expanded in 1932 to form *Fraser's Canadian Trade Directory*.

Wrigley Publications, Limited, founded by the late Weston

Wrigley, publish at Toronto, *Hardware in Canada,* established in 1909, and the *Retail Grocer and Provisioner,* established in 1910.

Roy Wrigley Printing and Publishing Company, Ltd., started in 1914 with *Western Fisheries* and in 1915 brought out *Storage and Distribution.* Then followed the *Canadian Hotel Red Book,* now *Wrigley's Hotel Directory.* The first of these, *Western Fisheries,* covers the commercial fishing industry of British Columbia, an industry with an annual turnover of around $40 million. *Storage and Distribution,* national in scope, serves the warehousing and shipping industry of Canada. It includes each month a comprehensive list of shippers in Canada, in the United States, and abroad. *Wrigley's Hotel Directory,* an annual, lists over 20,000 hotels in Canada and the United States and is used extensively by tourists everywhere.

An interesting fact about the brothers who founded the two Wrigley publishing houses is that their father, George Wrigley, born in 1847, at Wrigley's Corners, Ontario, established in 1879 at London, Ontario, the *Educational Journal,* the first publication of its kind in Canada. He also founded the *Canadian Farmer's Sun* in 1891. George Bernard Wrigley, a grandson, succeeded his father, Weston Wrigley, as president of the Wrigley Publications Limited in 1945.

Canada's Foundry Journal was founded in 1927 by the late Frank H. Bell, one of the best-known practical Canadian foundrymen in the Dominion. At one time he operated a foundry of his own in Dunnville, Ontario, and it was a molder's strike that closed down his foundry which gave him the opportunity to bring out *Canada's Foundry Journal.*

Motor Carrier is currently the sole publication of Wes-Trade Publications, Vancouver. It was launched as a business magazine for truck and bus operators, in 1940, by John B. Tompkins, its present editor and manager, in partnership with E. F. Carruthers. Their original capital was credit with the engravers and printers; their cash on hand, 25 cents. This magazine differs from other businesspapers in its field by reporting news of truck and busmen only in British Columbia and Alberta.

The *Fur Trade Journal of Canada* started in 1923. It claims to be the only fur-farming publication to survive the depression without going through liquidation or re-organization. Before the war it had quite a circulation in Europe, including subscribers in France, Germany, the Scandinavian countries, Italy, Russia, Belgium, Holland, and of course Great Britain.

The Health League of Canada, a voluntary organization in Toronto, publishes the quarterly magazine *Health,* founded in 1933. This features articles by prominent medical and health authorities.

The *Canadian Moving Picture Digest* of Toronto claims to be the oldest motion picture businesspaper on the American continent. Founded in 1915, its circulation covers every theater in Canada and includes the exchanges, or distribution centers, of the various head offices in Toronto and throughout the Dominion, as well as the affiliated film enterprises. On the import of British films into Canada, copies of the *Canadian Moving Picture Digest* are sent to producer and distributor subscribers in Great Britain and mailed to circuit theater owners in India, South Africa, and Australia. It boasts the first and only woman editor of a motion picture businesspaper, Ray Lewis. It is the official organ of the Canadian Picture Pioneers, an association composed of those who have been associated with motion pictures at least twenty-five consecutive years.

Canadian Business, the official magazine of the Canadian Chamber of Commerce, first appeared in 1930 under the title *The Commerce of the Nation.* In 1933 that name was changed. The publication specializes in business news and current interpretation of Canadian national affairs as they affect business. It also carries authoritative articles on the work of the Canadian Chamber.

Stone and Cox, Ltd., Toronto, publishers of businesspapers in the insurance field, was organized jointly by W. E. Stone, born in the United States, and Charles Cox, an Englishman. They were both connected with the Mutual Life of New York at its London office.

The year 1902 had seen the first edition of *The Policy,* which developed into a popular insurance journal. Charles Cox was responsible for the editorial content, and W. E. Stone for the business management of the paper. Following the launching of the journal, the idea of producing a manual showing the various companies' rates materialized. The *Red Book* was published the same year.

In 1904 the *Insurance Mail* for industrial insurance men was published and attained great popularity. It soon had the largest circulation of any paper devoted solely to insurance. From this point on, other statistical publications were produced, embracing not only fire and casualty but also finally all branches of insurance. In order to ensure speedy production, a printing department was formed in 1906; this was greatly expanded in 1924 and doubled in size in 1926.

In 1909, in conjunction with their insurance business, W. E. Stone and Charles Cox undertook for some considerable time the management of the London evening paper, the *Pall Mall Gazette*, owned by the late Lord Astor, but finally their attention reverted to their own business entirely.

With the appearance of the National Health Insurance Act, the house produced in 1912 another paper, the *National Insurance Gazette*, which has achieved a world-wide reputation and probably remains, as it was at its formation, the only social insurance newspaper in the world.

In 1912 the firm decided to expand further and, following a preliminary visit to Canada by W. E. Stone, Charles Cox came to Toronto to open up the field in Canada, publishing *Canadian Insurance* and gradually adding other life, fire, and casualty statistical publications, all of which are still being published. In addition, the *Insurance Law Service*, in ten loose-leaf volumes covering the laws for each province and one for the Dominion, is published. Both the English and Canadian publications reach all parts of the British Empire as well as Europe and the Far East.

On the death of W. E. Stone in 1932, Charles Cox acquired control of both the English and the Canadian businesses and divided his time between the London and the Canadian offices until his death in Canada in 1943. Control of the business now remains in the family.

The *British Columbia Lumberman* of Vancouver was originally printed in 1917 as the *Pacific Coast Lumberman*. The name was subsequently changed in 1924. It is the official organ of the following trade associations: B. C. Lumber & Shingle Mfrs. Assn.; B. C. Red Cedar Shingle Bureau; B. C. Loggers Assn.; B. C. Pulp & Paper Assn.; B. C. Retail Lumber Dealers Assn.; and Purchasing Agents Assn.

The Fullerton Publishing Company, Ltd., of Toronto, was established in 1905 to publish the *Canadian Music Trades Journal*, which was discontinued in 1931 but is now being revived in conjunction with the increase of piano production in Canada. The company's other publications include *The Canadian Publisher*, first presented in 1922 and edited for buyers in major Canadian industries the purchases of which are in excess of five billion dollars per year. The monthly *Sport Goods and Playthings* was established in 1923 under the title *Sport Goods Journal of Canada,* and in 1947 the Fullerton Company brought out the first issues of two new annual publications, the *Canadian Toy Trade Directory* and the *Canadian Sports Directory.*

In addition there are a number of strong smaller houses, and several publishers produce only one outstanding paper.

Businesspaper publishing in Canada has had a remarkable growth despite the comparatively small and spottily distributed populations as well as the use of two official languages in the country, French and English. Nearness to the United States and the influence of British industry and trade contacts have helped the growth of the Canadian business press.

The associations which serve the business press of Canada are the outgrowth of the Canadian Press Association, founded in 1858 by publishers of all kinds of publications. In 1919 it divided into different associations for the daily papers, the weekly papers, and the periodicals. At that time the Canadian National Newspapers and Periodicals Association was formed. The latter title has since been simplified to the Periodical Press Association, and this group embraces all important national periodicals including businesspapers. Its divisions include the Magazine Publishers Association, the Agricultural Press Association, and the Business Newspapers Association. Editors associated with the latter belong to the Canadian Conference of Business Newspaper Editors. This group used to meet once a year with the National Conference of Business Paper Editors (United States) alternating between the two countries.

The influence and importance of the business press in Canada is evidenced by the fact that, when Associated Business Publications, in the United States, offered an award for the best piece of editorial work performed during the year by any one of its 160 members in the United States and Canada, the first winner was a Canadian editor. H. L. Southall, then managing editor of *Hardware and Metal* and today manager of the Merchandising Newspapers Division of the Maclean-Hunter Publishing Company, won this first of many international awards which have gone to Canadian business newspaper editors for outstanding contributions to the fields they served.

Mr. Southall was president of the Business Newspapers Association of Canada.

Canadian businesspapers have a record of achievement which proves their impact on the affairs of the Dominion. They have been responsible for many reforms, both in business and government, and have made a major contribution toward raising the living standards of the Canadian people and the standards of practice of Canadian industry.

The prestige and practical value of the Canadian business press was more powerfully impressed on both business and government during the war years. It won high praise for its co-operation with and interpretation of wartime regulations, restrictions, and rationing, as well as for its promotion of wartime salvage and other emergency measures. Many editors played a prominent part in the home-front war effort, and other businesspaper editors served in the fighting forces. Some editors were loaned to the government for service in full-time senior administrative positions involving grave responsibility and requiring intensive technical knowledge. Others aided on a part-time basis. Members of the business press served on the Canadian Publishers War Finance Publicity Committee, which was responsible for all advertising and publicity for Canada's nine Victory Loans.

Several Canadian businesspaper publishing houses also publish consumer magazines, which in their early days depended to a considerable degree on the revenue from the business publications to support them.

Businesspaper publishers have been honored in a number of ways. W. A. Lydiatt, publisher of *Marketing,* a weekly periodical devoted to advertising developments in Canada, was first winner of the Association of Canadian Advertisers' gold medal award for outstanding services to advertising. Col. John Bayne Maclean received the association's silver medal, awarded to a publisher for service to advertising. The University of Western Ontario honored him with an LL.D. degree.

Growth of the trade press in Canada has paralleled the country's expansion. It is now entering a more stable stage of gradual and detailed development. More attention is being devoted to research and other services designed to aid the fields covered. In appearance, service, and readership the Canadian business press compares favorably with businesspapers originating in other parts of the world.

CHAPTER VIII

EXECUTIVE POSITION DESCRIPTIONS

Manuals: Many well-managed businesspaper publishing houses publish organization manuals containing formal descriptions of the content of all executive positions. In recording such information a distinction is sometimes observed between "specifications" and "descriptions." In other cases the two terms are erroneously regarded as synonymous.

Correctly speaking, position *description* is a written record of the functions, responsibilities, authority, and relationships of a particular position. It is concerned with the position itself, not with the executive. Position *specification* is a written record of the requirements or qualifications sought in the individual for a given executive position. It is concerned with the individual himself.

For example, a position description may state that a publisher must direct and coordinate all activities of the periodical or the firm producing the periodical. The position specification sheet for a publisher may state that he should have at least five years experience in editorial practice, five years experience in selling advertising space, and five years experience in circulation practice plus a bachelor's degree in liberal arts, a master of science degree in journalism, and a graduate degree in business administration.

Some manuals, as stated, combine descriptions and specifications. There is no uniform usage.[1]

When recruitment, hiring, and promotion are the objectives, the personnel director should prepare position specification sheets. Some firms publish "management guides" which describe the intangibles

[1] C. L. Bennet, *Defining The Manager's Job* (New York, American Management Association, 1958), p. 15. See also Scott, Clothier, and Spiegel, *Personnel Management* (New York, McGraw Hill Publishing Co., 1954).

of a position, the interlacing relationships, materials to inspire the individual holding a position to fulfill the ideals behind his job and all other jobs in the company. This sort of guide gives meaning to routine performance and illuminates the principles which are supposed to give the performance meaning.

The "position guide" is the core of the proper organization manual. The trend seems to be to reserve the term job description for wage and salary analyses and to use the term position guide for organization planning purposes. The position guide does not describe the incumbent's present responsibilities; it outlines the broad responsibilities that must be assumed if the position under study is to carry its weight in an integrated and balanced corporate structure.[2]

The executive position descriptions are supposed to supplement the facts discernible on a well drawn organization chart.

Here is a list of the advantages an executive position guide can offer:

1. compare internal and external compensation;
2. appraise performance;
3. develop managerial talents;
4. recruit, hire, and place personnel;
5. orient new executives;
6. establish promotion sequences;
7. afford self-analysis;
8. establish common agreement with a superior;
9. clarify and supplement organization chart;
10. analyze and improve organization structure.

Finally, every large firm should publish a statement of "The common responsibilities of all managers."[3]

Structure: Figure 4 shows the structure of a multiple businesspaper publishing house which, by the definition of *Standard Rate & Data Service,* is "a company issuing two or more separate and distinct periodicals under a single publishing house name."

Figures 5 and 6 show the actual structure of three different editorial staffs in a multiple publishing house.

In a company publishing only one periodical the organization chart may be simple or complex, depending upon how large the single periodical is and the field it covers.

[[2] See Standard Oil of New Jersey manuals.]
[3] See Chapter IX, section 8.

Figure IV
CHART OF A MULTIPLE BUSINESSPAPER PUBLISHING HOUSE

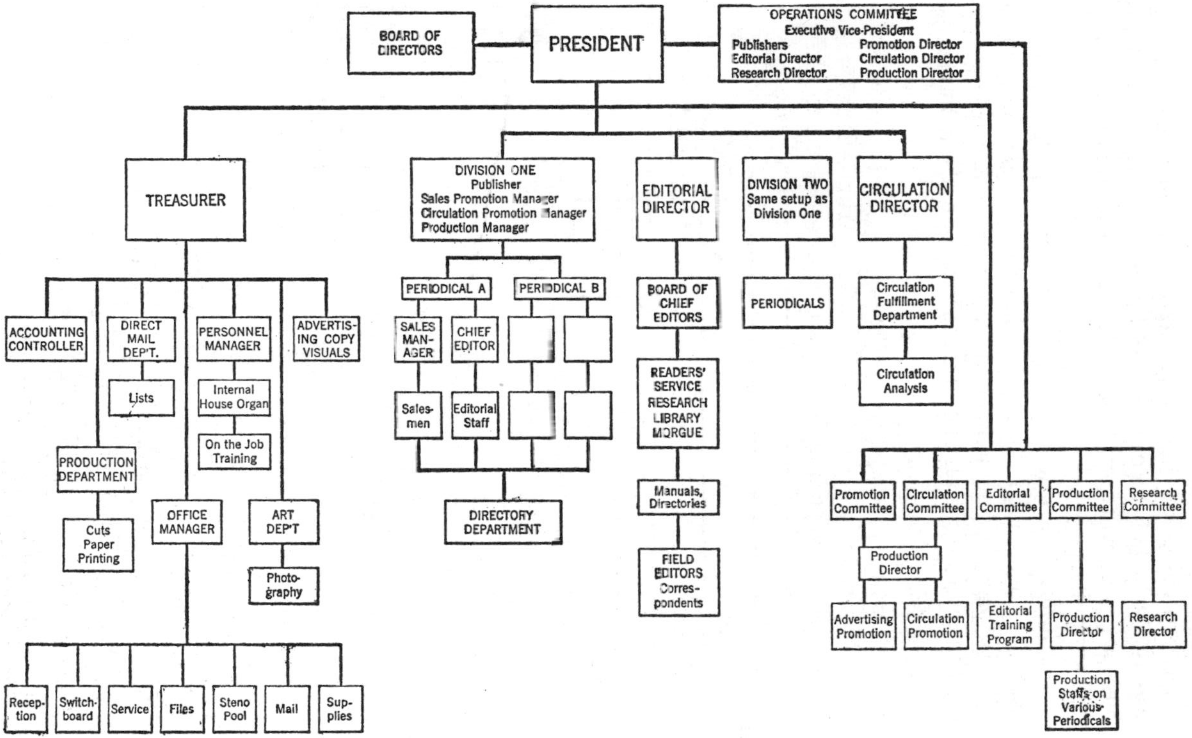

No two publishing houses operate exactly alike, but these charts, based on actual charts of several of the largest multiple publishers of businesspapers, will serve to indicate the distribution of responsibility and authority.

Mastheads: Few readers probably ever bother to look at the masthead of a magazine, which is the heading on table of contents or editorial page, and sometimes on advertisers' index page, supplying the names of executives and other information about the periodical.

Figure V
DIAGRAM OF A LARGE EDITORIAL STAFF

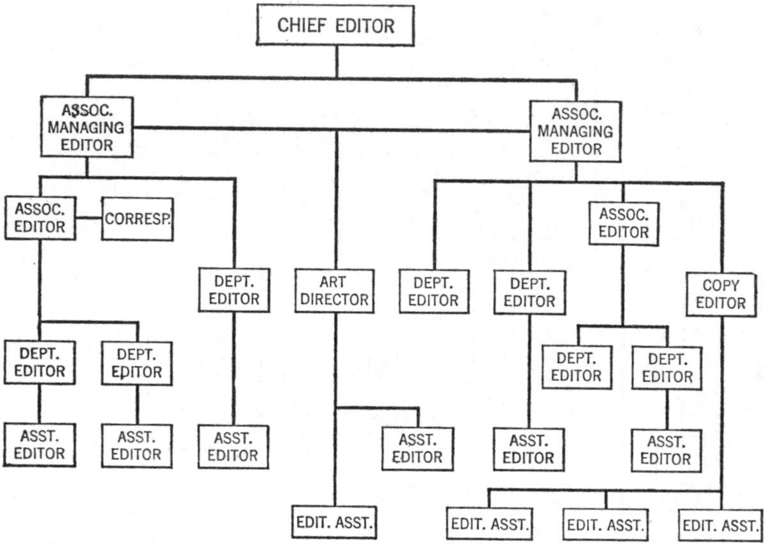

Professionals who analyze magazines see many things in a masthead. Some profess to see a reflection of owner attitudes; others see an expression of taste, good or bad.

Top name on the masthead is a matter of taste. Important periodicals place the name of their chief editor or editorial director at the top, followed by the names of the editor's associates and assistants: executive editor, managing editor, senior editor, associate editors, contributing editors, etc.

Now the publisher may feel his name should top the list. Some-

Figure VI
DIAGRAM OF A SMALL EDITORIAL STAFF

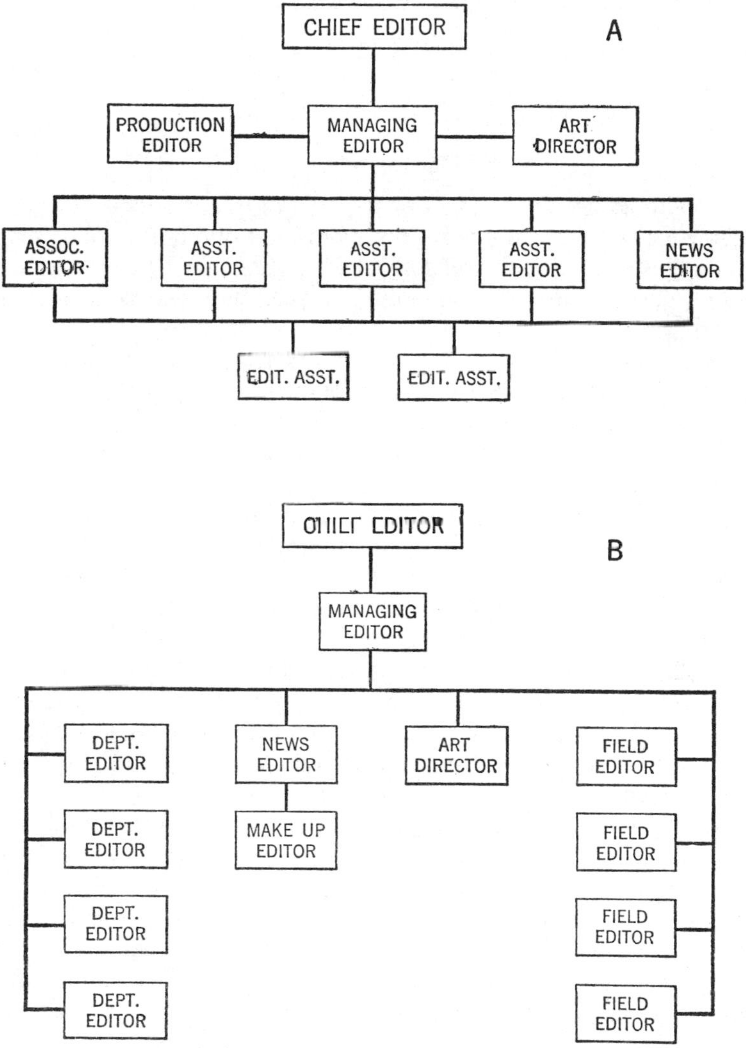

times the publisher and the president are two different individuals and there may be a third person of importance, the chairman of the board. And a fourth—the treasurer.

So some mastheads come out this way:

Chairman of the Board
President
Treasurer
Publisher
Editor (perhaps)

Sometimes a publisher retains the title of editor because he is the editor, or was for many years the editor. On the other hand, sometimes the title "Editor and Publisher" is retained by a person who does not function either as editor or publisher but *does* own the business.

We often wonder why any one would wish to be known as the editor of a magazine or newspaper when he is not performing that function. It recalls to mind what Sherwood Anderson once said:

"There are those who want to write and those who merely want to be writers."[4]

The publisher who merely wants to be the editor or the owner who merely wants to be editor and publisher may feel the title gives him distinction with the country-club set or in his *Who's Who* biography. Certainly no one in publishing or advertising circles is fooled.

"The greatest anomaly of all is that most [businesspaper] publishing establishments have no publishers,"[5] says R. O. Eastman.

There are mastheads on some magazines which, like some great daily newspapers, leave off the name of the editor. Is this because the editor is unimportant or a nonentity? We will leave the question unanswered.

The entire body of knowledge on the subject of journalism demonstrates that the editor will always be the most important name on any magazine or newspaper masthead. This is true because the editor is responsible for the product and guides his editorial staff in the creation of a new product every month, every week, or in some cases every day. It is also true because the personality of the editor gives personality to the periodical. By this personality it is possible

[4] Sherwood Anderson, "So You Want to be a Writer?" in *The Saturday Review Treasury* (New York, Simon and Schuster, Inc., 1957), p. 182.

[5] R. O. Eastman, "Why Is A Publisher," *Bulletin of the Eastman Research Organization*, N. Y., April 7, 1958.

to distinguish the periodical from every competing periodical, in the eyes of the readers, the advertisers, and those professionals who coldly analyze periodicals in order to counsel advertisers to buy or not to buy space; or who counsel owners to buy or sell the periodical itself.

It is thought to be better form to box off the names of the officers of the publishing corporation at the *bottom* of the editorial page or table of contents page or on the page called "Advertiser's Index" and leave the masthead to its creators, the editors, thus:

Editor-in-Chief
Managing Editor
Senior Editors
Associate Editors
Contributing Editors
Art Director
Research Director
Reporters

A final word about mastheads: be sure they are honest. List the staff accurately without screening their sex. Tell all in the masthead—especially tell for whom the publication is edited.

Editorial policy: It is a good idea, once in a while, to state the editorial policy on the editorial page. This is a sure way to find out if the periodical has an editorial policy. If it has, it should plainly state that the function of the business press is not to make advertisers happy but to serve the best interests of the readers. If it does this it will provide advertisers with a healthy market where they can find the happiness they deserve. The policy should also include a sentiment which the businesspaper publishers' associations prominently display and which member publishers publicly avow, such as:

The editor is pledged to publish no material in the editorial or news columns as a consideration for advertising space or any other end, except the welfare of the readers, and to refuse to withhold any legitimate news or editorial comment as consideration for advertising space.[6]

Further, each member of the Associated Business Papers, Inc. shall subscribe to and agree to conform to the following Standards of Practice:

1. *To refuse to publish paid "write-ups" and to measure all news by the*

[6] The seventh canon of business journalism, from Article X, Constitution and By-Laws, National Conference of Business Paper Editors, adopted 1919 (Revised June 1947) published in June 1953.

standard: "Is it real news?"; to publish no material in the editorial pages as a consideration for advertising space.[7]

The working press: In no business is there less use for an oversupply of top executives who sit on their surpluses (to borrow an expression of Ed Murrow's) than in business journalism. From the chairman of the board on down, except in the case of certain office administrators, such as the accountant and personnel director, every executive should be out of the office most of the time doing one of two things: (1) looking for new knowledge to help the readers or (2) selling advertising space or subscriptions to help the periodical stay in business.

Even accountants and personnel directors should be let out of the cage once in a while to find better ways of performing their tasks.

Doing their appointed rounds in the field among other business enterprises operating for profit, business journalists soon learn some basic truths that apply equally well to businesspaper publishing practice, namely: when any business bogs down its creative executives in endless red tape, endless office meetings, mountainous reports and memoranda, it is not long before the business is on the skids.

Thus the duty specifications and responsibilities outlined here should be approached with an open mind and also a sense of humor. Those duties within the office should be performed with a minimum of time and expedited by competent help, especially for those who must create the product and those who must sell the product—the *working* press.

According to Parkinson's Law:

The symptoms of bureaucratic illness are several. One of them is overwork because too many administrators make too much work for each other; there is too much work to do because there are too many of them trying to keep busy. For example, when the administrator is concerned with trivial details such as whether his pencils are sharpened or he has a sufficient supply of paper clips, office routine becomes an end in itself. The result of bureaucratic strangulation is that flexibility is lost, initiative is doomed, talent withered, new ideas throttled. In short the organization is well on its way to death.[8]

Every business organization should try to establish some ideal relationship between costs of administration and costs of production. If the

[7] From The Code of Ethics and Standards of Practice of the Associated Business Publications Inc., a folder.

[8] See Chapter IX, section 7.

ratio is firmly applied the only way to increase costs of administration is to increase production. The trick is to keep the tail in small relation to the head. If the tail gets too big—chop it off.[9]

1. Editorial Director

Primary function of the editorial director (or Chairman of the editorial committee) is to formulate and recommend over-all editorial policy, help the editors maintain their independence and editorial integrity vis-à-vis the business office and the advertisers, and act as liaison between the publishers, the business managers, and the editorial staffs.

Among his responsibilities is to see that the editors make editorial plans and keep within their budgets. He counsels editors, makes decisions involving editorial policy, makes recommendations for on-the-job training, maintains contact with specialists in the editorial and publishing fields, participates in outside activities which will advance the publishing firm or any of its publishing properties.

The editorial director will see that each editor holds periodic meetings of his staff. He himself will call periodic meetings of all editors on general matters inside the firm, or on outside problems of business which may affect them or their plans or which demand their consideration.

Above all, his responsibility is to see that the *readers* are guided as they expect to be—with intelligence and courage; that they are made to comprehend reality. Their interests and welfare are always his paramount responsibility.

The editorial director operates on authority directly from the chief executive of the publishing house. He serves on the operations committee, if there is one. He is chairman of the editorial committee, if there is one.

2. Editor-in-Chief

Primary function of the editor-in-chief of a single periodical is to strive to make his periodical the recognized leader among periodicals in his industry or profession, and to hold that leadership once it is attained. He is also charged, as a professional, with maintaining the independence and integrity of the editorial department, dramatizing

[9] Professor C. Northcote Parkinson, *Parkinson's Law* (Boston, Houghton Mifflin Co., 1957); see also Arthur Herzog, "A Visit with C. Northcote Parkinson," *Think*, Dec. 1958, p. 15.

the editorial content and simplifying the reading task. He is the principal contact with his readers and must live with them; make up and recommend his budget covering salaries, travel expenses, costs of photography, engraving, art, contributions, research, etc.; use the funds wisely; and keep within that budget once it is approved.

It is his duty to select and recommend competent editorial personnel and to train and develop them after they have joined his staff. He assigns the work of the staff, organizes, coordinates, and motivates their efforts.

He exchanges with other personnel in the company information which may be useful. He works with the art and research departments and sits in on conferences with the publication manager, the circulation, promotion and production managers.

He will participate in outside activities of the industry or profession his periodical serves, and also in the outside activities of his own profession, business journalism. He may delegate authority to junior members of his staff but he retains the responsibility and is accountable to the publisher for the editorial content.

The editor is responsible for the lead editorial page, which he usually writes himself and identifies with his personal signature. Sometimes, however, this page may be a composite of group editorial thinking, or contain contributions from other staff members.

3. Publisher

The publisher is the first line of defense for his editor against all pressures, outside or inside the publishing organization.

It is his duty to see to it that no member of the sales organization goes beyond the proper limits in advocating a client's case, under penalty of replacement.

It is his duty to stand up against improper use of advertising or circulation leverage on the part of any group within the industry to gain their objectives.

In a publishing firm with only one periodical the publisher may wear several hats. He may be the owner and the president of the corporation. He may call himself the editor.

In a multiple publishing company, the publisher is often appointed by the owners or the president and generally is the publisher of more than one periodical, sometimes as many as four. But one or four, his job is partly administrative, partly investigative and partly selling.

In the absence of a president or other higher official, he may make operational decisions. Otherwise, on the inside, his primary function as an administrator is to coordinate all the functions of the executives in his division, see that everything runs smoothly, and use as little of the time of the creative personnel as possible in meetings or memoranda.

Selling space being one of his primary functions, he must get out and sell the tough ones himself as well as supervise the sales efforts of his publication sales managers and their staffs of space salesmen.

Problems of hiring sales personnel, adjusting advertising and circulation rates, questions concerning the engineering and design of the periodical (editorial), problems involving the manufacture of the periodical, such as paper, printing, engraving, mailing, deliveries, postal matters (production) come within his jurisdiction. He must plan budgets, prepare and interpret reports, communicate top policy changes.

He may make the final decisions on all budgets, including the determination of the ratio of editorial space to advertising space.

He approves print orders submitted by the circulation manager and forwards them to the production manager who, in turn, transmits them to the printer.

He will recognize qualities in all those in his division and recommend them for salary increases and advancement on his own initiative, or approve such recommendations when they come from heads of the departments within his division.

He is directly accountable for revenue earned and the expenses incurred in his division and for profits or losses in his divsion.

The publisher, like the editor, must have an intimate knowledge of the magazine's audience. Just as the readers' problems are the concern of the editor, so the readers' buying, selling and influencing power, strengths, weaknesses, composition, history and future, are the direct concern of the publisher. He cannot know that audience from a swivel chair or from a research report. Half of his marketing job is done when he gets out and investigates his audience. Then he can successfully sell his understanding of the audience and intelligently criticize what others propose. Selling a periodical to a potential advertiser is (1) selling the audience and (2) selling the quality of the editors and the quality of the editorial content—the magazine personality. Like the editor, the publisher must place the readers' interest above everything else and make sure he has enough readers to interest a space buyer. Quoting R. O. Eastman: "That publisher serves his advertisers best who serves his readers first."[10]

The publisher of a businesspaper, however, holds a unique position, different from the management of any other business. He has two separate and different sales organizations selling two completely different sets of customers. His firm designs and manufactures a product for one set of customers and sells it to another. Subscriptions are sold to readers, and readers (as a market) are sold to advertisers. Even where the distribution is free, a separate circulation department is maintained to keep the reader "sold" and the circulation lists alive.

Circulation is the primary sales job in a businesspaper publishing house. Advertising is the secondary sales job, even if it produces most or all of the revenue, because without readers who are buyers you can't sell advertising space.

Mr. Eastman puts it rather neatly when he says a publisher rides four horses: "his engineering or designing (Editorial); his Production (even if he doesn't print the paper); and his tandem sales operations, Circulation and Advertising."[11]

4. President

The major functions of a chief executive are planning, organizing, co-ordinating, executing, appraising, controlling.

His objective, like the publisher's, is to serve the best interests of the readers.

He is also accountable to a board of directors (and perhaps to stockholders) for so managing the publishing corporation that it make a profit, shows steady growth, and attains other objectives laid down by the board.

He is responsible for the efficiency and morale of the entire organization and must see that its policies are properly carried out.

He is directly concerned with finances, financial planning, financing the operation; investments, pensions or profit-sharing plans; insurance; incentives; the acquisition or disposition of publishing properties.

[10] R. O. Eastman, *Bulletin of the Eastman Research Organization,* Nov. 17, 1958.

[11] *Ibid.*

He is concerned with the creation of new periodicals to meet the needs of new markets.

He must provide an example of creative leadership. The many corporations his editors serve, and his men sell, have presidents with basic functions similar to his. He must make it his business to know many of these presidents and to sell his own corporation on the highest levels.

Like his own exercise of influence on the policies and decisions of his corporation, the presidents of advertising agencies and the presidents of manufacturing corporations, exert an important influence in their companies. One of their functions may be to make the final decision whether or not his businesspapers are included in their present and future advertising schedules.

Moreover, many of his readers, indeed most of them, are executives in corporations, each of which has a president worth knowing and influencing.

Perhaps the president of a publishing firm considers it beneath his dignity to go out and sell subscriptions or advertising space. He can give it another name. For example, he can call it good public relations.

His four important publics are (1) the readers, (2) the advertisers, (3) the advertising agencies, (4) his employees. Those four publics can keep a businesspaper publishing corporation president quite busy selling his product, his service, and his good will.

5. Treasurer[12]

He actually relieves the president of the burdensome details of financing the publishing operation, but not of the responsibilities related to it.

The treasurer advises, and makes recomendations, on financial policies to the president. To help in reaching conclusions the treasurer may depend on his auditors, investment and legal counsel, and publishing consultants and draw upon other publishing corporation experience through his firm's membership in various publishing and auditing associations.

He sets up standards for evaluating performance, drawing up bud-

[12] For details of accounting practice in a businesspaper publishing house see J. K. Lasser, "Fundamentals in Businesspaper Accounting," *Businesspaper Publishing Practice* (New York, Harper & Brothers, 1952), p. 26.

gets, setting up administrative controls over costs: mechanical, advertising, editorial, and circulation costs.

He establishes credit policy for the acceptance of advertising contracts and sees that his own publishing house enjoys good credit standing with printers, engravers, suppliers, and contributors.

He supervises the negotiation of paper, printing, engraving and mailing contracts, subject to final approval by the president and the board of directors.

As treasurer he verifies the accounts of all other department managers and acts as a restraining or "controlling" power. He supervises the payroll and timekeeping functions, controls the accounting department and all budgets and budget-making.

His decisions on budgets are final but are always based on careful consultation with department heads.

6. Advertising Sales Manager

The advertising sales manager is the second line of defense for his editor against pressures from advertisers and prospective advertisers on the one hand and officers of the publishing house on the other. Naturally he does not want the periodical he is trying to sell to end up as a mere catalog of new products or "compendium of plugs." That would mean loss of readership because the catalog houses do a better job in their specialty. Since his primary function is to sell readership he is interested in his periodical's readers—both quantitatively and qualitatively.

As publication sales manager, his secondary function is to supervise the advertising space selling and subscription selling or (if the policy is free circulation) to supervise and control the distribution of the periodical.

In selling advertising space he is assisted by space salesmen and sales promotion and advertising specialists.

In increasing the distribution of the periodical he is assisted by circulation specialists.

He recommends appropriate advertising and circulation rates, allowances, short-rates, and rebates to the publisher for approval.

He draws up the budget for his own operation but also counsels on editorial and circulation budgets.

Like the editor and the publisher, his prime interest is the readers. It is his business thoroughly to understand the market he is trying to sell by intimate daily personal contact with it and with those clients and prospective clients interested in reaching it and selling it.

Like the editor and the publisher, he is charged with upholding the integrity of the editorial contents of each issue, and placing the readers' interests above the advertisers' interests whenever the two do not jibe.

He, or his assistant, keeps a tally on all salesmen's calls and reports.

He provides the publisher with lists of space sales, space contracts, expirations, new prospects, comparison reports on competitive periodicals.

He handles all telephone and mail inquiries relating to advertising.

He provides the production department with lists of advertisment space contracted for, with copy and art for each advertisement, or with complete plates.

He reads the advertising businesspapers constantly.

He maintains a personnel file for the industry.

He maintains close touch with the staff of space salesmen, furnishing them information on editorial plans, market information, and business predictions.

He supplies statistical information space salesmen request for advertisers

He maintains constant contact with circulation manager, feeding him information.

7. Space Salesman

His function is to sell: He sells two things: (1) the editors and the editorial product; (2) a market—the specific market his businesspaper claims to reach. To perform his job all the resources and know-how of the entire publishing organization he belongs to must be placed at his disposal.

To sell a market he must know the market from intimate personal contact with it. To sell the editorial product he must read the periodical and understand its editorial policy and objectives.

He must be provided with the latest, most complete information about the market—information that will satisfy the most curious and inquisitive advertising manager, company sales manager, advertising agency media man, or account executive.

He must be provided with the complete current story his competitors are telling.

He must memorize the advertising rates, contract terms, and circulation statistics.

He must be able, by education and cultural background, to discuss with ease, and on the same plane, the client's problems or the prospect's.

He will be assigned a territory in which he will call on both advertisers and prospects with the frequency necessary to adequately service accounts and sell space.

With the sales manager (his immediate superior) he will work out the most efficient itinerary and call schedule.

He will file complete, realistic, factual, and timely reports of his calls, including the correct names and titles and addresses of the key personnel on each account, correcting his records as soon as he learns of personnel or other changes affecting his accounts.

He will not only read but study every issue of his businesspaper (and the competition) so as to familiarize himself with the problems of his industry and the personnel involved in its activity.

He will read the advertising businesspapers.

He will exchange with other personnel of his company all information of mutual interest.

8. Promotion Manager

Since a businesspaper publishing organization has two products to sell—(1) a market to advertisers, (2) an editorial content to readers—its own sales promotional activity divides itself into two parts. In multiple publishing organizations there will be both advertising and circulation promotion managers, under the supervision of a sales promotion director. The basic functions are the same: to promote the business of the publisher.

He will work closely with those who research the market; those who report the market; with the salesmen who contact advertisers and prospects; and with the salesmen who contact readers and prospective readers.

He will draw up plans for company-wide promotions and promotions for specific periodicals and their special issues.

He will prepare his budget, requisition necessary art, paper, printing, lists, and other services needed for company direct-mail campaigns.

He will schedule and co-ordinate all efforts relating to company or publication displays at trade shows, exhibits, and conventions.

He will prepare and submit entries for national award competitions.

He will maintain accurate current records of all promotions and the results obtained.

He will maintain contact with promotion specialists, attend seminars, clinics, and workshops on the subject of sales promotion and marketing.

He will probe to learn who selects businesspapers for advertising or reading, what they want to know, who they are, and where they are.

He will seek to understand what editors are doing, trying to do, and why.

9. Circulation Director

Primary objective is to increase the circulation. Whether by subscription sales or free distribution, the objective is the same: to get maximum coverage and penetration of the field for the editorial messages and the advertising messages of his periodical.

He will work out and recommend to the publisher and sales manager circulation objectives, policies, and methods for the company as a whole and for individual periodicals.

He will work closely with the promotion managers.

He will work closely with all personnel who are in intimate contact with the market: editors, space salesmen, subscription salesmen, research people, circulation, and marketing specialists.

He will supervise the operation of the circulation fulfillment department, screen applicants for clerical jobs with his department and encourage their development into circulation specialists.

He will prepare print orders for the periodicals.

He will maintain contact with outside organizations of circulation specialists.

He will keep in practice by selling subscriptions himself occasionally—particularly at trade shows or professional meetings where the heaviest concentrations of prospective readership occur.

He will periodically review the company's conformance to approved circulation objectives and standards.

He will supervise all reports to outside circulation auditing bureaus and attend their meetings.

He will supervise the field force.

He will make special offers: extra copies, reprints, premiums, reduced prices, etc., when deemed advisable.

He will analyze and report to management his analyses of the circulation statements of all competitive periodicals.

He will conduct readership studies.

10. Circulation Fulfillment Manager

His primary function is to see that the readers receive the periodical and all other services they are entitled to.

He manages the department, seeing that it is properly staffed, trained, and equipped with the most modern filing and business equipment system.

He will recommend to the circulation director methods and procedures to improve efficiency and economy of operation.

He will prepare and recommend an operating budget and see that the department stays within the approved budget; maintains subscription records and prospect lists; compiles reports for the outside circulation audit bureaus; handles all correspondence on classification of readers; process renewals, expirations, and billings.

He will read the company's periodicals thoroughly to identify himself and his department with the major objectives of business journalism and also to pick up new names for the circulation list, note job changes and delete those who have died or retired.

He will constantly study and test improved methods and equipment for producing and maintaining desired circulation volume at costs within the operating budget or recommend changes in the budget to improve operating efficiency.

He will attend outside circulation meetings to improve his own technics and know-how.

11. Production Manager

Primary function is to direct the *manufacture* of the periodical.

He will negotiate contracts for printing, binding, engraving, purchase of paper, in accordance with operating policies laid down; prepare a budget for the operation of his department; and approve all bills involving his operation.

He will constantly study other methods of printing, binding, and engraving, to assure the most economical process in conformity with the quality standards set up by management.

He and his staff will maintain contact with printers and engravers on routine procedures: transmission of copy, plates, layouts, galley proofs, advertising proofs, page proofs, color proofs, preprints, reprints, etc.

Jointly with the editor he will supervise the folio of the periodical for each issue.

He will make decisions on schedule changes, authorize overtime, handle complaints concerning quality or service.

He is charged with the responsibility of giving notice and maintaining deadlines for copy, closing dates, folio dates, scheduling production to synchronize with other schedules of the office.

He maintains a record of all editorial and advertising material as it is received, sent to printer and engraver, returned to editorial and advertising departments, or to advertisers.

He will attend all meetings of production specialists to keep up with the new knowledge in his branch of the business.

He will maintain close contact with all departments of the publishing organization and strive for the most complete cooperation with all personnel.

12. Research Director

His primary function is to conduct research for editorial planning, circulation promotion, and advertising sales programs, and to provide information for clients of the company and related organizations such as advertising agencies, industrial designers, trade and professional associations, private corporations, and other research groups.[13]

He will maintain a complete library of current reference.

He will collect and classify all data obtainable on markets from the editorial columns of the businesspaper itself, from the advertising and promotion departments, from company reports, surveys by advertising agencies, newspapers, research groups, government bureaus, and other sources.

He will analyze and report conclusions on research projects of competitive publishing organizations.

[13] For complete details on six types of businesspaper research: editorial, advertising, circulation, media, mechanical, and selling, see Chapter V on Research, *Businesspaper Publishing Practice* (New York, Harper & Brothers, 1952), p. 153.

He will plan and develop research projects and methods of procedure for the publishers and publication managers, the editors, and the circulation director.

He maintains contact with competent outside research organizations and specialists and marketing organizations and keeps up membership in professional societies and organizations such as the American Management Association.

It is his duty to report periodically on research projects in process or completed.

He must be a professional, college-educated, trained, and experienced in the most modern technics and scientific methods of research and statistical analysis.

13. Personnel Manager

His primary function is to assist publishers, editors, and heads of other departments in procurement, orientation, and training of personnel.

The post requires a college-educated, professionally trained and experienced executive who thoroughly understands the requirements of each branch of the businesspaper publishing business and is expert in human relations.

Prepares and conducts aptitude tests.

Conducts preliminary screening interviews with applicants for professional, managerial, technical, and clerical positions, and for positions as salesmen.

Recommends appropriate compensation, rating and transfer in the promotion and demotion standards in the mechanical departments of the organization.

Establishes contact with sources of professional, technical, and clerical personnel.

Works closely with the office manager, all department heads, and the policy-making committees.

Formulates and recommends new personnel policies and revision of old ones.

Maintains contact with outside personnel specialists and continues own education in personnel direction, human relations, and traffic flow.

Introduces and maintains training programs.

Maintains job evaluation procedures, a medical program, grievance procedure, and gives counsel on personal problems of employees.

Recommends improvement in vacation programs, working conditions.

Sees that personnel engaged in creative editorial and production work are afforded privacy and quiet surroundings.

14. Office Manager

Primary function is to provide efficient clerical and mechanical services for management, to insure a smooth, economical operation:

Qualifications are good college education, good breeding, even temperament.

Must be specialist in human relations, and trained in modern office procedure and traffic flow.

Must thoroughly understand all the functions and objectives of businesspaper publishing practice.

Maintains inventory control of stationery and other office supplies.

Supervises delivery and receiving departments.

Responsible for telephone and reception, service files, stenographic pool, directory sales, reader service, and library.

Maintains contact with postal authorities.

Works closely with Personnel Manager and Treasurer.

15. Branch Office Manager

Primary function is to serve as representative of the company management in his city and the area assigned to that branch office.

Counsels and assists space and circulation salesmen operating out of that branch office, under the specific directions of the publishers and publication managers in the central office.

Carries out assignments for editors on their request.

Spends most of his time in the field, like other publication managers, contacting advertisers, advertising prospects, agency account executives, and media buyers, and readers of the businesspapers published by his firm whenever time permits.

Keeps his administrative office activities to an absolute minimum; gives most of his time and effort to his productive activities as a salesman for the company.

Provides research director with all possible information about the markets in his territory.

Undertakes research assignments in his territory for the company.

16. Art Director

His primary objective is to improve the physical appearance of the product the firm manufactures: the businesspaper.

His education and training must have greater breadth and depth than that secured in an art school.

He must have a deep knowledge and experience in journalism.

He must have a good knowledge of typography, photography, printing and engraving processes, paper, and ink.

He will conduct a training course among junior members of the editorial staffs, bringing them the latest know-how in visual technics.

He will act as consultant to the editors and all others who create and produce printed materials for advertising, circulation, and editorial promotion.

He will maintain a close contact with professional artists, photographers, printers, engravers, libraries, and archives of materials useful for illustrating articles.

He will supervise a staff of artists, give them their assignments, supply them with necessary equipment and material, and keep time records of their work.

He will budget the operation of the art department.

17. Copy Service Manager

Primary function is to prepare advertising copy when requested by the publication manager.

Staffs and directs a group of copywriters and advertising layout specialists.

Prepares an operating budget for his department.

Maintains contact with advertisers who require service—from original request for service, through preparation stages, production estimates, final approval of rough layouts, art and copy, engravers' proofs, composition proofs, and final proofs of advertisment.

Helps publication manager and space salesmen get business by preparation of speculative copy, layout, and complete campaigns.

Suggests improvements in advertising currently carried.

Cooperates in preparation of publishing company's own advertising and direct mail promotional campaigns.

Maintains contact with outside advertising groups and specialists.

Maintains contact with art director and heads of other departments.

18. Accounting Controller

Primary function is to maintain uniform system of accounting for profit and loss.

Keeps proper journals and ledgers, matches and passes all invoices, makes disbursements, handles and banks checks and money, issues billings.

Supervises payroll and timekeeping functions.

Compiles and prepares all tax returns.

Supervises handling of all insurance records: group life insurance, health and accident insurance, unemployment compensation. Maintains profit-sharing records.

Maintains records on credit policy.

Works closely with credit agencies.

Works under direction of the treasurer and makes no major decisions without treasurer's approval.

Supervises opening and distribution of incoming mail.

Reports on budgetary and accounting operations to treasurer.

Manages the accounting department, making requests for proper business machines and filing equipment in accordance with systems worked out with company's tax consultants and public accountants.

Attends outside lectures and seminars on accounting practice and reads professional publications to keep abreast of new time-, labor-, and cost-saving technics.

CHAPTER IX

AREAS OF RESPONSIBILITY AND CHALLENGE

"The Press itself is always one of the chief agents in destroying or in building the bases of its own significance."[1]

1. World's Biggest Classroom

If we now reread the definition of business, in the first chapter of this book, in the light of what we have learned in the chapters that followed, we become aware that the world, or at least that portion known as the free world, is one huge market place in which people can live together in free societies by freely exchanging what they have or know, for what they need or want; jointly advancing the technologies of peaceful progress; sharing the rich heritage of the past; pursuing a common ideal; all linked together by "a network of partial or complete understandings."

Edward Sapir, noted anthropologist, defines society not as a static structure but in terms of communications: ". . . a highly intricate network of partial or complete understandings between the members of organizational units of every degree of size and complexity. . . ."[2]

A free press bears a heavy responsibility to the free society from which it derives its freedom: the obligation to search out the truth, document it, give it meaning, publish it without restraint or favor.

Society is fed information and counsel from many kinds of media, but there is something special about the specialized business press.

[1] William Ernest Hocking, Emeritus Professor of Philosophy, Harvard University, *Freedom of the Press* (Chicago, University of Chicago Press, 1947), p. 232.

[2] Edward Sapir, *Culture, Language and Personality* (Berkeley, University of California Press, 1956).

It is more than a news-gathering and information-feeding agency. It is more than a purveyor of authoritative opinion.

The business press is modern man's chief source of postschool education all over the free world.

A continuous stream of textbooks called businesspapers are read periodically by the largest postgraduate class in the world—the managers of human enterprise.

Here rests a responsibility equal to that of the faculties of schools and colleges. Whatever spirit and sense of values, whatever good taste and high purpose has been impressed by the universities on their graduates, the business press must preserve, nourish, encourage, promote, and protect, throughout the postgraduate's life in the businesspaper classroom. From this classroom no one ever graduates except by retirement or death.

Those graduates of universities and colleges who enter law schools, medical schools, graduate business schools, or who continue their academic education in some other branch of the arts or sciences, now (perhaps for the first time) begin to read periodicals of the technical press which cover their specializations. In time these postgraduates themselves may become contributors to the columns of this press, as they come up with new technologies or know-how worth passing to the perennial students in the businesspaper classroom.

2. College Education Is the Prelude

There are still too many puzzled young men and women emerging from our halls of ivy every June: weak in such liberal arts as languages, history, economics, mathematics, and physical science; weak in the technics of research; unable to organize their findings; incompetent in verbal presentation; weak in making relevant judgments; and with the vaguest concept what to do with their degrees.

"Our university graduates," says Dr. Robert M. Hutchins, "have far more information and far less understanding than in the Colonial period. The degree does not stand for education; it stands for a certain number of years in educational institutions, and this is not the same thing."[3]

"Education is only begun in colleges and universities," says Mortimer J. Adler.[4]

[3] Robert M. Hutchins, *Education for Freedom* (Baton Rouge, La., Louisiana State University Press, 1947), p. 25.

[4] Mortimer J. Adler, *How to Read a Book* (New York, Simon and Schuster, Inc., 1949).

". . . I should like to stress the value of postgraduate studies," says Sir Richard Livingstone, former Vice-Chancellor of the University of Oxford. ". . . the course leading to the B.A. the 'college' stage in American university education is the prelude to postgraduate work . . . it gives little idea of what real knowledge is. . . ."[5]

As they enter the various fields of business the college graduates become the responsibility of the business press. Some corporations send college graduates who have joined their staffs back to college for postgraduate training; some give on-the-job training; but the great majority of corporate businesses provide their executive personnel and the assistants with the businesspapers specializing in their fields of activity and hope for the best.

The business press has a big stake in the kind of general education its future readers are getting while still in college. We appreciate the fact that each year the role of education becomes more difficult because of the expansion of knowledge and technology produced by specializations, and the growing complexity of the changing world. This makes a good general education all the more imperative, in our view.

The Report of the Harvard Committee showed that general education, as a preparation for stepping out into the world of business, had four aims:

1. *Effective thinking*: the test here is training in reading and listening and in the technics of creating ideas.

2. *Communication*: the ability to express oneself so as to be understood by others; the sharing of meanings. Visible-audible test is good writing and good speech.

3. *Making relevant judgments:* ability to project the whole range of ideas upon the area of experience; to tell good from bad.

4. *Discrimination of values*: a sense of the relative importance and mutual dependence of means and ends. Values (the Report says) are of many kinds. There are character values (fair play, courage, self-control); intellectual values (love of truth); esthetic values (good taste, appreciation of beauty in ordinary things).[6]

In short, a graduate should expect this of a good general education:

[5] Sir Richard Livingstone, *Some Tasks for Education* (London, Oxford University Press, 1946), p. 83.

[6] *General Education in a Free Society,* Report of the Harvard Committee (Cambridge, Mass., Harvard University Press, 1945).

1. Help to do those things in society for which he has the capabilities.

2. Preparation to be a responsible citizen fit to inherit a sharable world.

3. A synthesis of knowledge, a training to judge what is first rate.

4. Knowing how to think, what to think, with the ability to reflect, to voice a considered opinion, to make an intelligent decision.

Fourteen years have elapsed since the Harvard Report on General Education was published. It never reached the best seller list. Judging by the quality of the college output some observers feel the Report did not reach a large number of educators. Leaders in the field of education today are still calling for "bold and large-scale effort" to raise intellectual standards to a level adequate to meet the challenges and responsibilities created by new forces and conflicts of power in our modern society.

> Specialization, for example, is a vitality important force in the modern world but it is unfortunately true that for many individuals specialization is a dead end rather than an avenue to deeper and broader understanding. This need not be so and it is a challenge to our education to insure that it does not occur.
>
> The trend toward specialization has created among other things an extraordinary demand for gifted generalists—men with enough intellectual and technical competence to deal with the specialists and enough breadth to play more versatile roles—whether as managers, teachers, interpreters or critics.[7]

Whyte contends that in education the Soviet criteria of quality and the criteria of many big United States corporations are too much the same; the emphasis is on specialized technical knowledge. The corps of corporation recruiters, according to Whyte, fight tooth and nail for the new crop of engineering graduates each year, while hardly anybody gives a second glance at the liberal arts major.[8]

The President's Committee on Education Beyond High School (1958) says:

> *The country would be inexcusably blind if it failed to see that the challenge of the next twenty years will require leaders not only in science and*

[7] *The Pursuit of Excellence. Education and the Future of America,* Report V, Rockefeller Brothers Fund (New York, Doubleday, & Co., 1958), p. 11.

[8] Wm. H. Whyte, Jr., *The Organization Man* (New York, Simon and Schuster, Inc., 1956), pp. 112-113.

engineering and in business and industry, but in government and politics, in foreign affairs and diplomacy, in education and civic affairs.

3. Recruiting Business Journalists

The college talent hunt is getting bigger and more frantic every year. Placement officials estimate that up to 10,000 corporations now have active college recruitment programs. They say you can find anywhere from 100 to 300 companies interviewing on campus in one year at any large university.[9]

For instance, General Electric's needs for technical graduates (especially engineers) has grown from 400 in 1933 to 1,000 in 1958, and there are 500 other big corporations in the same predicament as G-E.[10]

"The shortage of college graduates who have majored in the physical or biological sciences and who can write is so great," declared Professor Marvin of Iowa State College, "that publishers of business-papers, industrial corporations and government agencies offer attractive starting salaries to such people.[11]

What educational preparation is expected of students preparing for business journalism? "A bachelor's degree in the profession (or specialism) with a minor in journalism plus a master's degree covering studies and research in the two fields," answers Marvin.[12]

The Council on Education for Journalism (1958) lists 46 colleges and universities with accredited schools of journalism. Some of them have accredited schools and departments in various fields of science and engineering.[13]

Attendance in journalism schools dropped 40 percent in 1958 from the peak in 1948. There were only 11,000 journalism students in 1958. Why has the attendance dropped? We have seen no analysis of the reasons why. Increased pressure on smart young men and women to enter other fields because of attractive promises held out to them in these other fields may be a reason. Another reason may be that, unlike the professions of medicine or law, a major in journalism

[9] *Acme Reporter,* official publication of the Association of Consulting Management Engineers, 1958 series, December.

[10] See Chapter II, section 3.

[11] K. K. Marvin, head of Department of Technical Journalism, Iowa State College, in *Quill and Scroll,* March 14, 1958.

[12] *Ibid.*

[13] Headquarters for the Council on Education for Journalism is Ernie Pyle Hall, University of Indiana, Bloomington, Ind.

is not required of a college graduate to become a journalist. Even a college degree is not absolutely essential.

However, as Dean Edward W. Barrett, of the Columbia University Graduate School of Journalism, observes: "*. . . for the average person going into journalism, the (journalism) training allows him to advance five, six or even ten years faster.*"[14]

Dr. L. A. DuBridge, president of the California Institute of Technology, makes a point:

"The fear of imbalance or conflict between science and liberal arts is due to failure to recognize that science *is* one of liberal arts. Every educated man needs an introduction to mathematics and physical science as well as literature, history and social studies.[15]

Dr. James R. Killian, Jr., attacks the charge that science fosters only materialism and is a contradiction of the spirit. "Science," he says, "is one of man's most powerful and noble means for searching out truth and for augmenting man's dignity by augmenting his understanding."[16]

More emphasis on all branches of higher education is the order of the day. Whether or not you consider science as one of the "liberal" arts, you may be sure science is the most liberating art in the history of mankind, and we believe it is now essential for a career in business journalism, or in anything else.

Everyone wants to know the facts of life. The most important fact in every person's life today is science.

Let us see what preparation is required of high school graduates in the U.S.S.R. in order to enter a Soviet university school of journalism. In 1955 the average Russian high school graduate had five years of physics, four years of chemistry, five years of biology, one year of astronomy, and ten years of mathematics, in addition to the orthodox liberal arts courses.

Now let us look at the preparation of a high school graduate in the United States for entering an American university school of

[14] *Time* magazine, January 5, 1959, "The Press," page 42.

[15] "Education in Review," *The New York Times*, November 17, 1957.

[16] James R. Killian, Jr., Special Assistant to the President of the United States for Science and Technology, speaking to a joint meeting of the Society of Sigma and Phi Beta Kappa Society, auspices of the American Association for the Advancement of Science, Washington, D.C., reported in *The New York Times*, December 30, 1958. Dr. Killian is president of The Massachusetts Institute of Technology.

journalism. In 1955 less than one third of the graduates had taken chemistry—for only one year; one fourth of the graduates had studied physics—for only one year; less than one seventh had studied any advanced mathematics.[17]

4. Soviet Education Is Not the Threat

The Soviet publishes more than 500 technical periodicals.[18] Some of these businesspapers may be examined and purchased in New York City and Toronto bookstores. Most of them are now being feverishly translated into English as soon as they arrive in our country.

In Moscow, American businesspapers have been translated into Russian and other languages of the U.S.S.R. for years. Indeed, for many years prior to World War II, Amtorg, a Soviet agency operating in New York, translated abstracts from American businesspapers and published, in New York, a monthly magazine of these translations (with charts and tables) which was mailed to Russian engineers and scientists in the U.S.S.R. The publishing cost was paid for by advertisements secured from large United States corporations eager to sell their products to the U.S.S.R. (Amtorg is a combination of the first letters of the agency, "American to Russian Government.") It was called *American Engineering and Industry.*

In his monumental study, *Soviet Education for Science and Technology,* Alexander G. Korol of the Massachusetts Institute of Technology points out that:

> The Soviet Union has committed the major part of the productive effort, skill and talent of its people to the maintenance and increase of communist capability for the aggressive expansion of communist power. It has mobilized a major share of the social and economic resources of the areas it controls to advance its technological means toward achieving this objective. It is this objective which the Soviet educational system is ultimately designed to serve.[19]

Mr. Korol, therefore, suggests:

[17] "Science Education," *Wall Street Journal,* November 13, 1957.

[18] See Chap. VII, section 16.

[19] Alexander G. Korol, *Soviet Education for Science and Technology* (New York, John Wiley & Sons, 1958), p. 410. Mr. Korol who got his secondary education in Russia and his higher education in the United States is on the Senior Research Staff, Center for International Studies, M.I.T.

We must maintain and decisively increase our technological, industrial and military lead—for self-defense in the last resort, but first of all in the hope that a superior weapons capability may effectively discourage any large-scale communist military aggression.[20]

But, in stating the goals of American education, Mr. Korol emphasizes the point that the threat to us is not Soviet education but Soviet communism:

The task of American education is infinitely greater, more difficult, and more challenging than that of Soviet education. It is greater because, in addition to the training it must provide on a very large scale in the rapidly expanding fields of modern technology and increasingly specialized vocational, industrial and professional skills, it is the goal of American education to afford enlightenment, to develop the independent, individual intellectual and moral stature requisite for and compatible with the responsibilities of informed and mature citizenship in a free society, and to encourage the maximum realization of individual capabilities and satisfactions.[21]

In essence, what Russian youth are getting is training and indoctrination, but it isn't education—not as we define it—and if the training is mainly in the physical sciences, mathematics, and technology, it is not enough, even as training. Accumulation of certain kinds of information is not education. Indoctrination is not education.

In his book Korol warns us that we can not maintain our combined scientific, technological and moral superiority by carrying on our educational efforts "as usual." He says:

"We free peoples must find a way to release a larger share of our aggregate resources and energy from nonessential material uses and devote them to the service of indispensable goals."[22]

5. Synthesis of Knowledge

How many graduates can give an intelligent definition of "university?"

We found the following explanation by Schrödinger in an old copy of *ETC*, the excellent little magazine of the Society of General Semantics. Schrödinger says:

[20] *Ibid.*, p. 410.
[21] *Ibid.*, p. 411.
[22] *Ibid.*, p. 146.

"We have inherited from our forefathers the keen longing for unified, all-embracing knowledge. The very name given to the highest institutions of learning (University) reminds us that from antiquity and throughout many centuries the universal aspect has been the only one to be given credit. But the spread, both in width and depth, of the multifarious branches of knowledge during the last hundred odd years has confronted us with a queer dilemma. We feel clearly that we are only now beginning to acquire reliable material for welding together the sum-total of all that is known as a whole; but on the other hand, it has become more than a specialized portion of it. I can see no other escape from this dilemma (lest our own true aim be lost forever) than that some of us should venture to embark on a synthesis of facts and theories, albeit with second-hand and incomplete knowledge of some of them—and at the risk of making fools of themselves."[23]

The most Reverend Geoffrey Francis Fisher, Archbishop of Canterbury, in 1946, on the occasion of receiving an honorary Doctor of Law degree from Columbia University, observed:

"*Universities are becoming aware of the danger of unrelated specialism and are seeking a way to teach a synthesis of knowledge.*"

Teaching a synthesis of knowledge is the role of the present day business journalist. To successfully teach his specialism he must *relate* it to everything around it, which means he himself must know what is going on around his specialism (see Chapter I, section 6).

An outstanding businesspaper editor who became a publisher, James Lyne, stressed this point at a meeting of businesspaper publishers which he addressed as their president:

Integration and synthesis, in contrast to specialization, are just as important in our economic life as scientific achievement [he said]. No industry or part thereof has any value standing alone . . . hence, a businesspaper which reports only the internal news of the industry with no reporting of monetary or tax matters (for example) is doing only half the job needed to help its readers in business.[24]

More and more we begin to appreciate that a private corporation is primarily a social institution which organizes and controls the behavior of its members very much like any political organization or church association. Its internal problems of worker-management rela-

[23] Erwin Schrödinger, "What is Life?" *ETC*, Spring 1946, page 208.

[24] James G. Lyne, president, Simmons-Boardman Corporation, former editor of *Railway Age*, before the Associated Business Publications, Hotel Astor, Feb. 20, 1953.

tions are also the concern of business journalists covering the field in which a particular corporation operates.

Leaders of business corporations, like the leaders of labor unions, need to know about all social as well as economic changes. They need precise and explicit knowledge of change or impending change and its probable effect on their actions. They need to know what science is really finding out about human behavior and how to apply the findings.

The experts are learning that money alone cannot satisfy the emotional needs of people who for much of their lives work in one place with one group eight hours a day and think and talk about it the rest of the time. What will satisfy these people? The programs and procedures for better human relations are now finding their way into the columns of the businesspaper as well as the columns of the employee magazine.

6. Scientism or Scientific Method?

Those who study fossiliferous rocks have discovered that many species of plant and animal life perished on this planet because they could not adapt themselves to the changing environment.

Why did man survive? Well, for one thing you can't defeat him. This was demonstrated in the powerful story *The Old Man and the Sea* by Ernest Hemingway. He also survives because he has developed the power to think. He underwrites his survival and progress because he creates tools to do his work better and faster, as he thinks up more work for himself and more ways to avoid work.

The most precise of these tools is scientific method. If we can supply this precision tool to the problems of the mind and human spirit the way small groups of men in modern times have applied it to the problems of the material world, some say we may underwrite our survival for a long time to come.

"We have never studied man-as-a-whole scientifically," writes Korzybski, ". . . in all aspects of his behavior, science, mathematics, and 'mental ills' included."[25]

The idea of a unified, exact science of man, with the same technics that worked in the physical sciences is, as Whyte says, "a cliche that has been kicked around for centuries.[26]

[25] Alfred Korzybski, *Science and Sanity* (2nd ed.; Lancaster, Pa., Science Press, 1941), pp. 17-18.

[26] William H. Whyte, Jr.: *The Organization Man*, Chap. III.

Dr. Bernard Berelson once observed that "some kind of communication on some kinds of issues brought to the attention of some kinds of people under some kinds of conditions have some kinds of effects."[27]

To reduce man or human society to an exact science like the physical sciences has, at least, produced a growth industry of formidable proportions in the contributive bracket of human activity. It is called "social science" and gives us the social engineer (self-styled), the personality-tester or brain-picker. What has been accomplished by the social engineer is rather dismal and frustrating according to the critics.[28]

You do not make something scientific by calling it scientific. Because of incomplete and half-baked "research," advertising agencies sometimes look on audience studies by periodical publishers with suspicion, and advertisers sometimes look on market surveys by advertising agencies with like suspicion. Inasmuch as advertising agencies are fed information by the research departments of publishing firms, and *vice versa,* misinformation about markets can reach epidemic proportions.[29]

How does science differ from scientism and why is this an area of responsibility for business journalists?

Scientific method is a method of thought and conduct which helps men understand the world they live in. Simply stated, it is the application of specific procedures to investigation; a method of orderly, honest thinking and scrupulous conduct toward anything you want to learn more about. As Stuart Chase says, "scientific method is the sole discipline where you can not lie even to yourself . . . you can not equivocate, crawl, dissemble, cover up or distort the figures."[30]

[27] Wilbur Schram, Ed., *Communications in Modern Society,* Urbana, Ill., University of Illinois Press, 1948), p. 172.

[28] F. A. Hayek, *The Counter-Revolution of Science: Studies on the Abuse of Reason* (Glencoe, Ill., The Free Press, 1952). See also Eric Voegelin, *Social Research,* December 1948; William H. Whyte, Jr.: *The Organization Man,* Chap. III, "Scientism"; Louis I. Bredvold, "The Invention of Ethical Calculus," *The Seventeenth Century: Studies in the History of English Thought and Literature from Bacon to Pope,* Richard F. Jones, *et al.* (Stanford, Stanford University Press, 1951); Martin L. Gross, "The Brain Pickers," *True* magazine, March 1959, p. 62.

[29] See *Businesspaper Publishing Practice* (New York, Harper & Brothers, 1952), Chap. 5.

[30] Stuart Chase, *The Proper Study of Mankind* (New York, Harper & Brothers, 1948), p. 304.

The bona fide scientist tackles a problem with an open mind, free of prejudices. He is humble. He listens. He observes. He has a wholesale curiosity and childlike wonder. How many of us outside the scientific circle know men like that? The scientist welcomes criticism. He *invites* the detection of error in his thinking or his conclusions. How many are there like that outside the scientific circle?

Many of us may think of the scientist as a fellow apart, above and beyond, when all the time he may be pretty much like the rest of us—except in one particular: he invariably uses a precision tool called scientific method. That tool is also available to the businessman, the business journalist, and all others who undertake communications research.

Some years ago we came across the "Schema of Scientific Method" as outlined by Dr. Russel Meyers, then Associate Professor of Surgery in the College of Medicine, State University of Iowa Hospitals.

First, Dr. Meyers drew a distinction between science and scientific method, terms which many people erroneously regard as synonymous.

Science (Dr. Meyers said) is a generic term embracing the body of technologic data (knowledge, know-how, know-what, etc.) which is at our command:

directions
formulae
laws, truths, etc.
constructs
technical achievements
principles
hypotheses

"Scientific method is the *modus operandi* through which we arrive at the bulk of this technologic data."[31]

Dr. Meyers illustrated scientific method with a 10 per cent solution of common table salt in water as an example:

1. Formulation of the question—what are you trying to find out? Definition of terms.

2. Accurate description of color, taste, weight, volume, other physical properties of the salt solution.

3. A catalog of the chemical agents with which salt solution is capable (and incapable) of reacting.

[31] Russell Meyers, "The Nervous System and General Semantics," *ETC.*, Vol. V, No. 4, Summer 1948, p. 231.

4. A statement concerning the uses now known and theoretically capable of being known to which the salt solution may be put.

5. Information concerning the distribution of salt and salt solutions on our planet and on other satellites or planets.

6. A symbolic representation of the ionized form of NaC_1 in solution.

7. A tabulation of whatever principles, laws, and other generalizations (abstractions) seem (in our day) relevant to the above.

8. The broad principles underlying the procedures by which such technologic data (as the above) was first acquired and later expanded and verified to such extent that qualified scientists in many lands and in successive periods of time have been able to concur with one another in regard to it.

This is scientific method.

Dr. Meyers pointed out that an individual may possess a considerable fund of knowledge and yet be incapable of formulating the procedures by which he and/or others have acquired it.

The pole vaulter (using Dr. Meyer's example) may turn in consistently near-record performances without being able to abstract the principles he regularly puts to use in the job of clearing the crossbar.

The pole vaulter, therefore, cannot communicate the principles to his team-mates when they ask him how he does it.

"A competent coach, even though he was never a pole-vaulter himself, would be able to discriminate, abstract and generalize the significant nuances of sensori-motor activities exhibited by the successful pole-vaulter, so as to improve the performance of other pole-vaulters," Dr. Meyers declares.

Schema of Scientific Method[32]

I. Formulation of the question. Definition of terms.
II. Collection of factual data through:
  Observation
  Experimentation
  Statistical analysis
III. Tentative ordering, arrangement, and classification of data
IV. Tentative derivation of generalizations
  role of mathematic treatment

[32] Russell Meyers, "The Nervous System and General Semantics."

role of principle of parsimony
role of general semantics

V. Further collection of data (see II above)
VI. Re-examination of generalizations in light of newly acquired data
VII. Retention, rejection or revision of generalizations as indicated by re-examination under VI
VIII. Repeat V–VII, etc., etc.

Employing the scientific method, the scientist has created machines to replace human muscle, human dexterity and even human brain power. He has given us new kinds of energy: hydroelectric, atomic, thermonuclear and solar.

Using the scientific method, medical scientists have conquered many diseases and extended the human life-span, and engineers have eliminated many physical burdens.

As the electronic machines accelerate the search for new knowledge and the speed of production, as men come up with more inventions, formulae and discoveries, challenging and even terrifying problems are created which, in turn, will require scientific method for their solution.

The employment of rational scientific methodology is sorely needed in the field of human relations and communications—particularly in business journalism research because of the important nature of the decisions management must make based on the findings of the business journalists.

The great biologist, Julian Huxley, in one of his books, emphasizes the task yet to be undertaken: the scientific exploration of human possibilities of spiritual development in the study of educational methods and psychological capacities—done scientifically and systematically.[33]

Huxley points to the fact that most people on earth are still substandard, underfed, sick, illiterate, ignorant, and superstitious. In his view:

"The highest and most sacred duty of man is seen as the proper utilization of the untapped resources of human beings."[34]

Huxley believes that man, through modern communications, can pool his intellectual resources so as to survive the violent changes

[33] Julian Huxley, *Evolution In Action* (New York, Harper & Brothers, 1953), pp. 170-176.

[34] Huxley, *op. cit.*, p. 171.

of environment that still lay ahead, and actually shape his own destiny.

In this the business journalist plays the lead role.

7. Cybernetic Revolution

Here is one of the most vital areas of responsibility and challenge business journalists must face up to: clarifying the current confusion and misrepresentation of the true meaning of automatic control and suggesting procedures for human adjustments—before too many people go off the deep end.

Some of the confusion that exists is based on ignorance and some is the result of what Ralph Cordiner, board chairman of the General Electric Company, describes as "a campaign of calculated confusion."

Confusion is the natural general reaction to change or impending change. Someone has said revolutions are half over before most people know they are in one. This is true of the Cybernetic Revolution which is characterized as the Second Industrial Revolution. Toynbee said the substitution of competition for medieval regulation which previously controlled the production and distribution of wealth was the chief cause of the First Industrial Revolution.[35] Now the system of competition has outgrown the brain capacity of man.

The United States plant is expected to increase its output more than 40 per cent by 1965 with an increase of only 11 per cent in the available work force. How can this be done?

We already have the answer: automation and cybernetics. We not only build automatic factories; we now build machines which can sense, remember, learn, beckon, observe, decide, act, command.

The total employment in 1956 was 65 million people. The gross national product (GNP) that same year was $412 billion. In other words, the consumer in 1956 demanded $412 billion of goods and services and there were 65 million people employed to extract, transform, distribute, and contribute to the business process.

Sylvania Electric's vice president, W. Benton Harrison, makes this point:

> If there had been a complete blackout on all technological progress and a blanket prohibition of further mechanization in the manufacturing plant during that period, 75 million people—a far larger number than

[35] Arnold Toynbee; *The Industrial Revolution* (Boston, Beacon Press, Inc., 1956).

were available—would have been required to produce the $412 billion. In other words, improved mechanization compensated for what would have been a shortage of ten million people in the working force."[36]

Mr. Cordiner believes increased automation will be evolutionary rather than revolutionary.

Others, however, are not so sanguine. For instance, Messrs. Chapple and Coon:

"Ever since the Industrial Revolution, the speed of technological change has been increasing geometrically. We no longer have a generation or two in which to absorb the shock of a new and basic invention."[37]

The rate of change, these observers say, has "skirted the threshold of the human capacity for learning."

Nor is Dr. Norbert Wiener, inventor of the term "cybernetics" so sanguine as Mr. Cordiner. In his second book, which clarifies portions of the first book, Dr. Wiener characterizes cybernetics as "The Second Industrial Revolution."[38]

"There is absolutely no reason," Dr. Wiener wrote in 1950, "why the same machine that works an assembly line cannot do the cost accounting for the assembly line, putting in the data directly as the motions are made. Even more, there is no reason why it can not do the sequential analysis for the quality control required in the assembly line."[39]

The giant "brains" used in industry and the military establishment currently are said to be only primitive prototypes of servomechanisms already on the drawing boards or in the fertile minds of the communications engineers and thermodynamics scientists.

A hundred years ago man's biologically generated energy (and that

[36] W. Benton Harrison, "Long Range Planning in a Dynamic Industry," booklet, *Planning Ahead for Profits* (New York, American Management Association, 1958), p. 50.

[37] Elliot D. Chapple of The Chapple Company and Carleton S. Coon, Associate Professor of Anthropology, Harvard University, "Technological Change and Cultural Integration," in *Conflicts of Power in Modern Culture* (New York, Harper & Brothers, 1947), Chap. XXII, pp. 260-261.

[38] Norbert Wiener, *Cybernetics, or Control and Communication in the Animal and the Machine* (New York, John Wiley & Sons, 1949) and *The Human Use of Human Beings* (Boston, Houghton Mifflin & Co., 1950). Dr. Wiener, who received his Ph.D. from Harvard at nineteen, is one of the world's most famous mathematicians. He teaches at the Massachusetts Institute of Technology.

[39] *Ibid.*

of beasts) began to be replaced by mechanical energy. Today (except in ant-heap countries like Red China, where manual labor is still the cheapest commodity) we rely on the human nervous system to do the world's work. This is the gist of the matter. It is the nervous system of man that is being rapidly replaced by automation and automatic control. Combined mechanical, chemical, and electronic machines simulate human behavior to do a better job than humans.

We are all familiar with machines which regulate themselves, such as the automatic pilot, the automatic elevator, the thermostat-oil burner, automatic gas water heater, automatic frypan or electric coffee-maker—although we may be less familiar with the electronic digital and analog machines and the feedback principle.

The price of a Mississippi mule has dropped from $300 to $30 in 15 years and serves to illustrate what automation has done down on the farm.

The tractor has replaced horse and mule, milking machines the dairy maid, and automatic feeding and artificial sunlight are commonplace.

In many factories you see electronic instrumentation and control. Electronic computers translate blueprints, put a machine's instructions on magnetic tape which is then fed to a control mechanism to automatically guide a milling machine, a lathe, or some other machine tool that once felt the skilled hand of a machinist.

The increased use of tools has raised the investment in an oil refinery to $300,000 per worker.

As more refineries, chemical plants, cracking plants, power utilities, and other types of factories come under automatic control serious employment problems are created for blue collar workers.

But there are twice as many white collar workers as blue collar workers and paper work is more easily placed under automatic control than production. Clerical workers cost business more than $30 billion a year. There are more than 10 million clerical personnel in the labor force. Faster, more efficient, and less expensive office operation is the order of the day.

Consequently banks, insurance companies, department stores, supermarkets, wholesale distributors, mail order houses, government bureaus, accounting firms, brokerage offices, are also scenes of the Second Industrial Revolution. Every day efficiency experts quietly install sophisticated machines to replace white collar workers with nothing but memories and poor ones at that—people doing routine jobs between coffee breaks.

It is not just a question of payroll economics, however.

Our technology, our modern system of competitive enterprise has outgrown the brain capacity of man (unaided by machines) to control the information involved in its management.

If management had to rely solely on personal memory today the whole thing called management would collapse. Science has provided many devices to serve the three basic functions of a manager's memory: (1) storage, (2) recall, (3) association.

Storage: For example, the library is no longer just rows of bookshelves. Yes, information is still stored in books, periodicals, pamphlets, and papers. It is also stored on punched cards, photographs, phonograph records, films, microfilm, magnetized wire, tape, punched tape, I.B.M. cards. "Univac Fac-Tronic System" can store any sequence of 26,000 different instructions.

Recall: By means of modern filing and classification systems, code numbers, catalogs, reference books, bibliographies, index cards, index tabs, file folders, accession sheets, routing slips, etc., all information can be recalled with little delay, using document control devices like the automatic Hollerith machines.

Association: Electronic machines from I.B.M., R.C.A., Sperry Rand, Remington-Rand, National Cash Register, Burroughs, and other makers of electronic office equipment, can be set to recall facts in particular patterns of association. These machines scan information, recognize patterns, reduce dictation to writing, translate, etc. "Uniprinter" reads metallic tape and converts coded magnetic dots into standard typewriter characters at 12 to 15 characters a second. Automatic machines translate languages.

Just what is cybernetics? Is it the same as automation? Wiener calls cybernetics, a Greek word for governor,[40] "the study of messages, and in particular the messages of control" Dr. Gulick in the following sequences explained the distinction between automation and cybernetics at a symposium back in 1950:

> As I understand the situation today, in the midpoint of this Century, we have now reached a point in human history at which we can create combined electronic, chemical, and mechanical devices which will:

[40] *Kubernētēs* or "steersman."

1. Examine a given set of factors and determine whether a specified condition exists or not. These machines can spot defects in a sheet of steel, they can inspect a product for "go" or "no go," they can identify off-color products, they can count, they can measure, they can listen, they can smell, they can feel. In short, they can perform all the functions of sense perception, and do it far more accurately and scientifically than can a human being, and over a far greater range of variation and calibration.

2. Machines can compute with complete accuracy not only in the field of arithmetic, with the development of straight line explanations and projections, but also in the field of the most complex simultaneous quadratic equations, involving non-linear past relationships and future probabilities. And what is of great significance, they can perform these computations at any desired speed. Machines already built have performed in 100 hours what it would have taken mathematicians with the best man-managed computers 100 years to do. This is known to man as "reckoning."

3. Machines can store and organize for ready use hundreds of millions of facts and bring such facts into use when called for. These facts may be statistical, or they may be non-statistical when properly coded. Such codes may be devised also for fact patterns, that is for a 'Gestalt.' This part of the equipment is as yet rudimentary and comparatively slow, but we know how to perform this function of storage and un-storage on demand, and can extend this performance in due course. This is known to man as 'memory.'

4. Machines can determine, on the basis of facts observed, facts stored up, and interrelations computed, a pre-determined type of action to be taken. This is known to man as 'decisions.'

5. Machines can communicate any fact or any decision over any distance.

6. Machines can take action on the basis of these decisions and communications.

7. Machines can observe the results of such action in the course of the doing and through the above processes modify such decisions, communications and action to conform with the changed situation. This is what Dr. Wiener calls 'feed-back.' When coupled with memory, it is the essence of the process known to man as 'learning.'

In other words—with limits at each stage—we can now build machines which can sense, remember, learn, reckon, decide, command, act, and observe the results of this action so as to make a new decision and take a modified line of action.

This is a very impressive list of faculties.

The significance of Cybernetics is not in the first part of this sequence.

It is in the last part: decision, action and feedback. What Wiener has done more than any other man, is to call attention to the management significance and the social significance of these developments.

The perfection of instruments of detection and measurement is not Cybernetics, though these are indispensable. The development of 'mechanical brains' and computers is not Cybernetics, though these too are indispensable. When you couple these thinking machines up directly to machines which act, and install feedback through control devices which actuate the mechanical brains again, then you enter the field of Cybernetics.[41]

The liberation of technology from the limitations of the human system has already elevated the standards of living for millions of people, which is to say, given them longer living and fewer working hours.

Mechanization has multiplied the output per man-hour in all societies possessing a high degree of know-how. In the United States it multiplied the output per man-hour by two in each generation for the past century.

If we now apply scientific method to social invention, cybernetic machines may not throw us for a loop when they release more and more men and women from boring, monotonous, often unhealthy, frequently tedious, sometimes unpleasant, and generally underpaid routine work. Says Dr. Wiener:

Any use of a human being in which less is demanded of him and less is attributed to him than his full status is a degradation and a waste.

It is a degradation to a human being to chain him to an oar and use him as a source of power; but it is an almost equal degradation to assign him to a purely repetitive task in a factory, which demands less than a millionth of his brain capacity.[42]

Cybernetics has been correctly called the Second Industrial Revolution. The effect on the pattern of employment, the cyberneticians say, will be revolutionary, rather than evolutionary, but not necessarily disastrous as in the case of the widespread unemployment following the First Industrial Revolution. Luther Gulick assigns four reasons for this conclusion:

[41] Dr. Luther Gulick at a symposium of the New York Chapter of the Society for the Advancement of Management, N. Y., November 16, 1950, on "The Cybernetic Revolution." From a pamphlet, *Cybernetics and Society* (New York, Executive Techniques, Inc., 1951), p. 28.

[42] Norbert Wiener, *The Human Use of Human Beings*, p. 16.

1. The breakdown of the feudal and family industry system—not the machine—caused widespread human suffering in the First Industrial Revolution.

2. Today, social inventions such as free education, public health and housing, social security, unemployment insurance, hospitalization and surgical insurance, pensions and profit sharing plans help to carry the unemployed through periods of economic adjustment without extreme hardship.

3. Rapid shifts from men to machines will come when it is relatively easy for individuals to switch to other activities. It will be speeded up only in the event of great manpower shortages, such as a third World War.

4. The cybernetic revolution will greatly increase national income (limited by such factors as exhaustion of natural resources, disproportionate population increases, destructions through war, destructive effects of manipulations by government).

Dr. Gulick adds:

> While I do not greatly fear the social and economic consequences of the cybernetic revolution, I would, nonetheless, urge as strongly as I can the need of making social adjustments to the changes which will come as surely as God made little apples to be made into applesauce by automatic machinery.[43]

We must look to that field of adult education called business journalism to make these human adjustments smooth ones.

"Management's problem," Wiener says, "is thinking out what to do with the leisure that goes with unemployment and the unemployment that goes with leisure."[44]

We agree with Peter Drucker that the responsibility of the managers (the audience of the business press) is moral, social, and economic—in that order of importance.

The responsibility of the business journalist runs along parallel lines.

8. Short Circuit Managers and Robot Executives

Business journalists have a continuing responsibility in all areas of management methodology. Discipline and control are important in a corporate society. No one will argue with that. But management

[43] Luther Gulick, in *Cybernetics and Society*.

[44] Norbert Wiener, in *Cybernetics and Society*.

should guide, not cramp, initiative. Management should stimulate, not stifle, creativity. Management should recognize, not smother, talent; encourage, not freeze, enterprise. Management should delegate functions, not tasks; goals, not specific jobs; the "what" rather than the "how."[45]

There is far less to fear in cybernetics than in robot executives. The machine simply replaces the non-thinking man but the robot manager filters out the thinking man at a time when the business needs him most.

Sensing the danger to the free enterprise system in the growing corps of robot executives, a number of people are sounding warnings, people like Lawrence Appley, president of the American Management Association, William H. Whyte, Jr., board chairman of Fortune, Ralph Cordiner and Moorhead Wright of General Electric Company, Dean Courtney Brown of Columbia University's Graduate School of Business, President C. H. Greenwalt and Lammont DuPont Copeland of DuPont, Dr. Robert D. Calkins of the Brookings Institution, and many others. These leaders echo a warning uttered a century ago by John Stuart Mill:

> *"Whatever crushes individuality is despotism by whatever name it may be called"*

"If," writes Mr. Whyte in *The Organization Man,* "the standards set up by many personnel managers were applied across the board, the majority of corporation executives would be out of jobs tomorrow. And if they had been well rounded they wouldn't have gotten to be executives in the first place."

References appear in the current literature of the American Management Association to a "short circuit" type of manager. Like a broken wire in a small motor, for example, which can short circuit an entire system, this manager can throw an entire business organization out of gear. The "short circuit" type is described this way: (1) he will not delegate authority; (2) he is afraid to surround himself with people who know more than he does or can do things better than he can; (3) his judgments are distorted by notions of self-importance; (4) he is afraid of new ideas; (5) he will not brook criticism; (6) he has no imagination or sense of humor.

[45] O. A. Ohmann, "The Leader and the Led," *Personnel,* November, December 1958, p. 14, American Magement Association.

These expressions are rarely or ever used by the "short circuit" type of manager:

I am proud of you!
You deserve the credit.
What is your opinion?
Good idea—let's try it.
May I suggest——
It's my mistake.
Thank you.

Self-management: John E. Raasch, former president of John Wanamaker, N. Y., who is a trustee of the New York University School of Retailing quotes a Hindu proverb: *There is nothing noble in being superior to another man; true nobility consists in being superior to your former self.*

These points were made by Edward Staley, president of W. T. Grant Company:

The secret of management success is the ability to manage yourself, control your vanity and your temper, your personal likes and dislikes. The tough top sergeant technic is a confession of weakness. When you misuse your power you are driving not leading. Be humble: acknowledge your own mistakes and errors. Know your business; if you bluff you lose the respect of those under you. Develop the habit of listening. Get the other side of the story. Let people explain their ideas and their point of view.[46]

Self-development: Many industrial firms have programs which are referred to as R&D (Research and Development) and which refer to product research and product development. Less is heard of the programs for the research and development of people, although some firms spend millions of dollars to develop people. Success is impossible if you do not have people *with* you and *for* you.

The facilities alone at the General Electric Management Research and Development Institute in Crotonville, New York, cost $2 million, and the firm spends $2 million a year to operate this human development center. Its director, Moorhead Wright, listed five principles of development in a talk to businesspaper editors and publishers recently:

1. All development is self-development—it isn't something you do to a man; it rests within a man.

[46] Edward Staley before The Eleventh Annual Conference, New York University School of Retailing, February 27th, 1959.

2. All development is individual—there is no average man.

3. Everyone must have the chance to develop—not just the P.Y.M. (Promising Young Men).

4. Forget personality traits—don't try to change the personality of the individual.

5. Responsibility to help pepole develop rests with the incumbent line manager—it is as much his responsibility as getting his work done.[47]

How can the business journalist go about keeping down top-sergeantism, robotage, and short circuitry in order to preserve the growth factors in private enterprise?

We suggest he devote some of his columns to the research studies in modern management method being conducted by many large corporations, graduate business schools, top consultants in the field, and by the American Management Association. There is a long bibliography of studies on which to draw.

9. A School for Publishers

"At Harvard University," writes Marquis Childs, "no one laughs any longer when the candidates for the Master's degree from the Business School are welcomed into 'the oldest of the arts and the youngest of the professions.' More and more the concept has grown up in the American business community of the *professional* responsibility of the businessman."[48]

Certainly no force has striven harder than business journalism to make business a profession; and since this is so, how very important it is for those pursuing or practicing careers as businesspaper publishers to act as if they were professionals.

The supervisors of hospitals being usually doctors, the judges of law courts being lawyers, the heads of churches being ordained ministers, and the heads of educational institutions being savants, it may be that A. J. Liebling's observation was an apt one, when he dedicated his own book on journalism:

"To the Foundation of a School for Publishers,
Failing Which,
No School of Journalism Can Have Meaning."[49]

[47] Moorhead Wright, "What Makes Good Managers?" Annual Eastern Conference, ABP, February 26, 1959.

[48] Marquis W. Childs and Douglass Cater, *Ethics in a Business Society* (New York, Harper & Brothers, 1954), p. 99.

[49] A. J. Liebling, *The Wayward Pressman* (New York, Doubleday & Co., 1947).

In his book Liebling points out that "journalism is the sole civilian 'profession' that can be exercised only as the employee of somebody else."

"Nearly all publishers of the present generation," he further points out, "inherited their publishing properties."

"Try to imagine," Liebling says, "the future of medicine, law, or pedagogy if their absolute control were vested in the legal heirs of men who had bought practices in 1890. . . ."[50]

A well-known authority of long standing in the field of business journalism research, R. O. Eastman, is not one to make hasty or ill-considered observations about businesspaper publishers. In a recent bulletin issued by his organization, Mr. Eastman observed:

"Few publications have a real publisher. There are plenty who carry the title. Some of them are glorified space peddlers who look upon the editorial department as a necessary evil and the circulation department as an unavoidable expense."[51]

Now, there can be little doubt that business is clothed with a public interest. If this were not true, the huge public relations industry would grind to a stop. It was once thought that only public utilities were so affected. Today we refer to our society as a corporate society and more and more of our corporations are publicly owned through common stock purchases. They are all affected with a public interest, and particularly the periodical publishing corporations, which may even be considered as *quasi-public utilities*. The periodical publisher is pledged to distribute a new product periodically, as agreed, whether each issue is profitable or not; or suspend publication and lose his franchise. He is pledged to furnish the reader a content which is at least one third editorial against two thirds advertising or run the risk of having an entire issue held up at the post office. The cost of distributing the product is partially subsidized by the Post Office Department. In addition, the publisher professes to be part of the educational system. He refers to his activity as adult education.

Thus, the businesspaper publisher's social responsibility will always be greater than the ordinary businessman's.

If any businesspaper publisher thinks of himself as a professional, then he cannot mean it when he says (as some have) that his *chief*

[50] *Ibid.*, p. 31.

[51] R. O. Eastman, *Eastman Research Organization Bulletin*, April 7, 1958.

objective is to make a profit. There is nothing wrong with making a profit or wanting to make a profit. The lawyer, doctor, engineer, scientist all want a profit as proof that their endeavors are wanted and appreciated. To conduct a non-profit operation you have to have a handout from someone or some group and you are no longer independent.

The professional man thinks of his debt to society and paying it back becomes his main consideration. To him profit must always be a secondary objective. There is another point:

The businesspaper publisher staffs his organization with college graduates. Those college graduates are his chief asset. What else does he have? Some magazine titles, a stencil list, a few pieces of office equipment? The publisher owns no printing plant or engraving shop, no paper mill. Anybody can compile a list of prospects. College-trained people are his chief asset. He gets an editor with an A.B., B.S. or engineering degree by the mere gesture of calling a placement bureau or inserting an ad in the help-wanted columns.

The ad cost three dollars. What did the job applicant cost society?

Does anyone think a professional man can be produced for the ten or twelve thousand dollars the parents invested in his education? To build an ordinary elementary school cost $2 million today and a high school costs $3 million.

You must calculate the cost of the elementary schools plus the high schools plus the colleges and universities: the cost of the plant, the laboratory equipment, the libraries, the buildings, dormitories, research facilities; the cost of projects, scholarships; the cost of the faculties and the staffs. (Not to mention the cost of thousands of years of accumulated knowledge and the cost of the age-old struggle for academic freedom.)

Take one school, for example, the Massachusetts Institute of Technology. In 1957 it spent $21 million for operating costs, $54 million for sponsored research projects.[52]

We are spending more than $19 billion a year for education, public and private, according to Marion B. Folsom.[53]

In 1955-1956 there were approximately 2,996,000 resident students

[52] *Time* magazine, December 15, 1958, p. 49.

[53] Marion B. Folsom, "Government and the Citizen," *Saturday Review*, January 17, 1959, p. 29.

enrolled in institutions of higher education in the continental United States and the cost to the public of this higher education was $3.5 billion. Today the cost is much higher because the enrollment is greater. The President's Committee on Education Beyond the High School, in its 1958 Report, indicated that over a quarter of a billion dollars more was needed to bring faculty salaries into line and $1.3 billion more would be needed each year between 1959 and 1970 to provide adequate physical facilities in colleges and universities.

Getting back to a School for Publishers: The effort of colleges and universities in the field of communications is still puny by comparison with the effort expended in other specializations. Of the less than fifty colleges with accredited schools of journalism in the United States (1958) only a few make any real attempt to prepare graduates for the technical duties and responsibilities of publishing. A few schools offer complete sequences in businesspaper publishing practice.

If the effort of the schools of journalism is puny, the effort of businesspaper publishers in the matter of grants and endowments to education is microscopic.

Just as industrial corporations give increased support each year to education, so the business press must begin to divert more of its profits each year to schools of journalism to establish scholarships and research grants, to underwrite better faculties and facilities, for better libraries, and for the one course which is indispensable to every school of journalism—*publishing practice.*

10. Exchange of Business Journalists

The Fulbright Act provides part of the cash held in foreign currencies from the sale of United States war surplus abroad for the exchange of American and foreign students. It has proved a valuable social invention for increasing world understanding.

Some 15 countries besides our own have networks of businesspapers today providing communication of know-how to the managers in their own economies (see Chapter VII). We suggest it would be a contribution to world understanding to promote the exchange of some of these business journalists with some of our own. We could learn much from these countries and they could learn from us. Dr. Ralph Nafziger, director of the Journalism School of the University of Wisconsin, learned from Professor Kouidiakov, Dean of the Faculty of Journalism of Moscow. Among other things he learned that the full journalism course of training at Moscow runs five years, one year better than in the United States. The students get six weeks of practical work on a newspaper the second year and eight weeks during the third year.[54]

No one is better qualified than the American businesspaper editor to explain in simple, understandable language, how this country, in four generations, with less than one-fifteenth of the world's population, 7 per cent of the land area, and 7 per cent of the natural resources, can produce and consume 35 per cent of the world's goods and services. And supply much of the capital for the rest of the free world to improve its production, living standards, and security.

The business journalist, better than one else, can explain what is meant when we say a country's greatest resource is not its mines or oil wells, farms or factories, power (energy) or people. He can explain why the greatest resource is know-how, because he deals in know-how; know-how is his stock-in-trade.[55]

He can best explain how this know-how has given the United States a living standard five times higher than the world's average and a thousand times higher than the substandard level of hundreds of hungry millions who inhabit the disease-infested areas of the Moslem, Chinese, Hindu, African, and South American wastelands.

The American business journalist abroad is still a teacher. He can teach business journalism or set up sequences in countries where no schools of business journalism exist. He can train future professors of busines journalism for countries desirous of extending their journalism teaching to include business journalism. He can discuss methods for establishing business journalism as a professional career within those countries where it is not so recognized.

He can discuss common markets of the human mind, the use of knowledge and energy in the service of life, "the use of life for the extension of the human spirit," and the necessity of world-wide cooperation among people in the distribution of goods and ideas.[56]

[54] "Report of International Center for Higher Training of Journalism, University of Strasbourg," *Editor & Publisher*, December 14, 1957, p. 59.

[55] See Chap. IV, section 7.

[56] See Lewis Mumford, *The Conduct of Life* (New York, Harcourt Brace & Co., 1951), p. 3.

11. Silence Is Not Always Golden

Professor Raymond Moley, conductor of the column in *Newsweek* called "Perspective," has this quotation posted over his desk: *"There comes a time when silence is not golden—just yellow."*

For a journalist to remain silent when something needs to be said is cowardly journalism.

The business press, at least that part of it represented by publishers' and editors' associations and societies, pledged itself long ago not to knuckle down to pressures—to let no considerations, advertising or others, induce them to withhold information the reader should have.

Newsweek was taken over in 1933 by Malcolm Muir, then president of McGraw-Hill, largest businesspaper publishing organization in the United States. Mr. Muir, who is now publisher of *Newsweek*, issued this publishing formula at the time (1933):

> News is to be presented fairly, impartially, and with scrupulous accuracy, together with its significance and meaning . . . news, plus opinion signed by qualified and responsible contributing editors speaking for themselves.

"I am concerned with what ought to be, not what I expect will happen," Moley wrote on the occasion of the magazine's 25th anniversary. "I could not in conscience tarnish the priceless privilege of free expression by avoiding an unpopular point of view. Nor permit frankness to lose its luster by dodging a controversial issue."[57]

12. Direction and Tempo in Technical Writing

The April 26, 1958, issue of *The Journal of the American Medical Association,* sent to me by its distinguished editor, Dr. Austin Smith, contains 260 pages, of which 100 pages are full-page and double-page advertisements plus five or six pages of smaller advertisements. I understand that this is an average issue. The large advertisements are professional and expensive looking. They are printed in four colors; some are four-color inserts.

Counting about 155 pages of editorial text, this would be a ratio of about 60-40 in favor of editorial text. This differs from the formula used by the majority of technical periodicals, where the ratio is usually the reverse: 60 per cent or more advertising and 40 per cent or less editorial pages.

[57] *Newsweek,* November 3, 1958, p. 112.

About 30 per cent of the advertisements in this issue of the *Journal* promoted tranquilizer drugs for such symptoms as hypertension, anxiety, insomnia, neurasthenia, emotional instability, high blood pressure, emotional tension, muscle spasm, hyperacidity, depression, etc. (These are the actual terms taken from the advertising copy and headlines.) Physician-readers are urged in these advertisements to prescribe some 25 or more nationally advertised brands of these tranquilizers for their patients.[58]

The table of contents of this excellent businesspaper is printed on the cover. I noted among the original articles these three: "Newer Drugs in the Treatment of Hypertension"; "Antihypertensive Drugs as a Cause of Acute Abdomen"; "Heart Failure, Fever and Splenomegaly in a Morphine Addict."

In the editorials I checked three:

"Why Do Females Live Longer?"

"Mental Health Week."

"High Pressure Telephone Securities Salesmen" (it seems the doctors are themselves confused, for they buy a lot of worthless stocks under high pressure).

In Questions & Answers Dept., I selected four subjects: "Noises in the Head," "Monthly Suicide Rates," "Cerebral Embolism," and "Alcoholism."

Let me assure you I am not trying to be funny. Mental illness has become the number one problem of our colleagues in medical journalism, because it is the number one problem of medicine. Over one-half the hospital beds in our country today are occupied by the mentally confused. Quoting from the editorial page in this April 26, 1958, issue of *The Journal of the* AMA, page 2185: "In addition to the more than 750,000 persons hospitalized because of mental disorders it is estimated that 16 million persons suffer from some form of mental or emotional disorder and are in need of psychiatric care."

The New York Times (May 13, 1958) published an article on outmoded mental hospitals by Dr. Harry C. Solomon, Emeritus Professor of Psychiatry at the Harvard Medical School and superintendent of the Massachusetts Mental Health Center in Boston. Speaking as president of the American Psychiatric Association, he said: "Care of

[58] Abstracted from a paper read by the author at the Fourth Arden House Conference of the Editorial Division of The Associated Business Publications, Harriman, N. Y., May 13, 1958.

the long-term mentally ill remains as one of the great challenges we have failed to meet and must somehow attack anew."

Mental confusion is also the problem of business journalism in other fields besides medicine, with much more than half the office desks in the business community surrounded by indecision, and an air of confusion prevalent in at least two thirds of the corporate board rooms today.

Last year 46 million prescriptions for tranquilizers were filled by druggists. I will not bore you with the tonnage statistics on narcotics, liquor, tobacco, and drugs consumed in a year by the business community. Five billion dollars worth of tobacco was consumed in the United States alone in 1953.

I simply raise this question: Could some of this mental confusion be the result of superficial reading, superficial listening, looking, and thinking? Could superficial writing be back of some of this confusion? Could there be too much running while reading or reading while running? Could indigestible digests be one of the causes of this mental constipation? It could very well be.

I am not fascinated or even impressed with the philosophy of speed reading or hit-and-run editing, exclusively picture-sequence stories, one-page-maximum articles, hundred-word-summaries, capsulized stories, boil-downs, digests, synopses, or, as Peter Roget would say, "abridgements, abbreviations, and truncations."

As applied to the technical press, the high-speed reading philosophy is a dangerous one which can lead to mental crack-up.

We have made reference to business journalism as adult education. No one goes to a university to read while he runs, to gobble down capsules of knowledge. Carroll Larrabee once described the businesspaper as "the businessman's university."[59] He did not mean a *Readers' Digest* type of university—of that I am certain.

Harvard's great philosopher and mathematician, Alfred North Whitehead said:

"What you teach, teach thoroughly."

If you can teach it thoroughly in 100 words—fine. If it takes 1,000 words, use them!

I find no objection to putting the essence or high points of a story or feature on the page with the story, in a box for example, or

[59] Editorial in *Printers' Ink*, November 26, 1954, "The Business Press—a business man's university."

boxed off in a heavier type, or to putting a summary of the writer's points above the story in the headlines or sub-headlines. These are good selling devices. I use them myself. Not as a substitute for an article but to draw the reader into the body of the complete story.

The reader of a businesspaper today has more time to read his businesspaper than ever before. The kind of economy in which he lives is constantly cutting down the hours of the day's work as it has already cut down the days of the week's work. His travel time is speeded up. As more readers move to Suburbia commuting time becomes reading time. At home labor-saving and time-saving appliances give him more time. Automation gives him more leisure. The businesspaper reader, to repeat, has more time than ever before, to do what interests him most. Our subject matter is his lifework—his job—his business—the source of all other satisfactions he may derive from life. So I say we have a head start on all other competitors for his time, whether it be radio, television, movies, or fiction. Our readers like to talk shop and to read shop.

"Show me the man who doesn't get a bang out of 'talking shop' with his fellows," says Paul de Guzman, an advertising agent specializing in media promotion. "They enjoy it more than talking about anything else, including the Milwaukee Braves or Brigette Bardot. And that includes any men right in your own shop who can see each other every day, then bump into each other next Saturday at some party. All right, challenge me—I dare you! I say that men can get a bigger bang out of 'reading shop' than reading anything else!"

Dale Carnegie quoted a former Dean of Columbia College, Dr. Herbert E. Hawkes, as saying that "half the worry in the world is caused by people trying to make decisions before they have sufficient knowledge."[60]

Your reader is living in a world of fast technological change. He can't hang on to old ways and old ideas. The new know-how is more technical, more highly specialized. The entire business press (as I have said) is a technical press, concerned with the technics for research and development, for extracting, processing, handling, and moving goods, services, and ideas: the technics for survival in a fast-changing, machine world.

Not just the medical journals and the engineering journals but all

[60] Dale Carnegie, *How to Stop Worrying and Start Living* (New York, Simon and Schuster, Inc., 1948).

business periodicals are filled with the symbols and formulae, the equations, charts, graphs, diagrams, tables, pictures, and drawings with which we try to communicate these new technics, this new knowledge, so it can be reproduced successfully somewhere else.

We editors often have to translate this new knowledge into new meanings. Our basic function is to lay it on the line for the reader, complete and factual, "technically or clinically explanatory, instructive, definitive."

Science has been defined as the most exact kind of reporting.[61] The description of a successful experiment is just as important as the experiment itself. By the use of mathematical symbols, weights, and measures and correct botanical and zoological terminology the scientist cautiously, meticulously, painstakingly describes his experiment, step by step, looking for error, inviting error, and as others reproduce his experiment they advance the progress of mankind possibly an inch or two.

The responsibilities of business journalists, outside the physical sciences, is just as important. The board chairman of the General Electric Company, Ralph Cordiner, pointed out to the business press three years ago:

> In the pace of today's world, where so many business decisions are made against the pressure of time, the time-honored standards of professional journalism—of reporting both sides of each issue objectively—have become more important than ever. It is also far too easy to accept a hasty conclusion that one isolated fact represents a trend. An editor who fails to do a thorough job of researching all available facts before reporting a trend can easily stampede his readers into unwise decisions.[62]

Lammont DuPont Copeland, finance chairman of the DuPont Company, said this at a meeting of the Associated Press Managing Editors Association:

> Historians will surely view this as one of the less happy periods in the life of our nation. Major problems harass us, and some observers wonder whether the philosophy on which our way of life rests is not now to be brought to its ultimate test.

[61] Joseph Garland, "Editorials and Medical Journalism," *New England Journal of Medicine, World Medical Ass'n. Bulletin,* Vol. 1, No. 1, January 1951, page 8.

[62] Ralph Cordiner, "New Opportunities for Multiplying Progress," an address before annual Eastern Conference, Associated Business Publications, New York, March 2, 1955.

That philosophy consists, I take it, of these concepts: that the individual citizen has the desire to gain information upon which important decisions can be based, that he has the wisdom to determine what should be done, and that he has the will to see that the proper course is followed.

If such a test does lie ahead, it will be no new thing in the history of the republic. But there is one important difference: We have very much less margin for error. In the past we could, and did, make mistakes without suffering more than temporary embarrassment. But today errors can be catastrophic.

We have enemies who make no secret of their intention of bringing us to our knees and who have been developing the muscles with which to tackle the job.

Future decisions will determine whether experience has brought to this country a wisdom that will enable it to avoid the collapse that has inexorably overtaken all earlier democracies—all, without exception. If we flunk the tests confronting us, it will not matter that we meant well.

Ignorance will be no excuse.[63]

For the business press the implication is obvious: we must not only inform accurately but we must teach thoroughly. We must interpret objectively. We must persuade eloquently. Ignorance will be no excuse. And the more intelligent our readers become, the more critical they will be, and the critical reader does not want his information in a capsule.

The concluding paragraph of a speech by John P. Cunningham before the Advertising Federation of America will wrap up this little essay on tempo and direction:

The printed page gives what to all of us at times, is the most desirable communication of all—the leisurely communion between man and the printed page in the most precious of atmospheres—the rich depths of silence![64]

[63] Lammont DuPont Copeland, "Tell Them It Can Happen Here" *DuPont Magazine*, February-March 1958, pp. 6-7.

[64] John P. Cunningham, president and chairman of the board, Cunningham & Walsh, Inc., "Magazines . . . up to now . . . and from now on," address before the 53rd Annual Convention, Advertising Federation of America, June 1957.

Appendixes

APPENDIX I

UNITED STATES BUSINESSPAPERS BEFORE 1900

SPACE does not permit the inclusion of all the numerous regional journals that made sporadic appearances (and disappearances) in the nineteenth century. For details see the four volume works of Pulitzer Prize Winner Frank Luther Mott, *A History of American Magazines*—Vol. I (1741–1850), Vol. II (1850–1865), Vol. III (1865–1885), Vol. IV (1885–1905), published by the Harvard University Press, Cambridge, Mass. A number of the periodicals listed here are mentioned in the text (Chapter VI).

1793–1810:	*New Hampshire Journal, or Farmers' Weekly Museum*
1795 ? :	*New York Prices—Current*
1796–1797:	*Monthly Military Repository*
1797–1824:	*Medical Repository*
1799–1800:	*Theological Magazine*
1804–1811:	*Philadelphia Medical Museum*
1805–1806:	*Theatrical Censor*
1805–1806:	*Thespian Mirror*
1808–1809:	*Medical and Physical Recorder*
1808– ? :	*Butchers and Packers Gazette*
1808–1817:	*American Law Journal*
1809–1809:	*Thespian Monitor and Dramatic Miscellany*
1810–1814:	*American Mineralogical Journal* (New York)
1810–1812:	*Agricultural Museum* (Georgetown, D.C.)
1812–1826:	*New England Journal of Medicine & Surgery* (Boston)
1815– ? :	*General Shipping and Commercial List*
1816–current:	*Congregationalist*
1818–1829:	*American Medical Recorder* (Philadelphia)
1818–current:	*American Journal of Science* (New Haven)
1818–current:	*Methodist Review*
1819–1838:	*Christian Spectator* (New Haven)

1819–1897: *American Farmer* (Baltimore)
1819–1823: *Plough Boy*, (later *Plough Boy and Journal of the Board of Agriculture*, Albany)
1820–1827: *Philadelphia Journal of the Medical and Physical Sciences*
1821–1824: *Journal of Foreign Medical Science & Literature*
1821–1821: *Journal of Jurisprudence* (Philadelphia)
1822–1830: *New York Medical & Physical Journal*
1822–1846: *The New England Farmer*
1822–current: *Episcopal Recorder*
1823–1828: *Boston Medical Intelligencer*
1824–1869: *Christian Examiner*
1825–current: *Journal of the Philadelphia College of Pharmacy*
1825–1826: *American Mechanics Magazine* (later *Journal of the Franklin Institute*)
1826–1839: *American Journal of Education*
1826–current: *Journal of Franklin Institute*
1827– ? : *Journeyman Mechanics' Advocate* (New York)
1827–current: *American Journal of the Medical Sciences*
1827–current: *Journal of Commerce*
1830–1830: *Mechanics Magazine* (Boston)
1831–1832: *North American Journal of Geology*
1832–current: *American Rail-Road Journal* (now *Railway Mechanical Engineer*)
1833–1837: *Mechanics' Magazine and Journal of the Mechanic's Institute*
1833–1836: *Military and Naval Magazine* (Washington, D. C.)
1834–1835: *American Musical Journal*
1835–1838: *Horticultural Register & Gardeners Magazine*
1835–1842: *Army & Navy Chronicle* (Washington, D.C.)
1836–1837: *Naval Magazine* (New York)
1836–1848: *Farmer's Cabinet & American Herd Book* (Philadelphia)
1836–current: *Thompson's Bank Note and Commercial Reporter* (later *Thompson's Weekly Report*, then *Thompsons Bank Report* and, in 1877, *American Banker*)
1837–1842: *American Medical Library & Intelligencer* (Philadelphia)
1837–1870: *American Presbyterian Review*
1838–1838: *Louisville Journal of Medicine and Surgery* (Kentucky)
1838–1840: *Journal of Education* (Detroit)
1838–1839: *American Journal of Homeopathy*
1838–1852: *Common School Journal* (Boston)
1838– ? : *Blast Furnace & Steel Plant* (started as *Pittsburgh American Manufacturer*)
1839–1909: *American Journal of Dental Science*

1839–1842:	*Musical Magazine* (Boston)
1839–1870:	*Merchant's Magazine & Commercial Review* (Later *Hunt's Merchants' Magazine* [New York])
1840–1855:	*Western Journal of Medicine & Surgery* (Louisville, Kentucky)
1840–1840:	*Union Agriculturist* (later *Prairie Farmer*, [Chicago])
1841–1842:	*Musical Cabinet* (Boston)
1841–1843:	*New York State Mechanic*
1842–1852:	*Philadelphia Law Journal*
1842–current:	*American Agriculturist* (New York)
1842–1854:	*New York Legal Observer*
1843–1879:	*Medical News and Library* (Philadelphia)
1843–current:	*Michigan Farmer*
1843–current:	*Southern Cultivator* (later *Southern Cultivator and Dixie Farmer*, [Georgia])
1843–1846:	*American Law Magazine* (Philadelphia)
1843–1860:	*New York Journal of Medicine*
1843–1853:	*Western Law Journal* (Cincinnati)
1843–1907:	*St. Louis Medical & Surgical Journal*
1843–1860:	*New York Journal of Medicine*
1844– ? :	*Price Current-Grain Reporter*
1845–current:	*Scientific American*
1845–1878:	*The Mining Journal*
1845–1917:	*Indiana Farmer and Gardener* (Indianapolis)
1845–1878:	*Mining Journal* (Marquette, Michigan)
1846–1880:	*De Bow's Commercial Review of the South and West*
1846–1848:	*Mechanics' Advocate*
1846–1875:	*Horticulturist*
1846–current:	*Banking Law Journal* (Boston)
1846–current:	*United States Economist and Dry Goods Reporter* (later *First-Dry Goods Reporter and Commercial Glance*, then *United States Economist and Dry Goods Reporter*; then *Dry Goods Economist* and currently *Department Store Economist*)
1847–1865:	*New England Mechanic* (Boston)
1848–1859:	*American Farmers Magazine*
1849–1872:	*American Railway Times*
1848–1864:	*Ohio Medical Journal*
1849–current:	*Astronomical Journal* (suspended in 1861 and resumed in 1886)
1849–1864:	*Ohio Cultivator*
1849–1852:	*Saroni's Musical Times* (New York)
1850–1861:	*N. Y. Medical Gazette*

1850–1851: *Insurance Advocate*
1850–1870: *Humphrey's Journal of Photography* (began as *The Daguerrian Journal*)
1850–1861: *Farmer and Planter Monthly*
1851–current: *Ohio Farmer* (Cleveland)
1851–1860: *Photographic Art Journal* (later *Photography and Fine Art Journal*)
1852–1857: *Bulletin of the American Geographical Society* (became *Geographical Review* in 1916)
1852–current: *American Law Register and Review* (later *University of Pennsylvania Law Review*)
1852–1867: *American Journal of Photography and The Allied Arts and Sciences*
1852–1881: *Wight's Journal of Music*
1852–1854: *Farmer's Journal*
1852–1933: *Ohio Journal of Education*
1852–1861: *Tucket's Insurance Journal*
1852–1895: *Wall Street Journal* (not related to current periodical of same name started in 1889)
1852–1867: *American Journal of Photography*
1852–1856: *Ink Fountain*
1852–1853: *American Telegraph Magazine*
1853–current: *American Insurance Digest & Insurance Monitor* (absorbed the old *Insurance Monitor* [1853]—oldest insurance businesspaper)
1853–1861: *Mining Magazine*
1853–1861: *American Cotton Planter*
1853–1854: *American Polytechnic Journal*
1853–1869: *Iowa Medical Journal*
1853–1861: *Pioneer Farmer*
1853–1854: *Pen and Pencil*
1853–current: *Pittsburgh Legal Journal*
1853–1873: *Railroad Record*
1854–1862: *American Medical Monthly*
1854–1884: *California Farmer*
1854–1894: *Fireman's Journal*
1854–1857: *Journal of Medical Reform*
1854–1857: *Railroad Advocate*
1855–1882: *American Journal of Education*
1855–1899: *Atlanta Medical Journal*
1855–1922: *Practical Farmer*
1855–1892: *Typographic Advertiser*
1855–1882: *U. S. Insurance Gazette*

1855–1856:	*Western Art Journal*
1855–current:	*Iron Age* (started as *Hardware Man's Newspaper;* absorbed *American Manufacturers' Circular*)
1855–1892:	*Typographic Advertiser* (Philadelphia)
1855–current:	*Hardware Age* (established 1855, succeeding and embodying *Hardware* [New York]; *Stoves and Hardware Reporter* [St. Louis]; *Western Hardware Journal* [Omaha]; *Iron Age Hardware* [New York]; *Hardware Reporter* [St. Louis]; *Hardware Salesman* [Chicago]; *Hardware Dealers Magazine* [New York]; and *Good Hardware* [New York])
1856–current:	*Railway Gazette* (later *Railway Age*)
1856–1921:	*Journal of Agriculture*
1856–1866:	*National Journal of Finance*
1856–1871:	*Northwestern Farmer*
1856–1888:	*Round's Printer's Cabinet*
1856–1869:	*Rural American*
1856–current:	*Wisconsin Journal of Education*
1857–1902:	*Age of Steel*
1857–current:	*Drug Topics*
1857–1883:	*Harness and Carriage Journal*
1857–1908:	*Western Railroad Gazette*
1857–current:	*Shoe & Leather Reporter* (New York)
1857–current:	*The American Druggists' Circular and Chemical Gazette*
1857–1883:	*Harness and Carriage Journal*
1858–1896:	*Journal of Materia Medica*
1858–1898:	*Medical and Surgical Reporter*
1858–1861:	*Oregon Farmer*
1858–1917:	*Pacific Medical Journal*
1858–1875:	*Printer*
1858–1871:	*Coach-Makers Magazine*
1859–current:	*Weekly Underwriter*
1859–1836:	*Dental Cosmos* (Philadelphia)
1859–current:	*American Gas Journal* (started as *American Gas-Light Journal and Mining Reporter*)
1859–current:	*Hub* (later *Automotive Manufacturer*)
1859–1878:	*American Life Assurance Magazine*
1859–1862:	*American Railway Review*
1859–1864:	*American Stock Journal*
1860–1922:	*Mining and Scientific Press*
1860–1864:	*American Medical Times*
1860–1871:	*Boston Musical Times*
1860–1922:	*Mining and Scientific Press*
1860–1905:	*National Educator*

1860–1861: *Plantation*
1860–1892: *U.S. Medical Investigator*
1861–current: *American Bee Journal*
1861–1920: *Legal Adviser*
1862–1864: *American Journal of Ophthalmology*
1862–1911: *Stockholder*
1862–current: *Trade of the West* (Later *American Manufacture and and Iron World,* later *Steel and Iron* [Pittsburgh])
1862–1886: *American Spirit and Wine Trade Review*
1863–1865: *Army and Navy Official Gazette*
1863–1906: *Chicago Journal of Commerce* (later *Iron and Steel,* later *Iron and Machinery World*)
1863–current: *Financier* (later *Bank Director and Financier*)
1863–1873: *Grierson's Underwriters Weekly Circular*
1863–current: *Kansas Farmer*
1863–1866: *Miller's Journal*
1863–1890: *Musical World*
1863–current: *Army & Navy Journal* (later *Army-Navy-Air Force Journal* [Washington, D.C.]; *The U.S. Army and Navy Journal and Gazette of the Regular and Volunteer Forces* [changed in 1926 to *Gazette of the Land, Sea, Air*]).
1863–current: *International Iron Molders Journal* (Cincinnati)
1864–current: *American Artisan and Patent Recorder* (now *American Artisan* [Chicago])
1864–1868: *American Mining Gazette and Geological Magazine*
1864–1888: *Brainard's Musical World*
1864–1876: *Cigar Makers Official Journal*
1864–1865: *Confederate States Medical and Surgical Journal*
1864–1874: *Kansas Educational Review*
1864–1902: *Maryland Farmer*
1864–1923: *Philadelphia Photographer* (became *Photographic Magazine* in 1889; *Photographic Journal of America* in 1915)
1864–1877: *Telegrapher*
1864–1867: *Pacific Index* (later became *American Mining Index* [New York])
1864–1896: *National Car Builder* (merged with *American Rail-Road Journal*)
1865–1905: *Philosophical Journal*
1865–current: *The Catholic World*
1865–1866: *Petroleum Gazette and Scientific Journal*
1865–current: *Commercial & Financial Chronicle* (split into 5 papers in 1928)

1865–1930: *Motor Vehicle Monthly* (formerly *Carriage Monthly* of Philadelphia)

1865–1872: *American Journal of Conchology* (Philadelphia)

1865–1930: *Carriage Monthly* [Philadelphia] (later *Motor Vehicle Monthly*)

1865–1915: *New England Farmer* (Boston)

1865–current: *U.S. Review*

1865–1865: *Petroleum Gazette anrd Scientific Journal* (Cincinnati)

1865–current: *The Tobacco Leaf*

1866–1872: *American Stock Journal* (Pittsburgh, Pennsylvania)

1866–1926: *Banking and Insurance Chronicle,* (later *Economic World*)

1866–1902: *Boston Journal of Chemistry,* (later *Popular Science*)

1866–1912: *Bulletin of American Iron & Steel Association* (Philadelphia)

1866–1886: *Inventors & Manufacturers Gazette* (Boston)

1866–1875: *Journal of Applied Chemistry*

1866–1886: *Midland Industrial Gazette* (St. Louis)

1866–1918: *New England Medical Gazette*

1866–1874: *N.Y. Musical Gazette*

1866–1890: *Printers' Circular* (Philadelphia)

1866–1875: *Printing Gazette* (Cleveland)

1866–1903: *Tailor's Review* (New York)

1866–1881: *Western Educational Review* (St. Louis)

1866–1880: *Western Musical Review* (Cincinnati)

1866–current: *American Law Review* (Boston)

1866–1907: *Chicago Mining Review*

1866–1875: *Journal of Applied Chemistry*

1866–current: *American Journal of Mining,* (Became *Engineering & Mining Journal,* 1869; absorbed *Coal & Iron Record, Mining Review, Polytechnic Review, Mining & Metallurgy, Mining Magazine, Mining & Engineering World, Mining & Scientific Press*)

1867–1888: *Advertisers' Gazette* (Changed in 1871 to *American Newspaper Reporter*) and supplanted in 1888 by *Printers' Ink*)

1867–current: *Insurance Graphic,* (formerly *Southwestern Insurance News Graphic,* Dallas)

1867–1882: *Iron Trade Review* (see *Steel,* 1882–current)

1867–1871: *Art Journal* (Chicago)

1867–1918: *Book Buyer* (later *Lamp,* New York)

1867–1905: *Keystone* (Philadelphia)

1867–1914: *Journal of the Telegraph* (New York)

1867–1882: *Masons Coin & Stamp Collectors Journal* (Philadelphia)
1867– ? : *American Journal of Photography*
1868–current: *N.Y. Spectator: An American Review of Life Insurance*
1868–current: *American Brewer*
1868–1896: *Manufacturers' Review and Industrial Record* (New York)
1868–1895: *American Journal of Art* (in 1872 became *American Builder* and, later, *Builder and Woodworker*)
1868–current: *Real Estate Record* (now *Real Estate Record and Builders' Guide*)
1868–current: *Textile World* (absorbed *Textile Manufacturers' Review* and *Textile Manufacturers' Journal;* started in 1868 as *Manufacturers Review and Industrial Record; Textile World,* 1888)
1868–1906: *American Journal of Philately* (New York)
1868–1908: *Dental Office and Laboratory* (Philadelphia)
1868–1884: *Newspaper Reporter and Advertisers Gazette* (New York)
1868–1896: *Manufacturers' Review and Industrial Record* (New York)
1868–1926: *Railway Review* (Chicago)
1868–1888: *Western Bookseller* (Chicago)
1868–1878: *American Booksellers Guide* (New York)
1868–current: *American Grocer* (New York)
1868–current: *Coal Trade Journal* (New York)
1868–current: *Country House Monitor* (New York) Later *Bullinger's Monitor Guide*
1868–current: *Publishers Auxiliary* (Chicago)
1868–1887: *Van Nostrand's (Electric) Engineering Magazine* [New York] ("Electric" was dropped from title in 1879; merger with *American Railroad Journal* in 1887)
1869–current: *American Grocer* (New York)
1869–1937: *Coal Trade Journal*
1869–current: *Jewelers' Circular-Keystone* (started in 1869 as *American Horological Journal*)
1870–1908: *Albany Law Journal*
1870–current: *Furniture World and Furniture Buyer and Decorator*
1870–current: *Insurance Index*
1870–1932: *American Cabinet Maker and Upholsterer* (in 1919 became *Furniture Buyer and Decorator,* and *Carpet Trade Review,* later *Carpet and Upholstery Trade Review;* subsidiary [1880-1932] was *Furniture Trade Review.*
1870–1877: *American Chemist*
1870–1872: *Petroleum Monthly* (succeeded by *Monthly Petroleum Trade Report* [1873-1882] and by *Oil City Derrick* [1871–current])

1870–1935: *Insurance Index* (New York)
1870–1895: *National Car (and Locomotive) Builder* (New York)
1870–1891: *National Live Stock Journal* (Chicago)
1870–1877: *Technologist* (New York)
1870–1886: *American Brewers' Gazette* (New York)
1871–1888: *American Journal of Fabrics and Dry Goods Bulletin* (later *Merchant World* [New York])
1871–1890: *Electrotyper* (Chicago)
1871–1929: *Dry Goods Reporter* (Chicago)
1871–current: *Insurance Law Journal* (St. Louis)
1876–1898: *Lumberman's Gazette* (Chicago)
1871–current: *Oil, Paint & Drug Reporter* (New York)
1871–1915: *Photographic Times* (New York)
1871–current: *Casket and Sunnyside*
1871–1929: *Dry Goods Reporter* (Chicago)
1871–1888: *American Journal of Fabrics & Dry Goods Bulletin* (later *Merchant World* in 1886)
1871–current: *New Remedies* (Changed in 1892 to *American Druggist;* merged *Pharmaceutical Record and Market Review* [1881-1893] and called *American Druggist and Pharm. Record*)
1872–current: *Standard*
1872–1879: *Clothier and Hatter* (split into *Clothier and Furnisher* and *Hatter and Furrier*, then *American Hatter Furrier; Clothier and Furnisher* merged [1927] into *Haberdasher* and was called *Haberdasher and the Clothier and Furnisher*)
1872– ? : *Pepper Trade Journal*
1872–1877: *American Journalist* (Philadelphia)
1872–current: *Banker and Tradesman* (Boston)
1872–1889: *Bee Keepers' Magazine* (Chicago)
1872–1908: *Boston Journal of Commerce*
1872–1893: *Grocer* (Cincinnati)
1872–1877: *Mining Review* (Denver)
1872–current: *Paper Trade Journal* (NewYork)
1872–1896: *Poultry World* (Hartford)
1872–current: *Publishers' Weekly* (New York)
1873–current: *Fur Trade Review*
1873–current: *American Miller* (Chicago)
1873–current: *Northwestern Miller* (Minneapolis, Minnesota)
1873–1928: *American Stationer* (Brooklyn)
1873–1912: *Grocers' Criterion* (Chicago)
1873–1886: *Grocers' Price Current* (Philadelphia)
1873–1877: *Industrial Age* (Chicago)

1873–current:	*American Furrier and Sol Vogel*
1873–current:	*Confectioners' Journal*
1873–1936:	*Insurance Age* (Boston)
1873–1924:	*Insurance Journal* (Hartford)
1873–1883:	*Patron of Husbandry* (Columbus, Miss.)
1873–1922:	*Price Current and Live Stock Record* (Later *Live-Stock Indicator;* later *Farmer and Stockman* [Kansas City])
1873–1891:	*Railway Register* (St. Louis)
1873–1895:	*Rhodes' Journal of Banking* (New York)
1873–1894:	*Sanitarian* (New York)
1873–1893:	*Sewing Machine Journal* (New York)
1873–current:	*Western Hotel Reporter* ([San Francisco]; now *Western Hotel and Restaurant Reporter*)
1873–current:	*Insurance Age-Journal*
1873–current:	*American Miller* (now *American Miller and Processor;* oldest milling journal; amalgamation of eight other milling journals)
1873–1893:	*Sewing Machine Journal* (New York)
1873–current:	*American Lumberman* (now *American Lumberman and Building Products Merchandiser*)
1874–1877:	*American Laboratory* (Boston)
1874–current:	*American Poultry Journal* (now three: *Egg Producer, Broiler Producer,* and *Turkey Producer*)
1874–1894:	*Cash Grocer* (Philadelphia)
1874–1907:	*Chicago Grocer*
1874–current:	*Crockery and Glass Journal*
1874–1924:	*Insurance World* (Pittsburgh)
1874–1874:	*Lithograph* (New York)
1874–1933:	*Painters' Magazine*
1874–current:	*United States Tobacco Journal* (New York)
1874–current:	*Engineering News Record: Engineering News* (consolidated in 1917 with McGraw-Hill's *Engineering Record,* which had been founded in New York in 1877 as *Plumber & Sanitary Engineer* and changed in 1880 to *Sanitary Engineer;* combined journals became *Engineering News-Record;* absorbed *The Contractor* [1891] in 1918)
1874–1931:	*Metal Worker, Plumber & Steam Fitter* (in 1921, became *Sanitary & Heating Engineering;* in 1929, became *Sanitary and Heating Age*)
1874–current:	*Western Tobacco Journal* (Cincinnati)
1874–current:	*Confectioners Journal* (now *Candy Industry and Confectioners Journal*)

1874–current: *American Fashion Review* (called *Sartorial Art Journal* since 1887; others are *Furnishing Gazette, Tailors' Review, American Tailor & Cutter*)
1874–1926: *New York Insurance Critic*
1874–current: *Electrical World* (started as a local telepraphers' journal in New York, in 1874; four mergers; *The Operator;* then *The Operator and Electrical World;* currently, *Electrical World*)
1874–current: *Crockery & Glass Journal* (merged with *China & Glass Guide* and Pottery half of *House Furnishing Goods Journal*)
1875–1887: *American Art Journal* (New York)
1875–1877: *American Meteorologist* (St. Louis)
1875–1890: *Carpet Trade* (Philadelphia)
1875–1920: *Fabrics, Fancy Goods and Notions* (New York)
1875–1887: *Grain and Provision Review* (Chicago)
1875–1890: *Grocer* (Philadelphia)
1875–1930: *Horse Shoers' Journal* (Detroit, Chicago, Indianapolis)
1875–current: *Hotel World* (Chicago, New York)
1876–current: *Millinery Trade Review*
1876–current: *Casket* ([Rochester], now *Casket and Sunnyside*)
1876–current: *Cheese Reporter*
1876–current: *American Architect* ([Boston], changed in 1890 to *Architecture & Building;* in 1921 absorbed *Architectural Review;* acquired by Hearst in 1929; in 1890 absorbed *Builders Magazine*)
1876–current: *Railway Age* (merged with *Railway Gazette,* 1908, as *Railway Age-Gazette,* 1909; changed to *Railway Age* in 1918)
1876–current: *Brewers Journal* (started as *Western Brewer*)
1876–current: *American Architect* (Boston)
1876–1893: *American Bookseller* (New York)
1876–1907: *American Dairyman* (New York)
1876–current: *Hotel Gazette* (New York)
1876–current: *Library Journal* (New York)
1876–current: *Millinery Trade Review* (New York)
1876–current: *Mississippi Valley Lumberman* (Minneapolis)
1876–1894: *United States Miller* (Milwaukee)
1877–current: *American Exporter* (New York)
1877–1921: *American Stockman* (later *National Stockman and Farmer* [Pittsburgh])

1877–current:	*American Veterinary Review* (later *Journal of The American Veterinary Medical Association* [Ithaca, New York])
1877–1879:	*Bentley's Book Buyer* (New York)
1877–1934:	*Retail Grocers' Advocate* (New York)
1877–1893:	*New York Mining Record*
1877–1904:	*Ice Trade Journal*
1877–current:	*Water Works Engineering*
1877–current:	*American Machinist*
1877–current:	*American Hairdresser* (now *American Hairdresser* and *Beauty Culture*; first in beauty industry as *American Hairdresser & Perfumer*
1877–current:	*Fire Engineering* (started as *National Firemen's Journal*)
1877–current:	*Geyer's Stationer & Business Equipment Topics*
1877–1934:	*Retail Grocers' Advocate*
1877–1902:	*Shoe & Leather Review* (Chicago)
1877–1893:	*Sewing Machine News* (New York)
1877–current:	*American Machinist*
1878–1914:	*American Antiquarian and Oriental Journal* (Chicago)
1878–current:	*Canning Trade* (Baltimore)
1878–current:	*Marine Journal* (New York)
1878–1901:	*Mining and Metallurgical Journal* (San Francisco)
1878–1895:	*Mining and Scientific Review* (Denver)
1878–1902:	*Poultry Monthly* (Albany)
1878–1913:	*Stoves and Hardware Reporter* (St. Louis)
1878–current:	*Marine Engineering & Shipping Review* (now *Marine Engineering/Log*)
1878–current:	*Rough News* (third oldest insurance journal)
1878–1913:	*Stoves and Hardware Reporter* (St. Louis)
1878–current:	*Spice Mill*
1878–1901:	*Mining and Metallurgical Journal*
1878–current:	*Modern Miller* ([Moline], started as *Grain Gleaner*; now *Modern Miller and Bakers News*)
1878–current:	*National Laundry Journal* (Chicago)
1878–current:	*Paper Mill & Wood Pulp News* ([Philadelphia], now *Paper Mill News*)
1878–current:	*Decorative Furnisher* (now *Furniture Retailer*)
1878–1902:	*Marine Record*
1879–current:	*American Builder*
1879–current:	*Syllabi* (later *National Reporter System*)
1879–current:	*Butchers' Advocate* (absorbed *American Meat Trade* and *Retail Butchers Journal* [1898–1920])
1879–current:	*Furniture Manufacturer*
1879–current:	*Textile Colorist* (Philadelphia)

1879–1893: *Pottery and Glassware Reporter* (Pittsburgh)

1879–1923: *Sewing Machine Advocate*

1879–1930: *American Contractor* (Chicago)

1879–1930: *Carpentry and Building* (in 1910 called *Building Age*)

1879–1913: *American Chemical Journal* (absorbed by the *American Chemical Society* [1879])

1879–1886: *Barbers National Journal* (Philadelphia)

1879–current: *Army & Navy Register*

1879–current: *Fishing Gazette* (New York)

1879–1890: *Baptist Review*

1879–current: *American Hebrew*

1879–current: *Dun's Review and Modern Industry* (formerly *Dun and Bradstreet's Review;* later *Dun's Review* [New York])

1879–1889: *Carpets, Wallpaper and Curtains* (Philadelphia)

1879–1893: *Carriage Journal* (Chicago)

1879–1905: *Grocers' Journal* (New York)

1879–current: *Insurance Salesman* (Indianapolis)

1879–1908: *Merchants' Review* (New York)

1879–1898: *Milling World and Chronicle of the Grain and Flour Trade* (Buffalo)

1879–current: *Music Trade Journal* (later *Review* [New York])

1879–current: *Textile Colorist* (Philadelphia)

1879–current: *Tradesman* (later *Southern Hardware and Implement Journal* [Atlanta])

1879–current: *Western Undertaker* (later *American Funeral Director* [Grand Rapids, New York])

1880–1902: *American Furniture Gazette* (Chicago)

1880–1935: *American Hatter and Furrier* (New York)

1880–1916: *American Tailor and Cutter*

1880–1932: *Furniture Trade Review* (New York)

1880–1903: *Textile Record of America* (Philadelphia)

1880–current: *Mining Record*

1880–1892: *American Engineer*

1880:1898: *Paper World*

1880–1884: *Steam*

1881–1909: *Glovers' Journal* (Gloversville, New York)

1881–1888: *Petroleum Age*

1881–current: *American Funeral Director*

1881–1901: (American) *Journal of Railway Appliances* (New York)

1881–1887: *American Merchant* (New York)

1881–1889: *Bowditch's American Florist and Farmer* (Boston)

1881–current: *Confectioners' Gazette* (later *Candy* [New York])

1881–1931: *Furnishers Gazette* (later *Haberdasher*)

1881–1890: *National Real Estate Index* (Kansas City)
1881–1893: *Pharmaceutical Record and Market Review* (New York)
1881–current: *Plumbers Trade Journal* (New York)
1881–current: *Southern Lumberman* (Nashville)
1881–current: *Tobacco World* (Philadelphia)
1882–1938: *American Silk Journal*
1882–1893: *American Metal Market* (merged *Tin and Terne and The Metal World* to become *The Metal World* [1893])
1882–1930: *American Elevator and Grain Trade*
1882–1929: *American Jeweler*
1882–current: *Wood Worker*
1882–current: *Steel* ([Cleveland]; started 1882 as the *Trade Review;* then *Iron Trade Review* [1888]; union of *Age of Steel* and *Iron and Steel* to make *Iron and Machinery World* [1902]; *Steel* in 1930) (Mott also gives 1867 as founding date for *Iron Trade Review*)
1882–1901: *Boots and Shoes* (called *Boots and Shoes Weekly* after 1899 [New York])
1882–1899: *Mechanics* (became *Engineering-Mechanics* in 1892)
1882–1887: *American Chemical Review* (Chicago)
1882–current: *Boot and Shoe Recorder* (known first as the *Great National Shoe Weekly*)
1882–1889: *American Electrician* (changed to *Electrician & Electrical Engineer* in 1884 and *Electrical Engineer* in 1888; finally merged with *Electrical World*)
1882–1933: *Miller's Review* ([Philadelphia]; moved to Atlanta, Georgia, [1924]; absorbed *Dixie Miller* [1892–1924] and called *Miller's Review and Dixie Miller*)
1882–current: *Manufacturer's Record* ([Atlanta, Georgia]; absorbed *Baltimore Journal of Commerce*)
1882–1915: *Printing Trade News* (New York)
1882–current: *American Metal Market* (New York)
1882–current: *American Press* (New York)
1882–1922: *American Woodworker and Mechanical Journal* (Cincinnati)
1882–1889: *Dow-Jones Letters* (forerunner of *Wall Street Journal,* 1889–current)
1882–1927: *Lutheran Church Review*
1882–current: *Electrical Review* (later *Industrial Engineering;* later *Maintenance Engineering;* later *Factory Management & Maintenance* [Chicago])
1882–1898: *Electrician and Electrical Engineer* (New York)
1882–current: *Glass Worker* (later *Commoner;* later *American Glass Review* [Pittsburgh])

1882–1926: *Harness Gazett* (Rome, New York)
1882–1931: *Lumber Trade Journal* (Chicago, New Orleans)
1882–1915: *Printing Trade News* (New York)
1882–1898: *Western Machinist* (later *Scientific Merchant* [Cleveland])
1883–current: *Gas Age* (formerly *Gas Age-Record & Natural Gas;* originally *Water-Gas Journal*)
1883–current: *Journal of the American Medical Association*
1883–current: *Electrical World* (absorbed *Operator* in 1885, and half dozen other papers)
1883–current: *Inland Printer* ([Chicago]; now *Inland and American Printer and Lithographer*)
1883–1934: *Keystone* ([Philadelphia]; merged with *Jewelers' Circular* [1934])
1883–1895: *American Agriculturist* (Wenham, Massachusetts)
1883–1913: *American Horse Breeder* (Boston)
1883–1885: *American Journalist* (St. Louis)
1883–1916: *Book Notes for the Week* (Providence)
1883–1890: *Bookmart* (Pittsburgh)
1883–1910: *Electric(al) Age* (New York)
1883–1908: *Inland Architect & Builder* (Chicago)
1883–1926: *Insurance News* (Philadelphia)
1883–current: *Leather Manufacturer* (Boston)
1883–current: *Telegraph* (*and Telephone*) *Age* (New York)
1883–current: *Bankers' Monthly* (Chicago)
1884–current: *Power* (called *Power-Steam;* in 1892 name reverted to *Power;* in 1908 absorbed *Chicago Engineer,* called *Power and the Engineer;* in 1904 bought by Hill Publishing Co., which became McGraw-Hill in merger of 1917; also absorbed: *Science & Industry, Mechanics Magazine, Steam Electric Magazine, Engineers Review, Safety Valve, The Stationary Engineer, Steam Engineering, The Mechanical Engineer*)
1884–current: *Editor & Publisher* (started as *The Journalist* [1884]; merged *Fourth Estate* [1894]; *Newspaperdom,* [1925])
1884–current: *Manufacturing Jeweler* (Providence)
1884–1930: *Milk Reporter* (Sussex, New Jersey)
1884–current: *National Glass Budget*
1884–1913: *Leather Gazette* (in 1888 called *Shoe & Leather Gazette,* St. Louis)
1884–current: *Street* (later *Electric*) *Railway Journal,* (later *Transit Journal*)
1884–1896: *Furniture Worker's Journal* (later *General Woodworking Journal* [Baltimore])

1884–1912:	*Hotel Register* (New York)
1884–1888:	*National Journalist* (Chicago)
1884–1913:	(*Shoe and*) *Leather Gazette* (St. Louis)
1885–1917:	*Midas Criterion of The Wholesale Whiskey and Wine Market*
1885–current:	*American Printer* (five mergers)
1885–current:	*Fibre and Fabric*
1885–current:	*National Coopers Journal*
1885–current:	*Hardware Age* (seven mergers)
1885–1894:	*Light, Heat and Power*
1885–current:	*Black Diamond*
1885–1929:	*Power and Transmission* (later *The Dodge Idea* [1909])
1885–current:	*Columbia Jurist*
1886–1898:	*Mining Industry*
1886–current:	*Tobacco*
1886–current:	*N. Y. Lumber Trade Journal*
1886–1918:	*Wine and Spirit Bulletin*
1886–1896:	*Street Railway Gazette* (later *Electric Railway Gazette;* later merged in *Electrical World*)
1887–current:	*American Wool and Cotton Reporter*
1887–current:	*Waterways Journal*
1887–1918:	*American Brewers' Review*
1887–current:	*Bakers Helper*
1887–1905:	*Wine and Spirit Gazette*
1887–1914:	*Grocery World*
1887–1908:	*Western Electrician*
1887–current:	*Harvard Law Review*
1888–1922:	*Spokesman and Harness World* (1884) and *The Harness World* (1888)
1888–current:	*Textile World* (2 mergers of older periodicals [1868])
1888–current:	*Printers' Ink*
1888–current:	*Pacific Drug Review*
1888–1920:	*Textile Advance News*
1888–1925:	*Newspaperdom* (purchased in 1925 by *Editor & Publisher*)
1888–1932:	*St. Louis Lumberman*
1888–current:	*American Produce Review* (split into three weeklies)
1888–1898:	*Seaboard* (later *Nautical Gazette*)
1888–1926:	*Sporting Goods Gazette*
1888–1942:	*Stone*
1889–1896:	*Electrical Industries* (later *American Electrician* [1896] and *Electrical World* [1905])

1889–current: *India Rubber World* (*Tire Review* [1934]; currently *Tire Review Convention News*)

1889–current: *Cotton Gin and Oil Mill Press*

1889–1896: *Electric Power*

1889–current: *Wall Street Journal* (forerunner *Dow-Jones Letters* [1882–1889]; purchased *Chicago Journal of Commerce* [1950])

1889–current: *Monumental News*

1889–current: *National Provisioner*

1889–current: *Lumberman*

1889–current: *Banking Law Journal*

1890–current: *Hardware Trade*

1890–1915: *Electrician and Mechanic*

1890–1909: *Hardware*

1890–current: *Men's Wear*

1890–1935: *Marine Review* (absorbed *Marine Record* in 1902)

1890–current: *Hide & Leather* (later *Leather and Shoes;* merged with *Shoe Factory*)

1890–current: *The Leather Manufacturer*

1890–1916: *Carriage Dealers' Journal*

1891–1907: *Ores and Metals*

1891–1898: *Street Railway Review* (later *Electric Railway Review;* absorbed by *Street Railway Journal*)

1891–1939: *Producer and Builder* (later *Granite, Marble & Bronze*)

1891–1917: *Grocers' Review*

1891–1906: *Electricity*

1891–current: *Normal Instructor* (*"The teachers' trade paper"*)

1891–current: *Yale Law Journal*

1891–1920: *Chef and Steward*

1891–current: *The Engineering Magazine: Industrial Review* (later became *Industrial Management,* combined with *Factory* in 1928; formed *Factory and Industrial Management;* now *Factory Management and Maintenance*)

1891–1891: *Ice and Refrigeration*

1892–current: *Embalmer's Monthly and National Funeral Director* (absorbed *American Undertaker* [1890–1904])

1892–current: *The Bricklayer* (renamed *Architectural Forum* in 1917; split in 1952, one half becoming *House and Home*)

1892–current: *Shears*

1892–current: *Foundry*

1892–current: *North Western Druggist* (St. Paul, Minnesota)

1892–current: *Brick & Clay Record* (originally *Clay Record* [1892]; *Brick* merged [1894–1910])

1892–current: *Hotel Monthly*

1892–1929: *Hay Trade Journal*
1892–1917: *Box Maker*
1892–current: *International Confectioner*
1892–1901: *Clothiers' and Haberdashers' Weekly*
1892–current: *Housewares Review* (oldest housewares and appliance magazine incorporating four other papers: *Home Equipment, House Furnishing Journal, Housewares Merchandising,* and *Creative Design*)
1893–current: *Caterer and Hotel Proprietor's Gazette*
1893–current: *Starchroom Laundry Journal* (Oldest in power laundry industry)
1893–current: *Pottery and Glass Salesman* (formerly *Glass and Pottery World*)
1893–1894: *Aeronautics*
1893–1929: *Hardware Dealers Magazine*
1893–1905: *Telephone Magazine* (later merged with *Telephony* [1901–current])
1893–current: *Daily News Record*
1893–1910: *Shoe Trade Journal*
1894–current: *Machinery*
1894–current: *Metal Finishing* (*Aluminum World* [1894]; absorbed *Brass Founder* in 1902 and *Electroplater's Review*)
1894–1911: *Coal and Coke*
1895–1916: *The Horseless Age*
1895–1900: *Motorcycle*
1895–current: *Journal of Electricity* (later *Electrical West* [1926])
1895–1913: *Pacific Lumber Trade Journal*
1895–current: *Automotive Industries* (Horseless Age—first auto businesspaper printed in English [1899]; *Automobile & Motor Review;* later, *Automotive Industries*)
1896–current: *American Shoemaking*
1896–current: *Retail Grocers' Advocate*
1896–current: *Power Engineering*
1896–current: *Weekly Bulletin of Leather and Shoe News*
1896–1940: *Automobile Trade Journal*
1896–current: *Southwest Hardware and Implement Journal* (first, *Cycle Trade Journal;* "Cycle" was not dropped until 1912)
1896–1924: *Cement and Engineering News*
1896–current: *Compressed Air*
1896–current: *Cigar and Tobacco*
1897–current: *National Underwriter*
1897–1908: *L. J. Callahan's Monthly*
1897–1910: *Modern Machinery*

1897–1918: *American Wine Press*
1897–current: *Marine Engineering*
1897–current: *Radford Review* (became *Lumber Review,* merger with *Lumber World* [1905] and *Chicago Lumberman* [1926])
1897–current: *National Engineer*
1897–1911: *Mining Magazine*
1898–?: *Metallographist;* later *Iron and Steel*
1898–1931: *American Trade* (became *American Industries* in 1902; official publication of National Association of Manufacturers)
1898–current: *Cotton*
1898–1929: *Shoe Retailer*
1898–current: *Luggage & Leather Goods* (originally *Trunks and Leather Goods*)
1898–current: *Grain and Feed Journals Consolidated* (formerly *Grain Dealers Journal*)
1898–1926: *Coal Trade Bulletin*
1898–1901: *American Knit Goods Review*
1898–current: *Dyestuffs*
1898–1923: *The Gas Engine*
1898–current: *Barber's Journal and Men's Hairstylist*
1899–current: *Sporting Goods Dealer*
1899–1902: *Motor Vehicle Review* (merged with *Automotive Industries*)
1899–1907: *Automobile Magazine* (merged with *Automotive Industries*)
1899–current: *Motor Age*
1899–current: *Cotton*
1899–current: *Columbia River and Oregon Timberman* (now *Timberman*)
1899–current: *Salt Lake Mining Review*
1899–current: *Coal Mining*

APPENDIX II

STYLE MANUAL FOR BUSINESSPAPER EDITORS

Introduction[1]

THIS manual had its beginning in a survey of business magazines, made to determine how such publications arrived at a consistent style. Done as a term project in Magazine 230, a seminar in the magazine, and originally intended to cover only magazines in the communications field, the survey was expanded to include all members of Associated Business Publications and National Business Publications which published five or more magazines. In the end, questionnaires were sent to twenty-five different firms, representing fields of considerable diversity.

The results of the survey strongly indicated that a general style manual for business publications was not only feasible but might fill a definite need. Of twenty-one respondents, eight had their own manuals or style sheets and four were preparing or revising manuals for themselves. All the manuals received were general rather than specialized in their approach, with reliance being placed on word lists, rather than rules, to clarify matters peculiar to a given field.

Sources of style rules varied little, either for those who had compiled their own manuals or those who currently used other manuals. In descending order, the choices were the *Style Book of The New York Times*, the Government Printing Office *Style Manual*, the University of Chicago *Manual of Style* and Skillin and Gay's *Words Into Type*. All fairly complete volumes, whose authority cannot be disputed, they are nonetheless unwieldy in their inclusion of many rules for which business publications have no need. Brevity can be of great value to the working editor, and it is for brevity I have striven in this manual.

The strength of those manuals which business publications have com-

[1]Compilation and Introduction by Peter R. Morehouse, Graduate Division, School of Journalism, Syracuse University, 1958, sponsored by the Editorial Division, Associated Business Publications, New York.

piled for themselves lies in their compactness. Weightier manuals may be the final authority, but a guide with more ready-reference characteristics can afford to sacrifice the narrower rules and more academic exceptions. If they have a weakness, it is in a lack of systematic organization to suit the business approach. Many give the appearance of having simply extracted the more general rules from the larger manuals, without due regard to condensation, simplification and meaningful categorization. The majority of them could be briefer still, and thereby gain rather than lose in practical value.

No pretense of comprehensive treatment is made for this manual: the content was selected and organized for the use of a specific branch of publishing. Much of the material used in small manuals has been omitted; some which appears only in the large manuals has been included. There are shortcomings to any condensation, but this one, at least, is simple. It should also prove as applicable for its size as anything now available.

Capitalization

General, Headlines, Trademarks

1. Capitalize proper nouns and proper adjectives, except where a meaning independent of the proper name exists.

   (America, American, india ink, roman type)

2. Capitalize common nouns when they form an essential part of a proper name, but not when standing alone as a substitute for such a name. An exception is when the common noun is well known and makes a specific reference.

   (Sagamore Hotel, the hotel, the Capitol, the Court)

3. Capitalize nicknames and other appellations.

   (Nutmeg State, Windy City, the Big Three)

4. Capitalize common nouns when they precede numbers or letters.

   (Local 1754, Type X, Volume V)

5. Capitalize the first word of a direct quotation when it comprises a complete sentence, not a fragment.

   (He called the idea "a good one.")

6. Capitalize the first word after a colon, except when the matter following is only supplementary.

   (Two men came: the editor and his assistant.)

7. Capitalize the names of historical documents, events and periods.

   (Declaration of Independence, Battle of the Bulge,
   The Dark Ages)

8. Capitalize the names of races and nationalities.

(Caucasian, Chinese)

9. Capitalize calendar divisions, but not seasons except when making a special reference.

(May, Tuesday, spring, the Fall fashions)

10. Capitalize holidays, special weeks and other events.

(Fourth of July, National Peanut Week)

11. Do not capitalize: school or college subjects, except languages; college classes or degrees.

(Spanish, calculus, sophomore, bachelor of arts)

12. In headlines, capitalize the first word in each line and all nouns, pronouns, verbs, adverbs—and other words of four or more letters. Also capitalize prepositions (and other words) when used to modify a preceding word or section. Capitalize both parts of a hyphenated word.

(Seventy-Five Magazines Go Far)

13. When a large initial letter begins a paragraph, capitalize all letters in the first word; if it has only one or two letters, also capitalize the next word. When the first word is part of a name or title, capitalize all letters therein.

(JOHN QUENTIN DOE went . . .)

14. Capitalize variety names, market grades and the registered part of trademarks; do not enclose in quotes. Descriptive nouns are not capitalized unless part of the trademark itself. Some trademarks have become generic terms and need not be capitalized—if in doubt, capitalize. Use the general term for a product unless its specific mention is necessary or desirable.

(Scotch tape, Contour Sheet, nylon, fiber glass, Fiberglas)

Abbreviation

General—Units of Measurement

1. Capitalize and punctuate an abbreviation if the word when spelled out is capitalized. Exceptions are in page references, which become lower case when abbreviated, and scholastic degrees, which are capitalized and punctuated without spacing.

(Co., Mass., Fig., but p., pp.; bachelor of arts, but B.A.)

2. Lower-case abbreviations of more than one word are punctuated but not spaced.

(m.p.h., a.m., e.g.)

3. Units of measurement, dates and designations of address are abbreviated only when directly connected with numerals. Note that numbered streets, but not dates, take an ordinal suffix; also that May, June and July are never abbreviated.

(17 in., but inches away; Jan. 17, but January, 1958; 64th St., but May 12)

4. Abbreviated units of measurement do not change in the plural; other terms add an "s."

(1 lb., 75 lb., Figs., Nos.)

5. Do not use symbols for units of measurement. Exceptions are in tabular matter, temperature and angular measurement.

(14 in., but 400° F., 30° 9′ 11″)

6. Do not repeat abbreviations unnecessarily. A hyphen may be used for *to* and *through*, but remember that such a range is always inclusive.

(15 to 20 per cent, 15-19.9 per cent)

Names, Titles, and Organizations

Abbreviation, Capitalization

1. First names of individuals should be abbreviated only to initials, unless contractions are used in business names. On first mention of an individual, the first name, or both initials, should be used.

(C. F. or Charles Smith, not Chas. F. Smith)

2. Capitalize a title preceding a name. A title following a name or standing alone is capitalized only when referring to officers of the United States or important state officers. A long or awkward title should always be placed after the name.

(Secretary Jones; the Governor; G. W. Smith, superintendent of public works)

3. Generally, abbreviate a title preceding the full name; spell it out when it precedes the last name only. Dr. and Mr. are used only in the abbreviated form (Mr. only when the last name stands alone). The following are never abbreviated: president, vice president, secretary, treasurer, chairman, commissioner, general manager.

(Sen. A. B. Jones, Senator Jones, President J. B. Smith)

4. Abbreviations of names of associations, government agencies, well-known corporations, laws and acts are capitalized but not spaced or punctuated. However, an abbreviation is hyphenated to follow spelled-out forms.

(ABP, NBP, FTC, AT & T, but T-H Act)

(5. On first mention, association, agency and business names should be capitalized and spelled out, except for these abbreviations of common nouns: Bros., Co., Corp., Dept., Div., Inc., Ltd. Except in all-initial abbreviations, other common nouns in official names (Manufacturers, Association, Board, Commission, Institute) should not be abbreviated at any time.

(Brown Bros. Manufacturing Co., Inc.)

6. Capitalize names of organizations, political parties, and their members or adherents.

(Rotarian, Democrat)

7. Capitalize federal, *state, government* and *administration* when those words are used in a specific sense.

(the Administration, the State Legislature)

8. Capitalize *the* when used as a part of a proper name or title.

(The Borden Co.)

9. Use the ampersand in names of partnership and companies—unless their usage dictates otherwise.

(Hodder & Stoughton, Simon and Schuster)

Addresses and Geographical Terms

1. Capitalize common nouns when used in conjunction with proper nouns (as part of such nouns) to denote specific regions, areas or places. Words of mere direction or description are not capitalized.

(the Midwest, the Atlantic Coast, the Orient, Pennsylvania Station, but western Oklahoma, the Florida coast)

2. Compass points are lower-case when spelled out; when abbreviated they are capitalized and punctuated, but not spaced.

(northwest, N.W.)

3. The names of all countries—except the United States and the Union of Soviet Socialist Republics—are spelled out.

(U.S. or U.S.A., U.S.S.R.—no space; England, Germany, France)

4. Except when used in business names, Fort, Mount, and Saint are abbreviated.

(Fort Wayne Plastics Co., Ft. Wayne, Ind.)

5. Avenue, street, boulevard, road, and building are capitalized and abbreviated when used with a number. Used without a number, but with specific reference, they are capitalized and spelled out. Drive, place, square, and other designations should not be abbreviated.

(Room 1620 Central Bldg., Central Building)

6. Street directions are capitalized and abbreviated with punctuation. When the name of a street is a number from one through ten, it is spelled; above ten the number is combined with its proper suffix, without punctuation.

(520 N. Liverpool St., Tenth Ave., 165th St.)

7. The names of states are abbreviated only when used with a city (Wilmington, Del., but otherwise Delaware). Idaho, Iowa, Ohio, Utah, Alaska and Hawaii are never abbreviated; the other states are abbreviated as follows:

Ala.	Ga.	Mich.	N.M.	S.D.
Ariz.	Ill.	Minn.	N.Y.	Tenn.
Ark.	Ind.	Miss.	N.C.	Tex.
Calif.	Kans.	Mo.	N.D.	Vt.
Colo.	Ky.	Mont.	Okla.	Wash.
Conn.	La.	Nebr.	Ore.	W. Va.
Del.	Me.	Nev.	Pa.	Wis.
D.C.	Md.	N.H.	R.I.	Wyo.
Fla.	Mass.	N.J.	S.C.	

8. Except in postal addresses, the following cities do not commonly require a state designation:

Akron	Denver	Philadelphia
Atlanta	Detroit	Pittsburgh
Baltimore	Duluth	San Francisco
Birmingham	Houston	Seattle
Boston	Indianapolis	Spokane
Buffalo	Los Angeles	St. Louis
Chicago	Milwaukee	St. Paul
Cincinnati	Minneapolis	Washington
Cleveland	New Orleans	
Dallas	New York	

Numerals

General, Figures, Fractions, Time

1. In general, spell out numbers from one through ten and use figures above ten. The commonest exceptions to this rule are: numbers in series, round numbers, dimensions, and other exact quantities, ages, time, figures in apposition and large figures.

   (Forty days, 5 minutes 12 seconds, 7-year-old)

2. Use figures for all numbers in a series if one is over ten.

   (5 tanks, 19 barrels, 2 cans)

3. When two figures are in apposition, spell out the first (unless spelling the second is less awkward).

   (Five 4-cycle engines, 263 four-cycle engines)

4. Figures are used for a number in conjunction with a common noun or an abbreviation; exception is made for numbered streets, which are spelled out when ten or under.

   (Section 7, Part 4, Fig. 9, 30 ft., 1215 Seventh Ave.)

5. Capitalize and spell out numbers or fractions which begin a sentence. But avoid this situation if possible.

   (Three-fourths of those present said . . .)

6. Mixed numbers should always be expressed in numerals. Fractions standing alone, however, are spelled out and hyphenated.

   (5½ tons, four-fifths)

7. Numbers of five digits or more (except telephone, house, and style or type numbers) should be pointed off with the comma. With seven or more digits, the ciphers should be dropped.

   (1000; 10,000; Model 16705; 5 million; $13 billion)

8. In money sums of integral dollars, omit the decimal and ciphers. This does not apply to tabular matter in which some entries include cents and uniformity is desired.

   ($75, $110, but in tables: $75.00)

9. Figures, not ordinal numbers, are used for all but one date.

   (Fourth of July, but July 3, 1957)

10. An inclusive period of years is indicated by the hyphen. If the period is in one century, two digits are used for the second date; if covering different centuries, all digits are used.

    (1937–57, 1875–1915)

11. Hours and minutes in clock time are separated by the colon; no ciphers are used for integral hours. Use a.m. and p.m. lower case, punctuated, and unspaced, and only in conjunction with a specific time.

(11:30 a.m., 3 p.m., not "in the A.M."; noon, midnight)

Punctuation

(Familiarity with the basic rules is assumed: the emphasis here is on more limited cases which may cause doubt.)

Period

1. The ellipsis—three periods—is used to show omission in a quotation, and occasionally for effect in column material.

(ending here . . . but starting again)

2. The period is used after letters or numbers in a series, in place of parentheses or dashes. (See parenthesis.)

(A. Books. B. Magazines.)

Comma

3. The comma sets off the state when used in a sentence with a city, or the year when used with a month.

(The Boston, Mass., division; January, 1958, was the time)

4. Omit the comma before *and* or *or* at the end of a series, unless clarity demands its use.

(Iron, steel, cobalt and magnesium)

5. Do not use the comma between a last name and Jr., Sr., or a Roman numeral.

(John Sears III)

6. Do not use a comma before an ampersand.

(Brown, Green & Co.)

Quotation Marks

7. Use quotation marks for names of articles, bulletins, catalogs and speeches. Names of newspapers, periodicals and books are italicized.

("Extension Bulletin No. 7"; *Newsweek*)

8. Commas and periods go inside quotation marks. Exclamation points and question marks go outside unless part of the quoted material; all others go outside.

(He said, "Did you find it?")

9. For quotations more than one paragraph long, use quotation marks at the beginning of each paragraph and at the end of the last.
10. Single quotes are used for quotations in heads and for quotations within quotations.

("Production is 'down to a trickle,' it appears.")

11. Do not use quotation marks when quoted matter is set in a different type face or on a shorter measure.

Apostrophe

12. To show joint possession, use the apostrophe with the last noun only.

(John Smith and Fred Brown's contract)

13. For the possessive of a compound noun, use the apostrophe with the last element.

(Brother-in-law's house)

14. Use the apostrophe to form plurals of letters and figures.

(P's and Q's, 8's)

Parenthesis

15. If paranthetical matter forms part of a sentence, the period goes outside it; if the whole sentence is in parentheses the period is used inside.

(This is a complete sentence.)

16. If parenthetical matter is more than one paragraph in length, begin each paragraph with a parenthesis and use a parenthesis to end the last paragraph.
17. Use parentheses to set off figures or letters used in series within a sentence.

(The buildings are (a) a school, (b) a courthouse and (c) a church.)

Italics

18. Italics may be used for emphasis. This should be achieved in other ways when possible, since an ordinary type face is easier to read.

19. Names of newspapers, periodicals, books, ships, aircraft and trains, are italicized. Automobile models are not.

    (*The New York Times*, *Twentieth Century Limited*, but Ford)

20. Reference letters are italicized; abbreviations in text matter are not.

    (*Fig. 1*, *Plate 16*, but i.e., e.g.)

Compounding, Hyphenation, and Word Division

(*For situations not covered here, the final authority is* Webster's New International Dictionary *(or a smaller edition). If in doubt about spelling, check the dictionary or accepted works within your field.)*

1. As a general rule, short prefixes and suffixes (one and two syllables) do not take the hyphen unless the adjoining letters of the compound formed are the same: in that case check the dictionary. The hyphen may also be used to avoid confusion or ambiguity and in long or unusual compounds.

   (Semi-independent; recover, re-cover; new-business department)

2. Hyphenate a combination of single units having equal strength.

   (Secretary-treasurer, kilowatt hour)

3. Hyphenate words used as a single adjective before a noun, except when the first word is an -ly adverb.

   (Half-empty bottle, fully developed plans)

4. Hyphenate combinations of a prefix and a proper name or date. Two names used together take the dash, not hyphen.

   (anti-American, mid-1957; Boston—Chicago flight)

5. A letter prefix is ordinarily capitalized and used with a hyphen.

   (V-belt, I-beam, but x-ray)

6. Ex- and -elect take the hyphen; other title prefixes and suffixes do not.

   (Ex-treasurer, Governor-elect, but vice president, general manager)

7. Always divide words at syllables: if doubtful, check the dictionary or pronounce the word aloud, slowly. Never divide a one syllable word.
8. Do not separate a one-letter syllable from the remainder of the word; do not separate -le and -ly endings from preceding consonants. If

possible, do not separate such consonants from vowels preceding them.

(Elec-tric, not e-lectric; many, not man-y; wrin-kle; poss-ibly preferable to possi-bly)

9. With doubled consonants, divide between the consonants.

(Expres-sive, compres-sion)

APPENDIX III

ABBREVIATIONS

AAA	American Arbitration Association
AAAA	American Association of Advertising Agencies (4 A's)
AAIE	American Association of Industrial Editors
AASDJ	American Association of Schools and Departments of Journalism
ABC	Audit Bureau of Circulation
ABP	Associated Business Publications
AEJ	Association for Education in Journalism
AFA	Advertising Federation of America
AIA	Association of Industrial Advertisers
AMA	American Marketing Association
ANA	Association of National Advertisers
ANPA	American Newspaper Publishers Association
ARF	American Research Foundation
ASJSA	American Society of Journalism School Administrators
BBB	Better Business Bureau
BNAC	Business Newspaper Association of Canada
BPAC	Business Publications Audit of Circulations
BPEA	Business Paper Editors Association (Canada)
BPEN	Business Publication Editor's Newsletter (Chicago)
CCA	Controlled Circulation Audit
CCAB	Canadian Circulations Audit Board
FIPP	International Federation of The Periodical Press
FTC	Federal Trade Commission
GNP	Gross National Product

IARI	Industrial Advertising Research Institute
ICC	International Chamber of Commerce
ICIE	International Council of Industrial Editors
INS	International News Service
MPA	Magazine Publishers Association
NBP	National Business Publications
NICB	National Industrial Conference Board
NSF	National Science Foundation
NYBPE	New York Business Paper Editors Association
OCC	Office of Certified Circulation
PAA	Premium Advertising Association
PANY	Publishers Association of New York
PIB	Publishers' Information Bureau
PPA	Periodical Publishers Association
SBME	Society of Business Magazine Editors
SIC	Standard Industrial Classification
SRDS	Standard Rate & Data Service
SPEA	State Pharmaceutical Editorial Association
VAC	Verified Audit Circulation

APPENDIX IV

BUSINESS PRESS ASSOCIATIONS

England:	The Periodical Trade Press and Weekly Newspaper Proprietors Association Ltd. (PTP and WNPA), London
Germany:	Deutscher Journalisten Verbank, Bonn, Munster platz 20
	Bernfsgruppe der Journalisten m I G Druckund Papier
	Verband Deutscher Zeitschriften Verlegen v Frankfurt am Main
Netherlands:	Netherlands Organization of Periodical Publishers (N.O.T.U.)
	The Hague, Holland
Switzerland:	Schweiz Fachpresse verband, Postfach 285, Zurich 32, Switzerland
	Schweiz Zeitungsverlager-Verband,
	Routgenstr. 16, Zurich 5, Switzerland
Sweden:	Foreningen Svensk Fackpress (Association of Swedish Trade Journals) Oraforanden-Vasagatan 38, Stockholm C Swedish Association of The Periodical Press, Stockholm
	Svenska Journalist forbundet (Journalists trade union) Stockholm
Denmark:	Vereingung Danischer Fachblatter and Zeitschriften, Copenhagen
United States:	National Business Publications (NBP) Washington, D.C.
	New York Business Paper Editors Association (NYBPEA)
	Agricultural Publishers Association (APA) Chicago
	Associated Business Publications (ABP) New York
	Society of Business Magazine Editors (SBME) Washington, D.C.

Norway:	Den Norske Fagpresses Forening, Oslo
France:	Federation Internationale de la Presse Periodique (FIPP) 54, rue René-Boulanger, Paris 117, Boulevard Saint Germain, Paris
Japan:	None. Source is Dentsu Advertising, Nishi-Ginza, Tokyo
Belgium:	Union de la Presse Periodique Belge, 47 rue Royale, Brussels
Australia:	None. Source: Australian Advertising Rate & Data Service, 75 Ultimo Rd., Haymarket, N.S.W., Box 3765, G.P.O., Sydney
Canada:	Agricultural Press Association, Toronto Business Newspapers Association of Canada, 137 Wellington St. West, Toronto (affiliate of Periodical Press Association)
USSR:	Only source is "Mezhdunarodnaya," Kniga, Moscow, or The Embassy of the Union of Soviet Socialist Republics

APPENDIX V

CHECKLIST FOR PERIODICAL PUBLISHERS

Author's note: This checklist is based on Recommended Standards compiled by the Publishing Division of the Special Libraries Association, 31 East 10th Street, New York. Mr. Ivan A. Given, editor of *Coal Age,* is currently Chairman of the Subcommittee on Layout of Periodicals, Sectional Committee Z39, of the American Standards Association, on the subject of Reference Data and Arrangement of Periodicals. Teachers, students, and publishers who desire copies of the complete revised code should refer to Z39.1-1943, American Standards Association, 70 East 45th Street, New York 17, N. Y

Format

General

Does your correct title, volume and issue number, parts and date of issue appear alike on cover, mastheads and/or contents page, and spine?

Does the name of your periodical and running date line appear on every page?

Does the volume number appear in Arabic numerals, not Roman?

Do you produce a sturdy, well-bound journal with readable print on good paper, with sufficient margins for binding?

Do you use continuous pagination throughout a volume (including ad pages)?

If possible, will you avoid change of size and title in the middle of a volume? (If this must be done, new volume numbering is desirable).

Does notice of change of title, merger, cessation or change of frequency of issue appear prominently?

If a merger, do you indicate clearly which title is to be continued and what volume number is to be used?

Masthead and Table of Contents

Do these features (frequently on the same page) appear in each issue in a uniform place? (If possible within the first four pages where postal notice must appear.)

Can these features be readily found? Does the cover indicate where to find them?

Does your masthead contain:

General business address
Editor's name
Publisher's name
Frequency of publication (Indicate summer schedule)
Different editions, if published

Does your table of contents:

List every feature of the magazine?
Give authors as well as titles of articles:
Call attention to special features, such as index, special supplements, etc.?
Indicate Parts 1, 2, etc., if issued in such manner?
Include title of such parts (if index, special supplement, etc.)?
List annual subscription price
List two-, three-, or five-year subscription prices
List foreign subscription price
State price per copy
State back copy price
State name of outside indexing services reporting contents (such as Readers' Guide, Industrial Arts Index, Engineering Index, etc.)

Indexes

General

Are weeklies indexed at least twice a year? Monthlies at least once a year? (Three times a year for weeklies and twice for monthlies is even more desirable, because of timeliness and necessity of binding large magazines at more frequent intervals than semi-annually or annually.)

Does the index appear in the concluding number of a volume?

Is the index issued separately?

Is it sent automatically to subscribers? If not, are instructions prominently printed as to how to obtain it?

Do you avoid:

Printing text with index?
Issuing 6-page folded index?
Printing on back of the title page?

Binding in issue so index cannot be removed to place in front of bound volume?

Content

Is your indexing done by a professional indexer?

Do you have an adequate subject authority list to insure consistency in index?

Do you use a consistent system of alphabetizing in each issue?

Are there sufficient cross-references?

Is there an author index?

Is there a company index?

Do you issue cumulative indexes?

Do you index all features, such as special supplements, special numbers, news items, parts, etc.?

Are symbols used to indicate illustrations, news items, maps, etc.? (This is helpful.)

Do you use bold face type for subject headings and alphabetical separations?

Do you use sub-headings to break down subjects?

Advertiser Index

Is there a separate index of advertisers?

Is this index arranged both by company and product?

Editorial Content

Content

Do special features appear in the same location and issue?

Are the more articulate members of your profession encouraged to submit articles for publication or to interpret important developments in your field?

Titles

Does the title relate to the subject matter?

Is it descriptive of the contents?

Is there a sub-title to abstract the article and attract those readers who really will be interested?

Biographical data

Is full information given as to author's business affiliation, title and background? (This establishes his authority.)

Do you include photographs of authors? (Libraries have increasing demand for pictures.)

Bibliography

Do you include bibliographical references with the articles? (Any arbitrary limit on number of such references is not recommended.)

Do these references include the following: Name of author including given name (initials are not enough), title, complete periodical reference (volume number, date of issue, and pagination); or publisher, place, and date of publication, if a book.

If citation is a document privately printed by an individual or by a little known organization, do you give address as well as name of issuing agency?

Do you use consistent abbreviations and symbols?

Corrections

Are corrections of errors previously printed conspicuously located and easy to find? (A notation on the contents page is desirable.)

Statistics

Are your charts, graphs and statistics fully documented?

Does this information include: source of data, details as to form of original information?

If you are citing government statistics, do you give the specific department and/or bureau issuing the data as well as title of publication, number, date, etc.?

If the original information is a separate publication, do you give author, title, date, and source of supply?

Pictures

Do you always carry credit lines?

Are they consistent as to location in your periodical? (It is desirable that the credit line appear with the picture, if possible.)

Are they consistent as to information given: source, page reference if previously published, and date? (Blanket credits are inadequate.)

INDEX